THE POPULATION
OF IRELAND
1750–1845

"THE POPULATION OF IRELAND

1750—1845 "

BY

K. H. CONNELL

GREENWOOD PRESS, PUBLISHERS
WESTPORT, CONNECTICUT

Library of Congress Cataloging in Publication Data

Connell, Kenneth Hugh.
    The population of Ireland, 1750-1845.

    Reprint of the 1950 ed. published by Clarendon Press,
Oxford.
    Bibliography: p.
    Includes index.
    1. Ireland--Population. 2. Ireland--Social
conditions. I. Title.

HB3589.C6 1975   301.32'9'415   74-9165
ISBN 0-8371-7620-4 (lib. bdg.)

Originally published in 1950 by the Clarendon Press, Oxford

This reprint has been authorized by the Clarendon Press, Oxford

Reprinted in 1975 by Greenwood Press
a division of Congressional Information Service
88 Post Road West, Westport, Connecticut 06881

Library of Congress Catalog Card Number 74-9165

ISBN 0-8371-7620-4

Printed in the United States of America

10 9 8 7 6 5 4 3

PREFACE

THIS book owes more than I can readily express to the teaching of the London School of Economics and to the encouragement and stimulus it gives to academic inquiry. It was the award by the School of a Leverhulme Research Studentship which enabled me to begin to read in Irish history, and the greater part of the work the book has entailed was done while I was a member of its teaching staff. In particular I am indebted to the Director, Sir Alexander Carr-Saunders, and Mr. H. L. Beales for initiating me into the ways of research, to Professor T. S. Ashton for his continual interest and for guidance on form as well as on substance, and to Professor D. V. Glass for showing me what could be made of early census statistics. Amongst my colleagues in the University of Liverpool I am grateful especially to Mrs. Ursula K. Hicks for her patient handling of drafts of early chapters and to Professor R. T. Williams for enabling me to make an excursion into the biochemistry of nutrition. Other scholars, upon whose time I could make the calls neither of a pupil nor of a colleague, helped me none the less generously. Dr. R. N. Salaman, F.R.S., took a lively interest in my work and allowed me to consult both his exhaustive notes on the history of the potato and the manuscript of his great book on the subject. Professor T. W. Moody and Professor D. B. Quinn read my typescript, and as the result of their comments the book has, I hope, lost something of the air of being written by a newcomer to Irish historical studies. To the names of these people who helped me personally I wish to add that of Professor George O'Brien whose pioneering *Economic History of Ireland* must underlie the many monographs that remain to be written in Irish economic history, as it underlies my own.

I have been rash enough to reject some of the guidance I have sought: none of the deficiencies of this book must, therefore, be attributed to those who have done so much to lessen their number.

An abridged version of the first chapter has appeared in *The Economic History Review* for 1946, and I am grateful to the Editor for his permission to use the same material here.

K. H. C.

NUFFIELD COLLEGE
OXFORD
February 1950

CONTENTS

LIST OF TABLES

I

THE GROWTH OF POPULATION

HITHERTO the focus of interest in discussion of the population of Ireland in the eighteenth and early nineteenth
centuries has almost inevitably been the spectacularly steep
increase which, according to the existing figures, began in the 1780s
and abruptly ended the more moderate expansion of earlier decades.
Mr. G. Talbot Griffith, in his *Population Problems of the Age of
Malthus*, says that while up to 1785 there was in Ireland 'a very
steady if slow increase' in population, at about that time it 'began
to increase at a phenomenal pace'.[1] 'If Young's estimate of the
population for 1779 is taken [and Mr. Griffith believes this figure
to be too high] the increase in the sixty-odd years from then until
the Census of 1841 is 172 per cent.; the increase in England and
Wales in the same period—from Rickman's estimate for 1780 until
the Census of 1841—is 88 per cent., which is only slightly more
than half the rate of increase in Ireland during the same period.'[2]

The fact that the population of Ireland increased steeply in the
latter decades of the eighteenth century is incontrovertible: there
is too much contemporary opinion on the subject, and it is too
nearly unanimous for any valid doubts to exist. But we cannot be
certain of the rate of increase, nor of the extent by which it exceeded that of any earlier period. It is not easy to verify eighteenth-
century statistics, and there has been some tendency to accept,
with as little modification as has been necessary in the interest of
consistency, the traditional series of population estimates.[3] We
must, therefore, begin our inquiry with an examination of these
figures, and with such revision of them as seems necessary.

The first problem is whether we can accept as broadly accurate
the early censuses in the decennial series. The first was taken in
1821, and it put the population at 6,801,827. There is reason for
believing that this figure is somewhat below the truth, for not only

[1] Cambridge, 1926, p. 47.   [2] Ibid., p. 50.
[3] 'Except as a point of academic interest it is not important to obtain estimates
of the population before the Census more accurate than these in all probability
are.' Ibid., p. 50.

were the enumerators inexperienced, but the traditional lack of confidence in the Government made householders loth to disclose to its agents information which might be made the basis for fresh oppression. The Rev. Horatio Townsend, in his *Statistical Survey of the County of Cork*, in accounting for the deficiency of some of the figures collected by the incomplete Census of 1813, refers to 'the difficulty of obtaining a fair return in consequence of the apprehension entertained by the inhabitants of its rendering them more liable to tax duty and militia service'.[1]

The Catholics [said Dr. James Doyle, the celebrated Bishop of Kildare and Leighlin] have ever been unwilling to make known their numbers to any agent of the Government. Having too often experienced from it what they deemed treachery or injustice they naturally distrusted whomsoever approached them in its name. Ignorant of its views in computing the number of its slaves, these latter rather feared they were to be decimated or banished, as if in the time of Cromwell, to some bog or desert if found too numerous, than that any measures were to be adopted for the improvement of their condition.[2]

However, when the census was taken in 1821, relations between the Government and people were easier than they were for some years before or afterwards, and the Catholic clergy, with their considerable power to lessen the desire of the people to deceive the enumerators, encouraged members of their Church to give accurate information.

Their efforts seem not to have been without success: the Census Commissioners of 1841, while they thought the 1821 figure was below, rather than above, the truth, did not regard it as sufficiently defective to make the margin between the 1821 and 1831 returns a materially inaccurate representation of the increase in population in these years, even though they believed that the 1831 figure tended to err in the opposite direction.[3]

The 1831 Census put the population of Ireland at 7,767,401, an increase of 14·19 per cent. over the 1821 figure. The 1841 Commissioners said that 'the numbers returned in 1831 were greater than the real population, or, at all events, that any error was one rather of excess than of defect'.[4] They based this view chiefly upon

[1] Dublin, 1810, p. 227.

[2] J.K.L. (i.e. James, Kildare, and Leighlin), *Letters on the State of Ireland*, Dublin, 1825, p. 96.

[3] *Report on the Census of 1841, Reports of Commissioners*, 1843, xxiv, p. viii.

[4] Ibid.

two considerations; that the enumerators believed, often with justification, that their payment would be in proportion to the number of people included in their returns, and that the taking of the census was spread over a considerable time.

The 1841 Census is, in many ways, a remarkable piece of work.[1] We can accept, as near the truth, the figure of 8,175,124 which it gives. The much-reduced percentage of increase between 1831 and 1841 as compared with the previous intercensal period (5·25 per cent. as compared with 14·19 per cent.) may reasonably be attributed to greatly increased emigration. The Commissioners of this census were able to do their work so satisfactorily, partly because they were able to profit by experience gained in previous censuses, and partly because of their zeal to follow a 'strict mode of enquiry': they had their returns made by a 'highly disciplined body of men', on the same day throughout the country, and they applied a 'method of verification'.[2]

It seems, then, that though the 1841 Census is probably the first with a really high degree of accuracy, the censuses of 1821 and 1831 are not seriously inexact. It is improbable that either strays beyond the margin of error that must be assumed to remain in even the most careful revision of pre-census figures. We may, then, accept the 1821 return as a reliable landmark in Irish demographic history.

There is no shortage of estimates of the size of the population of Ireland during the century and a half preceding the taking of the first census: especially in the closing decades of the eighteenth century was interest displayed in the subject. Thirty pre-census estimates have been collected in Table 1. With few exceptions they have been arrived at by multiplying the returns (modified or unmodified) of the number of houses in the country (made by the collectors of hearth-money) by an estimate of the average number of people in a house. This procedure is likely to be beset by two major sources of error: by inaccuracy in the figure used for the number of houses in the country, and by inaccuracy in the average number of people assumed to live in a house.

[1] It collected, for instance, statistics of the age of the mother at the birth of the child, not, however, because of any anticipation of the value of reproduction rates, but because the Commissioners wished to find evidence for or against a belief that the sex of a child was determined by the relative ages of its parents.
[2] Ibid.

Table i

Estimates of the Population of Ireland from the Time of
Petty to 1841

1672	1,100,000	Petty, *Political Anatomy*, ed. Hull (Cambridge, 1899), p. 141.
1676	1,200,000	Petty, *Political Arithmetic*, ed. Hull (Cambridge, 1899), p. 272.
1687	1,300,000	Petty, *Treatise of Ireland*, ed. Hull (Cambridge, 1899), p. 610.
1695	1,034,102	South, *Phil. Trans.* (1700), xxii. 520.
1712	2,099,094	Attributed to Dobbs.*
1718	2,169,048	Attributed to Dobbs.*
1725	1,669,644	Dobbs, *Trade and Improvement* (Dublin, 1729–31), pt. ii, 7.
1725	2,317,374	Attributed to Dobbs.*
1726	2,309,106	Attributed to Dobbs.*
1731	2,010,221	Returns by parochial clergy and magistrates.
1732	2,000,000	*Abstract of Protestant and Popish Families* (Dublin, 1736).
1754	2,372,634	Hearth-money collectors.
1767	2,544,276	Hearth-money collectors.
1767	1,908,207	Price, *Reversionary Payments* (4th ed., 1783), ii. 253.
1777	2,690,556	Hearth-money collectors.
1777	2,475,000	Laffan, *Population, Commerce, etc. . . . of Ireland* (Dublin, 1785), p. 1.
1778	3,000,000	Young, *Tour in Ireland* (2nd ed., 1780), ii. 354.
1781	2,500,000–2,750,000	Howlett, *Essay on the Population of Ireland* (1786), p. 2.
1785	2,845,932	Hearth-money collectors.
1788	3,900,000	Newenham, *Progress and Magnitude of the Population of Ireland* (1805), p. 94.
1788	above 4,040,000	Bushe, *Trans. R.I. Acad.* (1789), iii, facing p. 143.
1790	3,750,344	Beaufort, *Memoir of a Map of Ireland* (1792).†
1791	4,206,612	Hearth-money collectors.
1791	3,850,000	Beaufort, op. cit., p. 142.‡
1799	3,000,000	Duigenan, *Fair Representation of the Present Political State of Ireland* (1799), p. 239.

* Dobbs, in his *Trade and Improvement* (Dublin, 1729–31) did not, in fact, make the estimates given here for 1712, 1718, 1725, and 1726, but he gives the returns of the hearth-money collectors upon which they are based (pt. ii, p. 5). They are attributed to him in the *Report* of the 1821 Census Commissioners (*Reports of Commissioners*, 1825, vi, p. 7) and generally elsewhere.

† This total figure is not given by Beaufort. It is the sum of the estimates he gives for every county, with the exception of Tyrone, together with an estimate for this omitted county arrived at by multiplying by six Beaufort's figure for the number of houses contained in it. MacEvoy in his *Statistical Survey of the County of Tyrone* (Dublin, 1802), p. 142, says 'From a great number of views I have taken in different parishes I find the average of persons to each house rather exceeds six'.

‡ This figure is erroneously given in the 'Preliminary Observations' to the 1821 Census, and elsewhere, as 4,088,226. *Accounts and Papers* (1824), xxii. 416.

1800	3,800,000	Eden, *Estimate of the Number of Inhabitants in Great Britain and Ireland* (1800), p. 41.
1803	above 5,000,000	*Essays on the Population of Ireland*, by a Member of the last Irish Parliament (1803), p. 2.
1804	5,400,000	Census Commissioners, 1821, *Reports of Commissioners* (1825), vi. 7.
1804	5,395,436	Newenham (1805), op. cit., p. 134.
1813	5,937,856	Incomplete Census (amended), *Reports of Commissioners* (1822), xiv. 737–8.
1821	6,801,827	Census.
1831	7,767,401	Census.
1841	8,175,124	Census.

TABLE 2

Number of Houses in Ireland, as returned by the Collectors of Hearth-money

1712	349,849	Dobbs, *Trade and Improvement* (1729–31), ii. 5–6.
1718	361,508	Ibid.
1725	386,229	Ibid.
1726	384,851	Ibid.
1732	386,902	*Abstract of Protestant and Popish Families* (Dublin, 1736).
1754	395,439	Price, *Reversionary Payments* (4th ed., 1783), ii. 319.
1767	424,046	Newenham, *Progress and Magnitude of the Population of Ireland* (1805), p. 94.
1772	429,759	Howlett, *Essay on the Population of Ireland* (1786), p. 21.
1777	448,426	Newenham (1805), op. cit., p. 94.
1781	477,402	*Journal of the House of Commons of Ireland*, x, App. p. dxxii.
1785	474,237	Ibid., xii, App. p. cclvi.
1788	621,484	Newenham (1805), op. cit., p. 72.
1790	677,094	Beaufort, *Memoir of a Map of Ireland* (1792).
1791	701,102	*Journal of the House of Commons of Ireland* (1792–4), xv, App. p. ccii.

Census figures:

1821	1,142,000
1831	1,250,000
1841	1,329,000

In Table 2, there are shown all the hearth-money collectors' returns of the number of houses in the country which it has been possible to trace. What degree of reliance can be placed upon these figures? Hearth-money was introduced into Ireland in 1662[1] as part of a general revision of the Irish fiscal system. The Irish House of Commons in that year expressed its appreciation of His Majesty's 'great and abundant goodness by his freely parting with almost all the great forfeitures devolved to the Crown': in particular it noticed that the king had recently abolished the Court of

[1] 14 & 15 Car. II, c. 17.

Wards at the supplication of the people. The Commons felt that some recompense should be made, and proposed that 'the late precedent in England was worthy of imitation and that 2/- per annum be paid out of all chimneys, stoves and hearths'.[1] The tax was to be paid by the tenant of every house, with the exception only of people not able to get their living by work, and widows falling below certain property qualifications.[2] An attempt to check the widespread evasion of the tax was made in 1665[3] when fines were imposed for concealment of hearths, and it was provided that houses having no fixed hearth should be assumed for purposes of taxation to have two.[4] Originally the tax was farmed by auction to the highest bidder, but in 1682 this practice was abandoned, and the tax was gathered by collectors appointed for the purpose.[5]

Dr. Richard Price had little confidence in the accuracy of the returns of the collectors. He had been informed, he said, that the collectors' return 'is of no account, and deserves little credit'.[6] The Rev. Mr. Howlett, on the other hand, maintained that as the returns proceeded upon nearly the same footing from the Revolution to the time at which he was writing (a century later) they were 'as full and complete for the purpose [of estimating the progress of Irish population] as anything of the kind can well be'.[7] Price, unfortunately, seems to approach the truth more nearly than Howlett. The revenue of Ireland in the seventeenth and eighteenth centuries, like that of most other countries, was loosely administered. The collectors had insistent motives urging them to send in returns that were seriously deficient: laziness induced them to overlook houses in districts that were difficult of access: acquisitiveness induced them to include in their official reports fewer houses than those from which they collected tax. It was Newenham's opinion of the collectors in 1805 'that a majority of them still stand exposed to censure for negligence and supineness in the execution of the business incident to their office'.[8] He thought

[1] *Journal of the House of Commons of Ireland*, ii. 132, 8 August 1662.

[2] G. E. Howard, *A Treatise of the Exchequer and Revenue of Ireland*, Dublin, 1777, i. 89.   [3] 17 & 18 Car. II, c. 18.

[4] Wm. Petty, *Political Arithmetic*, ed. Hull, p. 272, footnote by Hull.

[5] T. J. Kiernan, *History of the Financial Administration of Ireland to 1817*, 1930, p. 91.

[6] R. Price, *Observations on the Reversionary Payments*, 4th ed., 1783, ii. 319.

[7] J. Howlett, *Essay on the Population of Ireland*, 1786, p. 2.

[8] T. Newenham, *A Statistical and Historical Inquiry into the Progress and Magnitude of the Population of Ireland*, 1805, p. 79.

they had improved in honesty and he was not inclined to charge those of his day with fraudulent practices. Nonetheless, he quoted Bushe's authority for their practice of suppressing in their abstracts houses whose yield of tax they kept to themselves.[1] He also quoted Thomas Wray, the Inspector-General of the Hearth-Money, who told the House of Commons in 1793 that, although in his inspection of the previous summer he came across no instance of collectors taking bribes from persons they exempted from the tax, he had evidence of 'every other fraud'.[2] Even if the collectors were industrious and honest their returns might well be appreciably insufficient: 'there were numberless dwellings in the country', said Dr. Doyle, 'which could not be discovered by a stranger, or, if discovered, would not be considered as abodes of men'.[3] Kohl referred to human dwelling-places which the traveller might overlook because 'the roof one side was level with the ground, and nearly of the same consistency'.[4] Moreover, the collectors seem to have been confused about the procedure they should follow in connexion with houses the occupiers of which were exempt from paying the tax they were collecting. 'Some, in their abstracts', wrote Arthur Dobbs in 1731, 'return them completely, some in part, some not at all'.[5] That things cannot have improved much in this respect in later years is suggested in a remark made to Newenham by Wray in 1804 to the effect that 'there was no truth of which he was more convinced than that not more than one half of the exempted houses were returned'.[6] If this statement be accepted, the deficiency of the returns for 1791 (the nearest we have to the period at which Wray was speaking) for this reason alone must have been upwards of 130,000. The relative absence in Ireland of the nucleated village complicated the task of the honest collector. He was further hampered by the unpopularity of his office: the hostility of a community could do much to conceal houses from him in a district with which he was not well acquainted, and, in the endeavour to combat dishonesty, it was the practice of the

[1] Newenham, 1805, op. cit., p. 78.

[2] Ibid., p. 79. Quoting *J.H.C.I.* (1793), xv, App. p. 337.

[3] J.K.L., op. cit., p. 96.

[4] Quoted by J. H. Tuke, *A Visit to Connaught in the Autumn of 1847*, 1847, p. 22.

[5] A. Dobbs, *An Essay on the Trade and Improvement of Ireland*, 1729–31, ii. 5.

[6] T. Newenham, *A View of the Natural, Political, and Commercial Circumstances of Ireland*, 1809, App. p. 21.

Government to move collectors away from districts they knew well, but in which they were also well known. A less serious deficiency in the hearth-money returns as the basis of population estimates arose from the deliberate omission from them of public buildings: colleges, hospitals, poor-houses, barracks, the residences of revenue officers, all were overlooked.

It is not easy to give any precise judgement of the degree of error present in the returns of the collectors. Of one thing we can be certain: that the error is one of deficiency, rather than of excess. The laziness of the collectors, their desire to embezzle, the isolated nature of much of the country in which they were working, the opposition of the people with whom they were dealing, all these factors co-operated to make the number of hearths they returned less than the real number. The provisions of the laws relating to hearth-money did something to make the collectors' returns of houses less seriously deficient than their returns of hearths. In a communication to Howlett, Beresford, then First-Commissioner of the Irish Revenues, pointed out that the collectors were required to cover their walks twice: the first time they had to make a list of the houses in each parish, the second time they collected the tax, adding to the list any additional houses they discovered. The collector was impelled more strongly to make a deficient return of hearths than of houses. An accurate return of houses did not prevent his appropriating part of the tax, but an accurate return of hearths did. Moreover, a supervisor with about four collectors under him made a survey of at least one walk a year: the collectors knew that he could more easily detect omitted houses than omitted hearths.[1]

Beresford believed that the returns of houses were not seriously misleading: even the most inaccurate of them, he thought, did not show a deficiency of one-twentieth. His confidence was misplaced. The actual return of houses for 1781 was 477,402. To make an allowance for deficiencies for hospitals, barracks, and for the residences of revenue officers, he put the total number of houses at not less than 500,000. But, seven years later, the still-defective returns, without correction for excluded buildings, put the number at 621,484. It is impossible to believe, in spite of the crudeness of the Irish cabin and the ease with which it was constructed, that in seven years the number of houses increased by 30 per cent. or

[1] Howlett, 1786, op. cit., p. 2.

144,000, a figure which, as net increase, would represent considerably more additional building.

The figures in Table 2 are, on the whole, consistent with one another until those for the 1780s are reached. It is surprising, in view of the marked increases in the preceding and following years that there should have been a decline of more than 3,000 in the number of houses in the country between 1781 and 1785. But it is even more difficult to accept the upward-bounding figures between 1785 and 1791 as a true reflection of house-building activity. According to these figures the net annual increase of houses between 1785 and 1788 was over 49,000, between 1788 and 1790 nearly 28,000, and in 1790–1, 24,000. That these figures are improbable, and more useful as an indication of the degree of error in the hearth-money returns than as a measure of the amount of house-building, is suggested by comparing them with other evidence of the number of new houses put up in the period, and with the more reliable evidence of the net annual increase of houses between the first and the second censuses.

Bushe, in the paper in which he estimated population for 1788 upon the basis of hearth-money returns for that year, said that the most accurate column of his table showed that 18,824 houses were newly built in 1788.[1] In 1792 21,868 houses were exempted from tax because they were newly built.[2] If it is permissible to take the average of these figures—say 20,000—as a measure of house-building from 1785 to 1788, we have some check on the degree of inaccuracy present in the return of 1785. The official return for 1788 was 621,484. At an annual rate of building of 20,000, 60,000 new houses would have been erected since 1785. Taking these from the figure for 1788 we arrive at 561,484 as the number of houses in 1785. This figure clearly tends to be below the truth, because the deduction represents total new building (including replacements as well as additions), not the net increase of houses: there were houses in occupation in 1785, which should have swelled the total for that year, but which, because they had been deserted by 1788, were overlooked by the collectors. This minimum figure of 561,484 for 1785 compares with a return for that year of 474,237. There appears, then, to be a minimum deficiency

---

[1] G. P. Bushe, 'An Essay towards ascertaining the Population of Ireland', *Transactions of the Royal Irish Academy*, vol. iii, 1789, p. 154.

[2] *J.H.C.I.* (1792–4), xv, App. p. ccii.

in the official figure, when compared with a later official figure (in itself seriously below the truth) of over 18 per cent.

As a second indication of the degree of inaccuracy in the return for 1785 we may start with the number of inhabited houses in 1821, given in the census, and deduct from it a figure for the net increase of houses between 1785 and 1821. In the ten years between the first and second censuses the number of inhabited houses increased from 1,142,000 to 1,250,000, or at the rate of 10,800 per annum.[1] Because of the smaller total number of houses in the period from 1785 to 1821 it would probably not be under-estimating the position to assume an annual net increase during these years of 10,000. This means that the aggregate increase in the period would be 360,000. Deducting this from the figure for 1821 we arrive at the estimate of 782,000 houses for 1785, which, if correct, would indicate a deficiency of 64 per cent. in the official return for that year.

There is other evidence that the later returns of the hearth-money collectors were deficient. The most spectacular leap between any two successive figures is the increase of 147,247 in the three years before 1788. In these years the Government tightened up considerably the administration of hearth-money. It had become convinced that revenue was slipping through its fingers because of the inefficiency or dishonesty of its agents.[2] Bushe, the First-Commissioner, said that in 1786 'although sworn officers were appointed to collect the duty, and after the frauds of several of them had been detected and punished, there were houses suppressed to the number of near 200,000'.[3] Before the tax was collected for 1788 a general interchange of collectors was made so that collusion between tax-gatherer and tax-payer might be lessened. The greatly increased return of 1788 is some indication of the wisdom of this policy, but a simple reshuffling of collectors, many of whom were lazy, careless, or dishonest, did not produce precision. Again between 1788 and 1790 and between 1790 and

---

[1] Between 1831 and 1841 the number of inhabited houses increased at the rate of 7,900 a year. The larger annual increase between 1821 and 1831 seems likely to approximate more closely the trend of the years before 1821 because, as the Commissioners of the 1841 Census pointed out, the natural course of the figures from 1831 had been disturbed by emigration 'to a very great extent', certainly of a much greater annual volume than between 1780 and 1821.

[2] Newenham, 1805, op. cit., pp. 75-6.

[3] Ibid., p. 78.

1791 there were very substantial increases which it may not be fanciful to associate with a continuance of the Government's zeal, stimulated by an active First-Commissioner of the Revenue, to increase the efficiency of its fiscal administration.

The Government's agents were under no illusions about the accuracy of their returns. Bushe, the First-Commissioner, discussing the return of 1788, computed that it omitted some 44,800 houses,[1] a deficiency of 7 per cent. His Chief-Inspector, Thomas Wray, a man appointed to his office in 1787, and taking his duties sufficiently seriously to visit 'every walk in every part of the kingdom',[2] had even less confidence in the accuracy of the collectors. As already mentioned, he told Newenham in 1804 that he was convinced that not more than half of the exempted houses were returned. The number of exemptions reported in 1791 was 134,422. If as many were omitted, this would represent a deficiency in the official returns of 19 per cent.

Newenham collected some local evidence to support the view that the returns of the collectors were often seriously deficient. He quotes from Tighe's *Survey of Kilkenny* the account of houses in corporate towns in the county in 1802, and compares the total of 4,131 with the total of 2,495 for the same towns reported to Parliament in 1800.[3] That there should be so serious a discrepancy in urban districts where the problems of the collectors were relatively easy, confirms the presumption that in isolated rural areas the collectors may often have been very wide of the truth. Newenham also quotes figures that Bushe arrived at in 1788 for 13 towns. Seven of these had then 17,567 houses, but only 12,717 were reported by the collectors in 1800: for the remaining 6 towns the hearth-money returns were in excess of Bushe's computation.[4] Finally, Newenham gives a list of houses in the principal seaport towns as returned by the hearth-money collectors in 1800. They are probably, he says, in most cases below the truth, and in some cases they can be found to be considerably so. Dr. Patterson found 1,458 houses in Londonderry, a figure which is 304, or 25 per cent. in excess of the official return. Beaufort, in 1791, reported the number of houses in Belfast as 3,107, 54 more than were returned in 1800.[5]

---

[1] Bushe, 1790, op. cit., facing p. 143.
[2] *J.H.C.I.* (1792–4), vol. xv, App. p. cccxxxvii.
[3] Newenham, 1805, op. cit., pp. 81–2.
[4] Ibid., pp. 82–3.
[5] Newenham, 1809, op. cit., App. p. 11.

What conclusions can we come to on the degree of inaccuracy present in the official returns of the number of houses? The evidence is too insubstantial to allow any certainty. Perhaps the nearest we can get to any statistical appreciation of the situation is through comparing the latest available returns with data derived from the first two censuses. The dangers are obvious: trends may have changed in pace, or even in direction in the half-century between the first of the hearth-money returns we shall consider and the second census. But at least we are on relatively firm ground when our starting-point is census material. The second column of Table 3 shows for each of the years between 1785 and 1791 for which hearth-money returns are available, an estimate of the number of houses derived from the number the census gave for 1821 and an estimate for the annual net increase before that year based on the net increase of the first inter-censal period.[1] The third column shows the percentage deficiency between the official figure and this estimate.

TABLE 3*

Amended Returns of Number of Houses

	Official return of number of houses	Revised estimate of number of houses	Percentage deficiency of official return
1785	474,237	782,000	64
1788	621,484	812,000	30
1790	677,094	832,000	23
1791	701,102	842,000	20

* It should be borne in mind when considering this table that for three reasons the estimated numbers of houses tend to be below the truth, and therefore to minimize the degree of error apparent in the hearth-money returns. In the first place, while it is thought that the 1821 Census is somewhat deficient, that of 1831 probably suffers from a contrary defect. The result is that the figures for the net annual increase of houses based on material coming from these censuses tend to overstate the real position, and that therefore the estimates for earlier years tend to be underestimates. Second, whatever the number of houses over-looked by the enumerators of the 1821 Census, the same number is omitted from these estimates. And, third, if we had applied a figure based on the annual percentage increase of houses between 1821 and 1831 to the earlier period, as would appear to promise greater accuracy, instead of the absolute figure of 10,000, we should have had a smaller aggregate increase after 1785, and therefore higher estimates.

[1] The figure taken for the net annual increase is 10,000: see above, p. 10.

Thomas Wray's authority may be used to support figures in the order of these estimates. It was his opinion[1] that there were as many exempted houses omitted from the returns as included in them. Doubling the number of exempted houses, and thus allowing merely for one of many probable sources of deficiency, would bring the 1791 figure to 835,542, as compared with the estimate of 842,000.

The evidence is insufficient, but what there is would make plausible the assumption that the returns of 1790 and 1791 were not less than 20 per cent. short of the truth. For the earlier years less faith can be placed in the calculations because of the lengthening of the period before the taking of the censuses. But a much more substantial deficiency is to be expected for other reasons: we have already seen that there is cause to believe that the return for 1785 is at least 18 per cent. more deficient than that for 1788: the endeavours of the Government after 1786 to tighten up the administration of the hearth-money would lead us to expect the greatest inaccuracy in 1785, and more in 1788 than in 1790. It would, perhaps, not be too rash to estimate the deficiency of the 1785 return as appreciably over 50 per cent.

What of the accuracy of the earlier returns? It is quite impossible to give any precise opinion. The fall of over 3,000 between 1781 and 1785, coming, as it does, both before and after periods of increase suggests that administrative reasons may have been responsible—that the return for 1785 was somewhat more deficient than that of 1781. Unless, through the century, the Government tolerated increasing laxity and dishonesty amongst its collectors, it is to be expected that efficiency would tend to increase if for no other reason than that as the country became more thickly populated the task of the collectors became less arduous. We may, perhaps, make the assumption that a 50 per cent. deficiency, which appears to be an inadequate allowance for the shortcomings of the 1785 return, at least does not exaggerate the omissions from the returns of earlier years.

The first possibility of serious error in the majority of seventeenth- and eighteenth-century population estimates lay in inaccuracy in the figure used for the number of houses in the country. We have seen that when the estimates rest on the uncorrected returns of the hearth-money collectors they are likely to be deficient,

[1] See above, p. 7.

probably to an even greater extent than 50 per cent. What of
the other possible source of major error, inaccuracy in the
average number of people assumed to live in a house? The estimates vary from the figure of 4·36 which Arthur Dobbs used in
1725 to Bushe's figure of 6·25 worked out for 1788. The variations,
however, seem to a much greater extent to be the result of differences in method of calculation than of real changes in the proportion of population to houses. Certainly the figures used show no
discernible trend or trends between 1650 and 1800. Petty, in
1672, worked on the assumption that the number was 5·5. Beaufort, in 1791, was still using this figure, even though he was aware
of, and made constant reference to, Bushe's calculations made
three years earlier which arrived at an average of 6·25. Dobbs's
low estimate of 4·36 was used for 1725, yet both the population
estimates commonly attributed to him for years from 1712 to
1726 (and including 1725), and the run of estimates for years from
1754 to 1791 all work on the assumption of 6 persons per house.

One point upon which there is agreement amongst a number of
observers at the end of the eighteenth century is that the average
number of occupants of a house was greater in Ireland than in
England.[1] Some plausible reasons are given to account for the
greater crowding in Ireland. Bushe[2] discusses two sets of factors,
both those which caused relatively few houses to be built in Ireland
in his time, and those which tended to increase the number of
inhabitants per house. It was the custom in Ireland for houses to
be put up by the tenants. When the tenants were impoverished
they would often be obliged to encourage a married son to continue to reside with his parents rather than help him build a house
of his own: when they had some money they would often prefer
to invest it in more land than in a new house. The customary
shortness of tenure combined (at least in Leinster, Munster, and
Connaught) with no general compensation for tenant's improvements made the occupier reluctant to endure deprivations to allow
building which would tend to lead to an increased rent. It is,
however, easily possible to exaggerate the obstacles in the path of
the Irish peasant or labourer when thinking of building a house.
'The young couple', said Arthur Young, 'pass not their youth in

---

[1] See Newenham, 1805, op. cit., p. 247; Howlett, 1786, op. cit., n. pp. 15–16;
Bushe, 1789, op. cit., p. 152.
[2] Bushe, 1789, op. cit., pp. 152–5.

celibacy for want of a nest to produce their young in.'[1] The countryman was poor, it is true, but no great outlay was required to put up a house as good, perhaps, as the majority of those recorded by the collectors of hearth-money. Outside walls, which were seldom more than five or six feet high, were commonly made of sods or mud, sometimes with the first two or three feet built of stone without mortar: inside walls were seldom required. The roof was formed by resting turfs on a foundation of branches and covering them with a layer of straw, rushes, or the stalks of potatoes or beans.[2] The trifling total expenditure required to put up such a house must have been much more in family labour than in money: there were few commentators upon social conditions in eighteenth-century Ireland who thought the typical peasant or labourer did too much work. It is, then, perhaps to a greater extent to factors tending to increase family size rather than to factors depressing the amount of new building that we must look to account for the relatively large number of residents per house in Ireland. It is certain that in the decades centring on 1800 marriage in Ireland took place at an early age: the evidence presented in Chapter III leaves this in no doubt.[3]

The tendency of early marriage to increase family size was reinforced by the cheapness of rearing a child, and by his value on his father's land from childhood until his marriage, and often until after this. The dominating position the potato had come to occupy by the end of the eighteenth century in the diet of the countryman throughout Ireland meant that the expense his children put him to for food was slight: nor did their clothing or schooling commit him to appreciable outlay. Children, then, absorbed little of the family resources, but early in life made a contribution to their expansion. 'A farmer', said Townsend (and he was stressing a point frequently made by his contemporaries), 'often estimates his riches by the number of his sons, whose labour precludes any necessity of mercenary aid.'[4] Arthur Young, when inquiring into the state of the poor, 'found their happiness and ease generally relative to the number of their children, and nothing considered such a great misfortune as having none'.[5]

[1] Arthur Young, *Tour in Ireland*, 2nd ed., London, 1780, ii. 197.
[2] T. Campbell, *A Philosophical Survey of the South of Ireland in a series of letters to John Watkinson, M.D.*, 1777, p. 145.
[3] See below, Chapter III, pp. 51–2.   [4] Townsend, 1810, op. cit., p. 202.
[5] Arthur Young, 1780, op. cit. ii. 198.

The single family, then, tended to be large, but the number of people living in a house was often further swollen by forces inducing more than one family to live together. We have already seen that poverty may have obliged parents to allow a married child to live with them: the wretchedness of the general standard of living made parents and children tolerant of the privations that the Irish cabin made inseparable from this practice. The system, too, of giving a son on his marriage a portion of the parental holding must have strengthened the tendency for him to remain living with his parents. The absence in Ireland of a poor law meant that when a labourer died his family was often divided amongst neighbouring households, and that when a couple became too old to work their land, and had no children living with them, they had to move to live with relations or others who would maintain them.

In the face of this evidence it is not difficult to believe that by the end of the eighteenth century there was typically in Ireland an abnormally large number of people living in a single house. To what extent was this position the result of recent developments? Bushe was willing to regard the figure of 5·5 occupants per house which Petty used in 1672 and his own figure of 6·25 for 1788 as largely, if not entirely, a measure of the change which had taken place in the intervening years. He pointed out that the scarcity of timber, which he thought appreciably retarded house-building in his own day, was probably not felt in Petty's time; that 'the wretched habitations' of Petty's day 'were worth but five shillings each, and could not hold two families'; that houses such as the peasant was used to could be easily built and that probably peasants did not have servants living with them, nor northern linen-weavers' apprentices, to the extent they had a century later.[1] These reasons do not appear to be sufficient to account for the discrepancy between Petty's figure and Bushe's: Bushe probably exaggerated the extent to which the house of his time was superior to that of Petty's. He does not consider how far the laying waste of much of Ireland in the years before Petty was writing tended to drive an abnormally large population into the remaining houses. Nor does he endeavour to estimate whether in Petty's time there were forces at work keeping up the size of the typical family as effectively as when he himself was writing. Certainly

[1] Bushe, 1789, op. cit., p. 152.

marriage was early in Petty's time as well as in the closing decades of the eighteenth century.[1] Nor can the contribution of early marriage towards high fertility have been seriously weakened by the inability of the people to make use of their children's labour. Perhaps a family cost a little more to rear in Petty's time: certainly there does not appear to have been the nearly complete dependence upon the potato that there was by the end of the following century.[2] But provision of the normal diet cannot have been a serious burden in a pastoral community. The food of the Irish, Petty said, 'is bread in cakes, whereof a penny serves a week for each; potatoes from August till May, mussels, cockles, and oysters near the sea; eggs and butter made very rancid by keeping in bogs. As for flesh, they seldom eat it, notwithstanding the great plenty thereof, unless it be of the smaller animals, because it is inconvenient for one of these families to kill a beef which they have no convenience to save. So as 'tis easier to have a hen or a rabbit than a piece of beef of equal substance.'[3] The tendency of the absence of a system of poor relief to increase the number of inhabitants in the average house was common to both the seventeenth and eighteenth centuries. It is almost only in regard to the practice of subdivision that we find an important factor in Bushe's time tending to increase crowding that may not have been operative when Petty was writing.

What evidence have we, and how reliable is it, of the average number of people living in a single house? Again, it seems wiser to start with the material provided by the censuses, and from this fairly certain base to push our inquiry back into years for which the information tends to become scantier and more questionable. According to the Census there were, in 1821, 5·95 persons on the average living in every inhabited house, in 1831, 6·2, and in 1841, 5·9. As in the case of the increase of houses between 1821 and 1841, the contrast between the trend of the twenties and that of the thirties is striking, and again the quickening rate of emigration seems to be largely responsible for it. The explanation of the very marked increase of crowding between 1821 and 1831 may perhaps largely be found in the factors we have already noticed tending to increase

[1] See below, Chapter III, p. 52.
[2] See below, Chapter V, pp. 125–35.
[3] Wm. Petty, *The Political Anatomy of Ireland*, *1672*, ed. C. H. Hull, Cambridge, 1899, p. 191.

family size, coupled with the increasingly common practice of the consolidation of holdings.[1] Consolidation was often accompanied by the tearing down of houses which, though they may have been superfluous from the standpoint of economic estate management, were often very much otherwise from that of the housing requirements of the rural population. The evicted tenants were obliged to seek shelter from their more fortunate fellows—and in doing so they tended to increase the size of the average household.

Does the limited statistical evidence we have for the decades before 1821 suggest that the increased crowding of the twenties was the continuance or the reversal of the trend of these earlier years? The most careful work on the subject was that which Bushe did for the year 1788. Bushe, the First-Commissioner of the Revenue, able to direct the collectors and supervisors of hearth-money, was more fortunately placed than other eighteenth-century writers interested in Irish population movements, and he made the fullest use of his opportunities. To find the average number of people living in a house he selected the most intelligent of the tax-collectors and required them to give an account of the number of persons in each house in their walks: if they were in doubt about the accuracy of the figure they were given for the number of residents in any particular house, they were instructed to omit it rather than give an unreliable figure. For each county Bushe found the number of houses in each of four categories: those occupied by widows and paupers, those with one hearth apiece which paid tax, those with more than one hearth, and new houses. He then extracted from the lists compiled by the chosen collectors, houses in each category amounting to one-twentieth of the county total for that category, and calculated the number of persons per house for his tolerably representative twentieth of the total number of houses. For those counties for which he did not have data for a representative twentieth of the houses he based his figure of persons per house upon a smaller sample, but one in which each category had its proper representation. These calculations gave a figure of 6·25—higher than any estimate in use before Bushe's time, but, he felt, inclined to err in the direction of under- rather than over-estimating the real position. The collectors, Bushe thought, were not ideally placed for getting correct answers to the question they put at each house on the number of occupants in

[1] Though see below, Chapter VI, pp. 174–80.

it: well-to-do people felt that the question coming from the collector was impertinent, the poor suspected that it was asked with some bad design. Either from carelessness or suspicion residents tended to be overlooked. Never, when Bushe was able to check the information provided on this subject by the collectors did he find that numbers had been exaggerated.[1]

If Bushe's figures could be accepted it would appear that the tendency towards greater crowding apparent in the first intercensal years was a reversal of the trend from 1788 to 1821, when the number of occupants per house would have declined substantially from 6·25 to 5·95. The resources at Bushe's disposal and the care he went to to see that his sample investigation was representative make us reluctant to make any substantial alteration in his figure. But it is difficult to reconcile it with other evidence that cannot be easily discarded. The Rev. Dr. Beaufort published his *Memoir of a Map of Ireland* in 1792. He was quite well aware of Bushe's work—he quoted appreciatively and frequently from it —but he showed no confidence in the accuracy of its figures for the average number in a household. Bushe gives seventeen county figures, but practically every one is considerably in excess of the figure Beaufort used to work out his own population estimate: the average[2] of Bushe's figures comes to 6·08, and of Beaufort's to 5·35. Beaufort's figure for the whole country was 5·5—lower by 0·75 than Bushe's.

There is other nearly contemporary opinion besides Beaufort's which would support the use of a lower figure for population per house than Bushe's. Newenham assumed that there were 6 persons per house because he believed the Irish figures were in excess of the English return of $5\frac{7}{8}$.[3] Howlett, writing in 1786, says he is satisfied that the number of persons to a house in England, exclusive of London, is about $5\frac{1}{3}$. From this he feels he may conclude 'with some probability' that the number in Ireland, inclusive of Dublin, is not less than $5\frac{1}{2}$.[4] Laffan, writing in 1785, adopted the same figure.[5] A number of writers of the *Statistical Surveys* of the

---

[1] Bushe, 1789, op. cit., p. 149.
[2] Omitting in both cases counties 'for which either writer, or both of them, give separate figures for the largest town in a county and for the county itself.
[3] Newenham, 1805, op. cit., p. 247.
[4] Howlett, 1786, op. cit., pp. 15–16 n.
[5] J. Laffan, *Political Arithmetic of the Population, Commerce, and Manufactures of Ireland*, Dublin, 1785, p. 1.

counties of Ireland published by the Dublin Society between
1801 and 1832 give for their counties figures based either upon
their opinions or upon surveys for part of the county. MacEvoy,
after taking into account 'a great number of views that I have
taken in different parishes' said the figure for Tyrone 'rather
exceeds six'.[1] Besides this equivocal testimony the only figure
supporting Bushe is given by Coote who says that in one barony
of Cavan there were from 6 to 8 people per house, but in the
other there were only 6.[2] Tighe's *Kilkenny*, though saying that a
figure of 6 to a house is not too high for country parts, records a
survey of 1,114 houses taken in 1798 in part of two baronies which
found that the average number of inhabitants was 5·7.[3] Fraser, in
his *Wicklow* (supported by enumerations made by Whitelaw, who
took the 1798 Census of Dublin, by Henry Tighe and others), says
he is unable to put the average number per house at more than
5·5, the figure arrived at by the Rev. James Symes after an
enumeration of his parish of Castle M'Adam, with nearly 3,000
parishioners.[4] Townsend, who wrote the very able *Statistical
Survey of the County of Cork*, supports as an average for town and
country the figure of 6 used by his friend Newenham.[5] Dubourdieu, for Down, as a result of counting both persons and houses
in his own parish of Annahilt, arrived at a figure of 5·25.[6] Sampson, for Londonderry, received from a resident 'an accurate figure'
for a coastal parish which put the average number of occupants
per house at 5·3. He made a survey in his own inland parish which
resulted in a figure of 5·2. He thought an average of 5·25 might be
extended to the country.[7] MacParlan assumes in his *Leitrim*, not
apparently as the result of any enumeration, that there were 5
people per house,[8] and in his *Sligo*, again with no supporting evidence, that 'as much as six . . . if not more' could safely be assumed
to be in a family.[9]

The authority of the 1813 Census, so carelessly and incompletely

---

[1] J. MacEvoy, *Statistical Survey of the County of Tyrone*, Dublin, 1802, p. 142.
[2] C. Coote, *Statistical Survey of the County of Cavan*, Dublin, 1802, pp. 90
and 239.
[3] W. Tighe, *Kilkenny*, Dublin, 1801, p. 453.
[4] R. Fraser, *Wicklow*, Dublin, 1801, pp. 107 and 240.
[5] Townsend, 1810, op. cit., p. 86.
[6] J. Dubourdieu, *Down*, Dublin, 1802, p. 243.
[7] G. V. Sampson, *Londonderry*, Dublin, 1802, p. 293.
[8] J. MacParlan, *Leitrim*, Dublin, 1802, p. 61.
[9] J. MacParlan, *Sligo*, Dublin, 1802, p. 69.

was it taken, must be used warily. Whatever weight it has supports a severe downward revision of Bushe's figure. The published returns, purporting to cover the entire country, with the exception of 6 counties and 2 towns, show an average household of 5·8 persons. This figure, quite consistent with the 1821 average of 5·95, is for a date 25 years later than Bushe's estimate, and the evidence is that during these years crowding was increasing.[1]

William Shaw Mason's *Statistical Account, or Parochial Survey of Ireland*,[2] 'drawn up from the communications of the clergy', like the census of 1813 must be considered with some reserve. It includes data upon the average number of people per house from 54 parishes scattered throughout the country. Thirty-three of these returns appear to be drawn from material compiled for the 1813 Census. The remaining 21 are based upon the opinion of the incumbent, or upon private surveys. These 21 figures suggest either that Bushe's figure for 1788 was above the truth, or that there was a remarkable decline in the proportion of people to houses in the following years: only 5 are higher than Bushe's 6·25. The remaining 16 figures in the series vary from 4 to 6: the average of the 21 is 5·2.

It seems, then, that, chary though we should be to modify Bushe's work, it might be wiser to accept a figure somewhat lower than his. Not only would the bulk of the statistical evidence support such a course, but to do otherwise would be to run counter to the trend that the social condition of Ireland would lead us to expect. The population per house in 1821, we have seen, was 5·95, and in the following decade it rose markedly, probably because of the united influence of factors tending to increase family size and the prevalence of consolidation followed by clearance. Consolidation at the pace at which it proceeded in the thirties was a new development, but since Bushe's time marriage had been early, a large family had been a cheap asset, married children had tended to live with their parents—in short, factors tending to increase the number of people living in a house had been operative. We should, it seems, in accepting a figure for 1788 allow for increased crowding between then and 1821, though at a slower rate than between 1821 and

---

[1] *Reports (Ireland)*, 1822, xiv. 737 f. The omissions are for Louth, Westmeath, Wexford, Cavan, Donegal, Sligo, and the towns of Kilkenny and Limerick. The returns for other counties were far from complete: see below, App. I, p. 258.

[2] Dublin, i, 1814; ii, 1816; iii, 1819.

1831. This would give us a rough upper limit of 5·8: as a lower limit we should not be justified in undercutting the figure of 5·5 upon which Beaufort, with perhaps excessive caution, based his calculations.

Our evidence on the average number of people living in a house in the century and more separating the work of Petty and Bushe is fragmentary. Much the most authoritative opinion is Petty's own. Petty was admirably placed for investigating the social conditions of Ireland. The 'Preliminary Observations' to the 1821 Census say of him that

> the circumstances in which he stood, with respect to this country, gave him great local advantages towards the solution of a question, to the investigation of which his mental powers and habits of study peculiarly qualified him. He had superintended the great Territorial Survey of Ireland, instituted during the Protectorate, for the distribution of forfeited property; the importance and accuracy of which may be estimated from the consideration, that . . . it still, after a lapse of more than two centuries continues to be the standard of reference, in the courts of the Judicature. . . .[1]

The value of Petty's population estimates, however, is lessened by his reticence on the procedure which allowed him to arrive at them. In *The Political Anatomy of Ireland, 1672*, Petty states that the country had 200,000 families[2] and 1,100,000 people, an average of 5·5 per house.[3] In the *Treatise of Ireland, 1687*, he assumes a slight change—that single-chimney houses average 5, and households with more than one chimney 6.[4] In neither work does Petty refer to any inquiry upon which these averages were based. Failing other evidence, and because of Petty's unrivalled opportunity for arriving at a correct estimation of Irish social conditions we may, perhaps, accept his figure of 5·5 as an approximation of the truth.

The next available information on the subject applies to the 1730s and indicates some decline from Petty's figure. Arthur Dobbs in his *Trade and Improvement of Ireland* said that 'from several returns made to me of the number of persons in each family in a great many contiguous parishes in Antrim I find the medium

---

[1] *Accounts and Papers (Ireland)*, 1824, xxli. 416.

[2] That Petty is using the word 'family' in the then customary sense of household is made plain by his division of families into three categories, those with no fixed hearth, those which have but one chimney, and those with more than one.

[3] *The Economic Writings of Sir William Petty*, ed. C. H. Hull, Cambridge, 1899, p. 141.

[4] Ibid., p. 610.

to be 4·36 per family'. He applied this figure to his estimate of the number of houses in the country to arrive at a population estimate which he was 'apt to believe is within the truth'.[1] The anonymous author of the *Abstract of the Number of Protestant and Popish Families in Ireland*[2] used a figure of five persons per household in connexion with a population estimate for 1732. He said that several gentlemen had had the curiosity to take an exact account of the number of men, women, and children in every house in several large districts and great towns. They found in some parts of the open country 4·33 to 4·5 people per house, in other parts where manufactures were carried on 4·75 to 5·0, and in large towns and cities from 5 upwards almost (in the case of Dublin) to 10. He pointed out that the discrepancy between county and city households is explained by the practice of the 'lower sort of people', who have few servants themselves, sending their children to wealthier families in the towns. He thought it reasonable to allow five to a family throughout the kingdom.[3] Only one opinion is available from the *Abstract* until the quickened interest in problems of Irish population in the seventies and eighties. This is in Price's *Observations on the Reversionary Payments*.[4] He made, very briefly, an estimate of the population of Ireland for 1767 on the assumption that there were 4·5 persons per house. He gave no explanation of how he arrived at this figure.

What use can be made of this very slight evidence to gauge the trend in the size of the average household during a century? It would be rash to take too seriously Price's figure for 1767. It would show that between then and 1788 the average number of persons living in a house increased by 22 per cent., even if we take the most drastic downward scaling of Bushe's figure that seems likely. More substantial evidence than Price's cursory reference would be needed to believe that so marked a change took place. Perhaps, though, Price's figure may be used to lend some support to the hypothesis that there was not a gradual increase in the size of the household from Petty's time to 1821, but that before the increase began there was a contrary trend. Both Dobbs and the *Abstract*

---

[1] Arthur Dobbs, *Essay on the Trade and Improvement of Ireland*, Dublin, 1729–31, ii. 7.

[2] Dublin, 1736.

[3] Reprinted in *Tracts and Treatises illustrative . . . of Ireland*, Dublin, 1861, ii. 535–6.

[4] 4th ed., 1783, ii. 253.

make it doubtful if Petty's figure was maintained until the thirties. We may, perhaps, assume, though with no certainty, that in the thirties a low level of between 5·0 and 5·25 persons per house was reached. Such an assumption would make allowance for the probability that the surveys in Antrim, upon which Dobbs's figure was based, did not include any considerable urban area, and that both his figure and that in the *Abstract* suffered, as was the tendency with private inquiries, from the householder's reluctance to give a full return.

Table 4, besides giving a revision of Petty's figure for 1687, shows for each year for which hearth-money returns are available, population estimates based upon two assumptions, first, that the hearth-money figures were defective by 50 per cent. up to 1785, that this deficiency dropped to 25 per cent. in 1788, and was 20 per cent. in 1790 and 1791; and, secondly, that the average number of persons to a household fell steadily from 5·5 in 1672 to 5·2 in the mid-seventeen-thirties, and thereafter rose to 5·65 by Bushe's time. The indications are that the error in these figures, which may well be substantial, is one of deficiency: they are based on conservative estimates both of the omissions from the hearth-money returns and of the average number in a household. Nonetheless, they are in almost every case considerably in excess of the traditional estimates shown in Table 1.[1]

Has the centre of interest in discussion of the growth of the population of Ireland legitimately been the 'phenomenal pace' of the expansion towards the close of the eighteenth century? Such revision of the traditional estimates as has seemed necessary allows still for substantial growth, but we should reckon, it seems, not, as Mr. Griffith supposed, with an increase of 172 per cent. in the sixty years before 1841, but with an increase that can scarcely have exceeded, and may well have been less than 100 per cent. This more modest expansion, from 4 to 8 millions in sixty years, brings Irish experience into the same category as that of Britain.[2] Not only does the quickening in the rate of increase of the popula-

---

[1] The methods by which the traditional estimates were arrived at, and the reasons for their divergence from the figures advanced here, are explained in Appendix I, pp. 255–60.

[2] Providing that Rickman's estimate for 1780 is much more nearly accurate than the work of some of his contemporaries interested in Irish population, and that the population of Britain did, in fact, increase by around 88 per cent. between 1780 and 1841.

tion of Ireland seem to be much more restrained than would appear from the traditional figures, but so also, in all probability, was the increase in the previous century. From Petty's uncorrected estimate for 1687 to Young's estimate for 1779 there appeared to

TABLE 4

Revised Estimates of the Population of Ireland

	Modified estimate of number of houses	Persons per house	Population estimate	Traditional estimates
1687	..	5–6*	2,167,000	*1,300,000*
1712	524,773	5·3	2,791,000	*2,099,094*
1718	542,262	5·3	2,894,000	*2,169,048*
1725	579,343	5·25	3,042,000	*{ 1,669,644–* *2,317,374 }*
1726	577,275	5·25	3,031,000	*2,309,106*
1732	580,353	5·2	3,018,000	*2,000,000*
1754	593,158	5·38	3,191,000	*2,372,634*
1767	636,069	5·47	3,480,000	*2,544,276*
1772	644,638	5·56	3,584,000	..
1777	672,639	5·56	3,740,000	*2,690,556*
1781	716,403	5·65	4,048,000	*{ 2,500,000–* *2,750,000 }*
1785	711,355	5·65	4,019,000	*2,845,932*
1788	776,855	5·65	4,389,000	*{ 3,900,000–* *above 4,040,000 }*
1790	812,513	5·65	4,591,000	*3,750,344*
1791	841,322	5·65	4,753,000	*3,850,000*
		Census figures		
1821	1,142,000	5·95	6,802,000	..
1831	1,250,000	6·2	7,767,000	..
1841	1,329,000	5·9	8,175,000	..

* Five in single-hearth houses; six in larger houses.

be an increase of 130 per cent. With the figures suggested in this chapter (and it should again be emphasized that all, and especially those for the century before 1780, may remain seriously inaccurate) the rate of increase is brought down to 80 per cent. What remains remarkable is the acceleration in the growth of population beginning in the 1770s: by the revised estimates a ten-yearly increase of some 9 per cent. before 1780 is succeeded by a ten-yearly increase between 1780 and 1821 of about 17 per cent. Still we are left with the problem that was so widely interesting to contemporaries: what caused the upward leap in the rate of growth? Was it that people were living longer, or that more were being born? Was it that there was a 'gap in the famines' or that people were marrying earlier? Had changes in the balance between tillage and pasture, or in that between large and small holdings, any relevance to the question? Did the unique importance of the potato in the diet of the Irishman, or the cheapness with which his house could be built, materially affect the situation? Did Grattan's Parliament bring a new political and economic climate favourable to population expansion? It is to these, and to related questions, that we must now turn.

II

BIRTHS AND MARRIAGES: STATISTICS

CLEARLY, the acceleration in the rate of population-increase which, according to the figures suggested in Chapter I, had begun by the 1780s, must have been the result of one or more of three factors: it must have been caused, singly or jointly, by an excess of immigration over emigration, by a rising birth-rate, or by a falling death-rate. Migration, directly, offers no help in explaining the rapid increase of population. Since the seventeenth century immigration into Ireland, though of some importance culturally and economically, has been numerically insignificant.[1] Emigration, far from helping to solve our problem, increases its magnitude: the last twenty-five years of rapid population-increase were also years of heavy emigration. It would be fruitless to attempt to discover what the population of Ireland would have been in 1845 but for emigration. The difficulties besetting any such calculation range from the manageable problem of determining the number of emigrants to the quite insurmountable difficulties of estimating both the fertility and mortality of the emigrants and their descendants had they remained at home, and the effect their presence would have had on the fertility and mortality of those who did in fact remain. As for the total number of emigrants, Professor W. F. Adams in *Ireland and Irish Emigration to the New World*,[2] gives estimates which put the total emigration from Ireland to America and Canada between 1780 and 1845 at about 1,140,000. The number of short-distance migrants to England and Scotland seems to bring the figure to around 1,750,000.

Professor Adams says that the three important sources of statistics of Irish trans-Atlantic emigration in the years before the Famine are the records, beginning in 1825, of sailings from English and Irish ports, those, beginning in 1819, of arrivals at ports of the United States, and those, beginning officially in 1828, of arrivals at Quebec. He points out that these figures are deficient, partly

[1] D. A. E. Harkness, 'Irish Emigration', in *International Migrations*, ed. I. Ferenczi and W. F. Willcox, New York, ii, 1931, p. 263.

[2] New Haven, 1932.

because they omit some of the emigrants carried by vessels that presented incomplete lists and all of those in vessels that failed to clear with the authorities, and partly because the customs officials presented in their reports the number of 'whole passengers' emigrating, either omitting children altogether or regarding two or three of them as the equivalent of one adult. The problem of estimating the number of Irish emigrants is further complicated by the difficulty of determining what proportion of the migrants leaving British ports were Irish. However, Professor Adams has revised the records available for the years after 1815 and has estimated that 1 million Irish went to Canada and the United States between then and 1845.[1] The figures for the years before 1815 are fragmentary, but we may be certain that emigration was slight in comparison with that of the following thirty years. Professor Adams says that, in the early eighteenth century, in only one year did as many as 3,000 Irish emigrate to the New World. Before 1774 an annual figure of over 6,000 had been reached but the average movement was around 4,000. Famine conditions in Ireland at the opening of the nineteenth century increased the number abnormally to about 6,000 a year for three years. From 1812 to 1814 emigration practically ceased: 'when, in 1816, the number again reached 6,000 it was considered extraordinary, and the 20,000 who followed in 1818 inaugurated a new era.'[2] We should, it seems, approach the truth as closely as is practicable by taking an average annual figure of 4,000 for the years 1780 to 1815. This gives a gross movement for these years of 140,000, to be added to the round million who emigrated in the thirty years before the Famine.

To this number of Irish who emigrated to the New World we have to add the very considerable number who went no farther than England and Scotland. The Census of Ireland of 1841 estimated that, in the previous ten years alone, Ireland lost 144,000 persons by migration to Britain, and by enlistment in the British Army and the East India Company.[3] According to the English census of 1841 there were then 419,000 people of Irish birth resident in England,[4] and this figure, however accurately compiled,

[1] Op. cit., pp. 410–26. The roughly comparable figure of 934,000 for the same years is given by Ferenczi in *International Migrations*, op. cit. i, New York, 1929, p. 99.   [2] Adams, op. cit., pp. 69–70.
[3] *Reports from Commissioners*, 1843, xxiv, p. xxvii.
[4] Ibid., p. x.

can account for only a proportion of the Irish who had taken up residence in Britain in the previous sixty years. We do not, it seems, exaggerate the extent of total emigration in the sixty-five years before the Famine if we put it at 1,750,000. But whether such an addition to the population resident in Ireland in 1845 would under- or over-assess the rate of natural increase it is impossible to say. We do not know whether the loss to Ireland of the emigrants and their children was more or less than offset by the tendency of their removal to make Malthus's positive check less insistent in its operation and to facilitate the marriage of those who remained at home. Certainly we may conclude that the rapid rate of increase shown in the population figures put forward in Chapter I reflects an even faster rate of natural-increase. We must, then, look for the entire causation of the doubling of population in the sixty years before the Famine to the mechanics of higher fertility or decreased mortality singly or in conjunction.

There is little statistical material earlier than that collected in the 1841 Census to help us to determine whether, in the whole or in any part of Ireland, abnormally high fertility helps to explain rising population. What parochial returns of births were kept applied only to the Protestant minority of the population, a group which differed from the remainder in occupation, custom, and wealth. Even had many of the minority's records survived they would be of little help in trying to estimate national or regional fertility. The compulsory registration of births was not extended to Ireland until 1863. It is, therefore, fortunate that the third Irish census, far more detailed than its predecessors, or than its contemporary in Britain, gives us some guidance on fertility in the closing years of our period.

Table A in Appendix II is derived from figures collected for this census: it shows, for the counties of Ireland, the annual average number of births between 1832 and 1841 per 1,000 of the mean population between those years. Table 5, below, gives figures for the Irish provinces and sets them beside comparable, and nearly contemporary, data for England and Wales. It is clear that there is no question of the crude birth-rate in Ireland being high by nineteenth-century British standards.

The crude birth-rate, however, is notoriously deceptive as a measure of fertility. Births are a function, not of total population, but of the number of women within the total population of child-bearing age: more closely they are a function of the number of married women of child-bearing age. Table 6, as an approximation to fertility-rates, shows for 1841 the proportions of children under

TABLE 5

Crude Birth-rate in the Provinces of Ireland, 1832–41, and in England and Wales, 1836–60

Rural and civic districts, 1832–41	Births per 1,000 mean population
Leinster	31·0
Munster	33·9
Ulster	32·1
Connaught	35·7
Ireland*	33·0
England and Wales (1836–46)†	31·43
England and Wales (1851–60)†	34·13

* Census of Ireland, 1841, *Reports of Commissioners*, 1843, xxiv. 459.
† G. T. Griffith, *Population Problems of the Age of Malthus* (Cambridge, 1926), p. 28. Births here are assumed to be baptisms plus 15 per cent.

TABLE 6

Children under 1 and Children under 5 per 1,000 Women 15–44, in Ireland and England and Wales, 1841

	Women 15–44	Children under 1	Children under 5	Number of children per 1,000 women 15–44	
				Under 1	Under 5
Ireland*	1,934,298	361,424	1,246,413	187	644
England and Wales†	3,802,373	427,600	2,099,194	112	552

* Census of Ireland, 1841, op. cit., p. 489.
† *Appendix to Ninth Annual Report of the Registrar-General, Reports of Commissioners*, 1849, xxi. 232.

1 year and under 5 per 1,000 married women from 15 to 44 years of age in both Ireland and England and Wales. If the figures there given are accepted they show a fertility in Ireland remarkably higher than in England: the proportion of children under 1 year is here 67 per cent. greater in Ireland than in England. This figure, moreover, according to the data in the table, would tend to under-

estimate the excess of Irish fertility. The much smaller excess, of 17 per cent., in the proportion of Irish children under five indicates, *ceteris paribus*, a substantially higher infantile mortality in Ireland, and this, presumably, would have had the effect of making the ratio of English infants to Irish smaller than the ratio of English births to Irish.

The great extent of the excess of Irish over contemporary English fertility shown by this table should make us question its accuracy. There is, however, other material that confirms its general conclusion. In order to test the validity of the theory that the sex of a child was usually dependent on the relative ages of its parents, the Commissioners of the 1841 Census collected information on the number of children born before 6 June 1841 to couples married in or since 1830, and presented it classified according to the ages of husband and wife. It is possible to extract from these data the number of children born in ten years to wives of various age-groups married in 1831 and thereby to obtain fertility data that are broadly comparable with information collected in the British fertility census of 1911.

TABLE 7

Fertility of Marriages of Ten Years' Duration, in Ireland, in 1841, and in England and Wales, in 1911

Age of wife at marriage	Children born before 6 June 1841 per 100 couples married in 1831 in Ireland*	Children born per 100 couples in marriages of ten years' duration in England and Wales†
Under 17 . .	356	374
17–25 . . .	383	320
26–35 . . .	326	209
36–45 (Ireland) ⎫ 36–44 (England) ⎭ .	135	149

* Census of Ireland, 1841, op. cit., pp. 460 ff. The Irish figures relate only to first marriages, that is, to 81·5 per cent. of total marriages.

† Fertility Census, 1911, *Reports of Commissioners*, 1917–18, xxxv. 338–9. The figures given here are calculated by averaging both fertility for wives at each year of age within the age-groups and fertility for marriages of 9–10 and 10–11 years' duration.

According to this table the youngest wives in Ireland and the oldest showed a lower fertility than wives in the same age-groups in England and Wales seventy years later. But in neither of these cases was the difference marked—a matter of 5 per cent. for wives under 17 and 8 per cent. for those over 36.[1] For wives in the intermediate age-groups the position was very different: fertility was greater in Ireland, and substantially greater. Irish wives married between 17 and 25 had practically 20 per cent. more children in the first 10 years of their married lives than the English wives in the same age-group: Irish wives married between 26 and 35 had 56 per cent. more. Table 14 makes it clear that in Ireland and England in the eighteen-forties the vast majority of marriages took place while the wife was in one of these age-groups of relatively high Irish fertility.

The data in the 1841 Census which have given these high national fertility figures have been used in Table 8 to show differences in fertility between the four provinces and between their rural and civic districts. Perhaps the most remarkable feature of this table is the excess it shows for every age-group of rural over urban marital fertility. For the two lower age-groups wives in rural districts had a fertility over 9 per cent. greater than that of those in urban districts: for wives between 26 and 35 the excess was 20 per cent., and for those from 36 to 45 it rose to 70 per cent. Not only was urban fertility relatively low, but it appears to have had an inverse dependence upon the size of the town. Dublin, Cork, and Belfast, the three towns which, because of their size, were treated separately from the civic districts of their provinces, show, as a rule (and always for the great majority of wives), marital fertility less than that of the entire civic districts of Ireland, and, with few exceptions, less than that of the civic districts of their own provinces.[2] For

[1] It is surprising to find that in Tables 8 and 9, which give marital fertility figures for both rural and civic districts of every Irish province and for all three of the large towns separately treated, the fertility of wives under 17 is lower than that of wives in the next, 17–25, age-group (with the two exceptions of Cork City in Table 8 and the civic districts of Connaught in Table 9). This unusual phenomenon is, perhaps, to be associated with the small number of pre-marital conceptions which, on the authority of most observers, took place in Ireland (see below, pp. 47–9): elsewhere, in all probability, a larger proportion of girls under 17 married 'because they had to'. The relatively low Irish fertility shown in Table 7 for wives above 36 may be the result partly of the inclusion in the Irish figures of women who married at 45 and were likely, therefore, to be highly infertile. Partly it may be attributable to earlier marriage (see below, Table 14): with more Irish women than English married before they were 36, and with women selected for marriage partly by the expectation of fertility, it is likely that those remaining unmarried at that age in Ireland contained an inflated proportion of sterile women.

[2] Wives under 17 in Cork City—but there were only 34 of them—show a higher fertility than members of the same age-group in the civic districts of

every age-group, except the oldest and smallest, Dublin had a lower fertility than Cork or Belfast.

TABLE 8

Fertility of Marriages of Ten Years' Duration in the Rural and Civic Districts of the Provinces of Ireland, in 1841*

Column (*a*) shows the number of marriages in 1831 in which neither partner was married before; column (*b*) shows the number of births to these marriages taking place before 6 June 1841, and column (*c*) shows the number of births per 100 marriages.

	Age of wife at time of marriage											
	Under 17			17–25			26–35			36–45		
	(*a*)	(*b*)	(*c*)	(*a*)	(*b*)	(*c*)	(*a*)	(*b*)	(*c*)	(*a*)	(*b*)	(*c*)
Rural districts												
Leinster . .	249	888	357	4,687	18,105	386	1,998	6,443	322	174	241	138
Munster . .	531	1,906	359	6,798	26,305	387	2,082	7,125	342	136	215	159
Ulster . .	457	1,671	365	6,021	23,373	388	1,863	6,132	329	224	281	125
Connaught .	468	1,721	367	4,756	18,492	389	1,129	4,199	346	73	155	212
Civic districts†												
Leinster . .	61	200	328	698	2,583	370	238	653	274	20	12	60
Munster . .	106	375	354	1,068	3,943	369	354	1,053	297	35	38	109
Ulster . .	40	145	362	469	1,727	368	115	359	312	11	2	18
Connaught .	40	116	290	297	1,053	355	64	172	268	6	9	150
Dublin . .	133	410	309	869	2,826	325	233	533	229	23	16	69
Cork . .	34	125	368	287	1,001	349	111	320	288	6	12	200
Belfast . .	36	117	325	273	956	350	58	179	309	9	5	55
Ireland												
Rural districts .	1,705	6,186	363	22,262	86,275	388	7,135	23,819	334	607	877	144
Civic districts .	450	1,488	331	3,961	14,093	356	1,173	3,269	279	110	94	85
Rural and civic districts.	2,155	7,674	356	26,223	100,368	383	8,308	27,088	326	717	971	135

* Census of Ireland, 1841, op. cit., pp. 460 ff.

† The Commissioners of the 1841 Census regarded the population of towns with at least 2,000 inhabitants as 'civic'. They realized that a town of 2,000 inhabitants seldom possessed any manufacture or trade of sufficient consequence to give it the principal characteristic of a town: nonetheless they thought the line of demarcation appropriate because in towns so defined the consequences of crowded habitations upon health began to be felt. (Ibid., p. viii.)

Secondly, the table shows an insistent tendency for rural marital fertility to have been greatest in Connaught, least in Leinster, and at an intermediate level in Munster and Ulster.[1] The differences between the 4 provinces are tiny for the 26–35 age-group, much the largest of the 4: wives in Connaught who married under 17 showed a fertility 2·8 per cent. greater than those of Leinster, those who

Munster. The other exceptions are in the age-group 36–45 where fertility in each of the three large towns exceeded that of the civic districts of its province. Here, again, there were very few city marriages in which the brides were between these ages—23 in Dublin, 6 in Cork, and 9 in Belfast.

[1] The only exception is in the 36–45 age-group where Ulster had a lower figure for rural fertility than Leinster.

married between 26 and 35, 7 per cent. greater, and those between
36 and 45, 54 per cent. greater.

Both of these trends in fertility—the rural-urban differential and
the tendency for the more remote provinces to have a higher
fertility—may be of great importance in explaining the rise in population. It would be unwise, however, to accept the existence of either
merely on the evidence of this table. The relative lowness of the
figure for urban fertility might, for instance, be the result of town-
dwellers forgetting to record a greater proportion of births than
rural-dwellers because a higher infantile mortality in the towns left
them without living reminders of more children born to them.
Table B, in Appendix II, has been constructed to reduce to a minimum the possibility of distortions from deficient returns of births.
It shows, according to the age-group of the wife at the time of
marriage, the number of couples married in each of the three years
before the census, together with the number of children born to
them before 6 June 1841. Table 9, below, shows the number of
births per 100 marriages. The births that parents were asked to
record in no case took place more than three-and-a-half years before
the enumeration: it is, therefore, unlikely that the returns are
seriously deficient because children who had died had been forgotten.

After examining the evidence of Table 9 we must still leave
standing the conclusion of the previous table that rural fertility
was markedly higher than urban: in every age-group, except the
youngest, the excess stands out; for the most numerous age-group
(17–25) it is a matter of almost 10 per cent., and for the next largest
it is 14 per cent. Still, for these same age-groups which have an
overwhelming numerical preponderance, Dublin, Cork, and Belfast show a fertility figure lower than those of the civic districts of
their respective provinces;[1] and still Dublin's fertility is lower than
that of either Cork or Belfast. The second lesson of Table 8, that
rural Connaught had a higher fertility than rural Leinster, is not
supported here: rather the reverse. Again, for the major age-group,
rural fertility is fairly constant throughout the provinces, though
the tendency is for Connaught to lag somewhat behind Leinster.
For the 26–35 age-group the figure for Leinster is rather more than
3 per cent. above that for Connaught.

---

[1] The 26–35 age-group in Belfast is the only exception: its fertility figure of
75 is the same as that of the remaining civic districts of Ulster.

TABLE 9

*Fertility to 6 June 1841 of First Marriages taking place 1838–40,
in the Rural and Civic Districts of the Provinces of Ireland and in
the Large Towns**

	Number of births before 6 June 1841 per 100 marriages taking place 1838–40 in which neither partner was married before			
	Age of wife at time of marriage			
	Under 17	17–25	26–35	36–45
Rural districts				
Leinster	65	93	88	52
Munster	53	92	94	57
Ulster	63	90	87	49
Connaught . . .	62	91	91	43
Civic districts				
Leinster	69	88	93	46
Munster	57	85	86	43
Ulster	62	83	75	18
Connaught . . .	90	88	92	47
Dublin	66	75	70	50
Cork	62	83	76	65
Belfast	61	78	75	26
Ireland				
Rural districts . .	60	91	91	51
Civic districts . . .	65	83	79	44
Rural and civic districts .	61	90	89	49

* Census of Ireland, 1841, op. cit., pp. 460 ff.

Some further statistical evidence is available on these two subjects. Table C, in Appendix II, relates, for the rural districts of
counties and for the civic districts of provinces, both births in the
single year 1840 and children under 6 to women from 16 to 45. In
Table 10, below, there are abstracted from the Appendix figures
for the rural and civic districts of the provinces: a further column
has been added to show the relationship between the total number
of births from 1832 to 1841 to women of child-bearing age.[1]

[1] This column has been inserted because the number of births in 1840 was
substantially below the average of the thirties. They amounted in that year to
249,538 as compared with an annual average of 260,873 over the period 1832–40.
(Census of Ireland, 1841, op. cit., pp. 458–9.) The significance of this divergence
may well be magnified by the tendency for a greater number of births for
years more remote from the enumeration to be forgotten, as well as by the virtual
certainty that the number of women of child-bearing age was lower throughout the thirties than in 1841.

TABLE 10

Proportion of Births in 1840, of Births from 1832 to 6 June 1841, and of Children under 6 per 1,000 Women, aged from 16 to 45, in 1841, in the Rural and Civic Districts of the Provinces of Ireland*

	Births in 1840 per 1,000 women 16–45 in 1841	Births from 1832 to 6 June 1841 per 1,000 women 16–45 in 1841	Children under 6 in 1841 per 1,000 women 16–45
Rural districts			
Leinster . . .	128	1,254	64
Munster . . .	130	1,353	70
Ulster	137	1,347	70
Connaught . . .	143	1,512	74
Civic districts			
Leinster . . .	114	1,021	46
Munster . . .	119	1,130	51
Ulster	120	1,152	54
Connaught . . .	122	1,225	53
Ireland			
Rural districts . .	135	1,367	69
Civic districts . .	118	1,096	50
Rural and civic districts .	132	1,322	66

* Census of Ireland, 1841, op. cit., pp. lxiii and 458–9.

Once more we have evidence of greater rural than urban fertility: the proportion of births in 1840 to women of child-bearing age was 14 per cent. greater in rural than in civic districts: the proportion of births recorded for a period of nine-and-a-half years was 25 per cent. greater: the proportion of children under six was 36 per cent. greater. There is support, too, for the proposition that Connaught was the most fertile province and Leinster the least: births in 1840 per 1,000 women of child-bearing age were 12 per cent. higher in Connaught than in Leinster: births over nine-and-a-half years were 20 per cent. higher:[1] the proportion of children under six was 15 per cent. greater.

[1] It should be borne in mind that the figures relating births over a period of nine-and-a-half years to women of child-bearing age in 1841 tend slightly to overestimate any amount by which the fertility of Connaught exceeded that of Leinster because the population of Connaught (and, presumably, the number of women of child-bearing age) increased more rapidly in these years than that of Leinster. The 1841 Census shows that the rural and civic population of Connaught increased by 5·58 per cent. between 1831 and 1841 while that of Leinster increased by 3·35 per cent.

If the evidence of Tables 6 and 10 be accepted as even broadly correct, we have as striking features of Irish demography before the Famine, first, a general fertility considerably higher than the level in contemporary England, second, within Ireland, higher fertility in the country-side than in the civic areas and, third, rural fertility higher in Munster and Ulster than in Leinster and higher still in Connaught. To what extent can these variations between Ireland and England and within Ireland be attributed to corresponding variations in the proportion of the total female population that lay within the child-bearing years? To what extent were they the result of a greater incidence of marriage or of earlier marriage?

TABLE 11

*Women of Child-bearing Age as a Percentage of the total Female Population in Ireland and in England and Wales in 1841**

	Total female population	Female population 15–44	Female population 15–44 as percentage of total female population
Ireland .	4,155,548	1,934,298	46·5
England and Wales .	8,136,562	3,802,373	46·7

* Census of Ireland, 1841, op. cit., p. 489; *Appendix to Ninth Annual Report of the Registrar-General, Reports from Commissioners*, 1849, xxi. 232.

If the figures of Table 11 can be accepted, it is clear that no part of the explanation of differences between the fertility of Ireland and that of England can be attributed to a difference in the proportions of women of child-bearing years in the total female population; the percentages are practically identical. Nor, within Ireland, as is shown by Table 12, can a partial explanation of regional differences in fertility be found in variations in the proportion of women of child-bearing years. Rural fertility was higher than civic in spite of the smaller proportion of rural women between sixteen and forty-five; similarly the rural fertility of Connaught was greater than that of Leinster in spite of Leinster's greater number of potentially fruitful women.

Was the higher fertility of certain areas associated with an unusually high incidence of marriage or with a tendency for marriage to take place earlier? Table 13 shows for the rural and civic districts of the provinces and of the whole of Ireland what percentage of the female population seventeen years of age and older was married in 1841. It makes clear that the areas of high fertility were also the areas where the greatest proportion of the

TABLE 12

Women of Child-bearing Age as a Percentage of the total Female Population in the Rural Districts of the Provinces and in the Rural and Civic Districts of Ireland in 1841*

	Total female population	Female population 16–45	Female population 16–45 as percentage of total female population
Rural districts			
Leinster . . .	769,231	351,777	45·7
Munster . . .	999,295	460,938	46·1
Ulster . . .	1,103,087	478,590	43·4
Connaught . .	668,237	293,235	43·9
Ireland			
Rural districts . .	3,539,850	1,574,150	44·5
Civic districts . .	615,698	314,392	51·1
Rural and civic districts	4,155,548	1,888,542	45·4

* Census of Ireland, 1841, op. cit., pp. lxi ff.

TABLE 13

Percentage of Female Population 17 years of Age and over Married and not widowed in the Rural and Civic Districts of the Provinces in 1841*

	Rural districts	Civic districts
Leinster . .	45	42
Munster . .	50	44
Ulster . .	49	45
Connaught . .	54	46
Ireland . .	50	43

* Census of Ireland, 1841, op. cit., *passim.*

female population was married. In the civic districts, where fertility was lowest, the smallest proportion of the adult female population was married: Connaught, which had the highest rural fertility, had also the greatest incidence of marriage; in rural Leinster, the lowest fertility went hand-in-hand with the smallest proportion of rural women married.

Age at marriage, as well as the incidence of marriage, tends to affect fertility. Table 14 shows the age-distribution both of all wives married in Ireland in the eleven years 1830–40 and of wives married in England and Wales in 1847. Unfortunately, precise comparisons between Ireland and England are out of the question because the age-groupings adopted for the two countries do not correspond. However, there is little doubt that higher Irish fertility can be associated with earlier marriage. While, of the Irish women marrying in the 1830s 28 per cent. did so in or before their twenty-first year, only 11 per cent. of English women marrying in 1847 did so in, or before, their twentieth year.

TABLE 14

Age of Women at Marriage in Ireland from 1830 to 1840 and in England in 1847

Ireland*			England and Wales†		
Age of wife	Number married	Percentage of total	Age of wife	Number married	Percentage of total
–17	16,914	3·1	..	..	..
17–20	136,398	25·0	–20	2,749	11·3
21–5	209,758	38·4	20–4	12,334	50·9
26–30	98,465	18·0	25–9	5,104	21·1
31–5	34,812	6·4	30–4	1,873	7·7
36–40	14,752	2·7	35–9	906	3·7
41–5	6,122	1·1	40–4	603	2·5

* Census of Ireland, 1841, op. cit., p. lxxix.

† *Tenth Annual Report of the Registrar-General, Reports of Commissioners,* 1849, xxi. 468.

Similarly, there would seem to be some association between regional differences of rural fertility and age at marriage. Table 15 shows the percentage of total first marriages recorded for 1831 which took place before the wife was 17 and the percentage before she was 26. In Connaught, in 1831, relatively twice as many women married before they were 17 as in Leinster: 84 per cent. married before they were 26 as compared with 69 per cent. in Leinster. Munster and Ulster, the intermediate provinces in the scale of fertility, are intermediate also in their proportions of early marriages.

The rural-urban differential in fertility cannot, it seems, be even partially explained in terms of earlier marriage. Dublin, conspicuous in Tables 8 and 9 for fertility lower than anywhere else, is here notable for a proportion of women marrying under 17 higher than

TABLE 15

Number of Marriages in which the Wives were (a) *under 17 and* (b) *under 26 per 100 Marriages taking place in 1831 in which neither Partner was Married before, in the Rural and Civic Districts of the Provinces**

	Total marriages 1831	Number of marriages before wife 17	Number of marriages before wife 26	Percentage of total marriages	
				Before wife 17	Before wife 26
Rural districts					
Leinster .	7,139	249	4,936	3·5	69
Munster .	9,572	531	7,329	5·5	77
Ulster . .	8,608	457	6,478	5·3	75
Connaught .	6,494	468	5,224	7·2	84
Civic districts					
Leinster .	1,019	61	759	6·0	74
Munster .	1,568	106	1,174	6·8	75
Ulster . .	638	40	509	6·2	80
Connaught .	408	40	337	9·8	83
Dublin . .	1,260	133	1,002	10·6	80
Cork . .	439	34	321	7·7	73
Belfast . .	377	36	309	9·6	82
Ireland					
Rural districts.	31,813	1,705	23,967	5·4	75
Civic districts.	5,712	450	4,411	7·9	77
Rural and civic districts .	37,522	2,155	28,378	5·7	76

* Census of Ireland, 1841, op. cit., pp. 460 ff.

that for any other district, urban or rural, and for a percentage of women married before 26 that falls little behind the figure for rural Connaught, the highest of all. In the civic districts as a whole there were nearly 50 per cent. more marriages under 17 than in rural areas and slightly more before 26; their lower marital fertility, it is clear, must have been the result of some force sufficiently powerful to offset the influence of earlier marriage.

On two points in connexion with fertility the Census of 1841 shows us the trend of earlier years: it gives an approximation of changes in the proportion of women of child-bearing age between 1821 and 1841, and it shows, in some detail, variations throughout the thirties in the age at marriage. Table 16 shows for the provinces the proportion of the total population which, in 1821 and 1841 fell between the ages of 16 and 40. Unfortunately the Census of 1821 did not distinguish males from females in its tables of ages (that of 1831 made no returns of age distribution that can assist us). If, how-

TABLE 16

Population from 16 to 40 Years of Age as a Percentage of the total Population, in the Provinces of Ireland in 1821 and 1841*

	1821			1841		
	Total population	Population 16–40	Population 16–40 as percentage of total	Total population	Population 16–40	Population 16–40 as percentage of total
Rural and civic districts						
Leinster .	1,757,492	734,192	41·8	1,973,731	830,045	42·5
Munster .	1,935,612	805,931	41·6	2,396,161	1,013,172	42·3
Ulster . .	1,998,494	808,467	40·4	2,386,373	924,916	38·8
Connaught .	1,110,229	455,937	41·1	1,418,859	566,254	39·9
Ireland .	6,801,827	2,804,527	41·2	8,175,124	3,334,487	40·8

* Census of Ireland, 1841, op. cit., p. lxvi.

ever, variations in the proportion of the total population between 16 and 40 can be accepted as an index of changes in the proportion of women of child-bearing age, there is no province in which we could expect such a change to make fertility in 1821 stray significantly from the level of 1841. In no province is the proportion of people in this age-group in 1821 greater or less than the proportion twenty years later by as much as 2 per cent.

Table 17, compiled from the fertility data of which we have made extensive use already, shows changes in the age-distribution of first marriages recorded for certain years from 1830 to 1840. The most remarkable feature of the table is the startling decrease throughout the country in the proportion of wives marrying at a very early age. In Connaught, where continuously (for rural areas) there was the largest proportion of marriages in which the wife was under 17, the percentage tumbled down from 7 in 1830 to under 2, 10 years later: in rural Leinster, with the smallest proportion, the figure fell from 3·8 to 0·76. The postponement of marriage was no purely rural

TABLE 17. *Age-distribution of First Marriages, in the Provinces and Rural and Civic Districts of Ireland from 1830 to 1840**

Column (*a*) gives the number of marriages, and column (*b*) the percentage of the total.

	Total number of first marriages	Age of wife at time of marriage								
		Under 17		17–25		Under 26	26–35		36–45	
		(a)	(b)	(a)	(b)	%	(a)	(b)	(a)	(b)
Rural districts										
Leinster										
1830.	6,967	264	3·8	4,704	67·5	71·3	1,798	25·8	174	2·5
1835.	7,112	150	2·1	4,891	69·0	71·1	1,880	26·4	167	2·3
1838.	7,060	74	1·0	4,617	65·4	66·4	2,111	29·9	225	3·2
1839.	7,071	43	0·6	4,413	62·4	63·0	2,356	33·3	231	3·3
1840.	6,206	47	0·8	3,935	63·4	64·2	2,304	32·8	171	2·7
Munster										
1830.	9,399	569	6·0	6,669	70·9	76·9	1,981	21·1	161	1·7
1835.	10,746	356	3·4	7,576	72·3	75·7	2,407	23·0	114	1·1
1838.	11,786	189	1·6	8,089	68·6	70·2	3,302	28·0	176	1·5
1839.	10,902	142	1·3	7,300	67·0	68·3	3,248	29·8	178	1·6
1840.	8,991	131	1·5	6,177	68·7	70·2	2,548	28·3	108	1·2
Ulster										
1830.	9,672	521	5·4	6,904	71·4	76·8	2,005	20·7	203	2·1
1835.	10,681	382	3·6	8,084	75·7	79·3	2,028	19·0	214	2·0
1838.	9,095	135	1·5	6,645	73·0	74·5	2,016	22·2	250	2·7
1839.	8,755	126	1·4	6,283	71·8	73·2	2,079	23·7	217	2·5
1840.	7,927	125	1·6	5,916	74·6	76·2	1,675	21·1	169	2·1
Connaught										
1830.	6,614	469	7·1	4,872	73·7	80·8	1,161	17·5	92	1·4
1835.	6,917	293	4·2	5,479	79·2	83·4	1,072	15·4	59	0·8
1838.	7,544	138	1·8	5,666	75·1	76·9	1,608	21·3	117	1·5
1839.	6,878	131	1·9	5,093	74·0	75·9	1,547	22·5	96	1·4
1840.	5,538	98	1·8	4,290	77·5	79·3	1,073	19·4	71	1·3
Ireland										
Rural districts										
1830.	32,652	1,823	5·6	23,149	70·9	76·5	6,495	19·9	630	1·9
1835.	35,186	1,181	3·4	25,970	73·8	77·2	7,387	21·0	554	1·6
1838.	35,485	536	1·5	25,017	70·5	72·0	9,037	25·5	768	2·2
1839.	33,606	442	1·3	23,089	68·7	70·0	9,230	27·5	722	2·1
1840.	28,662	401	1·4	20,318	70·9	72·3	7,330	25·6	519	1·8
Civic districts:										
1830.	5,701	477	8·4	3,985	69·9	78·3	1,095	19·2	132	2·3
1835.	6,402	287	4·5	4,813	75·2	79·7	1,161	18·1	119	1·9
1838.	6,381	155	2·4	4,609	72·2	74·6	1,432	22·4	159	2·5
1839.	6,529	120	1·8	4,615	70·7	72·5	1,572	24·1	200	3·1
1840.	5,941	93	1·6	4,350	73·2	74·8	1,341	22·6	139	2·3
Rural and civic districts:										
1830.	38,353	2,300	6·0	27,134	70·7	76·7	7,590	19·8	762	2·0
1835.	41,588	1,468	3·5	30,783	74·0	77·5	8,548	20·5	673	1·6
1838.	41,866	691	1·6	29,626	70·8	72·4	10,469	25·0	713	1·7
1839.	40,135	562	1·4	27,704	69·0	70·4	10,802	26·9	922	2·3
1840.	34,603	494	1·4	24,668	71·3	72·7	8,672	25·1	658	1·9

* Census of Ireland, 1841, op. cit., pp. 460 ff.

phenomenon, more than 8 in every 100 of the brides in all civic districts were under 17 in 1830, but less than a fifth as many in 1840. Nor is the movement a freak of the selection of particular years; everywhere, in 1835, there were fewer young brides than in 1830, and, with inconsiderable exceptions, fewer in 1840 than in 1838 or 1835.[1] It was not merely the very young marriages that were postponed. In rural Leinster and Munster there was a fall of between 8 and 9 per cent. from 1830 to 1839 in the proportion of wives marrying between 17 and 25 in spite of the tendency for this age-group to be inflated by the postponement of marriage in the under-17 group. Considering together the two lower age-groups, there was a decline everywhere between 1830 and 1839 in the proportion of women marrying below 26, though everywhere there was some return towards the former age-distribution in 1840.

It would be well, perhaps, before drawing conclusions from the statistics of this chapter, to ask whether an inquiry as searching as that directed by the 1841 Census Commissioners, pursued often in remote and difficult country, amongst a widely illiterate and sometimes hostile population, could give results that we can accept with any confidence. It may well be impossible now to determine the degree of error in this census; the discontinuity between Irish social history before and after the Famine makes comparisons with the results of later censuses quite useless. Those responsible for the enumeration in 1841 were best qualified to assess its accuracy and we have already seen that their belief was that the lessons they had learnt from the errors of earlier censuses, together with the precision of their methods and the careful checking to which they submitted their returns, had ensured reliable results.[2] Chary though we might be to accept the opinion of the Census Commissioners on this subject, the consistency between the various tables in this chapter is strong confirmatory evidence that they performed their work well. Whatever the test, fertility is shown to have been higher in rural than in civic districts: the result is constant whether the data are total births in a single year or in nine-and-a-half years, children born to couples married either for ten years or between six months and three-and-a-half years, or living children under six.

---

[1] The exceptions are for rural Ulster, where there was an increase of 0·1 per cent. between 1838 and 1840 and rural Connaught, where the percentage was the same each year.

[2] See above, Chapter I, p. 3.

In all these tests, save one, rural Leinster is shown to have had a lower fertility than rural Connaught, and this exception was not such as to have made the results mutually inconsistent. The tendency for nearly all marriages to have first and second births might well have allowed the co-existence of the slightly higher fertility which Table 9 shows in Leinster as compared with Connaught with higher general fertility in Connaught. Similarly, with the age-distribution of marriage: it would be most remarkable for a haphazard collection of information to display for every area the regular diminution in the proportion of early marriages between 1830 and 1839 shown in Table 17.

While then the accuracy of the statistical evidence is not beyond question, we should be over-cautious if we rejected out of hand its conclusions, particularly when they are not inconsistent with the literary evidence—and this seldom is the case. What is the guidance the tables give us in endeavouring to explain the increase in population? In the first place, they agree with almost all the literary comment that an unusually high fertility was at least partly responsible. This in itself is a point of some note because it is the current custom to attribute the increase in the population of England in the first half of the nineteenth century mainly to reduced mortality which is thought to have followed improvements in the cleanliness and public services of the towns. This is an argument that calls for re-examination, but in Britain, at least, there was the rapid urbanization to make it possible that advance in the theory and practice of medicine, better sanitation, and better water-supply should have had a critical effect on demographic history. In Ireland, however, overwhelmingly and persistently rural as she was, it is most improbable that mortality, reduced for such reasons as these, can help us in explaining a rate of natural-increase that seems to have outstripped that of Britain. The case is far from proven by this slight statistical evidence, but at least we have the suggestion to stand or fall in later investigation that in Ireland the burden of the explanation of rising population must be in terms of fertility.

The second conclusion we can draw—though it must be done with some hesitation—is that in rural Connaught, either the forces leading to high fertility were more fully developed than in rural Leinster, or they suffered from fewer restraints. Third, the tables point unequivocally to rural rather than urban or village life as the environment of high fertility. Fourth, we are left quite unable to attribute, even partially, either the relatively high national fertility, or the regional differences, to variations in the proportion of women of child-bearing age. Fifth, there is an association between the areas of high fertility and the areas where the smallest number of women remained unmarried.[1] It would not, therefore, be illegitimate to seek an explanation of high fertility partly in the proportion of the total number of women of child-bearing age who were married. But an explanation exclusively in terms of the incidence of marriage and the age at marriage would be wrong: the sixth conclusion is that in the regions of high general fertility there was an unusually high marital fertility. That the towns were areas of low *marital* fertility is given added interest by the common assumption that the modern and widespread rural-urban fertility differential is the consequence of the greater use of contraceptives by town-dwellers. We are led to ask whether other forces than the use of contraceptives contribute largely to depress modern urban fertility or whether in the civic districts of Ireland, before the availability of mechanical or chemical contrivances to prevent conception, the same end was achieved by other means.[2]

Seventh, any slackening in the rate of population-increase which other evidence might lead us to believe took place in the twenty

[1] The significant exception to this is the civic districts where marriage was early, but fertility low.

[2] It is possible that in part the lower civic marital fertility shown for every age-group in Table 8 and for the two that are vastly the most numerous in Table 9 may result from variations in the proportion of women marrying at different ages within the groups. Taking, in Table 8, the largest age-group (17–25), it is probable that a greater proportion of civic than rural brides were little over 17, because the civic under-17 group is relatively larger than the rural. If this were in fact the case, and if, as the lower fertility of wives under 17 than of those from 17 to 25 would make possible, these younger women were less fertile than members of the same age-group nearer its median, we should have an explanation of the lower fertility of urban wives. It is unlikely, however, for two reasons, that it is an explanation that would take us far. First, the proportions of the total number of wives falling within the various age-groups does not differ sufficiently widely between rural and civic areas to make significant changes in the composition of the groups probable. Second, as is made clear in Table 17, the proportion of women marrying between 26 and 35 is greater in rural than civic districts (especially is this the case towards the end of the eighteen-thirties), with the consequence of making it probable that in the rural areas the 17–25 age-group contained a greater proportion of wives little under 26, whose fertility, it is clear from Table 9, is more substantially below that of the 17–25 group than that of wives under 17. Any lower civic marital fertility of wives just over 17 would, then, tend to be offset by the relatively smaller number of wives just under 26.

years before 1841, can hardly be attributed to a diminution in the proportion of women of child-bearing age. Finally, the general and marked trend towards later marriage evident throughout the thirties makes it not unreasonable to attach an even greater weight to high fertility as a cause of population-increase earlier in the century than in the thirties.

III

THE STRUCTURE OF RURAL ECONOMY
AND THE DESIRE TO MARRY EARLY

IT is clear from Chapter II that although the available statistics tell us much about the marriage- and birth-rates of the 1830s and early 1840s, they give us little help in determining whether the acceleration in the rate of population-increase which had begun fifty years earlier was the result, wholly or partly, of rising fertility. For evidence on this central point in our investigation we shall be wholly dependent upon the literary sources. We must search them for evidence on three problems. First, did fecundity increase? Second, were there more illegitimate births? Third, was there higher marital fertility?

We can give no ready answer to the first question. Certainly there was no disposition amongst contemporary commentators to explain rising population in terms of increasing fecundity. The matter was seldom referred to: consciously or unconsciously the assumption was made that fecundity was constant. Campbell is one of the few writers to make the point explicitly, he did not suppose that in Ireland 'women are by nature more prolific . . . than in England'.[1] Sterility, there is some reason for believing, was not great in early nineteenth-century Ireland. 'Children', according to Townsend, 'abundantly follow [marriage] for barrenness is almost unknown among the lower classes.'[2] The testimony of Dr. Doyle, the Roman Catholic Bishop of Kildare, was similar: when married, he said, 'they seldom—at least in Ireland—fail to increase and multiply'.[3] But no available evidence suggests that a low level of sterility was the result of recent developments and could, therefore, help us to explain the quickening rate of population increase.

Second, it appears that our discussion must be concerned almost entirely with births within marriage: by practically all accounts extra-marital fertility was low. Townsend, it is true, said that 'the

---

[1] T. Campbell, *Philosophical Survey of the South of Ireland*, 1777, p. 147.
[2] H. Townsend, *Statistical Survey of the County of Cork*, Dublin, 1810, p. 89.
[3] J.K.L., *Letters on the State of Ireland*, Dublin, 1825, pp. 107–8.

common Irish' of Co. Cork 'have very imperfect notions of moral rectitude',[1] but his was a minority opinion. Curwen thought that, though the chastity of the unmarried Irish woman had often been doubted, 'these general imputations . . . have no foundation, and that by them great injustice is done to the sex. Instances of indiscretion among single women in the lower order, are, I am assured, by no means frequent: when the consequences become apparent their lovers seldom desert them.'[2] Dr. Doyle said that 'illicit intercourse . . . is restrained, as well by a natural decorum, which has ever characterised the women of this country, as by a strong and reverential fear of God, constantly kept alive and strengthened by the admonitions of the priests; when it once enters into our hamlets, love seeks its object, not by degrading the person and tainting the soul, but in that holy wedlock which our Redeemer has sanctified, and his Apostle declared to be honourable in all without distinction of rich or poor'.[3] A writer of the thirties, though he was prepared to regard Irish women as more drunken than English and Scottish, and generally more vicious and depraved in their habits, said that 'their chastity before marriage is superior to that of Englishwomen in the same rank'.[4] A French observer was 'certain that the Irish are remarkable for chastity: natural children are rare, adultery almost unknown'.[5] Michael Thomas Sadler thought that

[1] In W. S. Mason, *A Statistical Account, or Parochial Survey of Ireland*, ii, 1816, p. 311.   [2] J. C. Curwen, M.P., *Observations on the State of Ireland*, 1818, i. 171.
[3] J.K.L., op. cit., p. 108.
[4] *Observations on the Labouring Classes*, Dublin, 1836, p. 12.
[5] G. de Beaumont, *Ireland: Social, Political, and Religious*, ed. W. C. Taylor, 1839, ii. 35. The Select Committee on the State of the Poor in Ireland, which reported in 1830, was told by Frederick Page, the author of *Observations on the State of the Indigent Poor* (1830), that 'the moral character of the Irish women is very extraordinary. Colonel Colby, who is directing the Survey in Ireland, stated to me a fact as to the chastity of the Irish women; he told me that he had about 800 men employed all over Ireland, mostly soldiers, and who had almost all married there in consequence of the chastity of the women'. Bicheno, the author of *Ireland and its Economy* (1830), giving evidence before the same Committee, said that amongst the Irish poor 'the women appear to be more virtuous, and conjugal fidelity to be more constant than it is in England'. Marriage after pregnancy, he thought, was less common in Ireland than in England. (*Report of the Select Committee on the State of the Poor in Ireland, Reports from Committees,* 1830, vii, qq. 829 and 4234–5.) Nonetheless, 'the sure way to gain a man', which Arabella Donn's Wessex friends recommended to her, was not unknown in Ireland. John Revans, the Secretary to the Irish Poor Inquiry Commission, said that 'the peasant women constantly seek illicit intercourse with the view of inducing marriage', and, unlike Arabella, they saw more than the man's 'honourable nature' to assure them of success. In such cases, the priests invariably

whatever were the national failings of the Irish 'promiscuous connexion between the sexes is not one of them; there is, probably, less
of improper intercourse before marriage, and more fidelity afterwards, than in any other part of the empire, or of the world'.[1]

If there is no reason to believe that either fecundity or extra-
marital fertility increased, we must seek the causes of any rise in
the birth-rate in greater marital fertility. There are three possibilities: first, a greater reluctance of married people to limit fertility
deliberately; second, a greater incidence of marriage, and, third, a
tendency towards earlier marriage. On the first point, there is no
evidence that the Irish of the period under review, or earlier, made
any attempt to practise contraception. Those of the Irishman's
habits which his critics did not approve were the subject of such
frequent and such thorough-going admonition that the absence of
reproof for what almost every writer of the age who touched on the
subject regarded as a shameful sin, points to the conclusion that the
influence of contraception may be disregarded. Our knowledge,
moreover, of the social attitude of the Irish man and woman, and
of the mainsprings of their conduct, suggest that they would have
had little interest in birth-control, even had the knowledge and the
means been at their disposal. Children were not felt to be impediments in a struggle to clamber up the social scale: not only was
social ambition little developed, but a large family was regarded less
as a drain upon resources than as the promise of comfort and
material well-being in middle and old age. It is not evident that
Irish women showed any disposition to regard their traditional lot,
the routine associated with a large family, as anything it was possible

'recommended' (and this, to Revans, was the equivalent of their enforcing)
marriage, if the woman had previously borne a good character. If the injunctions
of the clergy did fail to induce the man to marry, the friends of the woman often
successfully threatened him with violence. As a last resort, the woman could
swear, or threaten to swear, rape, and then the magistrate's influence was also
brought to bear. (*Evils of the State of Ireland*, 2nd ed., 1837, p. 60.)

The author of the *Observations on the Labouring Classes*, attributed the superior
chastity of the Irish to the bastardy laws. (Op. cit., 1836, p. 12.) Harriet
Martineau, writing in 1852, from the north of Ireland, said that, as compared
with Protestants, 'Catholics are more honest, and the women more chaste—
facts which are attributed to the practice of confession by those who are best
aware of the evils belonging to that practice.' (*Letters from Ireland*, London,
1852, p. 7.) Wakefield, too, believed that 'confession . . . is a powerful restraint on
immorality'. (E. Wakefield, *An Account of Ireland, Statistical and Political*, 2 vols.,
1812, ii. 746.) But doubtless of greatest influence was the tendency for early and
general marriage to lessen the inclination towards extra-marital relationships.

[1] *Ireland: its Evils and their Remedies*, London, 1828, p. 150.

to mitigate. Nor can we believe that they or their husbands had any conception that by limiting the number of their children, each might be given a better chance in the world: certainly the economic and social life in which they played a part was not likely to generate such an idea or give it a wide currency. Sadler is one of the few commentators on the social condition of Ireland in the early nineteenth century who refers, however indirectly—and perhaps equivocally—to the possibility of contraception, and he does so only to absolve the Irish from the charge of practising it. The Irish, he said, 'have ever held in abhorrence' 'those unnameable offences which naturally flow from the discountenance of matrimony, and the substitution of "moral restraint" as it is facetiously denominated'.[1]

As to the second point, the incidence of marriage, a greater disposition to marry, even if we had evidence of it, could not go far to solve our problem. The proportion of Irish women remaining unmarried seems never, in the seventeenth and eighteenth centuries, to have been high. Ireland was a Roman Catholic country, but the opportunities for women to join celibate religious orders were few: the teaching of the Church was to encourage marriage, and the economic and social structure of rural Ireland gave little inducement to remain single. Writing at the outset of the period we are examining, Arthur Young said that 'marriage is certainly more general in Ireland than in England: I scarce ever found an unmarried farmer or cottar, but it is seen more in other classes, which with us do not marry at all, such as servants; the generality of footmen and maids, in gentlemen's families, are married, a circumstance we very rarely see in England'.[2]

The fact that in the generation before 1780 population was increasing may have affected the incidence of marriage more profoundly than could any greater eagerness to marry. If this increase were not entirely the result of middle-aged and elderly people living longer, there was, after 1780, an increasing number of

---

[1] Sadler, 1828, op. cit., p. 397. Certain statistics presented in Chapter II (see above, Tables 8–10, and p. 45) show, if they are reliable, that in the 1830s marital fertility was lower in the civic districts than in the rural districts. This suggested the possibility of the deliberate restriction of births in the towns. No other evidence has come to light that would confirm this hypothesis, and the statistics lend themselves to the not less plausible interpretation that sterility in the towns was higher than in the country-side. Certainly, as far as the great mass of the Irish are concerned, those living in rural areas, there is no available evidence to make us reluctant to agree with Sadler.

[2] A. Young, *A Tour in Ireland*, 2nd ed., 1780, ii. 198.

women in the age-groups in which marriage was frequent. Without any change in the propensity of women to marry, or, being married, in their propensity to have children, the crude birth-rate would have risen.

Earlier marriage, our third point, remains as the only agency that could have given the impetus to any substantial increase in fertility. There can be no doubt at all that, in the decades centring on 1800 the Irish married while unusually young. Table 17, in Chapter II, shows that in 1839 (after some years during which it had become increasingly difficult over much of the country for a couple to find a settlement) 70 per cent. of the brides in first marriages in the rural districts were under twenty-six. That only nine years before, 76·5 per cent. were so young suggests that in the previous half-century, when subdivision, the extension of arable and other agencies that we shall discuss in later chapters, provided settlements almost for all who wanted them, marriage took place even earlier. There is no dispute in contemporary comment that early marriage was an outstanding feature of Irish social life. Campbell, writing in 1777, said 'the only solace these miserable mortals have, is in matrimony; accordingly, they all marry young. Most girls are, one way or another, mothers at sixteen.'[1] In Co. Kildare, in the early years of the new century 'an unmarried man at twenty-five, or a woman at twenty, is rarely to be met in the country parts'.[2] In Kilmactige, in Sligo, a few years later, the women were said to marry at between fifteen and twenty, and the men at from twenty upwards.[3] From Cork came the report that 'among the peasantry the disposition to marry early operates with very powerful force: several couples marry whose united age scarcely exceeds thirty-five or thirty-six'.[4] In the Dingle district, where marriage was at an unusually early age, 'fourteen and thirteen, are common ages for the marriage of girls; fifteen is not considered at all an early age for marriage; and there are even instances of their having been contracted at so early an age as twelve'.[5] Bicheno, in the report in which he summarized for his colleagues on the Poor Inquiry Commission the great mass of evidence the Commission accumulated on social conditions, said that the labourers usually married in Galway at

[1] T. Campbell, *A Philosophical Survey of the South of Ireland*, 1777, p. 147.
[2] T. J. Rawson, *Statistical Survey of the County of Kildare*, Dublin, 1807, p. 23.
[3] W. S. Mason, *Statistical Account, or Parochial Survey of Ireland*, Dublin, ii, 1816, p. 360.   [4] W. Parker, *A Plea for the Poor and Industrious*, Cork, 1819, p. 15.
[5] H. D. Inglis, *Ireland in 1834*, 1835, i. 247.

from 14 to 21; in Leitrim from 16 to 22; in Mayo and Sligo usually under 20; in King's at from 17 to 20. A Kerry priest told of how he had 'married girls of twelve to thirteen, and at this moment there is a married woman in Templemore who has just had a child at the age of fourteen! A woman in the parish of Killarney had *two* children before the age of *fifteen*.'[1]

In the years of rapidly increasing population it is clear that marriage normally took place at an early age. But this is not to show that the acceleration in the rate of population growth was, even in part, the result of the higher fertility that followed earlier marriage. We should need proof of two propositions before we could establish such a causal connexion: first, that marriage, in these years, took place earlier than had previously been the custom, and, second, that earlier marriage did in fact lead to more births. On the first point, only occasional references have been found to the marriage habits of the Irish before the last quarter of the eighteenth century, and these would support the proposition that for long the Irish had married young. As far back as 1623, the *Advertisements for Ireland* pointed out that the mere Irish 'generally (be they never so poor) affect to marry timely or else keep one unmarried and cohabit with her as their reputed wife'.[2] According to Petty, writing in 1687, 'in England the Proportion of Marry'd Teeming Women, is not so great as in Ireland; Where they marry upon the first Capacity, without staying for Portions, Jointures, Settlements, etc.'.[3] Madden, in 1738, said that the Catholics have a 'general Custom (which has been of vast Service to repair the great Loss in this Island by War, etc.) of marrying very early, and consequently breeding fast, and as the *Protestants* do not follow their Example, in either of these particulars, they will possibly, in half a Century, outnumber us much more'.[4]

---

[1] *Report of the Poor Inquiry Commission, Reports from Commissioners*, 1836, xxxiv, App. H, pt. ii, pp. 669–70. That the reports of very early marriages quoted here from Inglis and Bicheno are not to be dismissed out of hand is suggested by Table 17 (p. 42) which shows that in the rural districts of Connaught, in 1830, the brides in 7·1 per cent. of all first marriages were under 17: certain districts may well have had a considerably larger proportion of young brides than this and, as pointed out above, it is probable that the age at marriage was lower earlier in the century than it was in 1830.

[2] Ed. G. O'Brien, Dublin, 1923, p. 43.

[3] W. Petty, *Treatise of Ireland, 1687*, reprinted in *The Economic Writings of Sir William Petty*, ed. C. H. Hull, Cambridge, 1899, ii. 608.

[4] S. Madden, *Reflections and Resolutions proper for the Gentlemen of Ireland*, Dublin, 1738, p. 98.

Early marriage was certainly no novelty in the 1780s. We are unable to prove that in these and the following years people were marrying even younger: nonetheless, as the present and following chapters will endeavour to show, in the half-century after 1780, the great mass of the Irish people were eager to marry while very young, and, what is more important, the economic and social scene made it increasingly possible for them to gratify their desire. A settlement was the preliminary to marriage, and settlements in these years were made more readily available by a swing from pasture farming to arable, by the subdivision of holdings, by reclamation of waste land, and by a more general dependence upon the potato as a foodstuff.

On the second proposition, that, granted earlier marriage, this was the cause of greater fertility, we are also unable to offer proof: nor is proof to be expected when next to no vital statistics are available for the years before 1831. Nonetheless, the probability is strong that the more of a woman's child-bearing years were spent in the state of marriage, the more children would be born to her.[1] Such, presumably, would tend to be the case if, as we have agreed, the influence of contraception can be disregarded.

Any movement towards earlier marriage must have been the result of two sets of causes, those which led to the desire to marry earlier, and those which led to the possibility of doing so. Before we can attempt to isolate from the Irishman's social environment any factors tending to make earlier marriage desirable, we must be clear whose wishes were effective in determining when marriage took place. Do we have to look for reasons influencing middle-

---

[1] Though, perhaps, the length of a mother's child-bearing period, as undoubtedly the length of her life, are partly dependent upon both the age at which her first child is born and the total number of her pregnancies. J. B. Bryan was one of the few contemporary writers on Irish social affairs to doubt the efficacy of earlier marriage to increase population. 'The ignorance of the Malthusians', he says, 'on the subject of prolificness of early marriages, is only to be equalled by the cruel, unjust, and immoral tendency of all their doctrines. Early marriages are less conducive to a permanent increase of the population than late ones. Firstly, as in late marriages the term of female prolificness is lengthened. . . . Secondly, the intensity of the prolificness during what remains of its customary duration is increased; and the mortality of the offspring of early marriages is so great as to check that comparative increase which the more rapid succession of a given number of early marriages would otherwise produce. . . .' (*A Practical View of Ireland* . . . , Dublin, 1831, p. 313.) I am assured by medical authorities that there is no reason for believing that if a woman bears her first child while she is unusually young she will cease to be able to bear children at a correspondingly early age.

aged or perhaps senile patriarchs who 'arranged' the marriages of their sons and daughters, or are we able to regard the bride and bridegroom as having been free themselves to determine when they married? Dr. Conrad Arensberg, an American anthropologist, lived for some years in the 1930s amongst the peasants of Luogh, in a remote part of Co. Clare, and made them the subject of a type of investigation that has usually been reserved for communities less easily accessible from western centres.[1] From his discussion of the prevailing social institutions and customs it is clear that there sur- vive to-day in the western fringe of Ireland modes of living which closely resemble patterns familiar throughout the country a cen- tury and more ago. Is the form of marriage which Dr. Arensberg describes, the form into which our discussion must be shaped? Dr. Arensberg found that in Luogh the first step along the un- romantic path to marriage was taken by the bridegroom's father who surveyed the neighbourhood for a suitable wife for the son to whom he intended transferring his farm. The qualities he sought in a future daughter-in-law were industry, skill in housework and in the woman's part of farm-work, and the promise of fruitful motherhood. Having made his choice, he approached the woman's father to obtain his consent to the proposed marriage, and to secure the promise of an appropriate dowry. Negotiations were sometimes lengthy, but if they were successful they brought about more far-reaching changes than the union of bride and bridegroom. 'The match', says Dr. Arensberg, 'unites the transfer of economic control and the advance to adult status. It is the only respectable method of marriage and the usual method of inheritance.'[2] With his son's marriage, the father, up till then a very real source of authority in the family, legally transferred the ownership of the farm to his son, and yielded to him responsibility for working it. The daughter, in return for the place in life which her marriage brought her, reinvigorated the farm with the fresh capital that made up her dowry.

Marriage such as Dr. Arensberg describes was certainly not unknown in early nineteenth-century Ireland. During the French Wars the Rector of Kilmactige, in Sligo, described the type of marriage common in his parish: it was similar, in all essentials, to that outlined by Dr. Arensberg.

[1] C. M. Arensberg, *The Irish Countryman: an Anthropological Study*, 1937.
[2] Ibid., p. 72.

Marriages [the rector said] are contracted, in most instances, without any regard to love, affection, or any of the finer feelings, and are concluded between the friends of the young people, without any reference to their choice or judgment; and it frequently happens, that the bride is dragged to the Hymeneal altar, bathed in tears, and compelled to take a companion for life, who is chosen by her parents from prudential motives. The chief time for marriages is from Christmas until Lent, being the season of the year when people have most leisure for settling such business.[1]

In Kerry, on Wakefield's authority, 'the match is frequently settled by the parents, without the knowledge of the intended bride and bridegroom'.[2]

References to aspects of the 'arranged' wedding, however, tend less to show its prevalence than the extent to which the customary marriage differed from it. The dowry, without which no match-making father would allow a new woman to take his own wife's place in the household, was more often lamented, than described or criticized. Almost every commentator regarded early marriage as a potent source of Ireland's ills: that marriage took place before a dowry could be accumulated was often pointed to as a reason for early marriage. The prudentially arranged marriage as described by Dr. Arensberg can be practised only by a community which rigidly adheres to a 'small-family system', or by one in which, typically, all children in a family, save one boy and one girl, seek their livelihood away from home. In Clare, to-day, unnaturally small families may have been achieved through the postponement of marriage, but, nonetheless, 'either at the match, or in preparation for it, comes the inevitable dispersal of the family': normally all but two of the children must travel—a boy succeeds to the family farm, and a sister of his can count on marrying the heir to a neighbouring farm.[3] But in pre-Famine Ireland

---

[1] Mason, op. cit. ii, 1816, p. 361.

[2] E. Wakefield, *An Account of Ireland, Statistical and Political*, 1812, ii. 764. The unknown author of *A Tour in Ireland in 1672–4* discussed the marriages of the Irish: they are made, he said, 'like bargains of old, like a pig in a poke, unseen; for the parents meet over a cup of nappy ale, when making some bargain for wheat, oats or any other necessary they want, at last strike up for a match between their son and daughter; this serves instead of wooing, by which means the first meeting is seldom till the man comes to fetch the woman to church, attended with a rabble of all their relations'. (Ed. J. Buckley, in *J. Cork Hist. & Arch. Soc.*, 2nd series, 1904, x. 98.)

[3] Arensberg, 1937, op. cit., p. 79.

there was neither a small-family system nor, at least until the decade or so immediately preceding the Famine, was there any great dispersal of brothers and sisters. The match is intimately linked with the custom of passing on the family farm intact to one boy: it was made possible only by the availability of openings overseas for his brothers and sisters. It needed, however, the experience of the Famine years for the Irishman to be taught the wisdom of keeping his family farm whole. At the close of the eighteenth century, and early in the nineteenth, it was the practice for the farm to be subdivided, and for cultivation to be pressed higher up the mountain-side, and farther in the bog, so that children for whom neither Irish towns, nor overseas countries, had adequate opportunities might settle near home. The son did not need to delay marriage until his father was disposed to relinquish ownership and control of his land: he did not need to accept his father's choice of bride as the condition for acquiring the means of livelihood that made marriage possible. If his father should refuse to give him a part of the family's land this was no insuperable obstacle to marriage: he could rent a scrap from a neighbour, and marry whom he pleased when he pleased. The woman, too, had not to wait until her father would endow her: the dowry is the price of being wife to a farmer; the cottar would take a bride without a dowry. Marriage, then, in the period of this study (in spite of exceptions concentrated, apparently, in the western fringe of the country, which either lingered on from an earlier time, or showed where later developments would lead) seems, in general, to have been the result of the free choice of the persons married. Wakefield's conclusion, when discussing the country in general, not any particular part of it, was 'that the sexes in general, unite, more through an anxious desire to escape parental authority, than from any other cause'.[1] If then we are to seek the motivation of earlier marriage, we must look for influences to which sons and daughters, not their parents, were sensitive.[2]

---

[1] Wakefield, op. cit. ii. 801.

[2] Indeed, parents frequently had reason to regret their children's marriage: John Kerrigan, a Mayo farmer, told the Poor Inquiry Commission that 'it is not always the father's fault that his children get married too soon; sometimes the father suffers more than the child. I was a comfortable man, and had four cows and a heifer, till my daughter got married, and played me a trick that a good many girls have done before: she ran off with a young man, and, after a week's

Perhaps the strongest motives urging young people towards early marriages were the wretchedness of their living conditions and their realization that no ordinary amount of self-denial or industry gave promise of better times. Contemporaries frequently regarded early marriage as one of the evils of poor living conditions. In the *Observations on the Reversionary Payments*, Dr. Price said:

I cannot help taking the opportunity to observe, that there is reason to believe that poor countries (provided the ground supplies them with plenty of food, and the poverty of the inhabitants consists only in their wanting *conveniences* and *elegancies*, in other countries deemed *necessaries*) increase faster than *rich* countries. The reason is obvious. The greatest enemies of population are the artificial wants, the accumulation of property, and the luxury and vices which are the constant attendants of opulence, and which prevent a regular and early union between the sexes. The inhabitants of poor countries are more simple, more healthy, and more virtuous; and, wanting little besides food, families are no burdens, and the prolific powers of nature have free scope to display themselves.—Perhaps IRELAND is one instance of this.[1]

To Dr. Doyle, who was constantly anxious to secure the postponement of marriage 'poverty and population act reciprocally upon each other, like cause and effect; remove the one, or lessen it, and you will thereby check the other'.[2] The Poor Inquiry Commission was told by a Catholic curate from Mayo that 'small holders are induced to marry by feeling that their condition cannot be made worse, or, rather, they know they can lose nothing, and they promise themselves some pleasure in the society of a wife'.[3] From Kilkenny—as, indeed, from most other counties—there came almost the same story: 'labourers get married under the idea that they cannot make their condition worse than it is. I have reasoned with some poor people who were about to take wives . . . more than one has replied to me, "At any rate, if it came to the

sport, he sent her back without having married her: she never stopped at me, saying that he wouldn't take her without a fortune, until I was forced to give her three of my cows, and money besides; moreover, I had to pay the priest.' (*Poor Law Inquiry (Ireland)*, Appendix F, *Reports from Commissioners*, 1836, xxxiii. 43.) More than any consideration of a fortune—for this was commonly dispensed with—the prospect of losing valuable labour must have inclined many a parent to dissuade his children from early marriage.

[1] 4th ed., 1783, ii. 318–19. [2] J.K.L., op. cit., p. 112.
[3] *Poor Law Inquiry (Ireland)*, Appendix F, *Reports from Commissioners*, 1836, xxxiii. 43.

worst, the wife can take to begging".' 'A comfortable farmer's son', another witness said, 'is very slow to marry; he not only marries late in life, but he always waits until he gets a girl with a fortune; below the class of middling farmers, unmarried men above 25 years of age are very uncommon in the country.'[1]

There is virtual unanimity amongst the writers on Irish social conditions in the closing decades of the eighteenth century, and amongst the witnesses that appeared before the numerous committees which inquired into the state of the poor of Ireland in the next half-century, that the general standard of living was exceedingly low. It was common to suspect that for a varying number of years previously things had been improving,[2] but such ideas did more to stress the bestiality of former conditions than the comforts of later times. Campbell, writing in 1777, referred to the nastiness of the streets in Ireland, and the squalid appearance of the *canaille*: 'the vast inferiority of the lower ranks in Dublin, compared even with those in country towns in England, is very striking.'[3] From Tipperary he supplied even stronger evidence: 'the manner in which the poor of this country live, I cannot help calling beastly. For upon the same floor, and frequently without any partition, are lodged the husband and wife, the multitudinous brood of children, all huddled together upon the straw or rushes, with the cow, the calf, the pig, and the horse, if they are rich enough to have one.'[4] That conditions improved little in succeeding years is suggested by the evidence collected in the blue-books. The *Report on the Employment of the Poor in Ireland*, published in 1823, said that

the condition of the Peasantry of those districts of Ireland to which the evidence refers [the west], appears to Your Committee to be wretched and calamitous to the greatest degree. An intelligent Scotch agriculturalist, who visited Ireland during the last year, alleges, 'that a large proportion of the Peasantry live in a state of misery of which he could have formed no conception, not imagining that any human beings could exist in such wretchedness. Their cabins scarcely contain an article that can be called furniture; in some families there are no such things as bedclothes, the peasants showed some fern, and a quantity of straw thrown over it, upon which they slept in their working clothes.'[5]

[1] *Poor Law Inquiry (Ireland)*, Appendix F, *Reports from Commissioners*, 1836, xxxiii. 49. See also pp. 37–81, *passim*.
[2] See below, Chapter IV, pp. 86–9.
[3] Campbell, 1777, op. cit., p. 29.   [4] Ibid., pp. 144–5.
[5] *Report from the Select Committee on the Employment of the Poor in Ireland*, *Reports from Committees*, 1823, vi. 335–6.

James Butler Bryan, a Dublin barrister and author of *A Practical View of Ireland*,[1] giving evidence before the 1830 Committee on the State of the Poor in Ireland, said that their condition was 'the most destitute and miserable that I have ever witnessed, more destitute than I have ever seen in foreign countries, and more miserable than I could possibly conceive any human being could sustain'.[2]

Wretched living conditions had a twofold effect upon the age at marriage. Dr. Doyle pointed out that thrown together in the same huts young men and women, who displayed as a national characteristic a familiarity and absence of reserve, formed intimacies which could end only in marriage or sin[3]—and the not inconsiderable influence of the Church encouraged its members towards the former goal. More important, the wretchedness of living conditions made marriage appear a welcome relief. 'They say of marriage', Doyle reported, 'as of other changes in their life, that "it cannot make them worse", but that it may give them a helpmate in distress, or at least a companion in suffering.'[4] Poverty, too, was sometimes the cause of parental pressure being exercised to encourage early marriage, and here, of course, its influence was felt when parents 'arranged' marriages. 'The parent also of the poor and unprotected female, who loves her as he does his life, when he finds himself unable to provide for her, and his end perhaps approaching, rather than leave her exposed to the dangers of the world, gladly gives her hand to a poor and virtuous companion, that her honour may not be stained, that she may not, by her misfortune, bring his own grey hairs with sorrow to the grave.'[5]

Hardly less than present wretchedness, the utter hopelessness with which he had to survey the future inclined the Irishman towards early marriage. His position was not such that ordinary —or even the most uncommon—industry and thrift could lift him from it. Unlike the apprentice, he had no inducement to forego marriage until he was a qualified craftsman, and neither, like the journeyman, could he persuade himself that by delaying marriage he could accumulate the capital that would secure his family's

---

[1] Dublin, 1831.
[2] *Report of the Select Committee on the State of the Poor in Ireland, Reports from Committees*, 1830, vii. q. 495.
[3] J.K.L., 1825, op. cit., p. 112. Doyle, *Rep. S.C. S.P.I.*, op. cit., q. 4571.
[4] J.K.L., 1825, op. cit., p. 110.   [5] Ibid., p. 111.

future, nor was he restrained from marrying by the prospect of a higher income when he was older. In spite of his critics (and they were too often his exploiters) the Irishman's wretchedness was not the result of his innate indolence and recklessness. He was the victim of economic and social institutions which, whatever the personal qualities he displayed, forced him down to a subsistence level, and often below it. There were many contemporaries who rated the Irish for their inborn idleness. There were others who supplied convincing explanations of why a people, inherently probably no less energetic than any other, should give the appearance of lack of industry. And there were men, like Sheridan, to explain that the peasants of Ireland were calumniated 'by those men who would degrade them below the level of the human creation, in order to palliate their own inhumanity towards them'; that, in fact, the Irish were enterprising was shown by their coming to England in search of employment; that they had affection for country and home was shown by their going back with their earnings; that they were not lazy was shown by their doing much of the hard work of London. The difference between their conduct in Ireland and in England could be attributable only to their gross misrule.[1]

Many reasons, some trivial, some substantial, were advanced to account for the Irishman's apparent lack of industry. Protestant critics, though religious intolerance may have moved them as much as zeal for the truth, emphasized the influence of the observance of the Roman Catholic holidays. The Rector of Grange Silvae, in Kilkenny, thought that 'the poorer classes are in general indolent, which is principally occasioned by the regular, indispensable observances of the numerous R. Catholic holidays'.[2] From another rector, in Co. Cork, came the testimony that 'many holidays are kept on Saints' days and Lady days to the great prejudice of industry, and the great emolument of ale-houses'.[3] Witnesses appearing before a Select Committee in 1830 testified that in the preceding years the number of holidays had been reduced,[4] but even so eminent a Catholic as Dr. Doyle told the Committee that, though there were only nine holidays per year, their observance 'especially at certain seasons is injurious to good morals,

---

[1] Hansard, 13 August, 1807, col. 1197.
[2] Mason, op. cit. i, 1814, p. 419.   [3] Mason, op. cit. ii, 1816, p. 311.
[4] *Rep. S.C. S.P.I.*, 1830, op. cit., qq. 8 and 159.

and to all the interests of the people'.[1] Nassau Senior attributed the agricultural labourer's indolence chiefly to the conditions of his employment—to its being almost always day-work, and, in great measure, a method of working out his rent.[2] To Petty (and many writers in the following century and a half would have agreed with him) the Irish people's 'Lazing seems . . . to proceed rather from want of Imployment and Encouragement to Work, than from the natural abundance of Flegm in their Bowels and Blood; for what need they to Work, who can content themselves with *Potato's*, whereof the Labour of one Man can feed forty; and with Milk, whereof one Cow will, in Summer time, give meat and drink enough for three Men'.[3] Professor O'Brien, too, thinks it probable that the introduction of the potato encouraged idleness, and he points out that between 1603 and 1641 there were no complaints of the laziness of the Irish: then 'the tenants were secured in their holdings by tenant-right, and there were no penal laws to sap the industrious spirit of the Catholics'.[4]

It was harsh to blame the Irishman for recklessly marrying early when, however long he postponed marriage, and however assiduously he worked in the interval he could not hope to soften the conditions under which his family would be reared. Why was he almost powerless to better his lot? What was the mechanism whereby the peasant, whatever the yield of his labour, was stripped of almost all save the barest subsistence?

Too often the degradation of the peasantry was implicit in the attitude of the landlord towards his estate. When property is recognized as carrying duties as well as rights, the well-being of the rural population and the fruitfulness of the soil are the measure of the landlord's fulfilment of his obligations.

There is no country in Europe in which the landlords are possessed of more unlimited power over their tenants, than in Ireland. So little does the legislature interfere with their prerogatives, that each proprietor is, virtually, a kind of potentate in the district over which he presides; and, whether his power is exercised in advancing the happiness

[1] Ibid., q. 4785.

[2] W. N. Senior, *Ireland in 1843*, *Ed. Review*, Jan. 1844, reprinted in *Journals, Conversations and Essays relating to Ireland*, 1868, i. 45.

[3] W. Petty, *Political Anatomy of Ireland*, 1691, reprinted in *The Economic Writings of Sir William Petty*, ed. C. H. Hull, Cambridge, 1899, i. 201.

[4] G. O'Brien, *An Economic History of Ireland in the Seventeenth Century*, 1919, p. 14.

of his subjects, depends, entirely, upon the interest he may feel in their welfare, and the moral obligation he may consider himself under to promote it.[1]

The cause of much of the destitution of the peasants, and much of the desolation of their land was that an exclusively mercenary attitude animated many landowners. However much the peasants suffered from the wretchedness of their living conditions, and from their primitive methods of farming, they were unlikely, by their own efforts, to make any serious improvements. They lacked, perhaps, the power to make any wholesale revision of their lot, but they lacked also the will. Temperamentally the Irish peasant was not restive under the grossest injustice, and, unfamiliar with the example of more comfortable living, he was prepared to live as his father had lived before him. If his life were to be made less bestial and his soil more fruitful; if he were to be secured from the danger of repeated famine, he needed attentive teaching and encouragement: he needed a landlord who would be 'the example, teacher, arbitrator, helper, friend of the poor, and patron of every good work'.[2] But, in fact, if he were typical, he was tenant to a landlord who, by origin, circumstance, and self-interest was inclined to be indifferent to the welfare of his tenantry, and was interested in his estate only as a source of income. That Irish property had its origin—and frequently a recent origin—in confiscation was not conducive to kindly relations between landlord and tenant. Many of the settlers themselves in the time of Cromwell were soldiers and traders who naturally applied their mercantile principles to landholding. There was no long tradition in Ireland binding the proprietor's family to the people who worked the soil. The grantee of Irish property, aware that his family might lose its title as swiftly as it had been acquired, too readily assumed the role of plunderer. So long, Dr. Sigerson pointed out, as a Stuart lived to intrigue for the throne the tenants of the last invasion felt insecure, and insecurity made them acknowledge none of the duties but exercise all of the rights of proprietors. 'Confidence in the future being absent, neither good husbandry nor good landlordism could

[1] W. R. Anketel, *The Conduct of the resident landlords of Ireland contrasted with that of the Absentees*, 1844, p. 3. In Ireland, according to McCulloch, 'infinitely more depends on the conduct of the landlord and his agent than in England'. (J. R. McCulloch, *Descriptive and Statistical Account of the British Empire*, 4th ed., 1854, i. 373.)

[2] Foster, 1846, op. cit., p. 216.

exist. Unfortunately, it was under such circumstances that the character of a large portion of Irish landlordism was formed.' On the decay of the Stuart interest the chief tenants became more secure, but by then 'the habit of oppression, of exacting high rents, and of caring nothing for the welfare of the cultivators, appealed to motives of self-interest and self-indulgence too powerfully to be shaken off. It had become ingrained.'[1]

The landlord's isolation from his tenants tended to perpetuate his undesirable attitude. Even though he lived in close proximity to them, they seldom became personalities to him. No middle class helped to narrow the social wilderness between proprietor and cottar, and, too often, social distinction was aggravated by diversity of language, religion, and national loyalty. Concern for their own safety did little to encourage the landlords to draw their tenants closer to them:

the Irish aristocracy has always had the misfortune of fearing nothing, and hoping nothing, from the people subject to its yoke; supported by England, whose soldiers have always been placed at its disposal, it has been enabled to give itself up to tyranny without reserve: the groans, the complaints, the menaces of the people have never tempered its oppressions, because popular clamour had for it no terrors. Did insurrections break forth in Ireland? The aristocracy of the country never stirred; it was English artillery that subdued the insurgents; and when everything was restored to order, the aristocracy continued to receive the revenue of its lands as before.[2]

Wakefield summed up the matter: 'Regard to present gain, without the least thought for the future', he said, 'seems to be the principal object which the Irish landlord has in view.'[3] Absenteeism, the middleman system, the prevailing type of tenure and exorbitant rents all demonstrated that the interests of the peasantry, and the fertility of the soil were readily sacrificed when they stood between the landlord and the greatest immediate monetary yield from his estate.

The effects of absenteeism were first widely felt in Ireland in the course of the seventeenth century.[4] The institution was rooted in the fact that many of the men who acquired land in Ireland

---

[1] G. Sigerson, *History of the Land Tenures and Land Classes in Ireland*, London, 1871, pp. 137–9.

[2] Beaumont, 1839, op. cit. i. 282–3.

[3] Wakefield, 1812, op. cit. i. 304.   [4] O'Brien, 1919, op. cit., p. 32.

were already well endowed with property in England, and that they and their families were firmly established upon English estates. The eighteenth-century attitude that colonies existed for the enrichment of the mother country, coupled with the belief that the Irish were a barbarous people among whom it was foolhardy to live, sanctioned the extension of absenteeism. According to Thomas Prior's *List of Absentees*, published in 1729, their annual income was £627,799.[1] Laffan, in 1785, put the figure at £1,200,000.[2] Wakefield thought the estimate of £2 millions a year given in a House of Commons Committee in 1804 was below the truth.[3] Ensor, giving evidence before a Select Committee in 1830, calculated that about £4 millions of the rental of Ireland was spent in other countries,[4] and, according to a writer in *The Economist*, by 1845, the drain was between six and seven million pounds a year.[5]

That the landlord was an absentee was no certain indication that the estate was ill run, nor was his residence a token of his concern for his tenants: the estate of Earl Fitzwilliam, an absentee, was the best cultivated that Wakefield saw in Ireland; that of Mr. Martin, the largest landowner in the British Isles, and a resident, 'exhibits every mark of the most wretched cultivation, or rather, of no cultivation at all'.[6] Daniel Leahy, a magistrate, farmer and land agent of Kanturk, giving evidence before the Devon Commission, said that 'the farmers of the country would rather have a farm from an absentee than a resident proprietor. Absentees are generally persons who can afford to let the land at a cheaper rate than the residents, and it is generally let cheaper than the land let by residents.'[7] The tendency, however, was for the landlord not reminded by daily contact of the needs of his tenantry to neglect or sacrifice them. At best the tenants suffered from the loss of the example a good landlord would have given in maintaining and improving the standard of cultivation, from the loss of assistance with building, draining and other expensive undertakings needing considerable capital, and from loss of the help they needed in times of distress. At worst they were oppressed by an owner who

---

[1] p. 19.　　　　　　　　　　　　　　　[2] Laffan, 1785, op. cit., p. 31.
[3] Wakefield, 1812, op. cit. i. 290 n.
[4] *Rep. S.C. S.P.I.*, 1830, op. cit., q. 5106.
[5] *The Economist*, 24 May 1845, p. 486. *Letters on Ireland*, No. 1, signed J.A.N.
[6] Wakefield, 1812, op. cit., ii, pp. 283 and 259–60.
[7] *Report of the Devon Commission*, 1845, 773, 90.

instructed his agent to 'send money, not arrears or expenses',[1] and by an agent, who, in the struggle both to fulfil his instructions and to make a distasteful job personally worth while, rack-rented, swindled, and indiscriminately evicted. When landlords are absentees 'there are none to give employment to those who, in an advancing state of society, are liberated from the lowest drudgeries of life; none to excite genius, or reward merit, none to confer dignity and elegance on society, to lead in the march of civilisation; to diffuse knowledge or dispense charity'.[2] It was the custom to attribute many of the evils of Irish life to lack of capital, and to blame the Irish themselves for this because their wild habits scared the English investor from sending his money across the Channel. But the native capital that absenteeism drained from the country could have replaced many a wretched house; it could have increased employment by improving agriculture and developing industry: perhaps, even, it might have made Ireland more tempting to the English capitalist by increasing tranquillity as it lessened discontent. The tendency of absenteeism to impoverish the country led to its being regarded as one of the mainsprings of emigration,[3] and a major cause of the expensive system of poor relief with which the country became saddled.[4] Because there were insufficient people to perform the duties elsewhere attended to by resident landlords, Ireland had to establish a paid magistracy.[4] Her hospitals, infirmaries, schools, loan-funds, and so forth, suffered because 'the absentees, in many, very many, instances, contribute nothing, and the wealthiest of them are not ashamed to figure in the subscription lists, with their names prefixed to sums which the smallest resident squire would blush to contribute'.[5]

Another feature of Irish land organization which reacted harshly upon the tenant was the interposition between him and the owner of the soil of one or more intermediaries. The system had an obvious convenience to the absentee landlord—he could hope through it to receive a regular income from one substantial tenant without the trouble that would necessarily attend his dealing with the people who cultivated the soil—but it had a *raison d'être* of its own in eighteenth-century Ireland. 'Middlemen', said Whitley

---

[1] J. Wiggins, *The 'Monster' Misery of Ireland*, 1844, p. 25.
[2] Sadler, 1828, op. cit., pp. 46-7.
[3] W. R. Anketel, *The Effects of Absenteeism*, London, 1843, pp. 14 and 15.
[4] W. R. Anketel, *The Conduct of the Resident Landlords of Ireland*, 1844, p. 18.
[5] Ibid., p. 20.

Stokes, 'are as necessary to Ireland as the shopkeeper is to London.'[1] When the land was crying out for capital, and both landlord and tenant were impoverished, there was room for a third party with capital to invest.[2] When the cottar was too poor to improve the land there was some temptation to the landlord to let to a middleman who could be expected at least to improve the part adjoining his residence.[3] By the 1820s, when the benefits the middleman had derived from war-time conditions were over,[4] and he was plainly a member of a dwindling class, there were laments for his passing.

The middleman took his rent in labour and produce, payment of which was easy: he lived in habits of easy familiarity with his tenant: if he was his master, he was also his companion and friend: he was his advocate and protector; but in those places where he no longer exists there is no link between the highest and the lowest; the poor peasant has no one to listen to his grievance, no redress from the oppression of the driver. His state is far worse than it was even under an oppressive middleman.[5]

It was seldom during the currency of the system that its praises were so extravagantly sung. To Dr. Doyle, middlemen were 'the worst description of oppressors that the curse of Cromwell has produced in Ireland': with their torture he was well acquainted, 'the most cruel that has ever been afflicted on any people, unless upon the Irish, and the slaves in the West Indies'.[6] To Arthur Young, middlemen were 'blood-suckers of the poor tenantry':[7] when they were resident 'surrounded by their little under-tenants,

---

[1] *Observations on Population and Resources of Ireland*, Dublin, 1821, p. 30.

[2] 'I discriminate between a wretch, who takes large tracts of ground, and relets at an enormous rent, without any lease, or at best a very short one, without making the smallest improvement, and the monied man of skill, who takes a great extent of waste ground, and, after reclaiming it by a great expenditure of money and industry, relets it at a rent, that, though moderate, will amply repay him, and put it in the power of those, whose want of capital and skill prevented it, to provide comfortably for their families.' H. Dutton: *Statistical Survey of the County of Clare*, Dublin, 1808, n., pp. 241–2.

[3] Young, 1780, op. cit. ii. 95.

[4] The Devon Commission attributed many of the evils it witnessed to the decline of the middlemen 'after the cessation of the war and the fall of prices'. 'The practice of letting land to middlemen', it found in 1845, 'is now rare'. (*Report from Her Majesty's Commissioners of Inquiry into the State of the Law and Practice in Relation to the Occupation of Land in Ireland, Reports from Commissioners*, 1845, xix, pp. 8, 15.)

[5] Resident Native, *Lachrymae Hiberniae*, Dublin, 1822, p. 23.

[6] J.K.L., 1825, op. cit., pp. 298–9.   [7] Young, 1780, op. cit. ii. 101.

they prove the most oppressive species of tyrant, that ever lent assistance to the destruction of a country. . . . Not satisfied with screwing up the rent to the uttermost farthing, they are rapacious and relentless in the collection of it.'[1]

The middlemen endeavoured to take an estate on as long a lease as possible—in Co. Cork for three lives or thirty-one years[2]—and sub-let it for short periods. Increasing land values would give the less extortionate middleman profit for his pains, and his unscrupulous fellow, each time a lease fell in could put the land up to auction and extort over the period of his tenancy a steeply increasing rent. On the authority of the rector, in Macroom, in Co. Cork, middlemen frequently drew three times as much out of the land as the real landlord.[3] In the parish of the Rev. Edward Barton, in Wexford, rents paid to landlords averaged 8s. an acre, but 'those paid to the middlemen, who are unfortunately too numerous, may be estimated, on the set of the last three years, at about £1.14.1½'.[4] The middleman had other channels of exploitation to tap besides rack-rents. 'Besides the payment of his rent, the cottager was also frequently burthened with many heavy obligations of supplying his task-master with men and horses to perform his work as well as eggs and poultry to supply his kitchen. The amount of rent, we may justly suppose, was so regulated as to leave the tenant no more than a bare subsistence.'[5] 'Personal service of themselves, their carts and horses, are exacted for leading turf, hay, corn, gravel, etc., insomuch that the poor undertenants often lose their own crops and turf, from being obliged to obey these calls of their superiors.'[6] The middleman, too, would bind his tenants on oath to pay their rent on a certain day, or he would accept in lieu of cash a promissory note at a distant date: either way, when the appointed day arrived, the tenant, committed to pay a wholly impossible sum, had no redress when the middleman had his cattle driven to the pound.[7] Where the middleman intervened, the influence which should have been the landlord's, and which in a well-ordered society would have been so beneficial to the tenantry, was transferred to the middleman and made one more weapon in his armoury of exploitation.

[1] Ibid., p. 97. [2] Townsend, 1810, op. cit., p. 183.
[3] Mason, op. cit. i, 1814, p. 567. [4] Ibid., p. 8.
[5] Townsend, 1810, op. cit., p. 185.
[6] Young, 1780, op. cit. ii. 98.
[7] Wakefield, 1812, op. cit. i. 287.

The peasant, so often the victim of a landlord less conscious of the duty to advance the well-being of rural society than of his power to strip his tenants of the fruit of their labour, and in daily contact with middlemen and agents as mercenary as their masters, but excelling them in the ingenuity with which they achieved their aims—the peasant, thus exploited, had particular need of the legal protection a fair lease might have given. He suffered in the courts from the disabilities which have always been the lot of the poor and ill educated when engaged in litigation with classes whose heredity or profession has skilled them in dealing with humble people, and his disabilities were heightened because the magistracy was recruited from the same more fortunate classes whose actions it was that brought the peasants to court.[1] Once the need to go to court arose the scales were tipped against the peasant and often to add to his misfortune, his lease was such that what, in justice, was the grossest oppression, was in law, no offence.

Wakefield, writing towards the end of the French wars discussed the length of tenure county by county: the most common periods were 21 or 31 years, or 21, 31, or 61 years and a life or lives.[2] The tendency then, and continuously until the Famine, was for the length of tenure to become shorter. Writing of Co. Cork in 1810, Townsend said that the usual leases some years earlier were for three lives or thirty-one years, but 'landed proprietors now, for the most part, let to occupiers only on leases of one life, or twenty-one years'.[3] The rector of Arklow, Co. Wicklow, wrote in 1816 that 'as old leases of three lives or thirty-one years terminate, new ones are substituted for the reduced term of one life, or twenty-one years. . . . This decrease in the tenure of farms, has latterly become very prevalent through Ireland.'[4] Pierce Mahony testified

---

[1] 'The execution of the laws lies very much in the hands of the justices of the peace, many of whom are drawn from the most illiberal class in the Kingdom. If a poor man lodge a complaint against a gentleman, or any animal that chuses to call itself a gentleman, and the justice issues a summons for his appearance, it is a fixed affront, and he will infallibly be *called-out*. Where MANNERS are in conspiracy against LAW to whom are the oppressed to have recourse? It is a fact that a poor man having a contest with a gentleman must—but I am talking nonsense, they know their situation too well to think of it; they can have no defence but by means of protection from one gentleman against another, who probably protects his vassal as he would a sheep he intends to eat.' Young, 1780, op. cit. ii. 128.

[2] Wakefield, 1812, op. cit. i. 285.

[3] Townsend, 1810, op. cit., p. 253.

[4] Mason, op. cit. ii, 1816, p. 41.

in 1823 that in Kerry, where Wakefield had found leases of thirty-one years and three lives common, there was considerable recent alteration in the state of tenures—'in fact you may call them all now tenants-at-will'.[1] In the country as a whole, by the time of the Devon Commission, 'the larger proportion of the land is occupied by tenants-at-will'.[2]

The movement towards shorter leases, begun during the wars, was doubtless associated with the rising land-values of those years. Rents rose probably even more spectacularly than in England: on Cairnes's estimate there was a fourfold increase in Irish rents between 1760 and 1815.[3] Partly the same causes were at work in both countries. British corn prices shot upwards as war both increased demand and placed in jeopardy the overseas supplies which rising population had made more and more necessary. For a while duties insulated Ireland from the increase, but in 1806 she was permitted to send grain to England duty free, and her rents responded to the new price situation. But it was not war-time conditions that began the increase: the quickening of economic activity which accompanied the greater legislative independence of the years before the Union had already been reflected in the trend of rents;[4] the movement from pasture farming to arable had doubtless also made a contribution.[5] Acute competition for land, before, during, and after the wars was a major cause. Partly this was the result of the increasing freedom given to Catholics to hold land. As the 'Williamite chief tenants passed from a state of insecurity to one of security, and as they feared no longer the Jacobite claimants, they gradually abrogated the Acts disabling Catholics from holding real estate'.[6] The first relaxation came in 1771, when, under conditions, Catholics were allowed to lease and reclaim bog. They were given permission, in 1777, to take leases for periods of up to 1,000 years, and, in 1782, to acquire freehold property for lives or by inheritance. Finally, in 1793, the forty-shilling franchise was extended to them.[7] It was not only legal

[1] *Rep. S.C. E.P.I.*, 1823, op. cit., p. 359.

[2] *Rep. Devon Com.*, 1845, op. cit., p. 15.

[3] Cairnes, quoted in G. O'Brien, *The Economic History of Ireland from the Union to the Famine*, 1921, p. 210.

[4] R. B. O'Brien, *Two Centuries of Irish History*, 1907, p. 210.

[5] See below, Chapter IV.

[6] Sigerson, 1871, op. cit., p. 138.

[7] *Rep. Devon Com.*, 1845, op. cit., pp. 7–8.

change that increased the competition for land; the rapidly increasing population had few other ways of obtaining its living than by working the soil.

There was some decline in rents after the wars but not in proportion to the fall in prices: 'all but what preserved the occupiers from absolute starvation was extorted from them.'[1] Dr. Doyle explained the extreme reluctance of the landlords to lower rents: during the wars they had risen in the world 'and when the peace came, and the value of lands fell, those gentlemen had establishments which could not easily be reduced, for we all know how painful it is for a man to descend from a certain rank to another below it. They endeavoured to keep up those establishments. Many of them also entered into marriage settlements, or borrowed money, and so created incumbrances upon their property, that they could not lower rents, or let their land for its value.'[2] The author of *Lachrymae Hiberniae*, after seven years of peace, explained that though the pounds had been filled with the cattle of defaulting peasants, there had been no reduction in rents.[3] Still, in the 1850s, the ruthless thinning of the population in the forties notwithstanding, 'the competition for land in Connaught is almost incredible: there is no rent you ask you will not be promised, and it is astonishing how well these exorbitant rents are paid'.[4] 'Land in Ireland is the common refuge; it is not enough to say, that land is desired in Ireland; it is envied and coveted; it is torn to pieces, and the pieces are fiercely contested: when it cannot be occupied by fair means it is seized by crime.'[5]

During the wars, with the impressive rise in rents, the landlord, when he saw the tenant at the end of a long lease paying substantially less than the current price, had little will to resist the temptation of short tenure. The example of the middlemen, too, often convinced him of the folly of long leases: the middleman, by giving annual leases to the people who worked the soil could make three or four times as much profit out of the land as he did himself. Though a landlord displayed the worst failings of his class he did not lack the insight and the initiative to deal directly with his tenants: the decline of the middleman went hand in hand with the

---

[1] Sigerson, 1871, op. cit., p. 173.
[2] *Rep. S.C. S.P.I.*, 1830, op. cit., q. 4409.
[3] Resident Native, *Lachrymae Hiberniae*, Dublin, 1822, p. 8.
[4] McCulloch, 1854, op. cit. i. 389.
[5] Beaumont, 1839, op. cit. ii. 237.

downward movement in the length of leases drawn up between landlord and cultivator. The withdrawal of the franchise from the forty-shilling freeholder in 1829 released one of the brakes on the movement towards shorter leases. A life-tenancy of a holding above a certain value had qualified the occupier for a vote, a vote the control of which the landlords regarded as one of the rights of property. The forty-shilling freeholders, O'Connell told a Parliamentary Committee in 1825 'are part of the live-stock of an estate. In some of the counties the voters are sold as regularly as cattle.'[1] A landlord from Co. Wicklow, giving evidence before the Devon Commission, showed very plainly with what freedom a section of his class thought their tenants might cast their votes. 'Contested elections', he said, 'are a means of destroying the relations which otherwise would exist between landlord and tenant. I have never known anything destroy it so much as a contested election. It is the greatest curse that can possibly come into the country.'[2] Before 1829 some of the landlords were sufficiently careless of wealth to prefer political influence to the larger rentals promised by shorter tenancies. With electoral reform the way was cleared to the yearly tenancies that were the rule in the Famine years.[3]

Short leases between landlord and working tenant had their champions. Plainly, evils that were dependent upon the intrusion of a middleman were ended; but the peasants, without his agency still found themselves beset with evils so nearly identical that they scarcely knew their origin had changed. 'Now', said Townsend, in 1810, 'proprietors for the most part let to occupiers only on leases of one life or twenty-one years. . . . [This] stimulates their industry, and strengthens the attachment which tenants naturally feel for a beneficent landlord. It tends also very materially to prevent that waste and injury so often committed, towards the termination of a lease, from the uncertainty of who shall come next.'[4] It was more general, however, to lament the effect upon the tenant of shorter leases. There is little evidence to suggest that the typical tenant had reason to prize a stronger attachment to his landlord,

[1] Quoted by M. MacDonagh, *Bishop Doyle*, '*J.K.L.*', London, 1896, p. 68.
[2] R. F. Saunders, *Rep. Devon Com.*, op. cit., *960*, 25. See also p. 166, n. 2.
[3] There is probably a tendency in much of the discussion of land organization in the period to exaggerate the extent to which landlords, in disposing of their property, were influenced by the enfranchisement of the forty-shilling freeholders. See below, Chapter VI, pp. 166–8.
[4] Townsend, 1810, op. cit., p. 253.

that he felt induced to keep his land in good condition as the period of his tenancy expired, or that, when the time came for the renewal of the lease, the claims of the occupying tenant were specially valued unless he outbid his competitors. Tenancies at the time at which Townsend was writing were yet to be severely foreshortened, but their uncertainty then did much to anticipate the evils later associated with their shortness. A life was customarily inserted in a lease (in part, at least, with the intention of securing a vote) and life tenure is uncertain. Wakefield explained how, on various occasions he tried to convince tenants of the wisdom of not overworking the soil, but his 'logic was of no use; the invariable answer was, "I hold my land only during such a person's life, he is advanced in years, and who knows how soon he may drop". But you will get a renewal: "I can't tell that." But it is most probable there can be no wish to change the tenant: "A high rent will be bid for the land if it be in heart." '[1] Short and uncertain tenures put a premium upon slovenly methods of cultivation: combined with other features of Irish land organization they made the industry the Irishman was berated for not displaying the promise of his ejectment and the measure of his landlord's enrichment.

That in Ireland (save in Ulster) there was no general recognition of the outgoing tenant's right to compensation for improvements he made to the land was a source of even greater grievance than in England because the Irish landlord accepted no responsibility for keeping the appurtenances of the land in working condition. In Ireland, the tenant 'generally comes to a naked farm without trees, without hedges, without house fit to shelter a human creature'.[2]

It is well known [the Devon Commission reported] that in England and Scotland, before a landlord offers a farm for letting, he finds it necessary to provide a suitable farm house, with the necessary farm buildings for the proper management of the farm. He puts the gates and fences in good order, and he also takes upon himself a great part of the burden of keeping the buildings in repair during the term. . . . In Ireland the case is wholly different. The smallness of the farms as they are usually let, together with other circumstances . . . render the introduction of the English system extremely difficult, and in many cases impracticable. It is admitted on all hands, that according to the general

---

[1] Wakefield, 1812, op. cit. i. 303.   [2] Townsend, 1810, op. cit., p. 186.

practice in Ireland, the landlord builds neither dwelling-house, nor farm-offices, nor puts fences, gates, etc., into good order, before he lets his land to a tenant.[1]

On moving to a new farm there were two courses open to the tenant. Either he could resign himself to living under bestial conditions, producing just the potatoes and the milk and the corn required for his family's sustenance and to pay the rent; or he could rebuild his house and the farm buildings, improve the land and cultivate intelligently. It is no wonder that the Irishman resigned himself to squalor, or that, indeed, he was often unaware that there was any alternative before him. Had he tried during an initial tenancy to make his farm an object of pride it is unlikely that he would have endeared himself to his landlord: the chances were that when his lease expired he would be treated as were his fellows, that there would be no preference shown for the occupying tenant, and that the new rent would exceed the old by an amount related to the extent to which the tenant's improvements increased the capital value of the property.

The practice of letting land by auction was most common in the south and west, but it was known elsewhere: it was especially prevalent on estates managed by the courts[2] or by middlemen. 'The usual practice', Wakefield reported from Kerry Head, 'is to expose land to public *cant* and he who bids most obtains it.'[3] In Co. Cork 'many landed proprietors advertise to let to the highest bidder, without any consideration for the claims of the occupying tenant. To these circumstances are imputed the frequent failure of tenants, and the generally unimproved state of the country. The farmer, who sees his lease drawing near its close, and feels no animating hope of a renewal upon reasonable terms, yielding to the emotions of despair, racks and impoverishes the farm he has so little chance of retaining.'[4] The highest bidder, said Wakefield of the country in general, 'whatever be his character or connexions, is invariably preferred; and if he can pay his rent, no inquiries are made whether he cultivates the land in a proper

[1] *Rep. Devon Com.*, 1845, op. cit., p. 16.
[2] It was the usual practice with estates under receivers in Court of Chancery, or Court of Exchequer, when a farm came out of lease for 'a sort of auction to be held in the Master's office, and the land was let to the highest bidder'. (*Rep. Devon Com.*, 1845, op. cit., p. 26.)
[3] Wakefield, 1812, op. cit. i. 263.
[4] Townsend, 1810, op. cit., p. 583.

manner, or ruins and exhausts it by mismanagement'.[1] 'When a lease expires', according to the author of *Lachrymae Hiberniae*, 'there is a public advertisement, with a notice annexed, that *no preference* will be given; that is the old tenant will not be preferred, and any person bidding higher will be put in possession. Thus the land is at public auction, and the old occupier, unwilling to remove, and having no place for himself and his family, through fear of losing a residence, has been bidding against himself, until he has raised the rent far beyond the value.'[2] It is no wonder that the typical peasant of Ireland, treated as the mass of his fellows, resigned himself to a life of degradation: it is no wonder that 'a farm is always left by the retreating tenant in the most impoverished state; the drains are choaked; the ditches and fences destroyed, the land exhausted and overrun with weeds; the house and offices fallen, or greatly out of repair, so that the farm is in reality of less value from five to ten shillings an acre than it was a few years before'.[3]

In Ulster the custom of 'tenant-right' gave some protection to the occupier, but beyond Ulster, our conclusion must be, the tenant's lease, even if he could get it unstintingly supported by the courts, was no safeguard against abuse. In general it was of uncertain duration, or it was short; sooner or later the time would come when it was no safeguard to the tenant against either eject-ment and the sacrifice of any labour he had devoted to improve-ment, or renewal at terms designed to pass to others produce surplus to his family's subsistence. But even the modest protection the lease purported to give could easily be, and in fact often was, lost to the tenant. A tax was imposed on leases: the peasant un-willing to pay it would say to his landlord ' "If your honour will only make a memorandum of the bargain in your book I shall be satisfied." '[4] But if the landlord or middleman were tempted by the general rise of rents to go back on his bargain, his notebook was of scanty protection to the tenant. Still, in the forties, 'in some cases where the landlord is willing, the tenants decline to take out leases, influenced, to a certain degree, by the high stamp duty'.[5] It was the custom, too, for the ingoing tenant to pay no rent for six, or

[1] Wakefield, 1812, op. cit. i. 304. [2] Op. cit., p. 10.
[3] Ed. Ledwich, *Statistical Account of the Parish of Aghaboe*, Dublin, 1796, pp. 51–2.
[4] Wakefield, 1812, op. cit. i. 276.
[5] *Rep. Devon Com.*, 1845, op. cit., p. 15.

perhaps twelve or fifteen months. This 'hanging gale' served a useful purpose; when the peasant was without capital he was not required to pay his rent until he had harvested the produce of his soil. But it ministered, too, to less worthy ends: if during the currency of the lease the landlord were offered more for a farm than the occupying tenant was paying, he stood a good chance of being able to evict him, without giving the courts cause to murmur, by demanding the arrears of rent. ' "The hanging gale" ', said Wakefield, 'is one of the great levers of oppression by which the lower classes are kept in a kind of perpetual bondage, for as every family almost holds some portion of land, and owes half a year's rent, which a landlord can exact in a moment; this debt hangs over their heads like a load, and keeps them in a continuous state of anxiety and terror.'[1] The Irishman 'always sees "the hanging gale" suspended over his head, as a menace, the obvious purport of which is, that if at the next harvest he should collect a few more sheaves than was expected, the profit shall not belong to him'.[2]

The Irish system of tenure was oppressive to the tenantry because leases were uncertain and short, and because it was within the power of the landlord to end when he pleased what the tenant had regarded as a lease of fixed duration: it was made even more burdensome by two obnoxious practices, one fairly general, the other occurring less frequently. It was common to have a clause inserted in a lease binding the tenant to work for the landlord at a given rate of wages; sometimes a lease would be renewed only upon payment of a fine. The vicar of Killegney, in Kildare, wrote, in 1812, that tenants in his parish, besides paying their rent, were also 'subject to the following: A fine, of at least, half-a-year's rent, as fees to the agent; duty-fowl for the consumption of his household; great requisitions of work, as often as they are called, for agriculture on his demesne of above 500 acres; the drawing of turf, coals, limestone, etc., the spinning of flax for the landlord's family, and various perquisites to the agent, who has only a nominal salary, and must be paid in various ways by the tenants.'[3] Wakefield recorded that when the proprietor of one of the best estates in Co. Down came of age 'his agent sent notice to all the tenants whose leases were expired, that there could be no renewal

---

[1] Wakefield, 1812, op. cit. i. 244.
[2] Beaumont, op. cit. ii. 228.   [3] Mason, op. cit. i, 1814, p. 459.

for them unless each consented to pay a fine of ten guineas per acre! But this was not all:—to those in possession of leases a threat was held out, that unless they surrendered their leases, paid the required fine, and took out new ones, a mark would be placed against their names in the rental book, and not only they, but their heirs and families, would be for ever excluded from any benefit of a renewal.'[1]

There is a further feature of Irish land organization relevant to our purpose of underlining that, whatever his industry or self-denial, the chances were that the peasant's family would be obliged to live upon slender resources.[2] Absenteeism, the middleman system, unfair leases, and rack-renting, though they had as an incidental effect the weakening of the incentive to increase yield, were all designed to draw away from the people who worked the land a maximum amount of their produce. It was otherwise with the partnership system: yield was kept down, but by the peasant's veneration for tradition, not by the landlord's profit-seeking. Wakefield gave the classic account of the 'rundale' or partnership system. It was common, he said, in Co. Galway, to grant leases to an indefinite number of persons, often twenty, who were by law joint tenants.

[1] Wakefield, 1812, op. cit. i. 256.

[2] In this chapter no attempt is made to give an exhaustive analysis of the institutions which forced the mass of the rural population to live on slender resources: omissions include matters as important as the methods of collecting taxes and tithes, the wage system, and the conacre system. The average daily wage, according to the data collected by the Poor Inquiry Commission was said to be 8½d. and the labourer was said, by and large, to be able to count on no more than 135 days' employment a year. (*Report of the Poor Inquiry Commission, Reports from Commissioners*, 1836, xxxiv, App. H, pt. i, p. 656.) Under the con-acre system, which was generally prevalent throughout the country, labourers and people with very small holdings, took plots of land for a single season so that they might plant potatoes. Sometimes the people letting the land did the ploughing and carted the manure, sometimes the labourer had to do all the work himself. Nominally the rent (of an amount varying from £5 to £10 per acre) was paid in money but frequently it had to be accepted, partially or wholly, in labour or in the potatoes the ground yielded. Bicheno discussed the system in the summary he prepared for the Poor Inquiry Commission of the evidence it collected on social and economic conditions. It appears, he said, 'that the average crops of con-acre produce as much or a little more (at the usual price of potatoes in the autumn) than the amount of the rent, seed, and the tenant's labour, say 5/- or 10/-'. The advantages to the labourer of a system, apparently so unreward-ing were that he hoped to work out all or a part of his rent (and so avoid the necessity of accumulating money) and that, in a good year, he secured his food-supply in the autumn and was thereafter independent of fluctuations in the price of potatoes. (Ibid., App. H, pt. ii, pp. 661–2.)

These people divide the land, and give portions to their children, which consist of a fourth, or a fifth of what they call a 'man's share', that is, of the land which originally belonged to one name in the lease. A certain proportion of the whole farm, or *take*, as it is styled, is appropriated for tillage, and this portion is then divided into lots, perhaps twenty or thirty. These lots are again subdivided into fields, which are partitioned into smaller lots, each partner obtaining one or two ridges; but these ridges do not continue in the hands of the same occupier longer than the time they are in tillage. The pasture is held in common, and the elders of the village are the legislators, who establish such regulations as may be judged proper for their community, and settle all disputes that arise among them. Their homes stand close to each other, and form what is here termed a village.[1]

Rundale displayed many of the disadvantages of the medieval strip system, but like it, it was appropriate to the environment from which it grew. When a community's population was fairly stable, or increasing slowly, when it expected its labour to produce only its subsistence, when its needs had to be satisfied almost entirely by its own land and stock, when the very continuance of tradition was a source of confidence and satisfaction—when these conditions were fulfilled it was needless to upset the partnership which for generations had shown that it could meet the requirements of its members. Partnership leases, said Townsend, in his description of Co. Cork, where they were well known, are 'a kind of tenure objectionable in many respects, yet not ill-suited to the circumstances of a poor tenantry whose chief riches consist in their labour. Two or more families, each bringing a little, are enabled thus, by combining their forces to accomplish what they were individually unequal to.'[2]

By the late eighteenth century, however, the conditions which had made rundale tolerable, if not desirable, had changed. The rapid increase of population left the peasants' requirements unsatisfied by the yield of the strip system: improving roads,[3] combined with the lessons learned from the necessity of finding an ever expanding money rent, made them more familiar with the outside market: knowledge of an improved technique of agriculture made clinging to tradition seem a foolish sacrifice of well-

---

[1] Wakefield, 1812, op. cit. i. 256.   [2] Townsend, 1810, op. cit., pp. 251-2.

[3] The great improvement of the roads of Ireland in the century before the Famine and the influence of better communications upon population history are discussed in my paper *The Colonisation of Waste Land in Ireland, 1780-1845,* shortly to be published in *The Economic History Review.*

being. As rundale became less appropriate to the circumstances of the partners there was, perhaps, a wider realization of the disadvantages inseparable from the system, and obvious to all commentators. The system was clearly an impediment to improvement. 'As long as this system exists, there can be no emulation for draining, enclosing, limeing, or carrying into execution any permanent plan for rendering the land more productive, since none of the party have any division which may properly be called their own. If one person should be disposed to improve, another, or perhaps the whole party may be averse to it, and thus the business of improving the farm is dropped altogether.'[1] 'The custom of running in common is a great evil, and produces much mischief among the peasants. It is frequently the cause of neglecting to make their fences, and suffering their cattle to damage the growing crops, and one or two lazy or indolent partners will introduce confusion, and damp the industry of others.'[2] 'Wherever this mode of letting land prevails, agriculture is execrable.'[3] It led to incessant quarrelling among the partners: 'fights, trespasses, confusion, disputes and assaults were the natural and unavoidable consequences of this system; these evils, in their various forms, were endless, and caused great loss of time and expense to the people attending petty sessions; and, of course, continued disunion amongst neighbours, was perpetuated.'[4] Tenants themselves were sometimes active in ending partnership leases,[5] but it was more usual for landlords to take the lead, the more liberal spurred on by a realization of the deficiencies of the system, the more covetous by the belief that, with individual tenancy the land might produce more, and pay a higher rent.

The partnership system was common in Wakefield's time, and known up and down the country: the 'greater part' of Mayo and 'fully a third of Galway' were subject to it, it was 'prevalent' in Donegal, 'frequently' to be seen in Kildare, and 'common' in Kilkenny and Tyrone.[6] But it was on the wane before Wakefield made his tour. In Clare, by 1808, 'from a conviction of its pernicious tendency, many proprietors have abolished this mode'.[7]

[1] Wakefield, 1812, op. cit. i. 244.   [2] Mason, op. cit. ii, 1816, p. 382.
[3] McCulloch, 1854, op. cit. i. 387.
[4] Lord George Hill, *Facts from Gweedore*, Dublin, 1846, p. 13.
[5] Mason, op. cit. ii, 1816, p. 384.
[6] Wakefield, 1812, op. cit. i. 249-78.
[7] Dutton, 1808, op. cit., pp. 145-6.

The curate of Kilrush, in a survey of his parish in 1816, said that the partnership system, though nearly abolished, still prevailed in some parts of the west.[1] In the same year, in Kilmactige, in Sligo, it was said that the 'tenants in common have been of late coming into the habit of dividing their several portions, casting lots on the divisions, and inclosing them'.[2] Rundale died hard. Still, in the thirties, McCulloch found it in every province: still Wakefield's description was quoted to show its leading features, but most references underlined that it was disappearing. In Clare 'partnership tenures [are] not so common as formerly'; in Cavan 'numbers of farms are held in common; but the practice is said to be declining'; in Donegal, 'partnership tenures [are] common, but diminishing'; in Mayo 'a good deal of land is let on the partnership or village system: it is said, however, that this system is on the wane'; in Roscommon, 'partnership tenures [are] diminishing'.[3]

Poverty and hopelessness were not alone as inducements to early marriage. When the Irish 'set a value upon the labour of their offspring from the earliest periods of infancy',[4] and when the peasants' 'happiness and ease [were] generally relative to the number of their children',[5] the desirability of marrying early was made plain to all. A certain recklessness which observers detected in the Irish temperament tended in the same direction. Few were dissuaded from marriage by concern for the added responsibilities it might bring. 'In other countries to make provision for a family is so serious an undertaking, that marriage is seldom ventured on at an early age, or until a man has acquired a competence sufficient for its support. Here marriage is delayed by no want, except sometimes the want of money enough to purchase a license—to Providence and their potato garden they commit the rest.'[6] 'Papists', said Madden, 'are careless as to Wealth or Portion, and will have Wives, let them be maintain'd how they will.'[7] 'It is customary to say', wrote a land-agent more than a century later, 'that the lower order of Irish will marry despite of the ruin which stares them in the face, and, to a great extent, the fact is true.'[8] A witness from

[1] Mason, op. cit. ii, 1816, p. 470.   [2] Ibid. p. 385.
[3] J. R. McCulloch, *A Statistical Account of the British Empire*, 2nd ed., 1839, pp. 382–3, 392–4.
[4] Wakefield, 1812, op. cit. ii. 690–1.
[5] Young, 1780, op. cit. ii. 198.   [6] Townsend, 1810, op. cit., p. 89.
[7] S. Madden, *Reflections and Resolutions*, Dublin, 1738, p. 206.
[8] Anketel, 1843, op. cit., pp. 16–17.

Co. Galway told a Royal Commission in 1835 that 'if I had a blanket to cover her I would marry the woman I liked; and if I could get potatoes enough to put into my children's mouths, I would be as happy and content as any man, and think myself as happy off as Lord Dunlo'.[1] The unattractiveness of the prospect of remaining single was another inducement to early marriage. The traditional division of labour between the sexes made working the land and running the house a co-operative enterprise between husband and wife: the single man or woman would find little satisfaction in trying to manage both, and it is improbable that the person who made the attempt would be the object of less scorn in the 1830s than a century later.[2] There were few alternative occupations in the country-side for the single adult: what day labour was required could be readily performed by married peasants.[3]

The attitude of the priests was held, by their critics, to sanction, even demand, early marriage. There is little doubt that if the legitimacy of a child were in dispute, priestly pressure would emphasize the desirability of marriage. Controversy arose on the question of whether the priests were disposed to encourage early marriage because their income was, in considerable part, derived from marriage fees and collections made at weddings.[4] It was Wakefield's opinion that 'the Romancatholic clergy . . . being dependent on their parishioners, are anxious to increase population as the best means of enlarging their incomes, and for this reason promote an early union of the sexes'.[5] Parker, the author of the *Plea for the Poor and Industrious of Ireland*, was so convinced of the evil consequences of the priests' dependence upon marriages for their maintenance that he regarded it as essential that the clergy be given an allowance from public funds in lieu of marriage fees.[6] Inglis, writing some years later, also urged that some public provision be made for priests, and that marriage and

---

[1] Quoted by Foster, 1846, op. cit., p. 146.

[2] See Arensberg, 1937, op. cit. p. 52.

[3] J. C. Curwen, *Observations on the State of Ireland*, 1818, i. 251.

[4] 'The marriage fee is established at 10/-. The priest now demands £1. Even at this price his gains are much diminished; for the custom of handing round the plate used to yield him from ten-fold to a hundred-fold what is got by fees from the married. A priest used to get sometimes a hundred pounds from the plate—in the days when priests kept horses and cars.' (H. Martineau, *Letters from Ireland*, 1852, p. 206.)

[5] Wakefield, 1812, op. cit. ii. 690.   [6] Cork, 1819, p. 53.

baptismal dues be abolished, so that 'it would be no longer the interest of the priest to encourage or countenance—as it is certain he often does—the unwise, and almost criminally early marriages of the peasantry'.[1] The case against the clergy is strengthened by the testimony of the Reverend Croly, himself a Catholic priest (albeit one whose work was the delight of his Protestant reviewers).[2] He emphasized the acquisitiveness of the clergy of his day: formerly they had been content with a standard of living very little different from that of the common farmers, but 'the country Priest now copes with the country Squire, keeps sporting dogs, controls elections, presides at political clubs, and sits "cheek by jowl" at public dinners and public assemblies with Peers of the land and members of Parliament'.[3] The priests' incomes were not large —'scarcely any parish yields four hundred per annum; and many a parish does not yield one third of that sum';[4] rich parishioners contributed little in proportion to their means: 'the main attention of the Clergy' had, therefore, 'to be directed towards the enlargement of their incomes'.[5] The temptation before the priest to encourage early marriage is plain, though the more serious abuse, in Croly's opinion, was the simony involved in the priest's driving a hard bargain with the families of the couple about to be married, and charging a fee in excess of that prescribed by Diocesan ruling.[6] Dr. Doyle angrily rebutted the charge against the clergy: 'Good God, how little are we, the Catholic Clergy of Ireland, known even to our friends, when one of them could represent us in parliament as encouraging the intermarriage of the poor for the sake of "base lucre"!—those poor who have nothing to bestow but their prayers and affection, and with whom we gladly divide every shilling which Providence places at our disposal.'[7] Perhaps the temptation to a bishop, poor though Doyle often was, to allow the prospect of fees to guide his conduct was less than to the inconspicuous parish priest, often desperately short of funds, and aware that fruitful marriage was esteemed by his Church.

In the late eighteenth and early nineteenth centuries it is clear that the Irish were insistently urged and tempted to marry early:

[1] H. D. Inglis, *Ireland in 1834*, London, 1835, i. 248.
[2] See *A Stipendiary Romish Priesthood, being a review of an 'Essay on Ecclesiastical Finance'*, Dublin, 1835.
[3] D. O. Croly, *Essay . . . on Ecclesiastical Finance*, Cork, 1834, p. 30.
[4] Ibid., pp. 29–30.   [5] Ibid., p. 28.   [6] Ibid., p. 33.
[7] J.K.L., 1835, op. cit., p. 109.

the wretchedness and hopelessness of their living conditions, their improvident temperament, the unattractiveness of remaining single, perhaps the persuasion of their spiritual leaders, all acted in this direction.[1] Not only, as we shall see in later chapters, was it easily possible for them to marry early, but, even though the literature of the age abounds with the most emphatic warnings, there was little in the experience of the peasantry to encourage its members to defer marriage. The desire to postpone marriage until the accumulation of capital, or the acquisition of a better farm would allow a higher standard of living could seldom, it is clear, have influenced action in Ireland in the period under review. Land organization was such that however long the peasant kept himself free of family responsibilities, however much capital he acquired, whatever his industry or efforts to move to a better farm, unless he lived on an estate owned or managed by a landlord or middleman of quite unusual quality, he was forced to live under conditions more fitting for his stock than for himself. Rents, it is Professor O'Brien's opinion, were so adjusted as to give the landlord almost the whole produce of the land.[2] There is abundant contemporary support for this conclusion. Where there is a middleman, said Wakefield, 'such as one of those who abound in every town of Ireland' 'whatever success attends the occupiers, the whole fruit of their labour finds its way into the pockets of this petty despot'.[3] 'The system of middle landlordship, which some years ago was almost universally prevalent, presented an almost insurmountable barrier to the exertions of humble industry. . . . The amount of rent, we may justly suppose, was so regulated as to leave the tenant

---

[1] The institutions which we have examined in this chapter for their tendency to make early marriage desirable (and the developments which we shall consider in later chapters for their tendency to make it possible) doubtless had more direct influence in shaping the conduct of men, than that of women. In dealing, however, with the influence of the age at marriage upon fertility we are more interested in the age of the bride than in that of the bridegroom. Our argument would not suffer in this respect if men normally chose wives of the same age, or younger, than themselves. That this was, in fact, the case, at least in the thirties, is shown by the marriage statistics of the 1841 Census. Of the 405,197 marriages recorded as taking place in the rural districts between 1830 and 1840, in 197,296, or 48·7 per cent., the wives were in the same age-group as their husbands, and in 182,484, or 45·0 per cent., they were in a lower age-group. (1841 Census, *Reports from Commissioners*, 1843, xxiv. 483.)

[2] G. O'Brien, *The Economic History of Ireland from the Union to the Famine*, 1921, p. 89.

[3] Wakefield, 1812, op. cit. i. 287.

no more than a bare subsistence.'[1] *The Times* Commissioner, writing from Co. Leitrim after the Famine, said 'If you ask the man why he bid so much for his farm, and more than he knew he could pay, his answer is, "What could I do? Where could I go? I know I cannot pay the rent, but what could I do? Would you have me go and beg?" In this manner the utmost worth of the land, beyond mere subsistence—I am assured beyond dry potatoes and water—is extracted from the tenants, and the tenants, seeing the inutility of productive labour, so far as they are concerned, seeing that whether they work or play they get little beyond mere subsistence, settle down content with mere subsistence.'[2] In Donegal 'such rents are extracted from the people, considering the low state of agricultural improvement, as do leave those who produce the rents with little beyond bare subsistence'.[3]

It was not only next to impossible for the peasant to raise the level of his material well-being while he remained a peasant: the virtual absence of a middle class robbed of all reality any dreams he or his children might have had of raising their social status by self-denial or frugality. In England the middle class was a cause and product of the growth of industry and commerce: in Ireland what shreds of a middle class did exist were largely the parasites of agriculture. Perhaps there was some truth in the suggestion frequently made that Ireland's industrial development was rudimentary because of the restraining influence of an antipathetic temperament and religion; of more consequence appears to have been the poverty of her mineral and power resources—though England had industries of international repute when her mining was little more than surface working, and when manpower was supplemented only modestly by wind and water. It is in large measure to her political subservience that we must attribute the fact that in Ireland there were so few representatives of social grades intermediate between landlords and peasants, and that those who did exist were so preponderantly of an unattractive type. Ireland's subject status had a dual influence. It meant, in the first place, that industry which would have bred a middle class was hampered, directly by prohibitions, and indirectly by restricted personal liberty. It meant, secondly, that those professions which had to exist however overwhelmingly agricultural the country,

---

[1] Townsend, 1810, op. cit., pp. 183–5.
[2] Foster, 1846, op. cit., p. 34.   [3] Ibid., p. 67.

were recruited at first almost exclusively, and throughout our period largely from a class disposed by heredity, religion, and education to become a minor appendage of the aristocracy rather than an independent middle class. The virtually exclusive Protestant domination of the professions and the more powerful and lucrative positions in public administration, industry, and commerce was broken down only in the closing decades of the eighteenth century. Before then the Protestant monopoly was enforced sometimes because Roman Catholics were legally incapacitated from occupying certain positions, sometimes because their general subjection made it impossible for them to acquire the education or capital required for their advancement. It was only the exceptional Protestant, qualified by an adequate income, who did not become assimilated with the landowning class, or at least strive to give the appearance of assimilation with sufficient success to convince any peasant who came into contact with him that he belonged, not to a middle class which the peasant's own children might aspire to join, but to the landowning class, membership of which was a wholly unreal—and not altogether desirable—proposition for the peasant's family.

With the relaxation of the penal code towards the end of the eighteenth century—in 1782 Catholics were allowed to buy and bequeath land (provided it was not in a parliamentary borough) and, on certain conditions, to become schoolmasters; in 1792 they were allowed to become solicitors and barristers, and the restrictions on the number of apprentices in Catholic trade were removed; in 1793 Catholics were not only enfranchised on the same terms as Protestants, but they were permitted to endow their own schools and universities and to receive degrees in Dublin University; then, too, they were freed of any remaining disabilities concerning personal property[1]—with this relaxation of the penal code there began to grow a middle class recruited from the population at large, and remaining distinct from the aristocracy. There came into existence the embryo of a class which promised to disseminate through the country some conception of more comfortable living conditions than the peasants were used to, and to provide, in the advancement of their sons, a reward for their industry and self-denial. But these effects were only occasionally felt in our period. All the time

[1] W. E. H. Lecky, *History of Ireland in the Eighteenth Century*, 1892, ii. 312–13; iii. 61 and 141.

it was exceptionally that the peasant was not robbed of what should have been the fruits of his industry. Industrial and commercial development was still slow: it was crippled by the absence of an industrial tradition, by shortage of capital, and by political unrest. Protestants still remained in the most desirable positions, and the rivalry of Catholics tended to drive them even more decisively than formerly into the society of the aristocracy.[1] Perhaps more frequently than in any other way, Catholics acquired a higher social status by becoming middlemen: they bettered their lot by becoming members of a declining class, a class parasitical upon the peasantry from which they had sprung. With advance to a higher status barred to them as effectively as the possibility of improving their lot while remaining peasants, it is no wonder that they were listless and lacking in self-respect: it is no wonder that, as a class, their lot was worsened by the individual's reluctance to postpone a marriage which promised him the solace that the degradation of his life made him crave.

[1] Beaumont, 1839, op. cit. ii. 112.

IV

THE BALANCE BETWEEN PASTURE AND ARABLE

THE desire to marry early was undoubtedly present in late-eighteenth-century Ireland, but without the opportunity for its gratification it could have had little influence upon the growth of population. It would seem, in fact, that a greater impatience to marry had less effect in increasing fertility than the social and economic movements which made it possible for people to marry while unusually young. Accounts of Irish social conditions, from the time of Petty onwards make it probable that any tendency of wretched living conditions to lower the age at marriage would have been felt to the full well before the 1780s. There is little reason for believing that the rise in the population-curve coincided with a worsening of living conditions. Indeed, wretched though conditions remained until, in 1845, the Devon Commission found that the sufferings of the labouring classes were 'greater . . . than the people of any other country in Europe have to sustain',[1] the nature of the evidence may well incline to make the historian's record more grim than the facts would warrant. There is from the time of Arthur Young until the forties a stream of evidence insisting that, hard though the peasant's lot undoubtedly was, it had been improving for some years past. Two of the principal sources from which most accounts of Irish social life in this period are derived are the mass of evidence accumulated by the Select Committees and Royal Commissions, and the accounts of travellers. State investigation was usually demanded, and granted, because of particularly acute distress: a famine or an epidemic likewise tended to attract private inquirers, a number of them journalists, others the agents of societies organizing relief. Both public and private reports, careful and honest though they may be, tend to give the reader the impression that all years were bad years. It is possible, too, that the observer left the Irish cabin over-impressed with the wretchedness of living conditions: certainly a people as addicted

[1] *Reports from Commissioners*, 1845, xix. 12.

to begging as the Irish—and they commonly had petitions ready drawn up to thrust into the hands of the chance traveller—would be careful to see that the observer was not left unaware of the depths of their misery. An utter neglect of cleanliness and tidiness (resulting, it may well be, from poor living conditions) contributed to heighten the observer's impression of wretchedness.[1] The peasants' experience, too, that any surplus above their requirements for subsistence normally found its way to the pocket of landlord or middleman encouraged them not to show a cheerful exterior. Harriet Martineau was convinced that 'the fearful apparent wretchedness of the people is no necessary indication of poverty. The five pigs wallowing near the bed's head is an instance. At the present value of pigs here . . . these five must be worth many pounds. Elsewhere we have seen a very fine cow, or perhaps two, belonging to a hovel so wretched that you would suppose the people had no prospect of another meal.'[2]

The wars with France, in spite of rising rents and taxes and the multiplication of middlemen, do not seem to have been accompanied by added hardships for the mass of the people. In discussing the position of the tenantry between 1793 and 1829, Sigerson pointed out that it 'was not altogether the unhappy one which an uncritical reading of the works of transient visitors would suggest. They judged it absolutely upon its demerits, not in relation to the country's past. Compared with that past, the cultivators had reason to regard its first years as their golden age.'[3] Writer after writer in Mason's *Statistical Account* maintained that by the late war years, in widely scattered parishes, social conditions had improved. A Sligo incumbent referred to the war as a 'golden age';[4] in a Co. Down parish 'within the last thirty years the progress in improvements of all kinds has been most striking';[5] from Antrim came the

---

[1] Patients were received in the fever hospitals, a medical observer wrote in 1819, with their bodies 'often so bronzed with filth that the natural colour of the skin could hardly be perceived. Their hair was filled with vermin, and the smell of many was so offensive as to render it a very disgusting office, on the part of the nurse-tenders to free them from the accumulation of dirt with which they were loaded.' (F. Rogan, *Observations on the Condition of the Middle and Lower Classes in the North of Ireland*, 1819, p. 78.)

[2] H. Martineau, *Letters from Ireland*, 1852, p. 96.

[3] G. Sigerson, *History of the Land Tenures and Land Classes of Ireland*, 1871, p. 159.

[4] W. S. Mason, *Statistical Account, or Parochial Survey of Ireland*, Dublin, ii, 1816, p. 381.

[5] Ibid. ii. 23–4.

report that 'the general appearance of the mass of the people, both males and females, is greatly improved within the last ten years'.[1] Frequent references to improved clothing support the impression of better times; in Kildare 'the appearance of the women is much bettered; for about 20 years ago they were ragged and barefooted; now no country girl is seen without decent clothing, shoes and stockings, etc.';[2] in Limerick 'the people are improving rapidly in manners and dress';[3] in Donegal 'dress has improved considerably within the last fifteen years'.[4] Housing, too, at least in certain areas, was getting better.[5] In Clare 'even the lower orders are of late years becoming more independent every day'.[6] At the end of the wars there was probably immediately some worsening of conditions. But by the thirties the weight of the evidence suggests that for ten years, at least, there had been improvement. Weld's is one of the minority voices: in the town of Boyle 'complaints were common of the stagnation of commerce and decrease of the country trade. It was an unvarying tale, that the peasantry who frequented the town were poorer than formerly; at least that they did not spend money as they heretofore used to do.'[7] The *Report on the State of the Poor in Ireland* is, perhaps, the most authoritative version of the general view. It stated that evidence had been brought to the Committee showing that the state of the peasants had improved rapidly in recent years: clothes, houses, and methods of agriculture had all been getting better; the Committee underlined the beneficial moral and economic influence upon Ireland of the steam packet service with Britain.[8] A coach proprietor pointed out in his evidence that peasants who had been accustomed to travel on foot were increasingly becoming outside passengers on coaches and that, while formerly country people travelled to their amusements on the 'common car' with a bundle of straw and a quilt, increasingly they were coming in jaunting-cars; he noticed, too, an improvement in the general condition of towns

---

[1] W. S. Mason, op. cit. i, 1814, p. 156.

[2] Ibid. i. 449.   [3] Ibid. ii. 101.   [4] Ibid. ii. 156.

[5] Ibid. ii. 33 (Arklow, Co. Wicklow), p. 452 (Kilrush, Co. Clare), p. 131 (Carrigaline, Co. Cork), p. 101 (Cahircorney, Co. Limerick).

[6] Ibid. i. 472.

[7] I. Weld, *Statistical Survey of the County of Roscommon*, Dublin, 1832, p. 203. The trouble at Boyle arose partly from the decay of the linen industry, and partly, Weld thought, from increased competition amongst shopkeepers which lowered profit-margins.

[8] *Reports of Commissioners*, 1830, vii. 4–5.

and shops, notably in the south.[1] Pierce Mahony felt bound to say that 'the state of the peasantry has improved very rapidly of late years', the peasantry 'are better dressed, and in every way seem to be more comfortable; their houses are improving'.[2] Another witness, a distiller from Limerick, thought that 'within the last twenty years . . . people have had more comforts than they had: on Sundays and holidays you can see that they are much better clothed than they were twenty years ago'.[3] R. O'Callaghan Newenham, an Inspector-General of Barracks and much travelled throughout the country, thought that the condition of the people had been advancing over forty years.[4]

It was only the rare commentator in our period, and he improbably one to be trusted, who thought Irish social conditions good. They were not good and their wretchedness and hopelessness predisposed those who suffered under them towards early marriage. But the origins of this tendency must be placed much earlier than the 1780s. Nor can we expect in these years to find in increasing misery the explanation of yet earlier marriage: rather the reverse; with the modest lightening of his discomforts which the peasant most probably enjoyed[5] it would be proper to expect some willingness to postpone marriage. Our problem, then, ceases to be the motivation of youthful marriage and becomes an exploration of the possibilities of marrying young. What changes in the late eighteenth and early nineteenth centuries allowed a people which had long wanted to marry early increasingly to gratify this desire?

The obstacle to early marriage for the greater part of the eighteenth century was the difficulty of acquiring a settlement upon which a new family might depend. Setting up a household was a matter of little concern: the cost of the cabin was typically no more than some days of the occupiers' labour and the assistance freely given by their neighbours. Only trifling additional expenditure went to the acquisition of its furnishings: these would not seem unusually deficient if they comprised only a bed of litter, a chair or two, a table, and an iron pot. The problem was to find

---

[1] Ibid., qq. 4338–42.
[2] Ibid., qq. 37–43.   [3] Ibid., q. 450.   [4] Ibid., q. 6789.
[5] This conclusion is not in accord with Professor O'Brien's findings. From the Union to the Famine, he says, 'the agricultural population of Ireland remained as poor as ever—or rather grew poorer from year to year'. (*Economic History of Ireland from the Union to the Famine*, 1921, p. 222.)

an occupation that would produce a flow of the necessities of life. Slowly growing towns and thwarted domestic industries made the land almost the universal provider. But the land, with a stagnant technique of farming, and a tendency for pasture to extend at the expense of arable, was not a bountiful provider. One son might succeed his father, but accommodation for his brothers was to be found only by encroaching on the heir's none too abundant birthright or in the modest amount of reclamation that was proceeding. Marriage, then, because of the difficulty of acquiring a settlement, tended to be delayed. But in the closing decades of the century developments in rural economy went far towards making marriage more easily possible for the peasant's son.

Five developments, in particular, are relevant to our problem. First, the increasing emphasis upon arable, apparent in Irish farming after the 1780s, both increased the amount of labour required in farming and, by producing a greater yield, allowed larger families to survive. Second, more nearly exclusive and universal dependence upon the potato as an article of diet made the problem of securing provision for a family less forbidding. Third, the spread of arable and the dependence upon the potato, in co-operation with other factors, brought widespread subdivision of holdings: with holdings tilled and the population living on potatoes, land which formerly had been adequate for only one family's subsistence could be parcelled among sons or other subtenants. Fourth, by pressing cultivation into bog or mountain, land which had been waste became settled. Finally, the spur given to economic activity, initially largely by the policy of the Irish Parliament and later by the war, tended to lower the obstacles confronting the peasant's son wishing to marry.

The tendency of a growing proportion of tillage after the 1780s to allow a quickened rate of population-growth was felt the more emphatically because it was the reversal of the trend towards more pasture which had persisted for at least a century and a half. Already, in 1623, according to the author of the *Advertisements for Ireland*, grazing was more profitable than tillage: it was the occupation of most of the Irish and seemed likely to oust the plough altogether if England's lead were not followed and measures taken to discourage its extension.[1] Ten years later it worried Spenser 'to have such huge increase of cattle, and no increase of

---

[1] Ed. G. O'Brien, Dublin, 1923, p. 33.

good conditions': he, too, wanted legislation to control the advance of grassland 'for otherwise all men would fall to pasturage, and none to husbandry'.[1] More than a century later, the Duke of Devonshire, meeting Parliament in 1741, commented on the scarcity of provisions in Ireland and urged its members to consider 'proper measures to prevent the like calamity for the future, and to this desirable end the increase of tillage . . . may greatly contribute'.[2] By the 1770s, of the ills of Ireland 'the first is, the suffering avarice to convert the arable lands into pasture. . . . Every man, connected with the interests of the graziers, or swayed by their prejudices, will tell you, very dogmatically, that tillage can never succeed in Ireland.'[3]

Few of the laments heard during the English inclosure movement of the sixteenth century were not echoed in Ireland in the seventeenth and eighteenth centuries. Livestock in Ireland were devouring men as they had devoured them in the days of Elizabeth. 'It is but putting ourselves', said Madden, 'a Degree or two above the *Savage Indians* . . . if we have only tame Beasts to roam about our Lands, instead of wild ones, for 'tis Demonstrable that the first devour more People than the latter.'[4] 'By running into the fancy of grazing, after the manner of the Scythians, [the landowners] are every day depopulating the country.'[5] There were complaints in Ireland, too, of a scarcity of provisions: the people were forced 'to send sometimes as far as Egypt for bread to eat'.[6] 'It is to our shame and reproach', said Madden, 'that as absolutely necessary as Tillage is to our well-being we have been careless about it, as if, like the *Jews* we expected Manna from Heaven to feed us.'[7] A spate of comment in eighteenth-century Ireland, as in sixteenth-century England shows how harassing was the concern for the country's future, should the graziers continue to lay down

---

[1] E. Spenser, *View of the State of Ireland*, 1633, reprinted in *Tracts and Treatises illustrative . . . of Ireland*, Dublin, i, 1860, p. 580.

[2] J. O'Rourke, *History of the Great Irish Famine of 1847, with Notices of earlier Irish Famines*, Dublin, 1875, p. 20.

[3] T. Campbell, *Philosophical Survey of the South of Ireland*, Dublin, 1777, pp. 294–7.

[4] S. Madden, op. cit., 1738, pp. 50–1.

[5] J. Swift, *Short View of the State of Ireland*, Dublin, 1727–8, ed. T. Scott, 1925, p. 87.

[6] J. Swift, *Answer to . . . 'A Memorial of the Poor Inhabitants . . .'*, 1735, ed. T. Scott, 1925, p. 111.

[7] Madden, op. cit., pp. 125–6.

arable to grass: perhaps the Irish commentators with a longer and fuller mercantilist tradition behind them were the more worried. 'Whether', asked *The Querist*, 'it be not a sure sign or effect of a country's thriving to see it well cultivated and full of inhabitants? And, if so, whether a great quantity of sheep-walk be not ruinous to a country, rendering it waste and thinly inhabited? Whether the employing so much of our land under sheep be not, in fact, an *Irish* blunder?'[1] 'As Things go on', said Madden, Ireland 'may become an uncultivated Desart in Time, inhabited by nothing but Beasts and Savages.'[2]

Further evidence of the extension of pasture and the reluctance of farmers to commit themselves to corn-growing is to be found in the trade-statistics and statute-books of the middle decades of the century. Newenham collected figures for the entire century showing the annual average excess of corn, ground and unground, exported from or imported into Ireland. His tables show that, while for the first third of the century native tillage produced substantially more grain than Ireland required, from the thirties until the seventies this position was reversed. From 1701 until 1732 Ireland had a net export of 819,616 quarters of corn and of 356,140 barrels of meal, but from 1733 until 1776, while she exported 71,844 barrels of meal, she imported 1,380,820 quarters of corn and 1,092,008 hundredweights of flour.[3] The diminution in the area under the plough was a matter which frequently attracted the attention of the legislature. Nine acts purporting to encourage tillage were passed between 1707 and 1780. Their very frequency suggests that they did little to redress the balance against the plough: indeed, the preamble to 'An Act for the further encouragement of tillage in this kingdom',[4] passed in 1765, admits defeat.

As for the causes of the extension of pasture, climate and soil over much of Ireland certainly favoured the pastoralist, but we cannot say that this was a new influence or one felt to be increasingly compelling. What Madden called a 'natural aversion' to

---

[1] G. Berkeley, *The Querist*, 1752, reprinted in *Tracts and Treatises illustrative . . . of Ireland*, Dublin, ii, 1861, p. 157.

[2] Madden, 1738, op. cit., p. 205.

[3] T. Newenham, 1809, op. cit., Appendix, p. 5.

[4] 5 Geo. III, c. 19. 'Whereas the laws heretofore made for the encouragement of tillage in this kingdom have not had the desired effect. . . .'

tillage may have reinforced the effects of climate. He thought that this was a characteristic the Irish had acquired from 'their good Friends the *Spaniards*, whose Pride and Sloth they are too apt to admire and Copy'. But there is no suggestion that reluctance to till was a recent development: Madden pointed out that Petty had discussed the matter and attributed it to the priests' teaching their flocks that to live by pasturage 'is more like the *Patriarchs* of old and the *Saints* of latter times'.[1] Perhaps the growing dependence upon the potato as the seventeenth century progressed was of some significance: the potato was capable of sustaining more people per square mile than corn crops, and, insofar as it took their place in the Irishman's diet, it may have released land for stock-farming. Troubled times too, penalized tillage. The risk of having their land over-run may have inclined farmers towards cattle and sheep, which could be driven to the hills in time of danger, and away from the corn which might have to be left to its fate in the fields. The difficulty under the Penal Laws for a Catholic to possess land, the general insecurity of his tenure, his chronic shortage of capital, and his ignorance of farming methods, all put a premium upon a type of agriculture in which little capital or effort had to be put into the soil. The collection of tithes, too, was so administered as to favour pasture-farming. The tithe-collectors, although there was no legal obligation upon them to do so, were guided by a resolution passed by the Irish House of Commons in 1735 to the effect that tithes should not be charged on pasture: this measure alone was said to have given 'pasture the advantage of tillage, by full £10 per cent'.[2]

Marketing conditions, often as a result of legal discrimination, did something to weigh the scales in favour of pasture. It is true that there was no approach to a consistent encouragement of the export of livestock and their products. In the 1670s a feeling that the export of cattle, then Ireland's principal trade, tended to lower rents in England led to legislation first restraining it, then prohibiting it altogether.[3] As a result, more sheep were kept, a fillip was given to the Irish woollen industry and its mounting export trade was a fresh source of concern in England. It was feared that

[1] Madden, 1738, op. cit., pp. 127–8.
[2] *Dissertation on the present Bounty Laws*, Dublin, 1780, pp. 23–4.
[3] 15 Chas. II, c. 7; 18 Chas. II, c. 2. See J. H. Hutchinson, *Commercial Restraints of Ireland*, Dublin, 1779, p. 86.

the high quality of the wool and the cheapness of provisions in Ireland would induce Englishmen to settle there to the great prejudice of the English manufacture. In 1698 duties were levied on woollen exports from Ireland: broad-cloths were to pay 20 per cent. *ad valorem* and new draperies, 10 per cent.; friezes, alone, were exempt.[1] The following year, because, in the words of the act concerned, 'the Irish trade would sink the value of lands, and tend to the ruin of the trade and woollen manufacture of England', it was forbidden to export from Ireland, elsewhere than to England and Wales, all goods made of, or mixed with, wool.[2] As there already existed prohibitory duties on the export of Irish woollens to England and Wales the new act was intended to complete a total prohibition of export. With the State endeavouring to ruin the Irish woollen industry, its organizers and workers emigrated: Catholics went to the north of Spain, some Protestants went to Germany, and others, despite the revocation of the Edict of Nantes, were received in France.[3] It can hardly have seemed reprehensible to these dispersed Irish workers to continue to draw their raw materials from the sources which had supplied them when they worked at home. Their local knowledge, personal and topographical, helped to establish a smuggling trade in Irish wool, the continued and thriving existence of which was guaranteed by a vast price-difference. In 1730 fleece wool in Ireland is said to have cost 5*d.* a pound and combed wool 1*s.*; in France, Irish fleece wool sold for 2*s.* 6*d.* and combed wool from 4*s.* 6*d.* to 6*s.*[4] The market for Irish wool was extended when in 1739, again for the benefit of the English woollen industry, duties were removed from woollen or bay yarn exported from Ireland to England.[5] Wool exports, however, were far outdistanced by exports of cattle and their produce.[6] The coming of peace opened profitable markets

[1] 10 Wm. III, c. 5.

[2] 10 & 11 Wm. III, c. 10.

[3] A. Dobbs, *Essay on the Trade and Improvement of Ireland*, 2 pts., 1729–31, reprinted in *Tracts and Treatises illustrative . . . of Ireland*, Dublin, ii, 1861, p. 335.

[4] J. A. Froude, *The English in Ireland in the Eighteenth Century*, 1895, i. 497, quoting *Proposals to prevent the Exportation of Wool to France*, 1730, 'by Mr. Knox'. (Manuscript in Dublin Castle.)

[5] Except worsted yarn of two or more threads. Hutchinson, 1779, op. cit., p. 119.

[6] According to Dobbs (1729–31, op. cit., ed. 1861, p. 345) on the average of the years 1719–26 the produce of cattle accounted for 48·9 per cent. of total exports and the produce of sheep for 12·4 per cent.

for Irish cattle and provisions on the Continent in 1714 and 1715 and murrain kept them open.[1] In 1758 the British market was made available to Irish cattle exporters. Ireland, then, in spite of much hostile legislation, was, throughout the eighteenth century, continuously able to find export markets for the products of her livestock. With grain British hostility had greater effect. The only potential market was in Britain, and, while imports from Ireland had to pay duties, bounties encouraged British exports to Ireland.

By the 1780s, perhaps earlier, there was a shift in the balance between flock and plough: the advance of pasture was held, if not reversed, and a swiftly increasing acreage of Ireland was tilled. There is a danger in pointing too readily to the extension of arable as a reason for the rise in population: contemporary writers were as willing to regard increasing numbers as the cause and extension of tillage as the consequence. Doubtless they were right: the pressure of population was an incentive to plough up pasture, but it was one incentive amongst many, and, as one that had operated (though with less force) in earlier decades when pasture had encroached upon arable, hardly the most effective. Once the swing towards arable became marked its influence on the rate of population growth could be felt: whenever a stretch of pasture was ploughed it required more people to work it; it produced more foodstuffs than formerly, and tended thereby to make more remote the operation of the positive check to population; perhaps most effectively, in a country in which few people had the capital or the skill to become large tillage-farmers, large- or medium-sized pasture farms became small tillage farms; subdivision became possible and a brake to earlier marriage—one of the most fruitful causes of population increase—was lifted.

The existence of a widespread movement from pasture to tillage in the half-century before the 1830s can hardly be questioned. It is reflected in the trade-statistics and was the subject of frequent comment in contemporary writings. Arthur Young in one of the earliest of such references pointed out that Belfast, until the year or so before his tour an importer of grain, had recently become an exporter.[2] The increasing attention being paid by Ulster farmers to tillage is again noticed during the French wars: from Ardstraw,

---

[1] Ibid., p. 337; G. O'Brien, *The Economic History of Ireland in the Eighteenth Century*, 1918, p. 108.

[2] A. Young, 1780, op, cit., 2nd ed. i. 163.

Co. Tyrone, it was reported in 1812 that for some years 'tillage has been improved and considerably extended':[1] in Dungiven, Co. Londonderry, many farmers were laying aside their old prejudices that soil and climate were totally unsuited for wheat:[2] in nearby Maghera, 'but little wheat is sown, but the farmers are likely to follow the example of some of the neighbouring parishes, in which it is beginning to be very generally cultivated'.[3] From the other provinces the reports are similar: in Aghaloe, Queen's County, nearly twice the area was under crops in 1812 as at the beginning of the wars;[4] in Co. Kilkenny, 'tillage seems to have much increased within the memory of man' and 'extends itself daily towards the summits of the hills';[5] in Co. Dublin, in spite of the great area near the capital devoted to market-gardening and milk production, 'the greatest exertions have been made by the farmers in breaking up lea for different corn crops; there never was an instance of so much ground under tillage in this county.'[6] McCulloch, writing in the thirties, said that in Meath 'grazing used formerly to be the principal occupation; but since the close of the American war, tillage has been gradually extending, until, at the present, about three-fifths of the county are under the plough'.[7] In Co. Cork, the Barony of Fermoy 'was formerly an open grazing country; it is now [1810] inclosed, tilled, and almost as full of inhabitants as the lands along the sea coast'; in the Barony of Kinalea, tillage 'is daily experiencing advancement both in quantity and quality'; even 'from Glangarriffe westward, some places excepted that skirt along the margin of the bay, to the furthest extremity of the Durzey islands, [where] the ground is coarse, mountainous, and rocky beyond description, population, however, even here has made great advances, and with it the tillage necessary to its wants'.[8] Waterford, one of the principal dairying counties, when visited by Arthur Young had not more than one-thirtieth of its area under the plough, but by the thirties 'the proportion of

---

[1] Mason, op. cit. i. 130.

[2] Ibid., p. 333.　　　　[3] Ibid., p. 603.　　　　[4] Ibid., p. 66.

[5] W. Tighe, *Statistical Observations relative to the County of Kilkenny*, Dublin, 1802, p. 260.

[6] J. Archer, *Statistical Survey of the County of Dublin*, Dublin, 1801, pp. 11 and 16.

[7] J. R. McCulloch, *Statistical Account of the British Empire*, 2nd ed., 1839, i. 375.

[8] H. Townsend, *Statistical Survey of the County of Cork*, Dublin, 1810, pp. 451, 543, and 393.

tillage is now . . . much larger'.[1] Connaught, with the slightest natural advantages for corn production, was no exception to the general movement towards tillage: Dutton's *Clare* reported an increase in the cultivation of corn in 1808:[2] in Galway, according to McCulloch, in 1839, 'there has, within the last dozen years been a very great increase in the growth of oats and barley', and in Roscommon 'latterly tillage has been rapidly extending'.[3]

In addition to the observations of contemporaries, there is some statistical evidence showing a remarkable increase in Irish grain production in the decades after the 1780s. Newenham, on the basis of a variety of statistics, endeavoured to calculate the extent to which the acreage of arable increased between 1784 and 1808. Import and export figures which he collected showed that Ireland, formerly dependent on imported corn, was, by 1807, exporting annually a surplus worth nearly £500,000, but this he regarded as an inadequate measure of the increased corn yield. To the increased exports had to be added allowances for the additional grain supplies sent to the distillers and brewers within Ireland and for the consumption of the augmented military establishment. Duty was paid in 1784 on 1,768,000 gallons of spirits, in 1807 on 5,704,000, and to this latter figure Newenham added 750,000 gallons to represent the increase in illicit distillation called forth by the virtual quadrupling of the spirit-duties between 1785 and 1808. For brewing, though figures were not continuously available, Newenham calculated that at least 800,000 more gallons of strong beer were brewed in 1808 than in 1784. With further allowances for the consumption of the 40,000 additional soldiers sent to garrison Ireland between 1785 and 1806, for their horses and for the increased number of horses used in agriculture, and after some calculations that make a greater show of precision than the materials they are based on would seem to warrant, Newenham concluded that the area of land under tillage must have increased by 200,000 acres since 1784.[4] An extension of arable acreage of this order of magnitude in a single generation could account for a considerable part of the increase in population: with family holdings as tiny as was customary in Ireland, and with families as large, it

[1] McCulloch, 1839, op. cit. i. 382.
[2] H. Dutton, 1808, op. cit., pp. 69–70.
[3] McCulloch, 1839, op. cit. i. 391 and 393.
[4] T. Newenham, 1809, op. cit., pp. 210–28.

H

would not be out of the question for each fresh acre of arable to provide the wherewithal for one person's maintenance.[1]

With what confidence can we accept Newenham's calculations? Without examining the accuracy of his figures for brewing, illicit distillation, or crop yields per acre—and it is unlikely that even the most painstaking modifications made to-day in his figures would reduce their error—it should be remembered that in part an increased acreage under corn may more accurately measure the growing dependence of the Irish on the potato than the absolute increase of tillage. In the period under review, if there had been any considerable substitution of potatoes for grain in the Irishman's diet, less land would have been required for the maintenance of the peasant's family and grain which had been kept for domestic consumption could have been sent overseas. It is impossible to measure the extent to which increased grain exports can be thus accounted for: if the conclusion of Chapter V is accepted, and it is assumed with Arthur Young that already by the time of his tour, the Irish were generally dependent on the potato, then only a fraction of the increased corn acreage could be the outcome of changes in food habits. On the other hand, tending to make us regard Newenham's figures as an under-estimate, is the fact that he made no allowance for the increased domestic consumption of grain consequent upon rising population: although potatoes were universally the rural staple, stirabout and bread, especially in the north, were not of negligible importance.[2] Newenham may have been too bold in his use of statistics, but there is no doubt that he was correct in his conclusion that there was a rapid extension in the area under tillage.

Tables D and E, in Appendix III, give a record, broken because statistics are not continuously available, of the corn trade in the century before the Famine. Figures for imports are much less complete than those for exports: in those years after 1770 for which information is available it shows that imports amount to only a fraction of current exports, and there is no other evidence that throughout this period, except in bad years, Ireland was a substantial importer of grain. There is a continuous series of export figures from 1772 to 1819. They show that in the forty years after

---

[1] It was Newenham's opinion that the area of tillage was increased without reducing the area of pasture (1809, op. cit., p. 218). See below, pp. 108–9.

[2] See below, Chapter V, pp. 138–41.

the seventies, the export of wheat increased nearly twentyfold; that of oats nearly tenfold, and of barley sixfold. In the seventies the official value of the entire produce of corn exported was only £65,000, but by the second decade of the new century the figure had risen to £416,000.

It is wholly inadequate, however, to measure the extension of tillage in Ireland by the increase in the yield of corn: if the export figures can be trusted, newly tilled land was used more generally to grow flax than corn. The export of linen cloth (as is shown by Table F in Appendix III) leapt upwards from 20 million yards in the 1770s to nearly 41 million in the nineties: there was a small diminution in the next decade because of poor yields from 1801 to 1803, but from 1810 to 1819 the figures rose and the decennial average was nearly 42 million yards. The official value of the produce of flax-seed increased from an annual average of £1,613,000 in the seventies to £2,647,000 between 1800 and 1809.

It is clear, then, that for at least fifty years before the 1770s, when the rate of population-increase was moderate by later standards, the tendency was for the graziers of Ireland to encroach upon arable land. In the next half-century, with rapid expansion in population, the old agricultural disequilibrium was reversed: though the yield of pasture farming may not have dwindled, it was the tiller, not the cattle farmer who was the more favoured, the colonizing element. To what change in circumstances can this shift in the balance between pasture and arable be attributed? First, population history doubtless helped to mould agricultural history: 'population, which in most places is very dense, having no other species of labour to resort to for subsistence, necessarily reduces the quantum of pasture, and obliges the inhabitants to become tillers of the soil.'[1] Cause and effect are intermingled: the extension of arable, because it was the product of a host of factors in addition to rising population, was able to contribute independently to population history; rising population, because its own causation was no less diverse, could help to shape the structure of agriculture. Second, the pre-eminence of pasture became less conspicuous with the weakening of some of the more transitory forces of which it was the result: climate and soil, doubtless, hindered the plough as much as ever, but with the troubles of the seventeenth century receding from men's memories, with the relaxation

[1] Townsend, 1810, op. cit., p. 610 (referring to the Barony of Imokilly, Co. Cork).

of the Penal Laws, perhaps, even, with some accumulation of capital by Catholics, the struggle between pasture and arable became less unequal. The extension of the potato, too, which in the mid-century had freed land for the then more attractive pasture farming, contributed after 1780, with the balance inclining towards tillage, to make room for corn or flax: as potato culture was pushed up the mountain-side, corn could succeed it in the more fertile areas.

Third, a movement towards smaller holdings, partly itself the result of the spread of tillage, though springing from other sources as well, contributed to make arable farming more attractive: if holdings were reduced in size to enable the landlord to have more voters on his estate, or to let him or the middleman enjoy a swollen rent-roll, the tenant had to till—and to till every inch—if he was to provide for his family. Fourth, and of greatest importance, the emphasis shifted from pasture to arable as a response by the farming community to a change in the relative productivity, measured in monetary terms, of stock and spade. It was, perhaps, rarely that any consideration of maximizing his personal fortune induced the peasant to rearrange his system of farming: whether his land was tilled or put to grass the structure of rural society was such that he and his family normally enjoyed only the most slender surplus above their requirements for subsistence.[1] It was not, then, the acquisitiveness of farmers that put land under the plough, but their response to the rising rents they were obliged to pay if they were not to be ejected from their land. If to acquisitiveness is to be attributed a share in the reshaping of agriculture, it is with the acquisitiveness of the landlords and middlemen who incessantly took higher rents that we must reckon. And a matter to be decided before heaping blame on them is whether the more remote source of rising rents was the landlord's acquisitiveness or the eagerness of his tenant, in a country where land was scarce, to outbid his fellows in the ransom he offered for the chance of securing a livelihood. As rents rose, so, within the limitations of his skill and labour- and capital-supply, the peasant had to maximize his marketable surplus: that, towards the end of the eighteenth century he should have found arable relatively more productive than formerly was the result of a variety of forces.

Partly, perhaps, there is here a further example of the impact of

[1] See above, Chapter III, pp. 82–3.

the growth of population upon agricultural developments. One of the determinants of the relative productivity of the different branches of agriculture is the relative proportions in which the various factors of production are available. Labour in Ireland by the end of the century was becoming increasingly abundant, land increasingly scarce; there was a continuous shortage of capital: it is no wonder that intensive, small-scale, arable farming became more prominent and large-scale pasture farming less so. But there were other, and less directly economic, reasons why Irish farming, under the inescapable obligation of increasing its money-yield, should have put greater emphasis upon tillage. Informed Irish opinion—mercantilist opinion—had been distressed since the seventeenth century at the extent to which the country was dependent on imports for her grain supplies. Writer after writer had urged the Government to follow Britain's example and encourage by bounties and duties the domestic cultivation of corn. Many Acts were passed with this as their professed objective,[1] but, either because the Government was less concerned than its critics at the decline in arable, or because it realized more forcefully than they that the remedy they pressed would seem to Britain an intolerable departure from the principles of colonial policy, there was no Act of any effect until 1757: then there was passed the first of the series of Acts subsidizing the transport of home-produced corn to Dublin and certain other Irish towns. Pressing hard on the constitutional changes which made the Government of Ireland more nearly master in its own house there came further solid encouragement to corn production: in 1784 Foster's Corn Law penalized the import of grain into Ireland, and subsidized its export. By then, too, the requirements of Britain from her Irish colony were beginning to change. When Britain had an export surplus of grain, Irish grain producers were treated as the nuisance they were, but as the mother country found, with increasing frequency, that her own harvests were inadequate to supply her people with bread there was some willingness to add corn to the list of primary products which it was proper for a colony to export. There was a special propriety in Ireland's sending grain to Britain. Coming so short a distance, supplies were unlikely to be interrupted even in time of stress and payment for them was made within the kingdom in remittances, of which many could hardly fail to find their way

[1] See below, Appendix V, pp. 272–3.

back to the mother country. Nonetheless, even by the time of the Union, English governmental opinion was still unreconciled to the idea of giving Irish corn-factors unrestricted access to the British market. Reflecting, presumably, the double concern of a war-time Parliament and a landlord's parliament for the farmer, the corn trade was made the one exception to the provision of the Act of Union, which arranged for the Irish fiscal system to be assimilated within the British.[1] A change in British opinion came when the experience of the next six years had shown that the native farmer alone, however actively patronized by the State, was unlikely to satisfy the nation's requirements of grain: these same six years gave fresh emphasis to the social and political undesirability of high food-prices in war time. From 1806, accordingly, Irish grain was freely admitted to the British ports. For a time, until an undoubtedly profit-determining rent swallowed his surplus, the Irish farmer was able to benefit from inflated British corn prices. Within half a dozen years, however, his contribution, on top of the increased domestic yield, brought prices down, even before the war demand had dried up. After the war the Irish supplies, increasing in spite of, or because of, the price-depression, continued: doubtless they allowed the British farmer to point to the competition of a potato-eating nation as a cause of his distress.

Three threads, in particular, in the closely woven causation of the swing towards arable merit a more detailed examination: first, the bounties on the transport of corn within Ireland, second, the export bounties and import duties, and, third, movements in grain prices. The bounties on the inland and coastal transport of corn to Dublin, paid over a period of forty years, were granted by a series of Acts of the Irish Parliament passed between 1757 and 1780. The original Act was introduced following the recommendations made in 1757 by committees of the House of Lords on the state of tillage in Ireland.[2] The committees collected statistics showing that in the five years before their inquiries, roughly two-fifths of the wheat consumed in Dublin were grown in Ireland, and three-fifths were imported. Most of the native wheat sold in Dublin came from the counties of Meath, Carlow, Kildare, Dublin, and King's;

---

[1] *Report of the Committee on the Corn Trade between Great Britain and Ireland. Reports of the Committees of the House of Commons*, ix, (1774–1802), 1803, p. 163.

[2] *Report from the Lords Committees appointed to enquire into the State of Tillage in this Kingdom . . .* , Dublin, 1757.

occasionally, Queen's, Wicklow, and Westmeath sent supplies. The committees inquired into the state of tillage in Clare, Galway, Limerick, Tipperary, and Roscommon,

and they find that those Counties have been, during a long Space of Time, and still continue mostly under Stock, although they contain great Tracts of exceeding good Land very proper for raising Corn of all Kinds, and particularly Wheat: That the Land in those Counties, being fresh, would produce much greater Crops than land, of equal goodness, nearer to *Dublin*, which has been worn by constant Tillage. That in many Parts the Land is become unwholesome for Sheep, from the length of Time it has been under Grazing, which would be a great inducement to those Counties to turn themselves to Tillage if they had any Vent for their Grain, but at present they raise little, if any, more than is necessary for their own Consumption. That the great Expence attending Land-Carriage, and the want of Granaries in *Dublin* for lodging their Corn, in case they should fail of an immediate Market, are the principal Causes which deter them from going largely into Tillage.

From all which it appears to your Committee, that if a Bounty was given, so as to ease the Price of Carriage from those distant Counties, it would probably induce them to go largely into Tillage: And that if publick Granaries were erected, in or near this City, for the Reception of Wheat, it would greatly encourage the Farmers, in those Counties, to raise Wheat for the *Dublin* Market, as they would not then be under the necessity of selling their Grain when the Market was glutted with that Commodity; and if a publick Officer was appointed, who should be directed to give a Receipt for each Parcel of Wheat lodged in those Granaries, a Paper-Credit would thereby be erected, which would be of singular Advantage to the Farmers in the carrying on of their Business.[1]

The Irish House of Lords resolved in 1757 'that the granting of a bounty on the carriage of wheat from remote counties would be a means of improving tillage and of better supplying the city with wheat of our own growth, and that the erection of public granaries will probably encourage the extension of tillage'. The first of the Acts offering bounties on the carriage of grain to Dublin was passed in 1757, the year of the Lords' resolution; others followed in 1767, 1777–8, and in 1779–80.[2] According to their preambles they were designed to achieve diverse benefits for the Irish people:

[1] Ibid., pp. 10–11.
[2] See Appendix IV, pp. 270–1, for details of this legislation.

navigation was to be encouraged, and the corn trade better regulated; the capital was to be safeguarded from a recurrence of distress caused by scarcity of corn and flour, and (of greatest importance to us) tillage was to be encouraged. To what extent did the laws achieve this last objective? An answer could be given readily, and the wisdom with which mercantilist law-makers chose means to achieve their ends demonstrated, if the returns of the quantities of produce on which the bounties were paid could be accepted as final evidence. These returns show that in the sixties an annual flow of under 200,000 hundredweights of grain and flour was subsidized: by the nineties, in every year for which the bounties continued (with one exception) more than a million hundredweights were subsidized. The cost to the Exchequer rose from £15,000 a year in the sixties to nearly £100,000 a year in the nineties.[1]

The danger of accepting the evidence of these figures as proof of the impetus the bounties gave to the extension of arable, is clear: there were, at the time, other inducements than the bounties on the carriage of grain to Dublin tempting farmers to put more land under spade or plough. How much of the general response can be attributed to the transport bounties it is impossible to say. There is, however, virtual unanimity amongst contemporary critics and supporters of the measures that their effect was substantial. Young, who made the most authoritative condemnation of the Acts, was opposed to them largely because of their success in leading to the ploughing of excellent pasture: the Acts, he argued, held a double bait before the farmer by offering, not only to relieve him of the entire cost of sending his produce to market if only he would grow corn, but also to give him an additional payment, equivalent to one-fifth of his transport charges, if he could get the corn ground locally.[2] Newenham, who gave his qualified support to the Acts, agreed with Young that they were the cause of the erection of many mills, some of them, perhaps, amongst the finest in the world. 'Several country gentlemen embarked very considerable capitals in the flour business; and a vast many others were allured into the pursuit of tillage by the ready markets which these different mills afforded for its produce. . . . The increase in the produce of corn, occasioned by this act, appears to have

[1] *J.H.C.I.* vi–xviii.
[2] A. Young, 1780, op. cit., 2nd ed., ii. 244.

induced foreign agents to come to Ireland for the purpose of procuring a supply.'[1] In Co. Cork, the transformation of the Barony
of Fermoy from open grazing country to thickly populated tillage
was dated from the building of the Rock Mills on the Funcheon
around 1775: the 'encouragement to the undertaking . . . was the
bounty on land carriage of flour to Dublin, which, during the
continuance of that bounty, received almost the entire produce of
those mills'.[2] Similarly, in Co. Clare, the bounty 'caused the erection of a great number of extensive flour-mills, and of course promoted the cultivation of corn in districts, where, from want of this
encouragement scarcely more was produced than supplied the
home consumption'.[3]

The dissentient voice from this testimony arguing effectiveness
of the bounty legislation was that of the anonymous author of *A
Dissertation on the Present Bounty Laws* published in 1780.[4] He
granted that the Acts were responsible for the erection of mills
throughout the country: 'the only consideration was, to get as far
distant as possible from the market they intended to supply' in
order that they should profit to the full from the excess of the
flour bounty over the cost of transport. The consequences were
that local grain was eagerly bought up and made into flour for
Dublin at the cost of depriving local people of their supplies unless
they were willing to pay prices higher than those of the Dublin
markets, and that grain which formerly was imported to feed
Dublin now had to be brought to feed the provinces. 'This bounty
has had little effect in increasing the general agriculture of the
kingdom, (in proportion to the greatness of the expense), only
destroying it in some places, and encouraging it in others.'[5]

The real contemporary controversy on the bounties centred,
not on whether they led to the extension of tillage, but on whether
the cost at which they achieved this end was disproportionately
great. A glaring anomaly in the Acts—but one that was made less

[1] T. Newenham, 1809, op. cit., pp. 136-7.
[2] Townsend, 1810, op. cit., p. 451.
[3] H. Dutton, 1808, op. cit., p. 70.
[4] The copy of the *Dissertation* in Lord Sheffield's collection, now in the Gold-
smiths' Company's Library of Economic Literature, is attributed in manuscript
on the title-page to 'D. Jebb, Esq., of Slane'. Newenham (1809, op. cit., p. 136)
says that among the excellent mills, the construction of which was occasioned by
the 1757 Act, was that of Mr. Jebb, at Slane.
[5] Dublin, p. 8.

severe by the legislation of 1778—was that originally they offered payments only on corn brought by road to the capital.[1] Young was indignant at 'the absurdity and folly with which such an idea is pregnant in a country blessed with such ports, and such a vast extent of coast. . . . Why not carry the corn in ships, as well as tear up all roads leading to Dublin by cars? Why not increase your sailors instead of horses? Are they not as profitable an animal? . . . The vast difference between the expense of land and water carriage should ever induce the legislature, though sailors were not in question, to encourage the latter rather than the former. From Cork there is paid bounty, $5/6\frac{1}{2}d$ yet the freight at 10/- a ton is only $6d$.'[2] Newenham plausibly explained, in terms of Ireland's colonial status, why her Parliament adopted so uneconomic a method of extending tillage and safeguarding Dublin's food-supply. English experience had made it plain to her that a sure way of encouraging agriculture and preventing scarcity would be by granting subsidies on the export of grain and imposing duties on its import. Such a policy, however, would have excluded British corn from the Irish market and would have reared up a competitor to the English farmer in foreign markets. At a time 'when the corn trade of England was at its height, and promised to become a most important branch of commerce'—a time when England supplied eight-ninths of Irish imports—it was quite out of the question for Ireland to experiment with such a policy. She had to be content with less satisfactory means of achieving her ends. Even bounties on coastal transport to Dublin were inadmissible: their effect would have been to encourage tillage all along the coast, with the result that English grain would have been excluded from the maritime towns, from, in effect, the whole of Ireland. Bounties on land-carriage alone were left, bounties that 'would seem to the last degree perverse and ridiculous, if the expedient were considered apart from the over-ruling policy of Britain; but considered in conjunction therewith, it appears to have been necessary'. Not until fifteen years after Britain had become a corn-importing country, when her rulers had had to

[1] It would seem from the wording of the preamble of 17 & 18 Geo. III, c. 29, that it was the practice, when grain or flour was brought partly by road and partly by inland navigation, for the bounty to be claimed in respect of the whole journey: the Act sanctioned the payment of only two-thirds of the full rate for produce coming by canal.

[2] Young, 1780, op. cit. ii. 268–70.

give up hope of a return of the profits of the export trade, was Ireland able to grant export bounties which gave a major impetus to her own tillage: not until three years afterwards, in 1767, was she able to give 'a trifling bounty, evidently the offspring of caution' on grain brought coastways to Dublin.[1]

Young was also the most forceful exponent of the second of the leading criticisms of the bounties: this was that the tillage they encouraged was bad tillage, and that it took the place of excellent pasture.

What is the tillage gained by this measure? It is that system which formed the agriculture of England two hundred years ago, and forms it yet in the worst of our common fields, but which all our exertions of enclosing and improving are bent to extirpate. 1. Fallow. 2. Wheat; and then spring corn until the soil is exhausted: or else 1. Fallow. 2. Wheat. 3. Spring corn; and then fallow again. . . . Let it not be imagined, that waste and desart tracts, that wanted cultivation, are only turned to this tillage. Nine-tenths of the change is in the rich sheep walks of Roscommon, Tipperary, Carlow and Kilkenny . . . the question therefore is reduced to this: ought you to turn some of the finest pastures in the world . . . into the most execrable tillage that is to be found on the face of the globe?[2]

There were few to disagree with Young that the new tillage was bad: the returns of the bounty bear him out that the greater part went to the grazing counties.[3] The dispute is over his claim that pasture farming receded as arable advanced. As far as the first point is concerned—the poorness of the new tillage—an attempt was made to remedy matters in the legislation of 1780, providing that no bounty was to be paid except on produce that sold for at least a certain minimum price, but before and afterwards there were general complaints of backward methods. There were in Co. Kilkenny, according to the *Dissertation on the Present Bounty Laws*

a multitude of little mills, which are carried on by persons of small capitals, who grind for the profit of the bounty alone; and as they receive the same premium for flour of the very worst quality, (which often does not sell for the amount of the bounty) as for the best, they make little or no distinction in the quality of the grain; the consequence is, that as

[1] T. Newenham, 1809, op. cit., pp. 132–6.

[2] Young, op. cit. ii. 275.

[3] Though it was these counties also that had largely supplied the Dublin market before the bounties. See *Report from Lords Committees appointed to enquire into the State of Tillage in this Kingdom . . .*, Dublin, 1757, p. 10.

the farmer can get as ready a sale for dirty, blighty corn, as for that which is clean and well coloured, he takes little pains in the culture. The best of our farmers are but slovenly, but the county of Kilkenny farmer exceeds all description; whereas before this bounty took place they were reckoned the best in the kingdom. There was flour sold in Dublin last year for two shillings and six-pence per hundred, which is the price of bran; and yet a premium was paid to bring this stuff to Dublin, of four shillings and six-pence per hundred.[1]

Newenham also agreed that the transport bounties tended to lower the quality of Irish grain: 'the quality of the grain and flour appears to have been overlooked, as no sworn officer was appointed to inspect it. And to that circumstance the actual general inferiority of Irish to English wheat is to be traced and ascribed.'[2]

We can, it seems, agree with Young that the tendency of the bounty Acts was to worsen the quality of corn produced, and that the impetus the Acts gave to tillage was concentrated in the grazing counties, but it is open to doubt that they diminished the country's yield of pastoral products. There would seem to be little statistical material bearing on the point besides the trade figures, the accuracy of which is open to question, though doubtless they give a fair indication of trends. They show that continuously from the inception of the Acts, the volume of pastoral products exported increased —and with the rapid rise in population that began within a couple of decades of the inception of the bounties it is probable that production rose still more to cater for greater domestic consumption.[3] Table 18, below, shows decennial averages of exports of pastoral products from the fifties onwards. Between the fifties (or sixties, according to the availability of figures) and the nineties, when the transport bounties ceased to be paid, the only item to show any diminution was barrelled beef, the export of which fell by 23 per cent., a deficiency, which, presumably, is to be explained

---

[1] Dublin, 1780, pp. 13–15.

[2] T. Newenham, op. cit., 1809, p. 137.

[3] It is possible, but improbable for two reasons, that the rising population consumed less pastoral produce: first, the changeover from milk and dairy produce to potatoes as the principal constituent of the Irishman's diet seems to have been carried about as far as ever it was by the 1780s (see below, Chap. V) and, second, low though the standard of living was from 1780 to the end of the French wars, there may well have been some modest amelioration in conditions during these years, and improvement would hardly have been accompanied by a more vigorous elimination of animal products from the general diet (see above, pp. 87–9).

by the rise of over 18,000 in the number of bullocks and cows exported on foot: bacon and pork exports swelled—from modest figures, it is true—the one to nearly nine times their former quantity, the other to four times; butter exports increased by 50 per cent. from a quite respectable level.

TABLE 18

Decennial Averages of Exports, 1753–1819*

	Flitches of bacon (000s)	Barrels of beef (000s)	Bullocks and cows	Butter (cwt. 000s)	Barrels of pork (000s)
1753–9 . .	. .	162	. .	203	31
1764–9 . .	8	199	1,171	286	41
1770–9 . .	17	190	3,086	262	58
1780–9 . .	19	157	10,647	276	89
1790–9 . .	70	124	19,782	300	125
1800–9 . .	158	100	21,529	311	108
1810–19 . .	386	113	44,841	419	138

* *Journals of the House of Commons of Ireland*, vi, App., p. cclxxxix; Ireland: Exports and Imports, 1764–1773, manuscript in British Library of Political and Economic Science; *Journals of the House of Commons of Ireland*, vii, App., p. xciv; *Reports of Commissioners*, 1823, xvi. 519 ff.

While, then, we can grant Young that the new tillage (like, indeed, nearly all Irish tillage) was poor, that it was concentrated not in the remote counties but in the more central pastoral areas, his case is far from proven that good grass was ploughed up to make bad tillage. The buoyancy of the exports of the pastoralists, in the absence of evidence of substantial improvements in their methods, goes to show that much land formerly waste, or grazing of very low productivity was ploughed under the stimulus of the bounties.

Secondly, we must examine the effect on the balance between tillage and pasture of the bounties offered for corn exports, and the duties levied on imports. The salient act is Foster's Corn Law of 1784—'An Act for regulating the corn trade, promoting agriculture and providing a regular and standing supply of corn.' According to Lecky, the Act was 'one of the capital facts in Irish history'. 'In a few years', he says, 'it changed the face of the land, and made Ireland to a great extent an arable instead of a pasture country.'[1]

[1] W. E. H. Lecky, 1892, op. cit. ii. 387.

It is distinguished neither in nominal intention, nor in mechanism from a series of Acts dating from the first decade of the century. Newenham made a thorough examination of these earlier Acts which purported to encourage tillage: all of them he was able to classify under the heading 'Irish Acts of an illusive and inefficacious Nature, professing to aim at the Attainment of public Benefits'.[1] The celebrity of Foster's Act follows either a change of heart in the legislators of Ireland—for the first time they wished to do more than appear to accept the advice of the advocates of tillage—or of a recently achieved freedom, the result of a shift in the requirements of the British connexion, to give real encouragement to Irish corn-growing.

To enable us to determine the probable effect of the Act we must look at its content in some detail. It provided, first, for export bounties of 3s. 4d. a barrel when the price of wheat was not above 27s. a barrel, of 1s. 7d. when barley was not above 13s. 6d., and of 1s. 5d. when oats were not above 10s.;[2] second, that there should be no export of any grain, or of flour, meal or malt made from it, when the price at the port of export or in Dublin, exceeded, if wheat, 30s. a barrel, if barley, 14s. 6d. a barrel, or, if oats, 11s. a barrel; third, that a duty of 10s. a barrel should be levied on imported wheat and barley when the respective prices in Dublin were below 30s. and 14s. 6d. a barrel, and a duty of 5s. a barrel on imported oats when oats were less than 11s. a barrel; fourth, that when Dublin's grain prices exceeded the levels at which these heavy duties were imposed, imports were to pay only the nominal duty of 2d. a barrel; fifth, that, in the endeavour 'to preserve that harmony and amicable intercourse which are essentially necessary to be maintained between the two kingdoms of Great Britain and Ireland', in the price ranges where foreign grain would have to pay the substantial duties British grain would be charged the nominal duties, providing Irish grain was given comparable privileges in the British market; finally—underlining the fact that the dominance of the potato over the diet of the Irish was less complete in Ulster than elsewhere—that whenever the export of oats or oatmeal was prohibited by the Act in any part of

---

[1] T. Newenham, 1809, op. cit., p. 122. Details of this legislation are given in Appendix V, pp. 272-3.

[2] Bounties were also payable on rye and on meal, malt, flour made from wheat, barley or oats; import duties were also levied on these products.

Ulster, Irish oats or oatmeal brought to that province should qualify for a bounty at the rate of 6*d*. per hundredweight if it came from Leinster or Connaught (except from Dublin), or at the rate of 10*d*. per hundredweight if it came from Munster.

This Act, unlike its predecessors, made no pretence of encouraging tillage by offering export bounties payable at a price-level never reached in the market. Table 19, below, shows that in the ten years after the passing of the Act on only two occasions did the

TABLE 19

Annual Average Prices of Wheat, Barley, and Oats per Irish Barrel in Ireland, 1784–93*

	Wheat and flour		Barley and malt		Oats and oatmeal	
	s.	*d.*	*s.*	*d.*	*s.*	*d.*
1784† . .	28	4	14	9	10	3
1785 . .	23	5	11	11	8	9
1786 . .	23	9	10	3	8	10
1787 . .	22	10	10	6	9	4
1788 . .	22	2	11	6	8	9
1789 . .	26	6	12	1	7	9
1790 . .	27	2	12	10‡	9	9
1791 . .	25	5	13	5§	10	2
1792 . .	22	2	15	4‖	9	4
1793 . .	25	5	14	9	10	4

* *Reports from Committees of the House of Commons*, ix, (1774–1802), 1803, p. 169: the figures given in the above table are the annual averages of the quarterly figures given here.

† August and November quarters only.
‡ February, May, and November quarters only.
§ May and November quarters only.
‖ May, August, and November quarters only.

annual wheat price not entitle farmers to the export bounty: the first was immediately after the Act became operative: the second was six years later when the annual average price was twopence above the level at which the bounty was payable. The export bounty amounted to 13 per cent. of the ten-yearly average price of 24*s*. 9*d*. With barley and oats average prices were above the qualifying limit for the subsidies immediately after the passing of the Act, and for only two years in the following nine: the barley subsidy amounted to 12 per cent., and the oats subsidy to 15 per cent. of the ten-yearly average price. Seldom was the bounty unrealizable because prices were above the limits within which exports were permitted and the bounty could be claimed: average prices of wheat and oats in the first ten years after the passing of the Act never exceeded this level, and barley prices did so on only three occasions. These same limits at which exports were forbidden were also the limits at which imported corn had to pay substantial duties—amounting, on wheat, to 40 per cent. of the ten-yearly average price, on barley to 78 per cent., and on oats to 54 per cent.: seldom, then, had Irish farmers to meet foreign competition with anything approaching its full force.

The provision of the Act, that, subject to the granting of reciprocal privileges, British corn imported to Ireland should pay only a nominal duty when foreign corn paid at high rates, can have had little adverse effect on the Irish farmer. Britain was in no position in these years to send considerable quantities of corn to Ireland: her own corn prices were not such as to allow her farmers to claim, with any frequency, the export bounties offered by her own laws, nor, indeed, in most years were they allowed to export corn at all. By an Act of 1791, when the price of wheat in England was below 44s. per quarter, a bounty of 5s. per quarter was payable on wheat sent to Ireland (and elsewhere). Between 1791 and 1806 only in the single year 1792 was the average price of wheat in England such as to permit export (and in that year it was sufficiently low for the export bounty to be claimed).[1]

Even more than in the case of the bounties on the carriage of corn to Dublin is it tempting to attribute much of the extension of arable to Foster's Corn Law. How legitimate it would be to do so it is impossible to say: there is no doubt at all that the bounties added solidly to the profits of the plough; that they did so to a greater extent than the carriage bounties would be easily defended, but to assess their relative importance compared with other factors affecting corn prices—the pressure of population, the desire to subdivide, and so forth—needs finer evidence than is available.

The third strand that we have to unravel in this discussion of the reasons for the extension of arable farming is the inducement that the persistently rising price of corn held before the peasantry to extend its area of tillage. Less intricate discussion is necessary to show its influence than in the case of either type of bounty

[1] *Report from the Committee appointed to consider the Corn Trade between Great Britain and Ireland*, 1802, *Reports from Committees of the House of Commons*, ix, (1774–1802), 1803, p. 168; and *Reports from Commissioners*, xxii. 9.

legislation. The peasants, compelled to find almost impossible rent-payments, strove to earn them by marketing more corn when the cessation of imports and the expansion of exports drove up its price. Table 20 shows that between 1791–5 and 1811–15 oat prices in Dublin rose by 59 per cent. and wheat prices by 61 per cent.

TABLE 20

*Price of Oats and Wheat per Irish Barrel in Dublin,
1786–90 to 1830–40**

| | Price per Irish barrel | |
	Oats	Wheat
	s. d.	s. d.
1786–90 . .	8 11	24 6
1791–5 . .	11 7	28 8
1796–1800. .	12 5	38 5
1801–5 . .	18 5	43 9
1806–10 . .	17 2	45 7
1811–15 . .	18 5	46 2
1816–20 . .	15 0	41 0
1830–40 . .	12 4	30 1½

* The prices for 1791–5—1816–20 are taken from *Estimates, Accounts and miscellaneous Papers relating to Ireland*, 1821, xx. 102–3, and those for 1830–40 from *Accounts and Papers*, 1840, xliv. 57. The prices for 1786–90 come from the *Report from the Committee appointed to consider the Corn Trade between Great Britain and Ireland*, 1802, *Reports from Committees of the House of Commons*, ix, (1774–1802), 1803, p. 169: they relate to the whole of Ireland and are not, therefore, strictly comparable with the other prices in the table which are for the Dublin market. Average oat prices for the whole of Ireland for 1791–5 and 1796–1800 are 10s. 4d. and 12s. 2d., as compared with the Dublin prices given in the table of 11s. 7d. and 12s. 5d. For wheat the Irish prices for the same periods are 27s. 6d. and 36s. 3d. as compared with 28s. 8d. and 38s. 5d. in Dublin.

None of the three developments which we have examined for their tendency to increase the attractiveness of arable as compared with pasture, survived the French wars: the bounties on the carriage of grain to Dublin were withdrawn in 1798; import duties and export bounties, in so far as trade within the British Isles was concerned, ceased in 1806; wheat prices, which in the five years ending in 1813 averaged 51s. 11d., were down to 40s. 3d. in the next five years, and they continued to fall.[1] To what extent was the ending of the wars followed by a swing back to pasture, with de-populating effect? 'Since the depression of the prices of agricultural produce', the Select Committee on the Employment of

[1] *Reports of Commissioners*, 1821, xx. 102–3.

the Poor reported in 1823, 'the necessity of consolidating many small, into one greater farm, seems to have been generally admitted and acted upon; and much of arable has been laid down for the purpose of rearing and fattening cattle, as well as for dairy'.[1] Some increase in the relative attractiveness of pasture there undoubtedly was, but not for another thirty years, not until the Famine demonstrated the perilous futility of the extreme parcellation of the land was there any general and long-lived return to pasture.

Much the most detailed analysis of the situation in the years between war and Famine is to be found in the report of the Poor Inquiry Commission. The Commissioners made, up and down the country, baronial examinations of local residents of the most diverse occupations—magistrates, labourers, landlords, agents, farmers, shopkeepers, and so forth—putting to them, in a vast field of inquiry, questions on the comparative advantages of grazing and tillage. The answers give us, for one or more baronies of twenty-one of the thirty-two counties in the kingdom, information on the balance between pasture and arable. For Leinster alone is there any considerable evidence of the continuation of the trend pointed out by the 1823 Committee towards the extension of grassland. In the barony of Balrothery, Co. Dublin, 'the comparatively high and the steadier prices of stock and meat have caused much tillage land to be converted to grass':[2] in Upper and Lower Philipstown, King's County, 'a great deal of land formerly in tillage has, of late years, been converted into grass land, and the effect has been to throw many labourers out of employment':[3] in Moyfenragh, Co. Meath, 'much tillage land has, of late years, been converted to grass, and the effect has been the throwing nine-tenths of the labourers upon such land out of employment'.[4] But even in Leinster though there were some fears for the future, the movement was far from universal. In Gowran, Kilkenny, 'the conversion of tillage land to grass has not yet proceeded to a sufficient extent . . . to produce any very serious effects upon the labouring classes; but as it is now rapidly increasing, in consequence of the low prices of corn, it is feared that it very soon will'.[5] At Clonlisk, King's County, 'very little land has been turned from

---

[1] *Reports from Committees*, 1823, vi. 337.

[2] *Report of Poor Law Inquiry Commission*, Appendix F, *Reports of Commissioners*, 1836, xxxiii. 230.

[3] Ibid., p. 247.   [4] Ibid., p. 259.   [5] Ibid., p. 224.

tillage to grass; the contrary has been the case within the last 20 years'.[1] In Upper Talbotstown, Wicklow, and in Portnahinch, Queen's County, some, but very little, conversion to pasture was recorded.[2]

The rest of the country was, apparently, almost immune from the movement: in many counties, indeed, tillage continued to show much of its war-time vitality. The Munster answers reported that, in the barony of Traghenackmy in Kerry 'land formerly grazing, has been converted into tillage . . ., and it must have given a regular increase in employment in the district';[3] in Lower Conello, Limerick, 'no land has been converted here of late years from tillage to grass, but . . . the reverse process has taken place';[4] the same trend was evident in Clare and Waterford.[5] From one barony of Limerick alone was there any mention of even the beginning of a movement towards pasture.[4] All the reports from Connaught were either of equilibrium between grass and tillage or of the extension of tillage: in Kilconnel, Co. Galway, it is true, farmers tended to decrease tillage, but 'the increase of population requiring a larger quantity of corn acre for the supply of potatoes, operates in some degree to counteract this: no great change can therefore be said to have taken place';[6] in Carberry, Co. Sligo, there was no conversion of tillage to grazing; in Dromahair, Co. Leitrim, there was more land in tillage than formerly.[7] Some of the reports from Ulster said that all, or practically all, of the land remained divided into tillage farms, others that tillage at least held its own; one from Co. Cavan, said that there pasture was being ploughed.[8] McCulloch, writing a few years after the Poor Inquiry, confirms the accuracy of its evidence that twenty and more years after the peace tillage was still the more actively expanding section of Irish agriculture. In none of his county surveys of Irish agriculture—not even in Leinster—does he refer to an extension of pasture, but frequently—in Kildare, Meath, Kerry, Limerick, Waterford, Galway, and Roscommon—he notices an extension of arable.[9]

The persistence with which the farmers of Ireland, at least until

[1] Ibid., p. 244.
[2] Ibid., pp. 267 and 271.   [3] Ibid., p. 283.   [4] Ibid., p. 288.
[5] Ibid., pp. 274, 300, and 305.   [6] Ibid., p. 208.
[7] Ibid., pp. 214, 224.
[8] Ibid., pp. 311, 312, 315, 318, 321, 323, and 325.
[9] McCulloch, op. cit. ii. 369–95.

the decade before the Famine, maintained under indifferent tillage, land which both fifty years earlier and fifty years later was largely good pasture needs an explanation—the more so because the artificial advantage accruing from state subsidies and a war-time price-structure had ceased to have effect for twenty or more years: whatever the explanation, it must be one flexible enough to account for the fuller response in parts of Leinster to the new marketing conditions.

It is by no means certain that the swing back to pasture in the immediate post-war years was either as widespread, or as swift as the report of the 1823 Committee suggests:[1] the elusiveness of other evidence of the extent and location of any such movement leaves its dimensions in some doubt. That, however, as a war-time expedient, some grass was ploughed which its owners were afterwards anxious to return to pasture is not surprising. The price-fall and loss of subsidies gave an added motive while the falling-in of many of the thirty-year leases granted after the relaxation of the penal laws in 1778, coupled with the simplification of the process of eviction in 1816, gave many a landlord the opportunity to have his estate used as he pleased. But it is tempting and wrong to single out corn prices when examining the impact on agriculture of marketing conditions: during the wars, graziers and dairy farmers—though admittedly to a less extent than corn growers—enjoyed inflated prices, and afterwards the prices of cattle and provisions fell in the general slump. Wakefield, writing during the war of the grazing country of Munster, realized that its well-being was precariously based.

The buyers of beef [he said] are few in proportion to the producers. The sub-contractors all act under one head, namely, the London firm, which has entered into an engagement for the season with the victualling board in that capital. This contract, indeed, depends on the continuance of war; but while it lasts, the holders of rich pasture lands all make fortunes. Should a peace take place their situation would be reversed, unless the inhabitants should create a demand by their own consumption.[2]

The post-war fall in the profits of grazing doubtless contributed to keep as tillage some of the land recently put under spade or plough. But there were other forces, and forces less readily burked,

---

[1] See above, pp. 113–14.
[2] E. Wakefield, 1812, op. cit., i. 319.

that determined there could be no general swing to pasture in the decades between war and Famine. Whatever the role of population-increase in the seventies and eighties—whether it was then cause or effect of the extension of arable—after the wars, rising population, linked with other, and peculiar, features of the Irish social scene, was an imperative cause of the continuance, often of the further extension, of tillage. By the time the wars ended, Ireland had had thirty or forty years' experience of a rural economy in which early marriage, endowed normally by the division of a farmer's holding among his children, was a crucial feature. It was an evil, self-destroying economy: once entrapped in it the Irish people were driven to go with it until the catastrophe it bred within itself was alone able to promise them a more secure life. Their holdings had become fragments: to wring a living from them they had to till almost every inch: if the landlord or his agent felt that there would be more profit or pleasure in pasture he had to be bribed to change his mind by the offer of more rent. The double pressure of rent and of the large families that followed early marriage drove the communities up the mountains and into the bogs: yet however barren their land, till it they must, because labour was abundantly available, and, given unlimited labour, there is little land that is more productive under grass.

Simple pressure of population is not enough to account for the retention of tillage: its full effect was felt only in conjunction with other features of the Irish social scene. The contrast with contemporary English experience is instructive: the population of England was rising (though probably less steeply than that of Ireland), yet post-war marketing conditions, largely identical with those facing Ireland, resulted in half a dozen years in the withdrawal of the plough from many of the additional acres to which war-time conditions had attracted it. The cause of the contrast, it would seem, lies largely in differences between the systems of landholding in the two countries, and in the existence in England and absence from Ireland, of a system of poor-relief. The immediate directors of the soil in the southern and midland counties of England—the regions that bore the brunt of the re-orientation that followed the wars—were not, as in Ireland, small peasants and cottars: in these areas the peasant-class, already hard pressed, scarcely survived the price depression. Those who determined whether land should be pasture or arable were the landlords and the substantial tenant farmers: if, to economize in labour, or to return land to the sub-marginal role that was its peace-time due, they decided upon a wholesale reduction of tillage, there was no class of petty occupiers to plead with them, or bribe them with uneconomic rents, to leave them to manage their land in the only way they could scrape a living from it. A dependent population there was in England, but to put tillage to grass did not obviously worsen its plight: it was dependent, not on land, often not on a wage, but on a dole, and the dole seemed neither more precarious nor more secure as the arable shrank within its pre-war boundaries. It is true that whatever the mechanism of support—whether through a system of small holdings or a system of doles and wages —southern and midland England, like Ireland, had a growing population to maintain, and its requirements were doubtless one of the factors limiting the extent to which pasture might be restored. But the limits were not restrictive; not only was the pressure of population less than in Ireland, but, in all probability, children could, to a greater extent settle beyond their immediate environment both in the towns of England and overseas. Some further latitude was given to those who determined whether the fields of England should be ploughed or not by the system of maintaining the mass of the population to a large extent through the rates: the overall obligation to produce at least an approach to the population's subsistence remained, but many a locality must have escaped through paying its taxes from substantial surpluses amassed in the war years.

That the growth of population was an influential cause of the retention of arable in Ireland after the wars was frequently stressed in the replies to the Poor Inquiry Commission's questions on the balance between pasture and tillage. In Galway, though 'tillage is not considered remunerating from the great decline of prices the demand of an increasing population for more arable counteracted any tendency towards an extension of pasture'; in Co. Down, the density of population and the comparative smallness of holdings meant that 'every possible spot of land is laboured'; in Clare, 'land formerly in pasture has in late years been converted to tillage because of the demand of the people for potatoes'; in Cavan, pasture was being tilled, as the increase of population led to subdivision. Even in Leinster, where the pace of population growth was more restrained, the process was known: in the barony of

Dromahair, in Leitrim, 'more land is in tillage than formerly owing to the increase of population'.[1]

The rapid growth of a population dependent on the utmost parcellation of the land was the over-riding reason why Ireland maintained her war-time arable, and even extended it, in thirty years of peace. Of an altogether smaller order of importance was a number of other factors: from Waterford it was reported that the extreme poverty of the peasants, causing them to sell their stock, led to the ploughing of grass:[2] in 1823, with pasture once more levied for tithe, there was ended one of the most anomalous of the causes which a century earlier had made arable increasingly unattractive. Widespread reclamation, because of the excellence of potatoes and rape in breaking-in new land, contributed to increase the tilled area, quite apart from the pressure of population on new land equally with old.

Why did Leinster cling less tenaciously than much of the rest of Ireland to its war-time tillage? In the examinations they held in those parts of Leinster where the tendency was evident, it was usually explained to the Poor Inquiry Commissioners as a response to marketing conditions: in Balrothery, Co. Dublin, it was the 'comparatively high and steadier prices of stock and meat [which] have caused much tillage land to be converted to grass': the same cause was at work in Kilkenny, Louth, Wicklow, and Meath—and in the latter county it was evident that its effect was reinforced by proprietors taking land into their own hands and saving themselves trouble by laying it down as grass.[3] Doubtless, being near the greatest port of the country, near the greatest centre of urban consumption, and enjoying, in all probability, the easiest means of communication, the farmers of Leinster tended to be more responsive to the fluctuations of the market than those of the other provinces. Nonetheless, if the market alone held the balance between pasture and arable it is surprising that no evidence has come from the hinterland of the other ports of the country, and from many coastal areas, of the sensitivity of agriculture to price variations. Moreover, there was no part of Ireland where the farmer, however poor, did not send to market a surplus above the subsistence of his family, and where he did not struggle to maximize the money value of this surplus: indeed, the greater his

[1] *Reports of Commissioners*, 1836, xxxiii. 318, 208, 274, 313, 214.
[2] Ibid., p. 300.　　　　[3] Ibid., pp. 230, 240–71.

poverty the stronger the presumption that an undue share of the fruits of his labour was enjoyed by others than the members of his household. The price structure is only a partial reason for the extension of pasture in Leinster: the burden of the explanation lies in the isolation of Leinster from some of the worst excesses of the socio-economic system which, in the rest of Ireland, allowed a pathological rate of population-growth, and the tiniest fragmentation of the land, and which made tillage indispensable. It is no accident that Leinster, the only province which allowed some of its arable to revert to grass, was the province with the slowest rate of population-growth and the least subdivision.

V

THE INFLUENCE OF THE POTATO

IN the eighteenth and early nineteenth centuries it needed no
more than observation of the lives of the mass of their fellow
men for the economists to arrive at a theory of population-
growth which pointed to the availability of the means of subsistence as the determinant of the size of population. We could not
apply to Ireland, without Malthus's celebrated revision, the doctrine as it left Adam Smith's hands. 'Among the inferior ranks of
people', the *Wealth of Nations* tell us, 'the scantiness of subsistence . . . [sets] limits to the further multiplication of the human
species; and it can do so in no other way than by destroying a
great part of the children which their fruitful marriages produce.'[1]
With Malthus we must allow that the niggardliness of nature led
to some postponement of marriage, and thereby checked population by preventing the conception of children, as well as by causing
their early death. That the population of Ireland began to increase
so rapidly in the closing decades of the eighteenth century clearly
presupposed an accomplished, or continuing, increase in the
availability of foodstuffs. Partly, the means of subsistence were
made more plentiful by the reclamation of waste and by the
increasing emphasis placed upon tillage at the expense of less
productive pasture-farming: partly, doubtless, a contribution was
made by the spurt in industrial activity following greater political
independence and the outbreak of war with France. But, towering
above both the spread of spade and plough and the growth of
industry and towns was the devotion of much of the tilled land of
Ireland to the potato, and the dependence of her peasants, their
families and livestock, upon a diet in which it was much the most
important constituent. No other western country has lived for so
long a period on a diet so largely dominated by the potato. Nor,
it is quite possible, in any other western country, in any half-century, has the number of births so vastly exceeded the number of
deaths as in Ireland before the Famine. The two facts are closely

[1] 1812, i. 121.

bound together: the potato loosened both the positive and the preventive checks to population. Growing potatoes, men forgot the niggardliness of nature: people who would have died of hunger or of the diseases it fostered, lived on potatoes; sons who would have been too unsure of the future to marry, planted potatoes on a scrap of land their fathers did not miss, or on a patch of mountain, and dug food for the families they reared.

How much more productive was the land of Ireland, in terms of the number of people it could support when growing potatoes rather than grain crops or dairy produce? Modern ratios of the yield per acre of potatoes and other products can help us little in solving this problem because of changes in the technique of agriculture since the eighteenth century. Nor can we work out any general ratio of our own because the necessary agricultural statistics are not available. Several contemporaries, however, were interested in the problem and their discussion gives us a broad idea of the scope for population-increase presented by a general shift from a diet of bread, stirabout, and dairy produce to one primarily of potatoes and milk. Arthur Young's estimate is the earliest: from the average of eight accounts[1] of a family's consumption of potatoes he concluded that a household of six would require practically a barrel of 280 pounds every six days. 'Now the average produce of the whole kingdom being eighty-two barrels per acre, plantation measure, one acre does rather more than support eight persons the year through, which is five persons to the English acre. To feed on wheat those eight persons would require eight quarters, or two Irish acres, which at present imply two more for fallow, or four in all.'[2] Making no allowance for the milk, or other foods that the potato- or bread-eaters would require, Young's calculations allow for a population four times as dense on potato-land as on wheat-land. Both Newenham and the author of the 1803 *Essays on the Population of Ireland* confirmed the broad accuracy of these calculations: they agreed that less than a quarter of the land required to maintain a family on wheat would maintain it on potatoes.[3] Andrews, in the essay for which the Royal Dublin

[1] See below, pp. 147–8.

[2] A. Young, 1780, op. cit., 2nd ed., ii. 120.

[3] T. Newenham, *A statistical and historical Inquiry into the Progress and Magnitude of the Population of Ireland*, 1805, p. 14; Member of the last Irish Parliament, *Essays on the Population of Ireland and the Character of the Irish*, 1803, p. 27.

Society awarded him its Gold Medal in 1835, reckoned that, on the average, an acre would produce $8\frac{3}{4}$ tons of potatoes or 16 cwt. of wheat. On the assumption that a man would require 9 pounds of potatoes a day, or 4 pounds of wheaten bread, an acre would support six potato-eaters for a year, substantially more than three times the number of bread-eaters.[1] The final estimate is McCulloch's: 'a given extent of land', he thought, 'planted with potatoes will support at least double the number of persons that it could do, were it planted with wheat, or any species of corn.'[2]

What conclusion can we come to about the relaxation of the limits to population-growth when the Irish became dependent on potatoes and milk? Our information, as is so often the case, does not allow us to give any precise answer. We know little about movements in the yield per acre between the two periods. We do not know the relative importance of milk and butter to bread and stirabout in the earlier period: if, as may well have been the case in so preponderantly pastoral a country, dairy produce bulked large, the eighteenth- and nineteenth-century ratios of the productivity of potato land to grain land may seriously underestimate the rate of population-increase allowed by the generalization of the potato. We have no measure of the relative proportions in which land was used for the subsistence of those who worked it in the two periods: if, in the course of the eighteenth century, as may well have been the case, absenteeism, the middleman system, and rack-renting transferred an increasing proportion of total yield to families other than those of the cultivator, then not the whole of any area which had produced means of subsistence in the seventeenth century would be available for potatoes in the nineteenth, and the full influence of the potato would not, of course, be felt. A guess, but one that almost certainly errs by excess of restraint in presenting the claims of the potato, is that its general adoption in any area of Ireland allowed at least a doubling of the density of population. And this, of course, is to put on one side the further freedom the potato gave to the rate of population-growth by making available for tillage and settlement mountain land which before its use had no, or virtually no, economic significance.

There are six major problems we must discuss if we are to

[1] W. G. Andrews, 'Essay on . . . the Potato', in *Prize Essays on the Potato*, Dublin, Royal Dublin Society, 1835, pp. 3–4.
[2] J. R. McCulloch, op. cit., 2nd ed., 1839, i. 436.

assess the demographic influence of the potato. The first concerns the period during which old foods were forsaken in its favour. If its general acceptance as the staple food of Ireland swiftly followed its introduction to the country late in the sixteenth century, then much of the release it gave to the pressure of population would have been spent before the period of really fast population growth. Still, without doubt, at the end of the eighteenth century, its impact would be felt as an agent of colonization: there still remained extensive moor and bog, useless for wheat or oats, but able, when broken into potato patches, to promise a family's subsistence to many a younger son. This effect would have remained, but surely, in nearly two centuries, the no less explosive potentialities of the potato as an instrument for doubling or trebling the population of existing settlements would have been exhausted. Malthusian theory would have supplied a most fitting frame for the facts: when potatoes were grown in place of grain fewer children would perish for want of food, fewer, as young adults, would be forced to forgo the pleasures of marriage. Generation after generation the process would have been repeated, but, with half a dozen repetitions, population would again have pressed upon subsistence, and the potato would have to share more freely with other agents responsibility for allowing the spurt in the population figures.

Second, we must examine the case for the dissemination, between the late eighteenth century and the Famine, of a more and more prolific potato. Plainly, if such were the case, without any more general or more exclusive dependence upon the potato the limits to population growth would be pushed yet farther back. Third, remembering that generalizations purporting to cover the whole of Ireland may be wildly misleading, we must investigate what regional evidence there is concerning the Irishman's diet: the less exclusively in any area the potato was his food, the less can we lean on it in interpreting that area's population-increase. Fourth, we need to know whether, continuously, regularly for part of each year, or occasionally in a bad year, the Irishman and his family went short of potatoes, and whether, in consequence the full stimulus to population growth implicit in a potato diet was not felt. Fifth, we must investigate the nutritional adequacy of the Irish family's diet. Did it, even in years or seasons of abundance, enjoy a diet favourable to a high survival-rate? Finally, we must look at the contribution made by the potato to the considerable reclamation of waste land which accompanied, and helped to allow, the rapid expansion of population.

I. *The Dissemination of the Potato*

Our first problem is whether the dominance of the potato followed hard upon its introduction, or whether, with piecemeal advance, it did not approach its greatest hold on the Irishman's field and board until immediately before, or during the period of rapid population-increase. The most recent contribution to the subject has been made by Dr. Redcliffe N. Salaman, F.R.S., in the Finlay Memorial Lecture for 1943.[1] Dr. Salaman believes that by 1630 the potato was the basic food of the Irish,[2] even though it had been introduced to the country not more than half a century earlier, possibly by Raleigh in 1588.[3] The conservatism of a peasant community in matters of diet, its reluctance to grow new crops, the moderate pace of agricultural change elsewhere in the seventeenth century, all make one question whether the dissemination of the potato and the general dependence upon it could have been achieved in so short a time. Dr. Salaman gives a series of convincing reasons to account for the eager acceptance of this new plant and new food: Irish natural conditions were admirably suited to potato culture; the destruction following war and revolution facilitated the introduction of a new crop, and the prevalent subsistence economy made people welcome one so prolific; that

[1] R. N. Salaman, *The Influence of the Potato on the Course of Irish History*, Dublin, 1943. This chapter was written some years before the publication of Dr. Salaman's *History and Social Influence of the Potato* (Cambridge, 1949). While it has been altered in only a few minor matters as the result of Dr. Salaman's kindness in showing me the manuscript of his book, if I had been able to draw on his work at an earlier stage my chapter might have been briefer and better in other respects. My dispute, however, with the conclusion of Dr. Salaman's Finlay Memorial Lecture on the chronology of the general dependence of the Irish upon the potato would have remained.

[2] Salaman, 1943, op. cit., p. 5.

[3] Professor D. B. Quinn has kindly sent me a note stressing the fact that there is no solid evidence for the belief that Raleigh introduced the potato to Ireland. The old assumption, he says, that Raleigh had collected specimens of the potato in the colony of 1585–6 known as Virginia and taken them to his Munster estates during his only known visits (in 1588 and 1589) is now regarded as botanically untenable. If Raleigh, on these visits, did take potatoes he must have got them from Spanish sources or from some of the English expeditions which touched on South America. A more plausible suggestion is that Raleigh collected specimens of the potato during his Guiana expedition of 1595 and sent them to Ireland.

landlords did not build the outhouses needed to store grain encouraged the cultivation of the potato which would keep in the
ground, and in Ireland, contrary to the experience of other countries, the advance of the potato was not hindered by the rigidity
of a three-field system or by religious prejudice. Less persuasive
than these reasons why the potato should quickly have become a
general article of diet is Dr. Salaman's evidence that it was, in
fact, widespread by 1630. He supports his case with three pieces
of documentary evidence. First, he refers to the Council Book of
the Corporation of Youghal which in 1623 gave a market toll for
'roots', which, turnips, parsnips, carrots and so forth being virtually unknown, he is able to interpret as affording 'strong evidence
that potatoes were grown in sufficient quantity to need special
consideration in the local market'.[1] Second, Dr. Salaman quotes
from the *Advertisements for Ireland*, written in 1623: the poor, it
says, 'feed altogether upon "moist meals" ', a term which, in his
opinion, excludes milk foods as they were known as 'white meats',
and would apply to potatoes. Third, he finds support for his
thesis in the work of Petty, who, 'writing somewhere about 1660,
tells us that the potato was already the basic food of the Irish
people'.[2]

This threefold evidence is not conclusive. It is unfortunate
that it should be the Youghal market that so early taxed dealings
in potatoes, suggesting, as it does, not that the potato had been
disseminated throughout Ireland, but merely that it was of some
consequence, whether as food for man or stock, in the area where
it may have been introduced to the country by Raleigh thirty-five
years earlier. Neither the author of the *Advertisements* nor Petty
is unequivocal in his testimony. If the term 'moist meals' does, in
fact, exclude milk foods the *Advertisements* would seem to be
inconsistent: 'the common sort', it says in another place, 'never
kill any [cows or swine] for their own use being content to feed
all the year on milk, butter and the like, and do eat but little
bread'.[3] This description of the Irishman's diet certainly does not

[1] R. N. Salaman, 1943, op. cit., p. 4.   [2] Ibid., p. 5.
[3] *Advertisements for Ireland*, ed. G. O'Brien, Dublin, 1923, pp. 8–9. Dr.
Salaman regards this quotation as evidence that by the time of the *Advertisements*
the potato 'had been accepted in every worker's home through the land'. The
Irish, he says, 'could not possibly have forsaken both meat and cereal in peace-
time, had they not by then found a satisfactory alternative food: that food was
the potato'. (Op. cit., p. 16.) Is it not probable that the additional food was still

exclude the potato, but neither does it rule out a continuation, perhaps modified by the introduction of the potato, of the food-stuffs of the sixteenth century, when according to Dr. Salaman, the staples were abundant milk, butter, and sour curds, oatmeal, and oaten bread.[1] Petty's support for Dr. Salaman's case is drawn from the *Political Anatomy*. But the *Political Anatomy* was not written until after 1670:[2] its testimony, however clear-cut, refers to a period more than forty years later than that with which Dr. Sala-man is concerned. And, moreover, even for this late period Petty's authority is of questionable use in showing that the potato was, in any sense, the Irishman's staple foodstuff. Perhaps the greatest emphasis Petty places upon it is to be found where he discusses the idleness of the Irish: 'what need they to Work', he asks, 'who can content themselves with Potato's, whereof the Labour of one Man can feed forty; and with Milk, whereof one Cow will, in Summer time, give meat and drink enough for three Men, when they can every where gather Cockles, Oysters, Muscles, Crabs, etc.?'[3] Here Petty may well be underlining the promise of the potato more heavily than its achievement: certainly, when he dis-cusses food in greater detail he is more restrained in his claims for the potato.

The Diet of these people [he said] is Milk, sweet and sower, thick and thin, which is also their Drink in Summer-time, in Winter Small-Beer or Water. . . . Their Food is Bread in Cakes, whereof a Penny serves a Week for each; Potatoes from *August* till *May*, Muscles, Cockles and Oysters, near the Sea; Eggs and Butter, made very rancid, by keeping in Bogs. As for Flesh, they seldom eat it, notwithstanding the great plenty thereof, unless it be of smaller Animals. . . .[4]

Petty here was surely pointing out, what we can readily believe, that the potato, three-quarters of a century after its introduction to the country, was, for the greater part of the year, a supplement

---

the oatmeal which in the sixteenth century had supplemented milk and milk-products? It is remarkable that if, in fact, the potato was in general use when the *Advertisements* was written, it is specifically mentioned in neither of its references to food.

[1] Op. cit., p. 12.

[2] C. H. Hull in his edition of *The Economic Writings of Sir William Petty* (i. 121–2) says that, though the first edition of the *Political Anatomy* was not published until 1691, Petty probably began to write it in 1671: one manuscript of the work bears the title 'The Political Anatomy of Ireland, 1672'.

[3] W. Petty, *Political Anatomy of Ireland*, 1691, ed. C. H. Hull, op. cit., 1899, i. 201.

[4] Ibid., p. 191.

to the traditional foodstuffs, not that it was 'already the basic food of the people'.

If there is no conclusive evidence of the primacy of the potato in the diet of the Irishman in the early seventeenth century there is authority, fully as convincing, supporting the proposition that a century later the potato was still far from occupying the place in the Irishman's life which it had achieved by the nineteenth century. In Madden's time the poor dug their 'wretched Potatoes' when bread was scarce.[1] Bread, in Madden's references to foodstuffs, was the staple, potatoes the substitute, forced upon the poor because of the 'epidemical Evil of over-running vast Tracts of Land, with such prodigious Herds of Cattle'.[2] Because of this spread of pasture, 'thinly peopled as we are, our poor live like *Nabuchadnezzar* on the Herbs and Grass of the Field, one 4th part of the Year, or on Potatoes without Bread, and for another 4th they must depend on the Courtesy of Foreigners, for what they please to extort from them for it . . . or live as the old *Irish* used to do, and the *Swedish* boors often do at this Day, on a mixture of Meal and Bark ground together'.[3] Even when religious observance restricted the peasant's diet he was not driven to depend on potatoes. The keeping of Lent, Madden pointed out, was not so destructive in warmer climates as in Ireland: in other countries, by Lent, gardens and fields had begun to supply the poor 'but in our Northern Regions there is nothing but Bread or a very little Milk to sustain them'.[4] The testimony of Madden's contemporaries is fragmentary and equivocal. Swift, on the one hand, lamented that 'to bestow the whole kingdom on beef and mutton' drove out 'half the people who should eat their share and force the rest to send sometimes as far as Egypt for bread to eat with it',[5] but, in the *Short View of the State of Ireland*, he referred to farmers, who, although they paid great rents, were 'living in filth and nastiness upon buttermilk and potatoes'.[6] In Maurice O'Connell's *Observationes Medicales*, written in the 1740s, 'those tuberous roots (commonly called potatoes)' are regarded as 'almost the continual and sole food of the poor and lower orders of the inhabitants of

---

[1] S. Madden, 1738, op. cit., p. 222.
[2] Ibid., p. 129.
[3] Ibid., p. 127.
[4] Ibid., p. 97.
[5] J. Swift, 1735, op. cit., reprinted in T. Scott, 1925, op. cit., vii. 111.
[6] J. Swift, 1727–8, reprinted in T. Scott, op. cit., p. 89.

this kingdom'.[1] But O'Connell was a Cork doctor and there is other evidence to show that in Munster, the province in which it appears to have been introduced to Ireland, the potato secured its dominance in the Irishman's diet earlier than elsewhere. One of Boulter's letters written in 1727 concedes the dependence of the poor on potatoes in winter, but by no means disputes the continuing importance of oats: 'last year the dearness of corn was such that thousands of families quitted their habitations to seek bread elsewhere, and many hundreds perished; this year the poor had consumed their potatoes, which is their winter subsistence, near two months sooner than ordinary, and are already, through the dearness of corn, in that want that in some places they begin to quit their habitations.'[2] *The Querist*, while disturbed by the necessity of importing grain, asked 'whether it is possible the country should be well improved, while our beef is exported, and our labourers live upon potatoes?'[3] A pamphlet of 1723 said that 'without plenty of' bread 'the poor must starve':[4] one of 1739 said that the poor Catholics lived on milk and potatoes.[5]

For the century intervening between the 1620s, when Dr. Salaman claims that potatoes were a basic food, and the comments of Madden, Swift, and Berkeley, information on the Irishman's diet is scanty—a fact which, in itself, should encourage one to question whether the major and unprecedented change implied in general dependence upon the potato had in fact taken place. Occasional references support the view that the potato had widespread and critical importance as a foodstuff before 1650: the majority encourage us to regard its generalization as a later development. Dr. Salaman finds that John Stevens's *Journal, 1689–91*, emphasizes the importance of the potato in these years.[6] Put in their context, however, the sentences Dr. Salaman quotes lose much of their force. They are here italicized in their place in Stevens's only major reference to the Irishman's food.

We had here [Stevens wrote at Carrigogunnell, four miles west of

---

[1] Quoted in 1851 Census, *Reports from Commissioners*, 1856, xxix. 389.
[2] Quoted in W. E. H. Lecky, 1892, op. cit. i. 185.
[3] G. Berkeley, *The Querist*, 1752, reprinted in *Tracts and Treatises . . . of Ireland*, Dublin, 1861, ii, qq. 138, 169.
[4] R.L.V.M., *Some Considerations for the promoting of Agriculture*, 1723, quoted in J. O'Rourke, *Great Irish Famine*, Dublin, 1875, p. 8.
[5] *Four letters, originally written in French relating to . . . Ireland*, Dublin, 1739, p. 2.
[6] R. N. Salaman, 1943, op. cit., p. 17.

Limerick] plenty of meat and barley bread baked in cakes over or before the fire and abundance of milk and butter, but no sort of drink. Yet there this is counted the best of quarters, the people generally being the greatest lovers of milk I ever saw, which they eat and drink above twenty several sorts of ways, and what is strangest for the most part love it best when sourest. They keep it in sour vessels and from time to time till it grows thick, and sometimes to that perfection that it will perfume a whole house, but generally speaking they order it so that it is impossible to boil it without curdling four hours after it comes from the cow. Oaten and barley bread is the common fare, and that in cakes, and ground by hand. *None but the best sort or the inhabitants of great towns eat wheat, or bread baked in an oven, or ground in a mill. The meaner people content themselves with little bread but instead thereof eat potatoes, which with sour milk, is the chief part of their diet,* their drink for the most part water, sometimes coloured with milk; beer or ale they seldom taste, unless they sell something considerable in a market town.[1]

The value of Stevens's testimony as evidence of the predominance of the potato is weakened not only by his self-contradiction: his evidence is drawn from a very limited area: he places such great weight on the place of milk and milk-products[2] as to make it probable that he is reporting the persistence of the food-habits of the nomadic and pastoral Irish who were obliged, until well into the seventeenth century, to live almost exclusively on the foods provided by their cows. Moreover, Stevens was writing during a period of war which tended to accelerate, perhaps only for a short time, the substitution of potatoes for other sorts of food.

Luke Gernon, writing in 1620, said that in the baser cabins 'you shall have no drink but Bonnyclabber, milk that is soured to the condition of buttermilk, nor no meat, but mullagham (mallabanne), a kind of chokedaw cheese, and blue butter, and no bread at your first coming in, but if you stay half an hour you shall have a cake of meal unboulted, and mingled with butter baken on an iron called a griddle, like a pudding cake'.[3] Fynes Moryson confirmed, for the early years of the century, the continuing predominance of milk-products and grain: 'their ordinary food for the common sort is of white meats, and they eat cakes of oats for bread, and drink

---

[1] *Journal of John Stevens*, ed. R. H. Murray, Oxford, 1912, pp. 138–9.

[2] In Co. Kilkenny, Stevens called at a farm and 'found a good will in the people but no great refreshment, they having nothing to eat or drink but milk, a diet I was not yet used to'. (Ibid., p. 49.)

[3] Ibid., quoted in Murray's Introduction, p. lvii.

not English beer made of malt and hops, but ale. . . .'[1] T. C. Croker concludes, rather sweepingly, from a poem called 'An Account of an Irish Quarter', published in 1654, 'that potatoes were ordinary food in the south of Ireland before the time of the Commonwealth'. The poet describes disparagingly his entertainment in Co. Waterford,

> And now for supper, the round board being spread,
> The van, a dish of coddled onions led,
> I'th'body was a salted tail of salmon
> And in the rear some rank potatoes came on.[2]

In 1644, the French traveller, le Gouz, though describing the foodstuffs of the Irish poor does not mention the potato: 'the poor', he said, 'grind barley and peas between two stones and make it into bread, which they cook upon a small iron table heated on a tripod; they put into it some oats, and this bread, which in the form of cakes they call Haraan, they eat with great draughts of buttermilk.'[3] Even the ardent champions of the potato are modest in the claims they make for its advance in Ireland. In 1663, Boyle showed specimens of it to the Royal Society and read a letter from his gardener at Youghal in which the potato was described as 'very good to pickle for winter salads and also to preserve'—but there was no commendation of it, even from this area of its introduction to Ireland, as a food of the people.[4] Forster, who in 1664 almost implored the English to grow more of the root, and excited their palates with recipes for pastries, puddings, custards, and cheese-cakes made from potatoes, together with references to potatoes stewed in wine, and baked in pies with sugar and spice, merely said of Ireland that there 'there is whole Fields of Them'—not that the worth of the potato was proved by the experience of a nation living on them. Moreover, the 'first and greatest Use of Potatoes' to Forster was for making bread, a use alien to Irish practice.[5]

The unknown traveller who wrote an account of his tour in

---

[1] Ibid.

[2] *The Popular Songs of Ireland*, ed. T. C. Croker, 1839, p. 55. The poem in question appeared in a volume entitled *Songs and Poems of Love and Drollery*, by T(homas) W(eaver).

[3] *The Tour of the French Traveller, M. de la Boullaye le Gouz in Ireland*, A.D. *1644*, ed. T. C. Croker, 1837, pp. 39–40.

[4] Quoted in 1851 Census, op. cit., p. 501.

[5] J. Forster, *England's Happiness increased . . . by a Plantation of the Roots called Potatoes*, 1664, pp. 2 ff.

Ireland between 1672 and 1674 did not give potatoes the leading place in the Irishman's diet: potatoes, presumably, are the 'roots' he refers to, but they are supplemented with oats, milk-products, and other vegetables. 'Their general food', he said, 'is a thin oatcake which they bake upon a broad flat stone made hot, a little sheeps-milk cheese, or goats milk, boyl'd leeks and some roots; but seldom eat flesh or drink strong beer. . . .'[1] Robert Leigh, on the other hand, writing of Co. Kilkenny in 1684 said that 'the graine this countye affords most plenty of is wheate, barly, and oates; yet it yeilds in many places beare, pease and beanes alsoe, particullarly in the Barronies of Forth and Bargye; in some parts it yeilds rye; but ye great support of ye poore sortes of people is thire Potatos, which are much used all over the County'.[2] John Dunton, in *Conversations in Ireland*, published in 1699, describes the Irish cabin as having behind it a potato garden: the food of the people he met between Galway and Kilkenny was 'Bonny-Clabber and Mulahaan, alias sowre milk and choak-cheese, with a dish of potatoes boiled'.[3] A contemporary author referring to the value of potatoes in time of war said that 'now they begin to spread all the kingdom over'.[4] Frequently, however, in the numerous pamphlets of the next half-century lamenting the decline in tillage, corn is regarded as the food of the poor. *The Groans of Ireland* attributes the frequency of famines to the lack of proper tillage laws and granaries, not to the failure of the potato.[5] Nor would the *Thoughts on the Tillage of Ireland* appear to be the work of a man discussing life in a potato economy: 'when bread is at a low price our labouring people can afford to work cheap; for which reason the price of labour always did, and always must depend on the price of corn.'[6]

[1] 'A Tour in Ireland in 1672–4', ed. J. Buckley, *J. Cork Hist. and Arch. Soc.*, 2nd ser., 1904, x. 95. The editor of the 'Tour' says the allusions of the author 'show that the oatcake continued to be, as it did for over half a century after, the staple diet of the people. The potato, although cultivated in the country, particularly in the South, had not yet attained a national popularity' (p. 85).

[2] 'A chorographic Account of the southern Part of the County of Wexford, written anno 1684 by Robert Leigh . . . ', ed. H. F. Hore, *Proc. & Papers Kilkenny and SE. Ireland Arch. Soc.*, n.s., ii, no. 24, Nov. 1859, p. 466.

[3] Quoted in 1851 Census, op. cit., p. 501.

[4] John Haughton, *Husbandry and Trade*, 1699, quoted in 1851 Census, op. cit., p. 502.

[5] Dublin, 1741, p. 5.

[6] *Some Thoughts on the Tillage of Ireland . . . to which is prefixed a Letter from the Rev. Dr. Swift . . .* , 3rd ed., Dublin, 1741.

Broken though it is, the evidence of the advance of the potato in the two centuries following its introduction to Ireland does suggest that by the last quarter of the eighteenth century it had become the main food of the mass of the Irish. Young's conclusion, when surveying the evidence he collected on his tour through the country was that 'the food of the common Irish [is] potatoes and milk'.[1] Cooper's *Letters on the Irish Nation*, written during his tour in 1799 are hardly less insistent upon the dominance of the potato.

The diet of the Irish peasantry [he said] is chiefly vegetables; his subsistence depending on a small spot of ground, which he generally sows with potatoes. Bread, which constitutes the ordinary and wholesome food of a civilised people, he is almost a stranger to. . . . Perhaps it might therefore be reasonably expected, that the peasant would often enjoy the nourishment of animal food. But the fact is otherwise: he is almost a stranger to it.[2]

There is other evidence supporting the conclusion (which is nowhere questioned) that the potato was the peasant's mainstay by the end of the eighteenth century, and suggesting that the nearly exclusive dependence upon it was a recent development. Dr. Salaman refers to a Mr. Irwin who, writing in the *Complete Farmer* in 1777, said that in time back the peasants were better off and the potato not much used, but '*now* . . . it had become their staple support'.[3] Arthur Young said that potato culture had increased twentyfold in the twenty years before his tour.[4] In Cork, when Townsend was writing in 1810, potatoes were 'the great staple commodity', but, he pointed out, 'formerly the use of them was limited to particular seasons, oatmeal having been used in Spring and Summer'.[5] An Antrim incumbent, a contributor to Mason's *Statistical Survey*, regarded the children of his parish as healthier, and more free from skin troubles in 1812 'in comparison with what they were 30 or 40 years ago, when a bit of oaten bread was put in their hands in place of a potatoe and salt'.[6] Dr. Doyle, in evidence before the 1830 Select Committee, regarded the potato as then the principal food of the poor, but pointed out that before

[1] A. Young, 1780, op. cit., 2nd ed., ii. 116.
[2] G. Cooper, 2nd ed., 1801, pp. 62–3.
[3] R. N. Salaman, 1943, op. cit., p. 20.
[4] Quoted in O'Rourke, 1875, op. cit., pp. 28–9.
[5] H. Townsend, 1810, op. cit., p. 88.
[6] W. S. Mason, op. cit. i., 1814, 257.

the French wars it was not in general use, except from the beginning of September until Christmas: it was the custom then for farmers to feed their labourers for the greater part of the year at their own tables on stirabout made of oatmeal, or on bread, together with meat two, three, or four times a week.[1]

On reviewing the seventeenth- and eighteenth-century accounts of the Irishman's food there is a strong case for regarding the generalization of a potato diet as a more gradual process than Dr. Salaman would have us believe. In place of the four or five decades into which his interpretation compresses the process it may well have been spread over more than an additional century: in some districts, doubtless, the potato early achieved dominance, but elsewhere it struggled with the calendar, slowly advancing from the position of seasonal supplement to the traditional foodstuffs to becoming their successor.[2] This conclusion is confirmed by the ignorance in which the sources of seventeenth-century social history leave us regarding the outlines, or even the existence, of the upheaval in the structure of rural economy which would have been quite inseparable from the revolutionary change in cropping and diet implied by general dependence upon the potato. Throughout the seventeenth century much of the land was occupied by graziers: it is not difficult to believe that in these areas, at least, dairy produce maintained something of its former prominence in the general diet. For the eighteenth century, on the other hand, we know that land was made available for the growth of the potato either by reclamation of waste, or by pasture yielding ground to arable; and we know that, towards the end of the century, as large farms gave way to small, almost every family gained the opportunity of growing its own potatoes. Nor need we be at a loss to explain why the potato gained ground in the eighteenth century. None of

---

[1] *Rep. S.C. S.P.I.*, 1830, op. cit., vii, q. 4533.

[2] Sir William Wilde's history of the potato in Ireland, published in the 1851 Census, concludes that the potato 'was grown in gardens as a rarity, used at table as a delicacy, and described by herbalists as an introduced exotic; but we do not find any warrant for believing that it was at all cultivated by the people as a general article of food until from the end of the seventeenth to the beginning of the eighteenth century'. (*Reports from Commissioners*, 1856, xxix. 501.) Elsewhere the same author says that 'from the researches which I have made it would appear that the cultivation of the potato was very irregular throughout the country; some localities, especially in Ulster, having adopted it generally within the memory of the past generation'. ('The Introduction and Time of general Use of the Potato in Ireland', *Proc. R.I. Academy*, 1853–7, vi. 360.)

Dr. Salaman's reasons explaining its advance before 1630 lost its drive in the following century and their total effect was then strengthened by the operation of new forces. Still, in the eighteenth century, the legacy of war and destruction made men eager for the benefits the potato could bring. Still living from hand to mouth, they felt impelled to grow the most prolific food crop: the more firmly they were held down by the oppression of absentees, middlemen, and penal laws, the less real became any alternative to the potato. The greater success of the graziers in the central decades of the eighteenth century in adding to their herds and fields—and neither the trade statistics, nor the laments of the mercantilists permit us to doubt this extension of pasture—gave fresh impetus to the advance of the potato. Scarcity of grain resulted and made an alternative foodstuff indispensable: that the potato would thrive on land the graziers did not covet made it, more certainly than ever, this alternative. The planting of potatoes on poor land may well have been further stimulated by the Act of 1742 'to encourage the reclaiming of unprofitable bogs'. Roman Catholics, till then, had been barred from occupying land: this Act made it lawful for them to occupy 50 acres of bog, together with half an acre of adjoining arable, and to enjoy immunity from tithes for seven years.[1] In reclaiming bog the potato was an ideal first crop, and on poor land it promised far better results than grain crops. Later in the century, with the engrossing of the graziers halted and reversed, the potato, which had benefited from the advance of pasture, benefited no less from the advance of arable. So acute was the shortage of capital that the men who took farms to grow corn had scarcely the money to pay their labourers, and it became customary to give them, in place of wages, the scrap of land they turned into a potato patch. In the last quarter of the century potato culture and subdivision, each both cause and effect of the other, became jointly cause and effect of the increase in population: the wilder the pace of population-growth, the more insistent was the trend towards a diet almost exclusively of potatoes.

II. *The Yield of the Potato*

In discussing the extent to which general dependence upon the potato released the restraints upon population-growth we have

---

[1] O'Rourke, 1875, op. cit., pp. 10 and 43.

made the implicit assumption that from the time of Young to the Famine, apart from the chance of season, the yield of the potato was constant. Much in the structure of Irish agriculture in these years would lead us to expect diminution rather than stability in yield: tracts of land of the poorest quality were brought under the spade; the cultivators lacked the tools, the knowledge, and the encouragement to make the most of even the meanest natural resources; their landlord-tenant relationship, with its rack-renting, short leases, and frequent change in occupier made it inevitable that much soil should be 'mined'. There were, however, two trends in agricultural practice which, in much of the country, more than offset any tendency for the yield of the potato-patch to dwindle —with, of course, the result of allowing a still denser population to settle even on land whose inhabitants had long since eaten potatoes in place of bread. First, though she lacked to a far greater extent even than contemporary Britain the capital, the knowledge, the stimulus, or the drive to agrarian revolution, Ireland probably did experience a real and widespread improvement in the tools and methods of agriculture, with noticeable effect upon crop-yields. Second, new and more prolific varieties of potato were introduced and planted generally.

General improvements in agriculture did not leave the potato unaffected. Increasing attention to fertilizers and drainage tended towards heavier yields. The more, in any area, farming was freed from the burden of fallow, and the more a better plough increased the yield of grain crops, the more land there was available each year to grow potatoes. The lazy-bed was, doubtless, better adapted to the Irishman's peculiar requirements than much contemporary criticism would allow,[1] but it is true, nonetheless, that the extension in the years before the Famine of the practice of drilling potatoes increased the farmer's return—to the extent, according to one writer, of nearly a third.[2]

---

[1] Appendix D to the *Report of the Select Committee appointed to take into Consideration the Means of promoting the Cultivation and Improvement of the Waste* . . . , 1795 (*Reports from Committees of the House of Commons, 1774–1802*, ix. 214), recommends a lazy-bed system of potato culture. In Dr. Salaman's opinion, 'Considering the equipment the cottier had at his disposal, and the undrained condition of much of the land, it will be realised that the lazy bed was an effective and intelligent method of cultivation, especially as it was frequently preceded by the burning of the top layer of the turf which afforded the potash it [the potato] so urgently needs'. (Salaman, 1943, op. cit., p. 10.)

[2] Mason, op. cit. i, 1814, p. 334. See also McCulloch, 1839, op. cit. i. 373.

Only inadequate material is available on the history of potato varieties in the century before the Famine, but it is clear that for half of this period, perhaps longer, the Irish had very generally become dependent on a more prolific potato than was common in the years before Young's tour: indeed, the increasing frequency of crop deficiencies after the 1820s and the extent of the disaster of the Famine may both have arisen partly from the greater susceptibility of the prolific potato to disease.[1] In the decade, or so, before the Famine the 'lumper' was much the most popular variety: this was 'an extremely ugly potato of poor quality',[2] 'little better in substance than a turnip'.[3] The agriculturalists recommended it extensively for stock,[4] but the pot which supplied the peasant's animals also supplied his family, and the heavy yield of the lumper, even without manure, on the poorest soil,[5] made it the food of man and beast. 'By the year 1838', Drummond's Railway Commission reported, 'the cultivation of "Lumpers" was universal in Ireland':[6] the *Edinburgh Review* confirms that at the time of the Famine, they were 'generally used'.[7]

The lumper was not the only new variety to have an unusually high yield. Townsend, in 1810, said that in one barony of Co. Cork farmers were introducing a new kind of potato, called 'cups' or 'minions', because it was more productive than the traditional varieties, though inferior to them in every other respect.[8] Cups, too, were important in Clare where their quality was more highly rated: more of them were planted, said Dutton, than of any other kind; 'they are reckoned not only more productive, but vastly more nutritive, being more difficult of digestion, and, as the country people say, "they stay longer in the belly" '.[9] The 'red-nosed kidney' and the 'early champion' are two other varieties introduced

---

[1] *Tate's Edinburgh Magazine* reported in 1845 that 'Lumpers suffered more than any other variety' from blight. (W. D. Davidson, 'History of Potato Varieties', in *Journal of the Department of Agriculture*, Irish Free State, 1935, xxxiii. 64.)

[2] R. N. Salaman, 'The Potato—Master or Servant?', in *New Biology*, 1945, i. 21.

[3] J. E. Bicheno, *Ireland and its Economy*, 1830.

[4] Davidson, 1935, loc. cit., p. 64.

[5] Davidson, 1935, loc. cit., quoting David Ferguson, in the *Farmers' Magazine*, Sept. 1853.

[6] Quoted in Davidson, loc. cit.

[7] 'The Irish Crisis', *Ed. Review*, Jan. 1848, lxxxvii. 232.

[8] Townsend, 1810, op. cit., p. 407.

[9] Dutton, 1808, op. cit., p. 43.

in the closing decades of the eighteenth century and noted for their high yields.[1]

In the fifty or more years before the Famine the potato changed not only in respect to yield: with similar effect in loosening the restraints to population growth, varieties were introduced which kept for a full twelve months. Formerly, however abundant the crop, if it would not keep from harvest to harvest there was danger of distress in the 'meal months'. As early as 1730 the 'black potato' was valued because it could be stored until the new crop was ready, but the most notable of the good keepers was the 'Irish Apple', first referred to in 1770 and 'extensively grown' in the following seventy years.[2]

III. *Supplements to the Potato*

The third problem to be considered in connexion with the potato concerns the degree to which, even in the period of its greatest use, it monopolized the Irishman's board. In certain restricted districts, even in normal times, the poor may have had to regard any supplement to a diet of potatoes and water as an unusual favour. In bad times there was more general dependence upon a diet exclusively of potatoes and with insufficient of them to satisfy hunger. But there is no doubt that in the century before the Famine there was a wide variety of regional supplements to the potato, and, indeed, in places, of substitutes for it. It was in the north-east of the country that the predominance of oatmeal persisted most doggedly. Especially in the north of Ireland, Richardson emphasized in 1816, there was more farinaceous food consumed than was generally supposed.[3] Almost every contemporary account of northern foodstuffs bore him out by emphasizing the importance of oatmeal. The incumbent of Holywood, Co. Down, reported that in his parish the diet differed little from what was general throughout Ulster: oatmeal and potatoes were the staples, together with fish, when in season, and bacon and cheese.[4] At Ballintoy and Aghalee,

---

[1] Davidson, 1935, loc. cit., pp. 61–2.

[2] Ibid., pp. 59–60; W. D. Davidson, 'The "Champion" Potato; History and Possibilities of its Revival', *Journal of the Department of Lands and Agriculture*, Irish Free State, 1926, xxvi. 109.

[3] W. Richardson, 'Simple Measures by which the Recurrence of Famine may be prevented', in *The Pamphleteer*, no. xv, viii. 168, 170.

[4] Mason, op. cit. iii, 1819, p. 199.

in Antrim, oaten meal, potatoes, and fish were the chief foods.[1] At Errigall-Keroge, in Tyrone, the diet was almost entirely oatmeal and potatoes.[2] At Killelagh, in Derry, the food was 'principally potatoes and oatmeal made into bread or stirabout'.[3] In Belfast jail, in 1823, the weekly food-allowance was 7 pounds of oatmeal, 35 pounds of potatoes, and 7 pints of new milk.[4] Meat, too, played no negligible part in the general diet in much of Ulster. Inglis, in 1834, found that in Fermanagh both Catholics and Protestants could afford butcher's meat three times a week, and that, in addition, they had as much milk and butter as they required.[5] McEvoy's *Tyrone* said that each October great numbers of horned cattle were killed and sold at market at from 30s. to £3 a carcass, and that the buyers were generally poorer people, three or four of them joining to make a purchase.[6] The north-east, too, had a number of foodstuffs other than meat to make its potatoes and oatmeal more palatable and more adequate nutritionally. Liquid milk, in one form or another, was drunk very generally,[7] and, in varying degree, milk-products were available. Cheese, generally little known in Ireland, was eaten in Ulster,[8] and butter was sometimes reserved for local use.[9] Fish was commonly eaten, at least in coastal districts,[10] and elsewhere pork, bacon, and eggs sometimes took their place.[11]

Leinster apparently fared less well than Ulster. Wexford seems to have been its one county that sometimes rivalled northern fare. 'The peasantry of Carne, [Co. Wexford]', the incumbent wrote in 1819, 'live uncommonly well in general: their breakfast consists of either barley bread and milk, or oatmeal stirabout and milk; very rarely are potatoes used at this meal: at dinner they have bacon or pork twice a week, and butter or herrings for the remainder of it'.[12] In Tacumshame, Co. Wexford, too, 'flesh meat is served up twice a week at least, at all farmers' tables, of which the cottiers and labourers partake; and fish or butter with potatoes, on other days. Oatmeal is rarely used; barley bread so hard that a hatchet is

[1] Ibid., i, 1814, p. 156; ii, 1816, p. 3.
[2] Ibid., iii, 1819, p. 159.   [3] Ibid., p. 229.
[4] T. Reid, *Travels in Ireland in the Year 1822*, 1825, p. 178.
[5] H. D. Inglis, *A Journey throughout Ireland during . . . 1834*, 5th ed., 1838, p. 294.
[6] 1802, p. 59.   [7] Mason, op. cit. iii, *passim.*
[8] Ibid., pp. 120, 199; ii. 87.   [9] Ibid., i. 120; ii. 87.
[10] Ibid. i. 156, 257, 312; iii. 199.   [11] Ibid. i. 120, 157, 312.
[12] Ibid. iii. 127.

almost necessary to cut it through, is eaten for breakfast, and potatoes with milk closes the culinary work of the day.'[1] Not everywhere in Wexford was food so varied. At Adamstown and Newbarn the lower classes ate chiefly potatoes with a little oatmeal:[2] at Enniscorthy it was only on festival days that there were supplements to potatoes and milk.[3] From Kilkenny the reports are all of potatoes and milk as practically the sole supports of the poorer classes.[4] In Meath, it was reported that potatoes made up three-quarters of the food of the mass of the people; oatmeal and churned milk were sometimes added; butchers' meat was a rare delicacy.[5] And so for Leinster the reports go on: potatoes and milk the staples, oats far from negligible, and only occasionally the addition of butter, eggs, or meat.

In Cork and Waterford potatoes were, perhaps, of even greater consequence than in Leinster: oatmeal is rarely heard of. For the whole year, according to Townsend's *Cork*, potatoes were the principal food of the poor: sometimes they had nothing to add to them, though the better sort had some condiment, salted fish or boiled seaweed near the coast, and inland some form of liquid milk.[6] When the peasant was not fortunate enough to possess a cow his diet suffered, though sometimes he was able to make do with ewe's milk.[7] In Stradbally, Co. Waterford, when fish were plentiful they supplemented the monotony of milk and potatoes.[8] In Drumcannon, Co. Waterford, the very poor had only potatoes, others had some oatmeal and cockles.[9] In the south-east of Ireland, according to Wilde, the people had a variety of 'kitchen': sometimes they used 'the milk of the cow of the roost', a flavouring made from eggs and water, sometimes onions or cabbage or lard through which a leek or a potato-onion had been allowed to grow, sometimes 'stags' (potatoes, that is, of the previous year's crop sweetened by frost), sometimes merely the head of a herring. The 'kitchen', with salt, was placed in the middle of the skib of potatoes, the members of the family gathered round and each, after skinning the potato with the thumb-nail, dipped it in the saucer of flavouring.[10]

---

[1] W. S. Mason, op. cit. iii. 410.   [2] Ibid. i. 4.   [3] Ibid., p. 350.
[4] Ibid. i. 366; iii. 243, 621.   [5] McCulloch, 1839, op. cit. i. 376.
[6] Op. cit., pp. 88, 221.   [7] Ibid., p. 237, and Mason, iii. 469.
[8] Ibid., p. 383.   [9] Ibid. i. 225.
[10] W. R. Wilde, 'The Food of the Irish', pt. i, in *Dublin University Magazine*, vol. xlii, Jan.–June 1854, no. ccliv, 127–8.

Along the west coast food seems to have been much as it was throughout Leinster and Munster. In bad years people in the west, even more than elsewhere, were driven to desperate expedients—in Sligo, to steal for food the seaweed strewn on the fields as fertilizer, around Tralee to dig up the potatoes recently sown, in the Aran islands to eat seaweed and limpets, in Mayo to boil and eat wild rape;[1] sometimes, throughout the country, people ate nettles and wild mustard.[2] In odd places the medieval custom of bleeding cattle in summer, and preserving the blood in cakes for winter food lingered on.[3] But, in general, potatoes were the standby. The northern tip of Donegal fared as well as the bulk of Ulster; oatmeal porridge, eggs, milk, bread, butter, and fish are all mentioned as general,[4] but elsewhere in the county people could not always count even on milk to go with their potatoes: sometimes they had to make do with salt or pepper-water as flavourings.[5] In Kilmactige, Co. Sligo, meat was available only at festivals: when potatoes were plentiful people had them three times a day; in the summer, the more fortunate peasants having saved part of their oats from the landlord's rent, were able to supplement dwindling stocks of potatoes with oaten bread or gruel.[6] Throughout Sligo the food was 'chiefly, almost entirely potatoes, with some oaten bread, flummery [made from wheat-flour or oatmeal], milk, eggs, butter, but mostly fresh or dried herrings and other sea-fish'.[7] At Kilrush, Co. Clare, buttermilk, eggs, and fish went with the potatoes.[8] In one barony of Mayo—and there were small variations in dietary throughout the county—the common food was 'potatoes, a little oaten bread, milk, butter, herrings, and, on two or three grand festival days in the year, some bits of flesh meat'.[9]

[1] W. Bennett, *Narrative of a Recent Journey of Six Weeks in Ireland*, 1847, p. 72; *Rep. S.C. State of Disease, Reports from Committees*, 1819, viii. 384; T. C. Foster, *Letters on the Condition of the People of Ireland*, London, 1846, p. 111; *Rep. Devon Com.*, 1845, op. cit. xx. 392.

[2] F. Rogan, *Observations on the Condition of the Middle and Lower Classes in the North of Ireland*, 1819, p. 12.

[3] Wakefield, 1812, op. cit. ii. 736.

[4] Mason, op. cit. i. 183; ii. 156.

[5] Foster, 1846, op. cit., p. 105.

[6] Mason, op. cit. ii. 452.

[7] J. M'Parlan, *Statistical Survey of the County of Sligo*, Dublin, 1802, p. 71.

[8] Mason, op. cit. ii. 452.

[9] J. M'Parlan, *Statistical Survey of the County of Mayo*, Dublin, 1802, pp. 86–90.

IV. *The Abundance of the Potato*

Could the peasant's family count on getting its fill of potatoes? Plainly, a community dependent upon one staple article of food is in a precarious position, and peculiarly so when that staple is the potato. The yield of the potato probably varies more widely from year to year than that of grain crops,[1] yet, if failure is imminent, the cultivator cannot detect it in time to plant any substitute. That the potato has great bulk in relation to its nutriment, that it is readily bruised and, in conveyance, sometimes develops dry-rot,[2] all make it difficult to transport, with the result that local deficiencies can cause serious hardship. That it cannot normally be stored for more than twelve months, and that many varieties will not keep for a full year, mean, both that the surplus of good harvests cannot be used to insure against deficiency, and that there is a tendency towards an annually recurring shortage before the new crop is lifted. A potato economy, too, is inherently likely to be a subsistence economy: the bulk of potatoes a family requires is one guarantee of this, another is the low position of the root on the hierarchy of desirable foodstuffs. With a peasantry unaccustomed to buy its foodstuffs a distributive apparatus has to be improvised to deal with what alternative foods charity or commercial enterprise may provide in times of scarcity: 'if the labourer's food of Ireland fail, or become scarce, he *dies*, or is half famished; because the barbarous custom of making the potato the *labour coin* of the country, deprives him of both food and money together.'[3]

[1] See Wakefield, op. cit. ii. 726; 'The Irish Crisis', in *Edinburgh Review*, op. cit., and McCulloch, op. cit., 1854, p. 443. Dr. Salaman, however, in a letter, tells me he is inclined to think that the yield of the potato is more stable from year to year than that of grain crops.

[2] Salaman, 1945, op. cit., p. 17.

[3] J. W. Rogers, *The Potato Truck System of Ireland* . . . , 2nd ed., 1847, pp. 6–7. Rogers illustrates his point by a quotation from T. C. Foster's *Letters on the Condition of the People of Ireland* (1846, p. 314)—though the quotation seems to comment as vividly on the morals of Irish pawnbrokers as on the ignorance of their customers. 'In Galway', says Foster, 'I was assured that so little do people know the commercial value of money they are constantly in the habit of pawning it. I was so incredulous of this that the gentleman who informed me asked me to go with him to any pawnbrokers to assure myself of the fact; and I went with him and another gentleman to a pawnbroker's shop kept by Mr. Murray in Galway. On asking the question the shopman said it was quite a common thing to have money pawned; and he produced a drawer containing a £10 Bank of Ireland note pawned six months ago for 10/-; a 30/- Bank of Ireland note pawned for 1/-; a £1 Provincial Bank note pawned for 6/-; and a guinea in gold, of the reign of George III, pawned for 15/- two months ago.'

The problem is aggravated because the simple equipment needed to prepare the potato—merely a fire and a pot—leaves the potato-eating community ill-equipped to make use of what grain it can acquire in bad years, and because the effect of the bulky potato in distending the stomach may make alternative foodstuffs less readily assimilated.

It may well have been something more than a reluctance to discard familiar foodstuffs that drove English working-men in the first half of the nineteenth century to dread that the Irish immigrants should bring a potato standard of living with them. Long before the Great Famine made the bold, classic demonstration of the insecurity of a potato economy, Irish experience had shown the major sources of insecurity. Wakefield pointed both to the great variations in the yield of the potato in good years and bad, and to the fact that failure appeared too late for the farmer to offset it by planting other crops.[1] Beaumont showed the dangers arising from the difficulty of transporting or storing the potato.[2] The *Edinburgh Review*, in 1848, examining the background to the Famine, said that in the past severe scarcity had often prevailed only fifty miles from districts in which there were potatoes in abundance.[3] It was clear from the experience of the west during the potato failure of 1823 that the peasantry suffered as much from not being accustomed to go to market for its foodstuffs or from not possessing purchasing power, as from actual shortage. A witness told the Select Committee of 1823 that, though the potato had failed, he had never known it much cheaper. In Mayo, one of the centres of distress, 'the granaries were stored'. 'There was no price for corn. . . . In short, there was plenty for every one; there was no deficiency of anything, but the means of buying.'[4] (A later answer qualified this last remark in so far as it applied to potatoes.) Referring to the export of grain from ports within the distressed districts—exports 'infinitely exceeding the imports'— the Report of the Committee said these districts 'presented the remarkable example of possessing a surplus of food, whilst the inhabitants were suffering from actual want'.[5] Before the Famine, literary comment showed a widespread awareness of the

[1] Wakefield, 1812, op. cit. ii. 726.
[2] G. de Beaumont, *L'Irelande Sociale, Politique et religieuse*, Paris, 1839, p. 376.
[3] 'The Irish Crisis', in *Ed. Rev.*, Jan. 1848, lxxxvii. 234.
[4] *Rep. S.C. E.P.I.*, 1823, op. cit. vi. 380-1.
[5] Ibid., pp. 334-5.

precariousness of a potato economy: nonetheless, for about eighty years centring on 1780 (when the pace of population-increase accelerated) surprisingly few of the risks materialized.

It is not easy, for these eighty years, to find contemporary accounts of deficiencies in the supply of potatoes. Disasters are often well documented, and this rarity of comment, in itself, gives some foundation to the theory that a 'gap in the famines' was, in fact, a cause of population-increase. Our starting-point, the first great disaster which Ireland suffered from a deficiency of potatoes, is well defined. The famine of 1740 and the following year was the result, not of a poor yield of potatoes, but of the damage done to the crop, either before it was dug, or when it was stored, by an early, severe, and prolonged frost. The shortage of food was aggravated by the difficulty of getting corn ground while the rivers were frozen. The winter and spring were seasons of drought, and the famine, accompanied by 'bloody flux' and fever, continued through 1741. Estimates of the mortality in the disaster, though they seem to be little better than random guesses, vary from Maurice O'Connell's figure of 80,000 to the alternative figures of 200,000 and 400,000 given by the author of *The Groans of Ireland*.[1]

The most tempting guide to the history of the potato in the following century is Sir William Wilde who, both in the 1851 Census and in a paper published over his own name, has given a lengthy list of crop failures, a list considerably fuller than any it has been possible to compile from alternative sources. The first deficiency he records after 1741 is in 1765. A series of unusually wet seasons, he says, preceded this year, which was memorable for the quantity of rain which fell in its early months and for the excessive drought of its summer. As a result the 'potatoes failed; they were scarce and small'. In 1770 there was another 'failure' attributed to curl. In 1795 the weather was 'uncommonly severe, the spring cold and late, the summer suffocatingly hot, damp, and rainy, while south winds were prevalent. There was disease among vegetables, especially potatoes and cabbages.' In 1800 'there was a partial failure of the potato owing to excessive drought'. In the following year there was a 'very general potato failure, attributed

---

[1] M. O'Connell, *Observationes Medicales*, quoted in 1851 Census, op. cit., p. 395; *The Groans of Ireland*, Dublin, 1741, p. 4; J. O'Rourke, 1875, op. cit., pp. 13–24.; J. Rutty, *Chronological History . . . of the prevailing Diseases in Dublin*, 1770, pp. 82–6; 1851 Census, op. cit., pp. 392–6.

to obstructed vegetation, while the sets were yet in the ground'. In 1807, a severe November frost destroyed nearly half of the crop. Two years later the curl was again evident, 'though not to such an extent as to deserve the name of a failure'. In 1811 excessive rain in the spring and early summer led to a partial failure. In 1816 the spring was unusually backward, the summer and autumn were late, and throughout the year there was more than average rain: 'the potato again failed very generally throughout the kingdom.' In 1817 the crop was 'very deficient'. In 1821, May and June were dry, cold, and frosty, while the autumn was unusually moist: in the wet and low-lying districts of the western seaboard the potato soured and rotted in the ground. In 1825 the seasons were mild, yet there was a 'partial failure of the potato crop, as may be instanced by the rise in prices'. In 1829, especially in August, the crop was beaten by heavy rains and severe storms, 'and a great quantity of the potatoes was lost'. In 1830 violent storms and heavy rains brought another failure to the west, especially along the coast in Mayo, Galway, and Donegal. In 1832 and for several years following 'an unmistakable epidemic attacked the potato in spring throughout Ireland': in 1833 the disease presented the appearance of curl, and likewise attacked the tubers in the pits. In 1834 a failure of early-planted potatoes, discovered in the spring, was, to a certain extent, remedied. In the following years Wilde frequently found rain the cause of a deficient yield: in 1836 it led to 'partial failure . . . in several parts'; in 1839 to 'unmistakable failure'; in 1841 to a partial destruction, especially in the south; in 1842 it 'injured' the crop. In 1844 partial failure preceded the catastrophe of the following year.[1]

It would be legitimate on Wilde's evidence to divide the century after the destruction of the potato in 1741 into an initial period of some seventy years in which failures were, on the whole, infrequent, and a second period of thirty years in which bad years were almost the rule. For the seventy years before 1815 Wilde records one occasion on which nearly half of the crop was destroyed, three 'failures' and four partial failures.[2] In the following thirty years he

[1] 1851 Census, *Reports from Commissioners*, 1856, xxix. 502–6, and W. R. Wilde, 'The Introduction and Time of general Use of the Potato in Ireland', *Proc. R.I. Academy*, 1853–7, vi. 363–7.

[2] In years when the crop was only slightly deficient it is probable that the peasant or labourer suffered little. A normal crop meant an abundance of potatoes, both for his family and for his stock, and it is unlikely that in lean years

lists four major and eleven partial failures—in all as many bad years as good. We are encouraged to distinguish these two periods by other evidence—and lack of evidence. The usefulness of Wilde's work is diminished both by his reticence on the sources from which he derived his information and by his omission, in many cases, of any indication of the location of a particular failure. No accounts have come to light, save for the years 1800 and 1801, of serious deficiencies in the first seventy years: nor, for these years, with the added exception of 1771, are there records of fever epidemics on the scale that characteristically accompanied the later potato failures. There is, on the other hand, a mass of evidence bearing out Wilde's description of recurring and major deficiencies in the yield of the potato after 1815.[1]

A good crop of potatoes was of critical importance to the survival of the pattern of rural life in Ireland. There was a double bond of dependence: it was the potato which made up the great bulk of the food of the people, and, by and large, it was the commanding obligation of securing the privilege of planting potatoes that determined the nature of other agricultural activities. But to bind the fortunes of a people to the fortunes of the potato was to court inevitable disaster. It is remarkable, but apparently true, that during eighty years of increasing dependence on the potato, even the rumblings of disaster were seldom heard.[2] The records, and the gaps in the records, give us no reason to doubt the accuracy of Arthur Young's comments on the great abundance of food enjoyed by the Irish at the time of his tour. Nor would his words lose their force if applied as a general commentary on the years from 1742 to 1815.

There is one circumstance, he said (referring to the potato diet of the

it was the family that bore the brunt of the shortage. The family's normal allowance, moreover, would seem to have permitted some temporary scaling down of consumption without seriously endangering health. (See below, pp. 153–6.)

[1] Failures are well documented, at least for the years 1816, 1821, 1830, 1835–7, 1839, and for the years immediately preceding the Great Famine: see *Rep. S.C. S.P.I.*, 1830, op. cit., p. 13; *First Report from the Select Committee on the State of Disease . . . in Ireland, Reports from Committees*, 1819, viii; 'The Irish Crisis', *Ed. Rev.*, Jan. 1848, lxxxvii. 235 ff.; J. O'Rourke, 1875, op. cit., pp. 30 ff.; T. C. Foster, 1846, op. cit., p. 222.

[2] This conclusion is at variance with Professor O'Brien's findings. He says 'the truth is that, throughout the whole of the eighteenth and the first half of the nineteenth centuries, Ireland had been living on the very border of famine, and that the border was not unfrequently crossed'. (*Economic History of Ireland from the Union to the Famine*, 1921, p. 223.)

Irish), which must ever recommend it, they have a belly-full, and that let me add is more than the superfluities of an Englishman leaves to his family. . . . I will not assert that potatoes are a better food than bread and cheese; but I have no doubt of a belly-full of the one being much better than half a belly-full of the other. . . . If anyone doubts the comparative plenty which attends the board of a poor native of England and Ireland, let him attend to their meals: the sparingness with which our labourer eats his bread and cheese is well known; mark the Irishman's potatoe bowl placed on the floor, the whole family upon their hams around it, devouring a quantity almost incredible, the beggar seating himself to it with a hearty welcome, the pig taking his share as readily as the wife, the cocks, hens, turkies, geese, the cur, the cat, and perhaps the cow—and all partaking of the same dish. No man can often have been a witness of it without being convinced of the plenty, and I will add the chearfulness that attends it.[1]

This conclusion—that for the first forty years of rapid population-increase it was only the isolated, untypical Irishman who had serious cause to worry lest his family should not get all the potatoes it required—is amply substantiated by records of the amount of potatoes actually eaten by the individual person or family. The earliest in a series of such estimates, and, apparently, the one based on more records and more widely distributed records than any of the others, is Young's own. In his tour he collected seven[2] accounts from six counties of the quantity of potatoes single families consumed weekly. The heaviest daily consumption was at Derry where a family of 5 required 80 pounds, the lightest near the Giant's Causeway where 6 people made do with 35 pounds: at Cullen, Co. Louth, 6 people used 80 pounds, and in the other examples, 4 families, each with 6 members, consumed 40 pounds. Making allowance for the smaller consumption of women and young children it would seem that to regard each of these families as equivalent in dietetic requirements to four adult men would tend rather to over-rate than under-rate their food requirements, and, therefore, to give a figure for average daily consumption somewhat lower than Young's figure would warrant. On this assumption we arrive at the conclusion from his data that the

[1] Young, 1780, op. cit. ii. 118–19.
[2] Young gives an eighth, from Shaen Castle, Co. Antrim, where in a week 6 people ate 30 pounds of potatoes and nearly 3 pounds of oatmeal. He takes this into account when arriving at his figure for average consumption, but as in doing so he uses an apparently arbitrary conversion-factor—that 20 pounds of meal are the 'equivalent' of 70 pounds of potatoes—it is here neglected.

adult man's daily intake of potatoes was over $8\frac{1}{2}$ pounds. The bulk of food that this figure represents is impressive, but its modesty is more conspicuous when it takes its place in the series of comparable estimates for the following seventy years. Either, the series of figures suggests, Young appreciably under-estimated the true position, or, between his time and the 1830s, the average consumption increased (possibly, though by no means certainly, because the potato was becoming more exclusively the Irishman's foodstuff). Young's figure is only a good third of one given by Dr. Doyle in 1830. Doyle had two opinions on the matter in his evidence before the 1830 Committee. In reply to the question, 'How many pounds of potatoes will sustain a man for 24 hours?' he said, 'I think in 24 hours a labouring man will require at least three half stones of potatoes, that is 21 pounds.'[1] Later he said that 'for the maintenance of a man and of his wife and children a barrel a week is necessary'.[2] With 280 pounds to a barrel, and assuming again family consumption to be equivalent to that of four adult men, we arrive at the more credible figure of 10 pounds a day—a figure which the evidence of two of Doyle's fellow witnesses would suggest to be on the low side. Major-General Richard Burke, who lived in Limerick city, thought that 14 pounds a day would be an ample allowance for an able-bodied man.[3] The Rev. Edward Chichester, the incumbent of Kilmore, Co. Armagh, said that a family of 6 would consume about 42 pounds a day :[4] again assuming this to equal the consumption of 4 adult men we get an average daily intake of $10\frac{1}{2}$ pounds. Young's figure, then, of $8\frac{1}{2}$ pounds, may well have to be scaled upwards before being applied to the half-century after the *Tour*. There is insufficient evidence before, and a substantial amount after 1830 supporting this conclusion. Townsend said of one barony of Co. Cork, where people lived almost exclusively on potatoes, that the average house would consume about 8 tons a year.[5] Again assuming a household with food requirements equal to those of four adult men, we arrive at a

---

[1] *Report S.C. S.P.I.*, 1830, op. cit., q. 4428. The Committee, apparently, had understandable doubts about the accuracy of Doyle's reply and asked him, 'Are those 21 pounds for the consumption of one individual?' He replied 'Yes; unless the potatoes are of the very best quality; because a man will eat of them three times a day, and he will eat at each time very nearly half a stone; there is a vast deal of offal, and the food itself is not solid.' (q. 4430.)

[2] Ibid., q. 4433.   [3] Ibid., q. 5216.   [4] Ibid., q. 5676.
[5] H. Townsend, 1810, op. cit., p. 229.

daily consumption of 12 pounds per man—providing (and the context is not clear on the point) that Townsend is including only the human members of the household, and not the livestock with which they may have shared a building. Andrews, in the methodical essay which was so highly commended by the Royal Dublin Society, estimated that a working man in good health consumed 9 pounds of potatoes a day.[1] Inquiries into Irish social conditions stimulated by the catastrophe of the Famine give us three further estimates. Jasper Rogers, a civil engineer employed by the Relief Committee, said that 'the average quantity of potatoes an adult peasant labourer consumes in the day is about ten pounds—his meal being usually a quarter of a stone each at breakfast, dinner, and supper'.[2] *The Times* Commissioner 'was assured that eight pounds of potatoes per day is but a *small allowance* for a labouring man'.[3] The authority of the *Edinburgh Review* supports a larger estimate—one of at least 14 pounds: it said that a hundredweight of potatoes would not last a man more than eight days.[4] Finally, Sir William Wilde, the Census Commissioner and early historian of the potato in Ireland, said that 'nearly a stone of the root was taken into the stomach of the Irish labourer per diem'.[5]

Our data, then, in arriving at an estimate of the Irishman's daily potato-consumption begin with Young's widely, and apparently firmly, based 8½ pounds for the 1770s; then there are Townsend's doubtful 12 for 1810, Doyle's wild 21 for 1830, dragged down towards reality by his own alternative figure of 10, and by his fellow witnesses' 14 and 10½; then, for 1835 we have Andrews's careful and authoritatively commended 9 pounds, and for the forties Rogers's 10, Foster's conservative 8, Wilde's well-informed 'nearly a stone', and the *Edinburgh Review*'s seemingly high 14, but a 14 which in so competent an article cannot be neglected. Perhaps if we take 10 pounds a day as the average potato-consumption of the adult man from the 1780s to the Famine we shall approach the real position as closely as our information permits:[6] it is

[1] W. G. Andrews, 'An Essay on . . . the Potato', in *Prize Essays on the Potato*, Dublin, Royal Dublin Society, p. 3.

[2] J. W. Rogers, *Facts for the Kind-Hearted of England!*, 1847, p. 31.

[3] T. C. Foster, 1846, op. cit., p. 75. Original italics.

[4] 'The Irish Crisis', *Ed. Rev.*, Jan. 1848, lxxxvii. 234.

[5] Wilde, 'The Food of the Irish', op. cit., xlii, Jan.–June 1854, no. ccliv, p. 131.

[6] When this was written I had not seen what is undoubtedly the fullest source of evidence on the Irishman's daily consumption of potatoes—that collected by the Poor Inquiry Commission. Up and down the country peasants and others

evident, however, that any such figure acquires its convenience at the cost of neglecting both any tendency there was for consumption per head to increase, and the undoubtedly wide regional variations.

There is very little material to guide us in estimating the quantity of milk the Irishman normally had to supplement his potatoes: doubtless it was an amount that varied regionally, seasonally, and according to whether a family's possessions included a cow—or a goat or a ewe. Milk was drunk in various forms—whole, skimmed, or as buttermilk, sweet or sour. The general importance of butter as a cash-crop would suggest that skimmed milk and buttermilk, at least, were freely available for much of the year to many an Irish family: it is difficult to believe, that much as the Irishman cherished his pig, he gave it milk which his own family wished to drink. Young thought there was more milk drunk in Ireland than in England and he warmly approved the practice. He admitted that the Irishman's cow might be ill-fed,

but ill-fed as it is it is better than the no-cow of the Englishman; the children of the Irish cabin are nourished with milk, which, small as the quantity may be, is far preferable to the beer or vile tea which is the beverage of the English infant, for nowhere but in towns is milk to be bought. . . . Generally speaking the Irish have a fair belly-full of potatoes, and they have milk the greatest part of the year.[1]

A number of references already quoted show that abundance was by no means always the rule: at times there was no milk at all for the more unfortunate families. Nonetheless, most writers referring to the subject imply that milk was not illiberally available: certainly the low value put upon it by the country community isolated from urban markets and the considerable quantities drunk to-day in remote parts of Ireland tend to confirm this. Amongst the few

gave their opinion on the quantity of potatoes a man required each day. 'A stone of potatoes', a Down peasant said, 'is little enough for a man in a day, and he'd want something with it to work upon.' ' "A labouring man", said another witness, "will consume a stone of potatoes in a day". "Ay", said M'Crome, "and he'd be hard set to do on it." ' (*Report of the Poor Inquiry Commission*, Appendix H, pt. ii, *Reports from Commissioners*, 1836, xxxiv. 692.) Bicheno, a member of the Commission, in the personal report he prepared for his colleagues, summed up the evidence on this point. 'A labourer, with a wife and three or four young children', he said, 'is stated to require daily, upon an average of the quantities mentioned by the different witnesses, three stone of potatoes to keep them in health and strength, varying a little according to the kind and the season of the year.' (Ibid., p. 667.) Taking the family's requirements as equivalent to those of four adult men we have further confirmation of the validity of the figure of 10 pounds which we have adopted.   [1] Young, op. cit., ii. 22.

early nineteenth-century records of milk-consumption that are available are the daily allowance of one pint at Belfast and Down-patrick jails in the twenties,[1] an amount which, as with jail diets in other respects, would seem to approach more closely the normal consumption of the urban rather than of the rural poor. That it under-estimates rural consumption is suggested by Andrews who, in making his calculations of the number of bread-eaters or potato-eaters a given area of land would support, allowed three pints of sweet milk per day with potatoes and 4 pints with wheaten bread.[2] Again we are guessing, but to take the Irishman's daily milk-consumption at one pint is to guess conservatively.

V. The Adequacy of the Irishman's Diet

If he had his 10 pounds a day there is little doubt that the Irish-man had his fill of potatoes. But how adequate nutritionally was a diet whose major and unvarying constituent was this great bulk of potatoes, supplemented usually by milk and, locally, modestly and often precariously by some meat, fish, eggs, and so forth? What, to focus attention on our major problem, was the bearing of the diet of the Irish upon the rapid increase in their numbers? Was their food sufficiently abundant and diverse to allow a higher survival-rate than in earlier Ireland, or in, say, contemporary England? Was it such as to cause any movement in fecundity or fertility that would help us to explain the population-increase?

These are not problems on which contemporary comment can give us any final guidance. Contemporaries, like their successors, were prejudiced both by custom and palate in assessing the relative values of foodstuffs, but, unlike them, they had no adequate science of nutrition to point to an objective assessment of the value of what they ate. Nonetheless, they showed no reluctance to give their views on the dietetic quality of the potato. Eminent opinion was divided. Adam Smith thought it a satisfactory food-stuff. 'No food', he said, 'can afford a more decisive proof of its nourishing quality, or of its being peculiarly suitable to the health of the human constitution.'[3] His opinion was heartily endorsed by Arthur Young who had heard the potato 'stigmatized as being unhealthy, and not sufficiently nourishing for the support of hard labour; but this opinion is very amazing in a country, many of

[1] Reid, 1823, op. cit., pp. 178–86.   [2] Andrews, 1835, loc. cit., p. 3.
[3] *Wealth of Nations*, 1812, i. 251.

whose poor people are as athletic in their form, as robust, and as capable of enduring labour as any on earth. . . . When I see the people of a country, in spite of political oppression, with well formed vigorous bodies, and their cottages swarming with children; when I see their men athletic, and their women beautiful, I know not how to believe them subsisting on an unwholesome food.'[1] Wakefield was much less happy about the potato: he quoted several writers who described its harmful effect in parts of Scotland, where it was held responsible for 'despepsia, fluxes, and dropsy in the belly'.[2] Doyle shared his uneasiness.[3] But it was left to Cobbett to provide the most thoroughgoing denunciation of the potato: even without poor rates, he wrote from Cork City in 1834, the people of Ireland 'never could have been brought to this pass without the ever-damned *potatoes*! People *CAN* keep life in them by means of this nasty, filthy, *hog-feed*; and the tyrants make them do it, and have thus reduced them to the state of hogs, and worse than that of hogs. . . . I will *never again give constant employment to any man* in whose garden I shall see potatoes planted . . . it is both my pleasure and my duty to discourage in every way that I can the cultivation of this damned root, being convinced that it has done more harm to mankind than the sword and the pestilence united.'[4]

Stomach and bowel complaints—dysentery, dyspepsia, flatulence, and fluxes—seem to have been common in Ireland,[5] and may well have been caused, or aggravated by an ill-chosen diet. The sheer bulk of the potatoes eaten and the resulting distension of the digestive organs may have tended towards pathological conditions. The belief, too, that the potato when only partially softened was more lasting than when properly boiled led to insufficient cooking and, perhaps, to digestive trouble.[6] Townsend made the plausible

[1] Young, 1780, op. cit. ii. 116.
[2] Wakefield, 1812, op. cit. ii. 716.
[3] *Rep. S.C. S.P.I.*, 1830, op. cit., q. 4533.
[4] 'Letters of William Cobbett to Charles Marshall,' in *Rural Rides,* ed. G. D. H. and M. Cole, 1930, iii. 899–900.
[5] See, for instance, J. Wiggins, *The 'Monster' Misery of Ireland*, 1844, p. 50, and Mason, op. cit. ii, 1816, pp. 247, 286, 453.
[6] F. Page, *Observations on the State of the indigent Poor in Ireland*, 1830, pp. 10–11, quoting *Report of Board of Health*, pp. 22–3. According to Sir William Wilde, 'the cabin-boiled potato was dressed in two ways: with or without the *bone*, or the *moon*, as it is universally called by the genuine Irish'. Wilde explains that when a half-boiled potato is cut, the sections exhibit a central disk, with a halo round it like the moon. 'In the latter form, the potato was done to the heart, equally mealy throughout, and bursting its skin with fatness. This was the supper

case that while the potato agreed with people when they were in health, it was an improper diet during many disorders of the stomach and bowels.[1] Several advocates of the potato held that it had the property, significant to population history if correct, of stimulating milk-yield in nursing mothers as well as in livestock. Lord Dundonald found that cows fed on potatoes gave 'a much *larger quantity of milk*, the milk *richer*, yielding more and better cream, than the milk of cows fed on cabbages or turnips'.[2] Richardson agreed that a potato diet increased the quantity, but thought it lowered the quality of a cow's milk.[3] Parmentier, the French champion of the potato, held that 'the property which of all others renders the Potatoe so valuable in the country, is, according to the testimony of the faculty of medicine at Paris, its improving the quality and encreasing the quantity of the milk of animals: it produced this effect on the nurses of the poor infants of the parish of St Roch'.[4] Infant mortality, too, Parmentier felt, was lowered by a potato diet which 'prevents many diseases to which children are subject, and by which great numbers are cut off, such as ulcers, diseases of the eyes, atrophy, etc.'[5]

Contemporary opinion does not take us far towards solving our problem of the nutritional adequacy of the Irishman's diet. What help can we get from recent assessments of a man's food-requirements and from analyses of the food-values of the potatoes and

when children and young persons were to partake of the meal; but when much work was to be done, or a long fast to be endured, the heart or central nucleus of the potato was allowed, by checking the boil at a particular period, to remain parboiled, hard, and waxy; and when the rest of the potato had been masticated in the usual manner, this hard lump, about the size of a small walnut, was bolted; and in this manner nearly a stone of the root was taken into the stomach of the Irish labourer per diem. Now, although this might be bad cookery, it was founded upon a certain knowledge of physiology. The stomach digested the well boiled farinaceous portion of the potato within the space of a few hours and that having been all disposed of, the half-boiled lumps remained behind, and a second digestion was commenced to assimilate this portion of food . . . which latter process lasted some hours longer, and thus the cravings of hunger were warded off for five or six hours after the original meal'. ('The Food of the Irish', in *Dublin University Magazine*, Jan.–June 1854, no. ccliv, xlii. 130–1.)

[1] Townsend, 1810, op. cit., p. 61.
[2] *Letters by the Earl of Dundonald on making Bread from Potatoes*, Edinburgh, 1791, p. 14.
[3] W. Richardson, 'Simple Measures by which the Recurrence of Famines may be prevented', in *The Pamphleteer*, 1816, no. xv, viii. 168.
[4] A. A. Parmentier, *Observations on such nutritive Vegetables . . .* , London, 1783, p. 15.
[5] Ibid.

milk that were so conspicuous on the Irishman's board? The Food and Nutrition Board of the National Research Council of the United States has published a table of 'Recommended Dietary Allowances' for adult men and women, graded according to their age and degree of activity, and for children and young persons for various age-groups up to twenty.[1] The Combined Food Board's publication *Food Consumption Levels* says that these allowances are recognized as liberal and that 'experience in the United Kingdom has shown that somewhat lower levels of intake of minerals and vitamins are compatible with a good general state of nutrition, although, doubtless, health could be improved if the full allowances were obtainable'.[2] The Board adopts the American figures for calories and protein in all cases, but scales down by 30 per cent. its recommendations for minerals and vitamins in the case of adult men and adult women (except for expectant and nursing mothers). Table 21 is designed to help us assess the adequacy, according to these standards, of the Irishman's diet in the years of rapid population-increase. The first line of the table shows the National Research Council's figures for the daily food requirements of the adult man engaged in moderate activity[3] as they are scaled down in accordance with the suggestion of the Combined Food Board. The second and third lines show, on the basis of a number of investigations of the chemical composition of potatoes and milk, the food-value of the 10 pounds of potatoes and the pint of milk which, our inquiries have shown, approximate the daily intake of the adult Irishman in the period under review.[4]

The table makes it clear that in the contemporary controversy over the adequacy of the Irishman's diet there was more justification for Young's commendation of the potato than for Cobbett's

[1] Quoted in Combined Food Board, *Food Consumption Levels*, H.M.S.O., 1944, p. 30.

[2] Ibid.

[3] Few of the sources of early-nineteenth-century Irish social history would justify a choice of the higher allowances recommended for the 'very active'.

[4] The table has been drawn up on the assumption that the potatoes eaten by the Irish a century and more ago, and the milk they drank, were similar in chemical composition to the samples more recently subjected to analysis. It would seem to be impossible to be certain that this was, in fact, the case. As far as the potato is concerned, I am told that if it keeps for any length of time its water-content cannot be unusually high, and that it is improbable that the relative proportions of the various solids present would have changed substantially, even over a considerable period.

TABLE 21

The Nutritional Adequacy of the Irishman's Diet

	Calories	Protein gm.	Calcium gm.	Iron mgm.	Vit. A International Units	Thiamin (Vit. B 1) mgm.	Riboflavin (Vit. G) mgm.	Niacin (Nicotinic acid) mgm.	Ascorbic acid (Vit. C) mgm.	Vit. D International Units[1]
Recommended by C.F.B.[2]	3,000	70	0·56	8·4	3,500	1·26	1·89	12·6	52·5	Probably 280[3]
Per 10 lb. potatoes[4,5]	3,459[6]	45[7]	1·92	21·34[8]	1,600[9]	5·76[10]	0·36–0·48[11]	22·67[12]	444–1,218[13]	Nil
Per pint fresh, whole milk[4,14]	393	19	0·71	0·41	797–3,983[15]	39·3[11]	0·59–1·77[11]	?[16]	171–1,650[17]	171–2,162[11,18]
Per 10 lb. potatoes and pint whole milk	3,852	64	2·63	21·75	3,990[19]	45·06	1·60[20]	22·67[21]	1,741[22]	280–1,764[23]

[1] Necessary only if not obtained from sunshine.

[2] Recommendation of the Food and Nutrition Board of the National Research Council of the United States of America modified according to the suggestions of the Combined Food Board Joint Committee, in *Food Consumption Levels*, H.M.S.O., 1944, p. 30. See above, p. 154.

[3] When not available from sunshine.

[4] Except where otherwise stated the analyses quoted of the composition of potatoes and milk are those given by R. A. McCance and E. M. Widdowson, *The Chemical Composition of Foods*, Medical Research Council, H.M.S.O., 1942.

[5] Except where otherwise stated the analyses quoted refer to potatoes boiled for thirty minutes, and peeled before boiling. The custom of the Irish was to peel their potatoes after boiling, and thereby, doubtless, they ensured a smaller loss in cooking.

[6] The experiments of McCance and Widdowson show that 10 pounds of potatoes contain 3,680 calories. The lesser figure given here takes into consideration the results of a series of experiments reported by H. C. Sherman, *Food Products*, 3rd ed., New York, 1933, p. 354, which show that, on the average, 94 per cent. of the carbohydrates of potatoes are assimilated.

[7] The figure of 64 gm. which McCance and Widdowson give scaled down to take account of the fact that 71 per cent. of the protein of potatoes is assimilated. (Sherman, 1933, op. cit., p. 354.)

[8] The figure of 22 mgm. given by McCance and Widdowson scaled down to make allowance for the fact that 97 per cent. of the iron in boiled potatoes is 'available'. (McCance and Widdowson, 1942, op. cit., p. 142.)

[9] Sherman, 1933, op. cit., p. 371. This is the content of 10 pounds of raw potatoes, but 'vitamin A values seem to be comparatively stable under ordinary cooking temperatures'. (p. 372.)

[10] B. Harrow, *Textbook of Biochemistry*, 3rd ed., Philadelphia, quoting U.S. Department of Agriculture, Publication 275. This is the average content of 10 pounds of raw potatoes.

[11] W. V. Thorpe, *Biochemistry for Medical Students*, London, 1938, pp. 400–1.

[12] W. G. Burton, *The Potato: a Survey of its History and of Factors influencing its Yield, Nutritive Value, and Storage*, 1948, p. 181. This figure is for potatoes boiled and eaten in their skin.

[13] L. J. Harris and M. Olliver, 'Vitamin Methods', in *Biochemical Journal*, 1942, xxxvi. 156. The figure given here makes allowance for the loss which the authors found took place in cooking.

[14] In the period with which we are concerned the Irishman frequently drank skimmed milk, not whole milk. A pint of skimmed milk contains 207 calories, 21 gm. of protein, 0·73 grm. of calcium, and 0·41 mgm. of iron (McCance and Widdowson, op. cit.). I have been unable to find accounts of the vitamin content of skimmed milk.

[15] Thorpe, 1938, op. cit., p. 400. Biological assay.

[16] I have been unable to find an analysis of the nicotinic acid content of milk.

[17] Thorpe, op. cit, gives the average ascorbic acid content of 10 pounds of raw potatoes as from 3,414 to 33,002 International Units. The International Unit is one-twentieth of a milligramme.

[18] In winter, 171–389; in summer 1,366–2,162.

[19] Average vitamin A content of milk.

[20] Average vitamin G content of milk and potatoes.

[21] Potatoes only: see note 16.

[22] Average vitamin C content of milk and potatoes.

[23] Winter and summer averages.

extravagant denunciation. If, in fact, the adult Irishman was able day by day to consume the 10 pounds of potatoes that a conservative interpretation of the available data suggested as probable, then, even if he took no additional food whatsoever, with nearly 3,500 calories he comfortably exceeded the allowance which the biochemist regards as desirable. In his potatoes alone there were available many times as much vitamin C as he required, more than four times as much vitamin B1, two or three times as much calcium and iron, and nearly twice as much niacin. With the pint of milk which we have argued was frequently, if not invariably, available, his intake of vitamins A and D was made adequate[1] and there remained only two deficiencies, one of 11 per cent. in vitamin G and one of 9 per cent. in protein. These deficiencies are not immoderate and it is doubtful if they were chronic: a daily cupful added to our conservative estimate of milk-consumption would have eliminated them altogether. If milk were scarce, the food-value of this additional third of a pint may often have been found in some of the other foodstuffs which supplemented potatoes and milk.

We can conclude that, except when the potato was deficient—and we have seen that there were few bad years during the first three or four decades of rapid population-increase—the Irishman was well nourished. Good nutrition tended to influence population history in two ways: it tended to lower the incidence of disease, and, by making provision for a family seem no problem, it tended to encourage earlier, and more fruitful, marriage.

VI. *The Potato and the Reclamation of Waste Land*

We are here concerned with only one aspect of the general contribution made by the reclamation of waste land to the growth of population. The potato was not a crop that would succeed only on a narrow range of soils: good yields could be won from land that had recently been 'mountain' or bog. One of the technical experts, asked to report to the Commissioners who, in 1810, examined the possibilities of reclaiming the bogs of Ireland, told them that potatoes 'have such an affinity (if the expression may be allowed) for Boggy soil, that farmers always prefer planting the

---

[1] Though, in general, the Irish countryman could doubtless obtain from sunshine the vitamin D he needed.

seed that has been raised on Bog to any other'.[1] Population in pre-Famine Ireland pressed hard upon cultivated land; the staple foodstuff could be produced on the unoccupied land that was so conspicuous a feature of the Irish landscape: it is not surprising that there was a spontaneous colonizing movement. The success, moreover, of what commercial reclamation there was, was partly dependent on the suitability of the potato as a first crop. The potato, then, played its part in facilitating the earlier marriage which we have pointed to as a leading cause of the increase in population, not only by allowing a couple to marry when they could secure the tiny holding that would yield their food if they ate potatoes, but also by allowing many of them to acquire this holding, not by persuading an existing occupier to subdivide, but by marking out a new patch in the limitless bog.

Early in the history of the potato in Ireland it was used as an instrument of colonization. Smith's *Kerry*, published in 1756, said that 'since the culture of the potatoes was known, which was not before the beginning of the last century, the herdsmen find out small dry spots to plant a sufficient quantity of those roots in for their sustenance, whereby considerable tracts of these mountains are grazed and inhabited, which could not be done if the herdsmen had only corn to subsist on'.[2] The Act of 1742 which made it legal for Roman Catholics to lease half an acre of arable and 50 acres of adjoining bog depended for its success on the readiness with which the tenant could get his living from potatoes grown on the bog.[3] Later, when population had begun to grow rapidly, a report of 1795 on the improvement of waste recommended the inclosure of waste by the cultivation of potatoes on lines very similar to the Irishman's much criticized lazy-bed. It showed, too, by a number of examples, that potatoes were, in fact, being successfully grown on bog. A Mr. Leslie 'reclaimed bogs by draining and then dunging for Potatoes; the crop 320 bushels per English acre; afterwards excellent pasture.' 'At Mercra, in Ireland, the greatest crops are gained from bogs; fifty bushels per acre more than from grass land. Much the best was of improving bogs; but they must have a little dung. Mr. Irwin, in Ireland, tried if

---

[1] *Second Report of the Commissioners . . . to enquire into the Nature and Extent of the several Bogs in Ireland, Reports, etc. (Ireland)*, 1810–11, vi. 592.

[2] p. 88. Quoted in C. Creighton, *History of Epidemics in Britain*, Cambridge, 1894, ii. 252.

[3] O'Rourke, 1875, op. cit., p. 43.

paring and burning would do to improve a boggy moory mountain. It answered greatly, and yielded the best potatoes in the country.'[1] Some years later a writer outlining *Simple Measures by which the Recurrence of Famines may be prevented*, was enthusiastic in his claims on behalf of the achievements and potentialities of the potato as a means of cultivating waste. He knew of no other crop that could, without great delay or expense, encroach upon coarse unbroken ground. Potatoes could be grown in the first year: there would be a better crop the following year, and thereafter the ground would be in the highest order for whatever crop its nature would allow it to produce. Without the aid of potatoes, cultivation in Ireland would never have been able to press upon the edges of the bogs, or advance up the side of the mountains. Within living memory, much of northern Ireland was covered with 'scroggs', ground never broken up by man and covered by woods long destroyed: 'nine tenths of these scroggs have disappeared in my own time, the ground once so occupied, and of little value, now under culture, undistinguishable from the rest of the arable; yet I venture to say that every acre of these scroggs was commenced with, and brought in by the potatoe. The thick coat of whins which clothed so many of our small hills, and particularly our steep *braes* . . . are vanishing rapidly from the face of our country, and exclusively by potatoe culture. Our *soft bogs* as well as our steep braes, are inaccessible to the plough, as is also our rocky ground: but a potato crop with a trifling addition to the expence can be had from all these, and after the second crop the soil is so completely mellowed, that grain can be put in by the spade alone, with little labour.'[2] Later in the century, when landlords were anxious to 'consolidate and clear', there is evidence that a number were able to dispose of occupying tenants by apportioning scraps of bog as potato-land.[3]

The potato, with comparable effect on population history to its facilitating reclamation, sometimes allowed farmers to dispense with fallow. It was reported to the Poor Inquiry Commission from Wicklow that 'a general increase in the sowing of potatoes, has

[1] *Report from the Select Committee appointed to take into Consideration the Means of promoting the Cultivation and Improvement of the Waste . . .* , 1795. *Reports from Committees of the House of Commons*, 1774–1802, ix. 214.

[2] Richardson, 1816, op. cit., pp. 179–80.

[3] *Poor Law Inquiry (Ireland)*, Appendix F, *Reports from Commissioners*, 1836, xxxiii. 88, 93. See below, Chapter VI, pp. 174–5.

almost entirely superseded fallow in this and most other districts'.[1] The more readily fallow could be dispensed with, the more willingly a father could agree to his son's settling on a fragment of the family holding and the smaller the holding the son could regard as sufficient to allow him to marry.

Our discussion of the history of the potato in Ireland shows that it was of quite fundamental importance in permitting and encouraging the rapid growth of population in the sixty or seventy years before the Famine. It permitted the growth of population because, in early eighteenth-century Ireland, population had been pressing on resources: any substantial expansion of population implied a parallel expansion of the means of subsistence, and in large measure it was in an abundance of potatoes that the increasing number of people found its sustenance. Statistical proof of the contention that population had been limited by resources—by, that is, the resources that the double exploitation of landlord and Government left for the subsistence of the people—is out of the question: proof—or support—is to be found only in the belief that births, of a number approaching the physical maximum, normally followed marriage, which was neither widely avoided nor unnaturally postponed, and that the social conditions enforced by political and economic exploitation were conducive to high mortality.

It is not difficult to see how the potato lifted the restraints to the growth of population. When people had been living largely on grain, the substitution of the potato allowed their land to support at least twice as many people as before: when, as with the Irish before their general dependence on the potato, pastoral products had bulked large in the popular dietary, at least a quadrupling of the density of population became possible. At the same time, land which to a pastoral or grain-producing community had been of next to no economic importance became capable of yielding satisfactory crops of potatoes, and of allowing, therefore, a further measure of population-increase.

If, as is argued in this chapter, the general acceptance by the Irish of the potato as their dominant foodstuff was a slow process reaching its culmination only towards the end of the second century after its introduction to the country in the late sixteenth century, the substitution of potatoes for the traditional foodstuffs is an

[1] Ibid., p. 108.

important lever in the mechanism which allowed population to increase with such explosive force in the half-dozen decades before the Famine. That it is not the entire mechanism is suggested by the fact that, as far as we know, there was no striking extension of the habit of potato-eating immediately before the 1780s. The substitution of potatoes had been proceeding piecemeal for a number of generations, yet, even though population had been pressing on resources, there had been no spectacular increase in its size. Perhaps, in part at least, the explanation is that as 'white meats' and grain were forsaken for potatoes, and as, therefore, the proportion of the peasant's land needed to produce his subsistence shrank, the proportion devoted to securing money (or produce) for rent and allied charges was inflated.

It was not only through the substitution of the potato for the traditional crops that its influence was felt in relaxing the limits to population growth. There is evidence that, in the fifty and more years before the Famine, the potato itself was undergoing a process of substitution. Increasingly the traditional varieties were losing ground before new and more prolific types, which allowed a further increase in the density of the population of the areas where they were grown.

Within the provinces, and from province to province, there was, of course, no uniformity in the extent to which potato-culture permitted the expansion of population. In Munster, for instance, where there it appears that the potato achieved its primacy in the peasant's dietary earlier than elsewhere, it would be legitimate to suppose that its demographic influence was partially spent by 1780, and that, accordingly, it shared more liberally with other agencies responsibility for increasing the means of subsistence. Similarly, in Ulster, where the potato never became so nearly the single food as elsewhere, it must be allotted a less prominent role.

The potato provided not only a prerequisite for the growth of population; it provided also a mechanism: it not only permitted, but encouraged increase. As potatoes were substituted for the traditional foodstuffs, a family's subsistence could be found from a diminished section of its holding. There tended to appear on every tenancy a margin of land that was needed neither to provide the peasant's subsistence, nor the landlord's customary rent. The tendency of landlordism was to force up rent until this margin had to be entirely assimilated with the section of the holding devoted to producing the crops that were disposed of to pay the rent. But in the closing decades of the eighteenth century circumstances developed under which the landlord's response to his desire for more rent was not merely to increase the payments exacted from his existing tenants. For reasons that we have examined elsewhere, higher rents were to be obtained from arable farmers, than from pasture farmers.[1] But there could be no simple swing by the mass of the peasants from pasture to arable farming: they probably lacked the skill, as they certainly lacked the capital to make a success of grain production on holdings of the size of those they had been occupying. The landlords, accordingly, if they were to tap the increasing profitability of grain-production, were obliged to set land in smaller tenancies: they were obliged to tolerate a larger population on their estates, even though this meant that the sector of their property devoted to the tenants' subsistence expanded at the expense of the sector devoted to securing the rent. Increasing dependence on the potato, then, in conjunction with the new emphasis on arable farming allowed subdivision. It allowed—and obliged—the peasant to break up his holding and give portions to his children. Always anxious, because of the degradation and hopelessness of their lives, to marry young, the children now had the opportunity of doing so. The potato, then, by helping to allow subdivision, tended towards a lowering of the age at marriage, and earlier marriage was followed inescapably by higher fertility.

The potato had a further, more direct, influence on population history. We have seen that for the first forty or so years of rapid population-increase an abundance of potatoes was the mainstay of a diet which probably approached nutritional adequacy more closely than did the contemporary—or, indeed, very often, the more recent—diet of the mass of the people of most other countries. We have seen that this tended to influence population history in two ways: it tended to prolong life by lowering the incidence of disease and it tended to encourage earlier marriage (and therefore higher fertility). What, in fact, were the relative contributions of the potato in this context to the reduction in mortality and the increase of fertility we can only guess. To give an accurate estimation we should want to know for how long a period before the 1780s the Irishman had been well nourished: the increasing use

---

[1] See above, Chapter IV, *passim*.

of the potato over a period of nearly two centuries and the absence, since 1741, of records of major food shortages suggest that the quickening in the rate of population growth did not coincide with a marked improvement in diet. On the other hand, we are able to explain, with some plausibility, how, throughout the period of rapid population-increase, high fertility went hand in hand with early marriage. Perhaps, then, the contribution made to the expansion of population by the nutritional excellence of the Irishman's diet was felt more by allowing the survival of an increasing number of children born, than by prolonging the lives of the number of people which would have existed, had fertility remained constant.

In the thirty years immediately preceding the Famine, with deficiencies in its yield becoming chronic, the potato obtrudes itself more starkly in the history of social conditions, but it assumes a more restrained role in the causation of the growth of population. It can no longer be argued that by lessening the incidence of disease it contributed to the prolongation of life: its failures, year after year, meant famines, widespread or localized, and fever joined hands with famine to raise mortality. Strengthening this depopulating tendency, there was the growing stream of emigrants, impelled, many of them, by the failure of their potatoes. Nonetheless, throughout the years of distress, population continued to grow: while failures of the potato heightened the despair that was the incentive to youthful marriage, they did not, with any effect, teach the dangers attending fruitful marriage in a potato economy.

VI

SUBDIVISION AND CONSOLIDATION

THE argument of Chapter III, that early marriage appears to have been the most influential factor tending to increase fertility, gives to the subdivision of holdings a leading place amongst the economic developments which reacted upon population history. Much of the impetus which the growth of population derived from dependence upon the potato and the spread of arable was felt indirectly through the division of farms: when a family lived on potatoes rather than on grain or pastoral products, when it turned pasture to tillage, it could more readily agree to live on less than its entire holding. For other reasons, too—and not least because of the rapidity of population growth—after the 1780s landlords and tenants were eager to see the number of tenancies multiply. As farms were divided, so sons and daughters, for long ready to marry as early as they could, found fewer obstacles to setting up homes of their own. The availability of land was the great determinant of age at marriage, and the more subdivision there was the more readily was land available.

There are, apparently, no statistics which allow us to mark the progress of subdivision throughout our period. We can, however, determine with some confidence the extent to which the movement had proceeded by the forties. Table 22, compiled from figures collected in the 1841 Census, shows the distribution of holdings of various sizes in the provinces. No account is taken at all of the doubtless considerable number of holdings of one acre or less.[1] In the whole of Ireland, if the figures are to be trusted, 45 per cent. of holdings did not exceed 5 acres and 81 per cent. did not exceed 15. These figures hide the more extreme subdivision of some areas. In Connaught fragmentation was most acute: of all holdings there above 1 acre 64 per cent. were not more than 5 acres; 93·5 per cent.

---

[1] A return of 1849—made, that is, when several years of famine had brought widespread abandonment and consolidation of tiny holdings—put the number of holdings of less than one acre at 7 per cent. of the total. (*Accounts and Papers*, 1849, xlix. 13.)

were not more than 15 acres. In Ulster, although, doubtless, its insistent contrasts with Connaught recur in the motivation of subdivision and in the lessons it pointed to, the process itself was pressed nearer the Connaught extreme than elsewhere: 43 per cent. of the holdings were not more than 5 acres, and 86 per cent. were not more than 15 acres. Munster and Leinster had a broadly

TABLE 22

Distribution of Holdings by size in the Rural Districts of the Provinces of Ireland in 1841*

	Total number of holdings above 1 acre	Size of holdings in acres							
		Above 1 to 5		Above 5 to 15		Above 15 to 30		Above 30	
		Number	Per cent.	Number	Per cent.	Number	Per cent.	Number	Per cent.
Leinster .	133,220	49,152	36·9	45,595	34·2	20,584	15·5	17,889	13·4
Munster .	162,386	57,028	35·1	61,320	37·8	27,481	16·9	16,557	10·2
Ulster .	234,499	100,817	43·0	98,992	42·2	25,099	10·7	9,591	4·1
Connaught	155,204	99,918	64·4	45,221	29·1	5,790	3·7	4,275	2·8
Ireland .	685,309	306,915	44·8	251,128	36·6	78,954	11·5	48,312	7·0

* Census of Ireland, 1841, *Reports from Commissioners*, 1843, xxiv. 454–5.

similar distribution of holdings: both had substantially more larger farms than Connaught or Ulster. In Munster 35 per cent. of the holdings were 5 acres or less; 73 per cent. were 15 acres or less: in Leinster the corresponding figures were 37 and 71. The pattern of the conclusions of these figures is confirmed by Table 23—which, for certain purposes, is the more valuable table as it does not grade holdings by size, irrespective of the quality of the land. It shows that for the whole of Ireland more than half of the holdings were valued at under £5. In Connaught 54 per cent. were valued at less than £4 and 84 per cent. at less than £8: in Leinster 44 per cent. were valued at less than £4 and 62 per cent. at less than £8. That Ulster's tiny holdings were less a mark of poverty than Connaught's is suggested by Ulster's better showing in the table of valuations: Ulster has, though only by a small margin, a smaller proportion of holdings valued at less than £4 than any other province.

What were the causes of the movement towards small holdings? When did it begin? To what extent was it offset before the Famine by a counter-movement towards the consolidation of farms?

Doubtless the strongest motive for subdivision was the growth of population itself and the desire, or willingness, of the farmer to provide for his children by endowing them with land. In Waterford, Wakefield was told that 'when the eldest daughter of a farmer marries, the father, instead of giving her a portion, divides his farm between himself and his son-in-law; the next daughter gets one half of the remainder, and this division and subdivision is continued as long as there are daughters to be disposed of. In regard

TABLE 23

Distribution of Holdings by Valuation in the Province of Ireland (exclusive of the Boroughs) on 1 January 1846*

| | Valuations | | | | | |
| | Under £4 | | At and above £4 but under £5 | | £5–6 | |
	Number	Per cent.	Number	Per cent.	Number	Per cent.
Leinster .	105,446	44·46	12,874	5·43	10,786	4·55
Munster .	112,991	43·56	16,153	6·23	13,552	5·22
Ulster .	146,711	41·67	29,980	8·52	24,424	6·94
Connaught .	128,613	58·68	20,920	9·54	14,435	6·59
Ireland .	493,761	46·24	79,927	7·48	63,197	5·92

| | £6–7 | | £7–8 | | £8 and over | | |
	Number	Per cent.	Number	Per cent.	Number	Per cent.	Total Number
Leinster .	9,625	4·06	7,672	3·23	90,777	38·27	237,180
Munster .	10,969	4·23	9,593	3·70	96,118	37·05	259,394
Ulster .	21,098	5·99	16,812	4·77	112,938	32·08	352,035
Connaught .	11,189	5·10	8,130	3·71	35,948	16·40	219,185
Ireland .	52,881	4·95	42,207	3·95	335,781	31·45	1,067,794

* *Accounts and Papers*, 1849, xlix. 498.

to the male children, they are turned out into the world, and left to shift for themselves as best they can.'[1] In Co. Cork 'the farmer, who has half a dozen sons, may, perhaps, for one or two of them find trades; the rest are provided for by an equal partition of his land. By such means, the farmers of this county are, for the most part, reduced to petty cottagers'.[2] That, after the 1780s the fragmentation of the parental holding was increasingly possible resulted partly from factors we have already discussed—the dependence on a foodstuff which allowed each family to get its subsistence

[1] Wakefield, 1812, op. cit. i. 280.
[2] Townsend, 1810, op. cit., pp. 80–1.

from a tiny area and the greater reliance upon tillage than upon pasture farming for producing the surplus sent to market to pay the rent. Other factors accelerated the process of subdivision, some of them influencing the tenants, others the landlords. The common law of inheritance, lingering on from the custom of gavel-kind was said to predispose the peasant to believe that all his children had the right to inherit equal parts of his land.[1] The practice in the linen manufacture for the workers to be part-manufacturers, part-agriculturalists was often pointed to as a cause of extensive subdivision in Ulster and other flax-working districts.[2] Throughout the country if tillage were to spread, the poverty of the tenants meant that holdings had to be small: the difficulty, too, of finding money for wage payments, tended towards the creation of the host of tiny patches in the form of which many labourers received their remuneration.

Landlords are commonly said to have been influenced by two motives when they encouraged subdivision: the prospect of a larger rent roll and the desire to enjoy political influence. 'A landlord, if he sees his tenant making money by dividing his farm, looks forward with anxious hope to the expiration of the lease, when he expects to enjoy the benefits of alienation, mud cabins, and tillage, instead of grass lands: he therefore favours rather than opposes the custom.'[3] The acute competition for land among peasant cultivators and their ability to drench their holdings with labour, led them to offer rents that would be wholly uneconomic to a larger farmer. This, coupled with the general eagerness of the landlord or his agent to order his estate so that a maximum of rent was promised, irrespective of other losses, undoubtedly gave a free rein to many a father anxious to provide for his children.

It is open to doubt whether the landlord's prospect of political gain from increasing the number of tenancies had an influence at all comparable with that of his prospect of financial gain. Certainly contemporary opinion very generally regarded the Act of 1793[4]

[1] Wakefield, op. cit. i. 251.

[2] McCulloch, 1839, op. cit. i. 386, 392. Wakefield, op. cit. i. 249. John Hancock in evidence before the Devon Commission, *Reports from Commissioners*, 1845, xix. 92, 55. In the published evidence taken before the Devon Commission each witness is given a number and his answers are numbered in a series of their own. In references here the witness's number precedes the number of the question and is italicized.

[3] Wakefield, op. cit. i. 285.

[4] 33 Geo. III, c. xxi.

which extended the franchise to Catholic forty-shilling freeholders as responsible for much of the later fragmentation of holdings.[1] The Government's patronage was guided by members of Parliament, who, landlords were said to argue, would remember those who controlled solid blocks of voters.[2] 'The 40/- freehold system', said the author of *Lachrymae Hiberniae*, 'means that if a tenant has a larger portion than 2–10 acres *he is called upon*, as soon as his sons attain the age of 21, to demise a portion of it to each, to make him a freeholder. Freeholders are brought by the driver to the registry: many express great reluctance at taking the oath, conscious that it is false.'[3] 'A very intelligent and active agriculturalist' in Co. Cork believed that 'parliamentary influence is very much looked to in all leases; consequently every proprietor has an army of freeholders.'[4] An incumbent in Londonderry, regretting the evils that followed excessive subdivision, marvelled 'that some landlords could be so blind to their own real interests, and so indifferent to the happiness and prosperity of their tenants, as to encourage this ruinous system, from miserable views of increasing their political influence'.[5]

For several reasons it is legitimate to doubt whether the forty-shilling franchise was as potent a cause of subdivision as was sometimes thought. A witness told the Select Committee of 1830 that, though there was no franchise on ecclesiastical land, it was as much, if not more, divided than land in lay hands.[6] It is a matter of doubt, too, whether Irish landlords, with conspicuous exceptions, valued political influence at all highly: the absentees were not characterized by any enthusiastic interest in Irish political affairs and many of the resident owners had alternative diversions. Electoral statistics confirm that there was little competitive zeal among landlords to send the greatest number of tenants to vote. There was published in 1829 a return of the number of electors who had polled at contested elections since 1805:[7] in seven counties

---

[1] The qualification for the franchise as far as the freeholder was concerned was the same in Ireland as in England: he had to have a forty-shilling interest for life. It was customary in Ireland, but not in England, to insert lives in all leases, and voters were, therefore, freely created in Ireland without being possessed of any property. See J. R. McCulloch, 1825, op. cit. p. 46.

[2] 'Resident Native', *Lachrymae Hiberniae*, Dublin, 1822, p. 5.

[3] Ibid., p. 5.   [4] Townsend, op. cit., pp. 461, 468.

[5] Mason, op. cit. i, 1814, p. 310.

[6] *Rep. S.C. S.P.I.*, 1830, op. cit., q. 5023.

[7] *Accounts and Papers*, 1829, xxii. 1–24.

there was no contested election at all in these twenty-two years: in eleven more there was only a single election. Nor does this return suggest that, in what elections there were, the landlords had the support—or opposition—of more than a tiny fraction of the number of freeholders on their estates. In 1806, thirteen years after the enfranchisement of the forty-shilling freeholders, elections were recorded for six counties: the average poll was under 3,000. For the twelve elections of 1826 the average was under 5,000. While, then, political influence may sometimes have been an incidental benefit of subdivision it is probable that there were comparatively few landlords for whom it was a more compelling motive than the prospect of financial gain.

The subdivision of holdings, begun before the wars with France, was stimulated during the war years by the extension of the acreage under grain, by high prices which allowed peasant farmers to offer high rents, and, to a certain extent, by the political value of a numerous tenantry. How general was subdivision in the years between war and Famine? Did it continue to be a major factor in allowing the growth of population?

We have seen that both peasants and landlords in the years before 1815 wanted to press on with subdivision. The social structure of rural Ireland made it unlikely that the peasants would wish to slacken or reverse the process unless, either the pressure of population were reduced, or holdings reached the minimal size at which the peasants were convinced that further fragmentation would make subsistence impossible. Until the volume of emigration expanded in the thirties there is no reason for believing that there was any significant slackening in the rate of population growth, and, still, in the thirties, with a decennial population-increase of over 5 per cent., there remained the incentive for fathers to divide their holdings. Much literary opinion in the post-war years believed that fragmentation had proceeded dangerously far—and the Famine showed that it was right. But the peasant's conduct was not guided by literary opinion: there is no reason for believing that there was any considerable willingness on the part of the peasantry to leave children without provision so that a holding might remain intact. Indeed, looking only to the *Report* of the Devon Commission, there are accounts from every part of Ireland of the eagerness of the peasantry, right up to the forties, to divide their holdings.

It was the landlords, not the peasants, who, in the post-war years, changed their minds about the wisdom of subdivision. 'Every man that is not a fool is endeavouring to counteract it', said Dennis Browne, a member of the 1823 Committee when questioned by his colleagues on the prevalence of the system of dividing land.[1] Three years later the Select Committee on Emigration reported that 'from the uniform tenor of the evidence given by the Irish witnesses, it appears that there is now among the Landowners in Ireland a growing conviction (already almost universal) of the mischief of the system of an under-tenantry and of the excess of population which attends it. They are satisfied that the best chance for the improvement of their estates and the amelioration of the condition of the people is the removal of this grievance, by the ejectment of that excess of tenantry.'[2] John Musgrave, in evidence before the 1830 Select Committee, agreed that there was a general disposition among the landlords of Ireland 'to consolidate their farms, and to clear their estates of the pauper population'.[3] The district reports of the Poor Law Commission showed that practically throughout the country it was the custom to insert clauses in leases forbidding subdivision.[4]

Several reasons contributed to make landlords revise their attitude towards subdivision. First, smaller holdings had proved to be less desirable in practice than in anticipation. Hopes of a greater income from rents had been largely disappointed; whatever had been the political value of a numerous tenantry, it became elusive in the years before 1829, when Catholic voters showed greater independence, and it disappeared afterwards with the disfranchisement of the forty-shilling freeholder. Second, there was a widespread feeling among landlords that subdivision was responsible for the overrunning of their estates by a pauper population, undesirable both socially and, after the Poor Law of 1838, because of the danger of its becoming chargeable on the rates. Third, there was a fairly general desire amongst landlords to 'improve' their estates, to get tenants with more capital who would treat the soil

---

[1] *Rep. S.C. Employment of the Poor in Ireland, Reports from Committees*, 1823, vi. 53.

[2] *Third Report from the Select Committee on Emigration, Reports from Committees*, 1826–7, v. 230.

[3] *Rep. S.C. S.P.I.*, 1830, op. cit., q. 904.

[4] *Poor Inquiry (Ireland)*, Supplement to Appendix F, *Reports from Commissioners*, 1836, xxxiii. 427 ff.

with greater consideration than the peasant. Fourth, in so far as landlords in some districts found it profitable to extend pasture, they required larger tenancies. On a smaller scale a desire to discriminate against Catholic tenants, and to end both the middleman system and common farming inclined the landlords towards larger holdings.

On the question of rents, the small man, it seems, regularly offered more than the large. Even in Leinster, where one might expect a stronger tendency towards larger holdings than elsewhere, this was the case. In Co. Dublin the Poor Inquiry Commission was told the rent offered for small farms was 10 to 15 per cent. more than for large; in Meath, 15 to 20 per cent.; in Queen's up to 30 per cent.: in Louth the small man offered an extra 5 to 10s. per acre.[1] The promise of rent, however, was no measure of the landlord's profit. With the fall of prices at the end of the wars many middlemen and petty occupiers were unable to pay the high rents they had offered.[2] Then, and afterwards, landlords felt it better to accept the somewhat lower rent promised by the larger farmer because there was less risk of his defaulting. In Tipperary there had been much subdivision, but landlords 'finding that the smallholders do not and cannot pay this promised rent, they naturally wish to consolidate their farms, and to let them to more responsible tenants'.[3] From Kilkenny it was reported that 'the necessary consumption of many tenants would leave less to meet the rent than that of a few. The poor man will *promise* more, but the large holder will *pay* more.'[4] Not only, with larger holdings was there the chance of larger payments, but these were collected with less inconvenience to the landlord or his agent.[5]

The prospect of larger rents from small tenancies proved illusory in the post-war years: so, soon, did the prospect of rising to political influence through the votes of a numerous tenantry. Tenants became increasingly critical of their landlords' politics, and largely, doubtless, for this reason in 1829 the vote was withdrawn from the holders of property worth less than £10. Thereafter 'many of those who had encouraged or compelled their tenantry to divide their farms, and who had risen to rank, as well as, in many cases,

---

[1] *Poor Inquiry*, 1836, op. cit., Appendix F, pp. 90 and 98–103.
[2] *Rep. S.C. S.P.I.*, 1830, op. cit., p. 7.
[3] *Poor Inquiry*, op. cit., Appendix F, p. 119. See also pp. 116 and 123.
[4] Ibid., p. 92.   [5] Ibid., pp. 89, 101, 131.

to power through their support, were the most indefatigable supporters, both in theory and in practice, of the "clearance system" '.[1]
Where, after 1829, the landlord still wished for numerous voters on
his estate his course was clear: it was to amalgamate small holdings
until he had a maximum number of £10 freeholders. In Co. Meath
there were 'wholesale ejectments' after 1829; in Limerick there
were junctions because small tenants no longer had votes; in
Waterford there was a desire to get rid of the forty-shilling
freeholders 'who are now a useless class'; in Co. Dublin there
was consolidation of holdings to increase the number of £10
voters.[2]

The Poor Law of 1838 brought to a head concern which had
previously been felt that subdivision was leading to a dangerously
rapid multiplication of an impoverished population. The 1830
Committee pointed to the 'general impression . . . produced in
the minds of all persons, that a pauper population spread over the
country would go on increasing, and the value of the land at the
same time diminishing, until the produce would become insufficient to maintain the resident population'.[3] Fear of poor rates,
even before 1838, made landlords disposed to consolidate.[4] Support for the Act came from people who thought that it would
facilitate consolidation. Nicholls, the Government's adviser on the
Irish poor law, thought it would ease the change from small
holdings to the 'better practice of day labour for wages': Cornewall
Lewis reported confidentially to the Chancellor of the Exchequer
that 'in the present condition of Ireland I can conceive no other
means except a strongly guarded poor law of restoring to the
landlords their power of doing what they will with their own'.[5]

Allied with their concern over the multiplying of a pauper
population was the landlords' desire to 'improve' their estates
through consolidation—to get a more responsible class of tenant,
people with more capital and able to cultivate more skilfully. 'Som(
landlords consider it a kind of disgrace to have what is called &
numerous pauper tenantry upon their estates, and especially if
near to their own residence.'[6] In 1830 landlords were consolidating

---

[1] W. R. Anketel, 1843, op. cit., p. 21.
[2] *Poor Inquiry*, op. cit., Appendix F, pp. 101, 116, 122, and 90.
[3] *Rep. S.C. S.P.I.*, 1830, op. cit., pp. 7–8.
[4] *Poor Inquiry*, op. cit., Appendix F, pp. 101, 103.
[5] Quoted in G. O'Brien, 1921, op. cit., p. 190.
[6] *Poor Inquiry*, op. cit., Appendix F, p. 103.

to put an end to this disgrace:[1] they found the smartness of the larger farmers 'more flattering to the appearance of their estates than the more homely cut and general habits of the small'.[2] Sometimes there was consolidation to give the occupier a holding large enough to get a decent subsistence,[3] but no less influential than the landlord's interest in the welfare of his tenantry was his concern for the state of his land. The small man was driven to overwork his holding. The high rent he had contracted to pay meant that 'not the breadth of your hand can they afford to let idle':[4] every scrap had to be tilled, and tilled every year. Abundant family labour made such intensive cultivation possible, but lack of resources and knowledge meant that the cost was often the deterioration of the soil. The Devon Commission reported in the forties that 'the cause which most frequently, at the present day, tends to the eviction of a number of tenants on a particular estate, is the wish of the proprietor to increase the size of the holdings, with a view to the better cultivation of the land'.[5]

The fourth of the series of factors mentioned above which induced the landlords to favour larger holdings was the tendency for arable to be laid down to grass. The great relative advantage of the small man was his cheap labour, but this was an advantage he felt less fully when his land was under grass: then, too, the general lack of capital worked less effectively in his favour. The 1823 Committee reported that already holdings were being amalgamated to make farms large enough for graziers. The Poor Inquiry Commissioners in their regional investigations found numerous instances of consolidation for grazing in Leinster where the swing to pasture was most pronounced.[6] Occasionally the process occurred elsewhere: in Leitrim 'in changing from small holdings, the portion of land devoted to tillage has usually been diminished';[7] in Tipperary 'most of the gentlemen are getting into the habit of laying down the land in clover, and they say they would rather let it out into sheep-walks and feed cattle'.[8]

There is little reason for believing that dislike of Roman Catholic

---

[1] Bourke's evidence, *Rep. S.C. S.P.I.*, 1830, op. cit., q. 5221.
[2] *Poor Inquiry*, op. cit., Appendix F, p. 98.
[3] Ibid., p. 88.   [4] Ibid., p. 126.
[5] *Reports from Commissioners*, 1845, xix. 20.
[6] *Poor Inquiry*, op. cit., Appendix F, pp. 90 ff.
[7] Ibid., p. 83.
[8] *Rep. Devon Com.*, op. cit., 550, 32.

tenants was a substantial cause of eviction and consolidation: nonetheless it operated occasionally. In Cavan tenants were turned out because they were Catholics 'although it was said that in general Roman Catholics were better rent payers, that is, were content to live more poorly than Protestants, and give a greater portion of the production to the landlord . . . this odious system of religious persecution was not more justly denounced by the Roman Catholics than it was strenuously upheld by the Protestants'.[1] In Meath, too, there were said to be clearances because landlords disliked their Roman Catholic tenants for their religious as well as their political views. In Kerry, and doubtless elsewhere, if tenants in common were unable to pay their rents, landlords evicted them and let their holdings to one or two tenants.[2] With the decline in the post-war years of the middleman system, and with the reluctance of the landlord to put himself or his agent to the trouble of dealing with a host of petty tenants, there was a desire to consolidate.

There can remain, it is clear, little doubt that in the thirty years following the French wars landlords fairly generally revised their ideas on the desirability of allowing their tenants to subdivide their holdings: the gains of tiny holdings had been illusory or were short-lived, their dangers were becoming increasingly menacing. Facilities to prevent subdivision increased with the desire. The Ejectment Act of 1816[3] made it easier for the owner to regain possession of land occupied by tenants who had absconded, who refused to leave when their tenancies had expired, or who were in arrears with their rent. It is said to have enabled a landlord to evict an obnoxious tenant in two months at a cost of £2, while in England a similar process took twelve months and cost £18.[4] The Act, moreover, made it lawful for the landlord to seize as distress for arrears of rent any potatoes, grain, and other produce growing on the estate, to harvest them at an appropriate time, and deduct from any residue due to the tenant the costs incurred. The preamble to the Subletting Act of 1826[5] pointed to the expediency of ensuring the fulfilment of covenants in existing leases for preventing subletting, and of making more effectual in the future provisions for its prevention. It provided that no sublease would be

---

[1] *Poor Inquiry*, op. cit., Appendix F, p. 127.
[2] Ibid., p. 112.
[3] 56 Geo. III, c. 88.
[4] O'Brien, 1921, op. cit., p. 157.
[5] 7 Geo. IV, c. 29.

valid unless it had the landlord's explicit approval, that the owner could recover possession of land when the tenant violated provisions against subletting, and that a tenant could not bequeath his land to more than one person.

In the thirty years after 1815, the landlords of Ireland, in spite of the legislature's sympathy with their new-found appreciation of the benefits of consolidation, were generally unable to halt the movement towards subdivision which they had encouraged so warmly during the wars. To have ended it would have been to redraw the pattern of Irish social life, but this had to await a force more compelling even than any possessed by the landlords hand in hand with the State. Landlords found a variety of reasons to account for the halting, piecemeal advance of consolidation. First, and probably of greatest importance, was the opposition of the peasantry to the ejectments that had to precede consolidation. Sometimes the matter was taken to law; more often there was the use of force. Sometimes the situation was so dangerous that no tenant could be found for the enlarged farm; sometimes the landlord was deterred from eviction by the contempt in which he would subsequently be held by the local population. In Queen's County some of the peasants were said to challenge ejection by legal process:[1] in one barony of Tipperary they 'resist ejection in almost every case. . . . The ejector has always recourse to the sheriff, assisted by a military force. In most cases the ejected tenantry threaten those who take their farms, and in hundreds of cases outrages have been committed in consequence of ejection . . . the fear of outrage has prevented ejection.'[2] In Leitrim there was 'resistance to ejection for any other cause than the non-payment of rent. . . . Ejected tenants threaten those who take the enlarged farms in an under-growl, and even openly. Cattle are sometimes injured.'[3] Fear of outrages was an impediment to consolidation in Meath, 'or, at least, if not actual outrage, that degree of personal odium and obliquy which is almost as bad, and, perhaps, more painful and insupportable, because more lasting and difficult of cure'.[4]

Secondly, landlords were often restrained from ejecting because they were reluctant to cause distress to their tenantry. In some

---

[1] *Poor Inquiry*, op. cit., Appendix F, p. 103.
[2] Ibid., p. 121.
[3] Ibid., p. 84.
[4] Ibid., p. 100.

parts, it is true, 'the fear of causing an extension of distress has never operated to prevent the junction of small farms; for whatever the present distress it may occasion to the occupiers of them, the proprietors consider that it is not so great as that into which they eventually sink by clinging to these very small holdings'.[1] Certainly, in one of the baronies of Tipperary humanitarian sentiment did not slow down an economically desirable movement: 'it is agreed by all that the fear of causing an extension of distress does not prevent the landlord from ejecting; his own pecuniary interest is too pressing to permit his feelings of sympathy to operate.'[2] From up and down the country, however—from Galway, Leitrim, Sligo, Kilkenny, Meath, Kerry, Limerick and Armagh—came reports that there would be more large farms, but for the fear of increasing distress.[3] Occasionally, landlords were able to provide for some, at least, of the ejected tenants by giving them grants to assist emigration, or by allowing them to reclaim portions of bog:[4] and, doubtless, their consciences then permitted more rapid consolidation.

Finally, the progress of consolidation was sometimes halted by the difficulty of finding men with sufficient skill and capital to manage large farms, by the long leases of some sitting tenants, and by the revived, or still continuing tendency in some areas for grass to be laid down to tillage.[5]

Not always, by any means, were landlords frustrated in their desire to consolidate. There is considerable evidence drawn from the thirty years before the Famine showing that some landlords were enforcing ejectments and thereby creating considerable distress. The 1823 Committee reported that 'since the depression of the prices of agricultural produce, the necessity of consolidating many small, into one greater farm, seems to be generally admitted and acted upon; and much of arable has been laid down for the purpose of rearing and fattening cattle, as well as for dairy:'[6] the 1830 Committee agreed that clearances had been proceeding since 1815.[7] Nonetheless we should do well to read in conjunction with this the *Report* of the Devon Commission. 'Upon a review of the whole subject', it said, 'we feel bound to express our opinion, that

[1] Ibid., p. 97.   [2] Ibid., p. 121.   [3] Ibid., *passim.*
[4] Ibid., pp. 88, 93, 48.
[5] Ibid., pp. 88–110.
[6] *Rep. S.C. on the Employment of the Poor*, 1823, op. cit., p. 337.
[7] *Rep. S.C. S.P.I.*, 1830, op. cit., p. 8.

there has been much of exaggeration and mis-statement in the
sweeping charges which have been directed against the Irish landlords.'[1] Nor was it only amongst contemporaries that there has
been exaggeration of the rate at which landlords, before the Famine,
ejected tenants and amalgamated farms. The standard *Economic
History of Ireland* tells us that 'the dominant feature of Irish agriculture in the early nineteenth century was the consolidation of
holdings, and the consequent evictions'.[2] Both the Poor Inquiry
Commission and the Devon Commission collected voluminous
evidence from all parts of the country on the progress of consolidation: the reports of both Commissions make inescapable the conclusion that, until the mid-forties, however ardently landlords
wished for larger farms, in no county were they able to obtain
them in other than exceptional cases.·

The Poor Inquiry Commission sent to landlords, priests, clergy,
magistrates, and other prominent residents a series of fifty questions on the condition of the small tenantry. To the question, 'To
what extent has the system of throwing small farms into large
ones taken place in your parish, and what has become of the dispossessed tenants?'[3] it published more than 1,500 replies drawn
from every county. There was not a single county in which more
than a small fraction of the replies reported any considerable
amount of consolidation. In view of the established belief that
these were years of ruthless ejectment, and of the importance of
the matter to population history, it is worth our while to examine
the replies in some detail.

In Ulster, even more than in the other Provinces, the replies
point to consolidation only on a trivial scale—and much of what
there was was not imposed by landlords on a suffering peasantry,
but was caused by the more comfortably placed tenants buying
neighbouring land, often when its occupant emigrated. In a Co.
Down parish 'the only instances of small farms being thrown into
large ones . . . are cases of individuals choosing to emigrate to
America, who sell their farms to persons remaining in the neighbourhood': in Cavan 'when farms are enlarged, it is done by
purchasing from those who emigrate to America'. An Armagh
incumbent reported that consolidation 'is never done by the landed

[1] *Rep. Devon Com., Reports from Commissioners*, 1845, xix. 20.
[2] O'Brien, op. cit., p. 60.
[3] *Poor Inquiry*, op. cit., Appendix F, pp. 428–819.

proprietors; . . . farms, however, undergo changes, the industrious improving tenant frequently purchasing the whole or a portion of the adjoining farm from the sluggard who has contracted debts and adding it to his own farm'.[1]

In all, the Commission printed nearly 500 parochial reports from Ulster, but in only five cases was appreciable consolidation mentioned: the Marquis of Waterford was said to have tried the system 'in many instances'; in four other parishes there was 'considerable' consolidation. From every county the mass of the replies were in such terms as: 'this system has not been introduced'; 'it has not prevailed at all in this parish'; 'not acted upon in a single instance'; 'rather the contrary practice of splitting up farms prevails'; 'the system has very partially operated here'; 'in a very trifling degree'; 'in one instance three small farms have been thrown into one; I know no other.'[2]

From fewer than twenty-five of the 450 parishes of Leinster from which reports were sent are there accounts of substantial consolidation: sometimes, in these parishes, the consequences were severe. The priest of Castletown Devlin in Westmeath said that farms had been thrown together 'to a most unbounded extent . . . in most instances where leases have expired, the tenant, *no matter what his character for punctuality in his payments* or moral rectitude, the moment his lease expires he is *at once ejected*, and cast, himself and little family, at once upon the world': in a Meath parish consolidation was practised 'some years since to a vast extent'. 'The unfortunate victims were sent adrift; some of them in crossing the seas to procure a livelihood in a foreign land, met with a watery grave; more of them this moment languishing in hospitals and goals; and the rest of them dying in bogs and morasses, or pining away in beggary and want, in sight of their once-happy homes and birthplaces.'[3] Such hardships were without doubt inflicted, but it would be wrong to build a general agrarian history upon them. In Wexford, King's, and Dublin not a single parish mentioned considerable consolidation, and in the great mass of Leinster parishes 'this system has not taken place'; 'nothing has been done here these 27 years past'; 'five persons dispossessed'; 'there have been no small farms thrown into large ones, but several good farms have been thrown into small ones; no tenants dispossessed'; 'such a practice has gone on on a very small scale'.[1]

In Munster twenty-eight parochial reports out of some 400 recorded considerable consolidation. A dozen of these were from Co. Cork: 'in three estates 86 houses had been razed to the ground by orders from the proprietors'; a landlord elsewhere said he had carried the system of consolidation 'to a great extent'; the Catholic curate of the island of Sherkin said there was 'very much' consolidation. But far outnumbering these reports were more than 150 from Co. Cork typical of those of the rest of Munster: 'no such proceedings'; 'there is but one instance of this kind in the memory of man'; 'this occurred only in one instance'; 'only in two instances of any note'; 'the contrary is the practice'.[2]

From Connaught a Mayo priest said that 'this system has not as yet taken place in this parish, but I am told it is in contemplation by some of the landed proprietors, or at least by their agents, who are in general a selfish, merciless, and tyrannical set of men'. There were some other fears for the future, but, with a dozen exceptions, the Connaught reports were of the same tenor as the mass of those from the other Provinces: 'in two instances only has this horrid and heart-rending system been acted on in this district'; 'instances of such are rare'; 'one about ten years ago'; 'no such system prevails in this parish, but the contrary practice of throwing small farms into still smaller ones.'[3]

The evidence given a few years later before the Devon Commission presents a similar pattern to that of the correspondents of the Poor Inquiry Commission. From Connaught the evidence was overwhelmingly that there was much subdivision and only occasional consolidation. In Leitrim there was 'very little [consolidation] indeed', though landlords wished for more. Subdivision, on the other hand, was prevalent 'to a great extent': landlords did not sanction it, but took no steps to prevent it. From Mayo, one report said that consolidation was effected by landlords on the expiration of middlemen's leases and on political grounds, but others that it was 'very little effected', or 'not to any extent': subdivision, however, was 'prevalent to a great extent'. Similarly, in Sligo and Roscommon there was evidence of only slight consolida-

---

[1] *Poor Inquiry*, op. cit., Appendix F, pp. 469, 482, 489, 493, 545.
[2] Ibid., pp. 633, 593, 607, 608, 590, 591, 592, 600.
[3] Ibid., pp. 449, 429, 445, 457, 467.

tion, but of widespread subdivision, carried on, often, in spite of the wishes of the landlord. Only from Galway was there any reference—and this an isolated one—to 'very much' consolidation, and there was no suggestion that subdivision was any less the normal procedure there than in the rest of Connaught.[1]

Ulster, like Connaught, made to the Devon Commission few complaints of radical consolidation. Landlords were generally anxious to throw farms together: sometimes the more prosperous peasants helped them by taking on neighbouring holdings. But in Tyrone consolidation was little practised: in one or two parishes of Monaghan it was reported to be 'prevalent', but elsewhere it was 'almost impossible to effect', or 'not practised to any extent'. In Londonderry there was a great desire for consolidation, but little took place: in Down it was 'effected cautiously' or 'going on very slowly'. In Fermanagh, Donegal, Cavan, and Armagh there was little. The references from Antrim suggest that there there was rather more force behind the movement: in one parish it was 'always attempted on the expiration of leases'; in another it was effected to a 'considerable extent' on some properties, but elsewhere 'little change has taken place in the size of farms during the last thirty years'. Almost invariably when people with experience of Ulster referred to subdivision they had to report its prevalence as a means for providing for children: in most counties, however, there were some witnesses who thought the practice was less prevalent than formerly.

Complaints about consolidation would seem, from the evidence heard by the Devon Commission, to have had more justification in parts of Munster than in Connaught or Ulster, though the system was far from universal in Munster. In Kerry, though landlords were anxious to throw farms together, and did make some consolidation on the expiration of middlemen's leases, the system was 'not adapted to this part of the country'. 'There is a want of capital among the tenantry, and the land is not adapted to consolidation

[1] These summaries of the evidence given before the Devon Commission on the progress of consolidation and subdivision in the four provinces are each based on the statements of some fifty or more witnesses. It has been thought unnecessary to give the 200 or so references in full. They may readily be found, classified by counties, under the headings 'Consolidation of Farms', and 'Sub-division of Farms' in the detailed index (which is, in effect, a most useful summary of an enormous body of evidence) included in the fourth volume of the *Rep. Devon Com., Reports from Commissioners*, 1845, xxii. 453–61, 739–49.

because it is naturally poor.' In Waterford there were odd instances, but consolidation was not prevalent to any extent. In Tipperary, on the other hand, there were some parishes where there were numerous ejectments, often for the sake of extending grazing land. In Cork, Clare, and Limerick, too, there were as many reports commenting on the prevalence as on the absence of consolidation. But in spite of the sometimes considerable consolidation in Munster, there was no county in which subdivision was still not very active, though sometimes it was said to be less regularly practised than formerly.

In parts of Leinster there was considerable consolidation. One parish in Kildare reported that it was 'generally taking place', another that it was the cause of the eviction of 'numerous tenants'; in Kilkenny it was 'increasing very much' and 'effected generally by the emigration of small proprietors at the proprietor's expense'; in Longford it was 'effected by the removal of a great number of small tenants to increase holdings to 20–25 acres'. Leinster landlords, however, did not all act alike. In Louth there was the disposition to consolidate, but all that one parish could report was a single instance in which two or three tenants were removed, and in another, ten years previously there had been some consolidation on two or three holdings. In Co. Dublin, where proximity to the capital strengthened the position of the small holder, landlords were reported to have 'made no great efforts' to consolidate: one reporter could remember a single instance twenty-five years previously, but there had been little since then. Even in counties where the reports suggest that consolidation was most considerable it seems to have made little interruption to the progress of subdivision. In Kildare, though one report spoke of less subdivision because of the efforts of the landlords, another said it was prevalent because covenants in leases forbidding it were not enforced, and another that it was 'effected to a great extent'. In Kilkenny and Longford, though, perhaps, there was less than formerly, subdivision was widely carried on as a provision for children, often in violation of leases: elsewhere in Leinster it continued, frequently in the face of strenuous opposition from landlords.

What conclusions can we come to concerning variations in the size of holdings between 1815 and 1845, and their reaction upon population history? First, we seem to be justified in modifying

descriptions of wholesale clearances and consolidation following a
largely hypothetical swing from arable to pasture,[1] or following
the ejectment and subletting acts and the disfranchisement of the
forty-shilling freeholders. Certainly many, perhaps most, landlords
eagerly desired a more solid and skilful tenantry, men who would
be better able to avoid the danger of mining the soil, who would
pay their rents more steadily, and who would be less likely to
become dependent upon the ratepayers. Nor is there reason for
believing that they were less ruthless and despotic in managing
their estates than their forerunners. But their own mismanagement
and their fathers', coupled with the colonial status of Ireland, had
robbed them of the opportunity of doing what they would with
their own. Their estates had become overrun with a peasantry
whose way of life presupposed subdivision and who would subdivide, however strong the disapproval of the landlords. The
peasants, on their side, had stronger allies than the penalties of
the Subletting Act or the visits of the bailiffs: sometimes they
could move their landlord to hold his hand by pity for their lot;
more often they could put him, or his nominee to the tenancy of
a consolidated holding, in fear of his life. Not until the potato
blight of the forties brought famine and mass emigration to their
side could the landlords proceed as they wished. Before this, on
scattered estates, most of them in Leinster and Munster, some of
them being put down to pasture, there was consolidation, but we
cannot agree with the view that 'consolidation, accompanied by
clearances, advanced very rapidly during the twenties. . . . After
1830 the process of eviction progressed very rapidly, and was
prevented from depopulating the whole country only by the widespread fear of the Whiteboys. . . . The evidence before the Devon
Commission demonstrated that ejectments were still being pursued with as much energy as ever.'[2] Such views would seem to be
based on the great distress caused by such ejectments as there
were rather than on the frequency of consolidation.

When consolidation did take place there can be no doubt that
its tendency was to slacken the local rate of population-growth.
Witnesses vary in their estimate of the amount by which enclosure
curtailed the demand for labour, but they were almost agreed that,
whether the new farms were tilled or put to pasture, only a fraction

[1] See above, Chapter IV, pp. 113–20.
[2] O'Brien, op. cit., pp. 53–6.

of the labour formerly expended on them was necessary. Sometimes after consolidation there was an initial spurt in the demand
for labour: in Leitrim, for instance, 'the condition of many of
those who were ejected is certainly better than when they held
land inasmuch as they find constant employment in works of
improvement in progress on the estate', but this happy result, as
the witness pointed out, was only temporary.[1] When these works
were completed demand for labour fell away, partly because there
was less intensive farming, partly because horses did work formerly
done by men: estimates of the amount of labour ultimately made
superfluous varied from half to two-thirds. When arable land was
turned to pasture the effect on the peasantry was catastrophic:
often only one-twentieth of the former labour-supply was needed,
sometimes one-tenth.[2]

In general it is only when ejected families left the country that
we can say categorically that consolidation slackened the general,
as distinct from the local, rate of population growth. Detailed facts
on the subsequent history of those who remained in the country
are elusive. Most in Waterford are reported to have become
labourers, though odd people became carmen, publicans, farmers,
shoemakers, fishermen, and paupers. In Louth 'the few of the
ejected tenants who had anything left after paying their rent and
debts, became pig-dealers or higglers, and a very few met with
other farms, but most of them became labourers, and many of
them homeless wanderers dispersed over the whole country and
neighbouring towns, wherever they could find a temporary shelter'.
Sometimes landlords settled them—or allowed them to settle—on
bog or mountain land.[3] Such people were not invariably worse-off
than the general run of the peasantry. In Leitrim 'latterly several
have been provided with houses and portions of waste land which
they are to occupy rent-free for a number of years': some of these
cabins were superior to the general run. 'I am quite confident',
said one witness, 'that they are now better off than they were
formerly.' Many settled precariously in the towns, others became
wandering beggars.[4] The demographic history of the dispossessed
must be a matter of speculation. Certainly their lot differed little
from that of the mass of the Irish in that wretched, hopeless lives

[1] *Poor Inquiry*, op. cit., Appendix F, p. 84.
[2] Ibid., pp. 98, 104, 99, 101.
[3] Ibid., pp. 123, 95, 83, 92, 110.
[4] Ibid., pp. 83, 84, 92.

predisposed them towards early marriage. Not always did the ejected lack opportunities for marrying early. For every land-lord who consolidated there were several who, willingly or grudg-ingly, tolerated subdivision: on their estates, on mountain or bog, or on the earnings of casual work in the towns—sometimes on the gifts of a kind-hearted people—the modicum of security conventionally necessary for marriage was sustained. When mar-riage was not possible for the dispossessed we do not know the incidence amongst them of illegitimacy: nor do we know their mortality experience.

We can conclude, not only that consolidation in the decades before the Famine (apart from the encouragement it gave to emigration) is unlikely to have slackened seriously the general rate of population-growth, but also that subdivision continued to per-mit early marriage and high fertility as it had done in the war years. Some success did attend the landlord's efforts to prevent subdivision—and their achievements are doubtless reflected in the higher emigration figures of the thirties—but, apart from the literary evidence, the statistics of landholding for 1841 show that there can have been little interruption in the movement towards tiny holdings. Taking no account of patches under one acre, 45 per cent. of all holdings in the country were then of not more than 5 acres.[1]

[1] See above, Table 22, p. 164.

VII

THE DEATH-RATE: BACKGROUND AND STATISTICS

WE saw in Chapter II that the acceleration, which appears to have begun by the 1780s, in the rate of growth of the population of Ireland must be attributed entirely to increased fertility or diminished mortality, singly or in conjunction. Unfortunately, we lack the statistics that would permit us to trace the course of the birth- and death-rates and determine with precision the extent of their relative contributions. We have, however, found both literary and statistical evidence indicating that Irish fertility in these years was unusually high, and we have examined a number of features in the structure of rural economic and social life which tended to increase fertility by encouraging and permitting earlier marriage. It remains for us now to re-examine the material of social and economic history for guidance on the second of the possible causes of more rapid population-increase. Was mortality in these years after 1780 lower than in preceding years and did, therefore, a falling death-rate add to the effect of a rising birth-rate? Or are we forced to the conclusion that the increase in fertility was sufficiently steep to accelerate the pace of population-growth in spite of the retarding tendency of mounting losses from death?

We may proceed on lines parallel with those of our investigation of fertility and look, before examining the literary evidence, at the statistical information on two problems. First, we want to know whether the expectation of life in Ireland between 1780 and the Famine was unusually long or unusually short: second, we want to know the nature of any differences between the provinces in their mortality experience. Our conclusions here will have to be borne in mind when we try to assess the relative contributions of the birth- and death-rates in leading to the growth of population in the country as a whole and in its divisions. But we can expect from the statistics alone no final guidance, partly because they are available only for the closing years of our period and partly because we cannot be confident of their accuracy.

We shall then look for developments in social and economic life which tended to extend or curtail the expectation of life. It would be natural for us here to seek guidance in the current explanations of the contemporary rise in the population of England—the more so as these explanations place such heavy emphasis upon the contribution made by falling mortality. But such guidance we must accept with reserve. Not only were the social and economic systems of England and Ireland utterly disparate, but, on the surface at least, there appears to be a number of unresolved problems which should make us reluctant to accept these explanations of English population history. On the one hand, the agrarian changes of the eighteenth and early nineteenth centuries are said to have created the new abundance of food which, *The Principle of Population* made plain, was the prerequisite of any lengthening of life that was not merely compensatory for lower fertility: on the other hand, it has been asserted that the foodstuffs of the mass of the people, in town and country, were deteriorating in quality, and often in quantity. On the one hand, we are told that improved water-supply, drainage, and paving made the towns healthier places to live in, while, on the other hand, Chadwick's reports on the towns of the 1830s and 1840s leave us curious to discover how either townsmen or countrymen in the early eighteenth century could have lived in an environment more likely to have shortened their lives. Fundamentally, with the exception of food-supply (and this, we have noticed, is uncertain support for an argument), the developments that are said to have prolonged life are developments, which, if they had appreciable effect, must have had it in the towns. It was not merely that the countryman can hardly have been aware of improved water-supply and drainage. The hospitals were built in towns and only the adjacent minority of rural dwellers were not cut off from them by the difficulty of transport if by nothing more. Much, too, is made of medical advances and of a growing conviction that dirt aggravated the cost of disease, yet there is little evidence to show that country doctors were in the van of medical progress, or that their numbers were multiplied sufficiently to ensure that their skill was available to all. Nor is it easy to substantiate the theory that the homes and bodies of country families became cleaner in years during which the standard of rural housing appears to have deteriorated; when lack of fuel often made hot food out of the question, let alone hot water for washing persons or clothes; when it is far from certain that employment became steadier, or that the standard of living rose; when self-respect was undermined by loss of land and stock, by loss of the respect of others more fortunately placed in the social scale, and by maladministration of the poor law. The evidence, then, seems to point to the conclusion that if life was prolonged in England in the years of the Industrial Revolution, the agencies responsible were selective in their operation: they singled out the townsmen as their beneficiaries, and in so far as they affected the countryman at all their force may have been at least partially offset by contrary developments. Now, if these urban developments were to play a large part in moulding population history they must, indeed, have been potent, for town-dwellers throughout the period were a minority of the population. Yet we must doubt their potency when we hear that so high was mortality in the towns that often their population scarcely replaced itself, relying for its undeniable augmentation on recruitment from the healthier country-side.

The contrast between the Irish and English social and economic structures reinforces our reluctance to seek in Ireland any close counterpart of the forces said to be responsible for a falling death-rate in England. England was the mother-country; Ireland her colony. England's industries, long established and vigorous, were developing in size and technique as never before, while, through most of the years of population-increase, the few industries Ireland's subject status had permitted her to acquire, stagnated or decayed. The towns of England doubled and redoubled in size, partly because they held positive attractions to the countryman: the slower growth of the towns of Ireland was the accretion of the destitution of an impoverished country-side. In English agriculture enterprising and capitalist landowners and farmers remodelled the system of land-tenure so that larger-scale, profit-seeking farms should emerge, capable of employing wage-labour and of practising more efficient technical methods: in Ireland, the landlords' struggle to maximize rents, unattached to what should have been its corollary, a policy of increasing yield, led to the continuance of subsistence farming on ever tinier holdings.

Such contrasts as these help to point to the futility of looking in Ireland for the operation of a number of forces which are said to have lowered the death-rate in Britain. It is fanciful, first of all, to

suppose that improved public hygiene could have had any significant influence in Ireland. Not only do we lack evidence of substantial improvements in drainage and water-supply, but the towns,
to which any such improvements must have been confined,
accounted for too small, and too slowly growing, a proportion of
total population for purely urban developments to be conspicuous
in national population history: moreover, in the closing years of
our period, the people of the towns appear still to have had a
remarkably shorter expectation of life than those living in the
country.[1] Second, we cannot expect greater cleanliness to have
lowered the incidence of disease. Almost every reference to the
subject by travellers and doctors underlines the filthiness both of
the persons of the mass of the Irish and of the interior and surroundings of their cabins: all point to conditions of gross overcrowding, with whole families, or sets of families, living in one or
two rooms, with sick and healthy sleeping often under the same
covering. To this lack of evidence of greater cleanliness must be
coupled the undeniable existence of a number of agencies combining to allow standards of cleanliness to stagnate or fall away. We
have seen in an earlier chapter that one of the shortcomings of the
Irish social structure was that it included so few representatives
of a class intermediate between peasants and labourers, on the
one hand, and landlords, on the other, and that many members of
the small middle class that did exist were alienated from the mass
of the people by their occupation and religion. The peasant's
family, then, was often unfamiliar with any higher standard of
comfort or cleanliness to which it might aspire. And, indeed, even
if the peasant did become aware of other ways of living, few
aspirations except the most ascetic (and they were unlikely to
make him cleaner) were realizable in an economy which diverted
from the producers almost the entire surplus of the yield of their
soil, beyond the meanest subsistence. As the Famine approached,
in a succession of disastrous years, shortage of fuel and shortage
of food robbed the peasant of the desire or the opportunity even
to maintain his existing standards: fever and the threat of fever
left people dejected and preoccupied; shortage of fuel meant that
the poor, in the endeavour to keep warm, piled on all the rags
they could find, left them on day and night, stopped doors and
windows, and seldom had hot water to wash clothes or bodies.

[1] See below, Table 27, p. 193.

We must, in the third place, be restrained in our expectations of a lengthening of life in Ireland because of medical advances. The sheer physical difficulty, over much of the country, of bringing patient and doctor together, denied many of the Irish any formal medical attention at all, and the problem was aggravated by the popular prejudice against doctors and the unshakeable faith of the mass of the people in quacks and traditional remedies of doubtful efficacy. The Irish evidence, however, does suggest as worthy of investigation two ways in which advances in the theory and practice of medicine may have had considerable influence in saving life: we must examine, first, the effect of the extension of hospitals, fever-hospitals, and dispensaries in the half-century before the Famine and, second, the degree of success that attended the efforts of the doctors and others in the eighteenth and nineteenth centuries to immunize the people from small-pox, long one of the major causes of premature mortality.

One prerequisite for lower mortality existed in Ireland more surely than in England. We have seen in our discussion of the potato that in the first forty years of rapid population-growth there was normally available for the mass of the population a supply of food adequate both in bulk and nutritive content. But even if this abundance had been a new development it would not point unequivocally towards longer life. Any earlier stringency of food-supply could have been reflected as clearly in low fertility as in high mortality; as, indeed, the abundance of food after 1780 seems to have been vividly reflected in earlier marriage and a rising birth-rate.

We have, then, three headings for our inquiry into mortality: first, the statistics of the 1841 Census; second, the dissemination of hospitals and dispensaries; and, third, the progress of inoculation and vaccination. A fourth subject that needs inquiry is the history of fever, the characteristic Irish disease of these years: it was responsible in the thirties for nearly a tenth of all deaths, far more than were attributed to any other single cause.[1]

The only considerable mortality statistics collected in Ireland before the Famine are those of the 1841 Census.[2] Unfortunately,

[1] For the years 1831–41 1,187,000 deaths are recorded in the 1841 Census: of these 112,000 were attributed to fever. (*Reports from Commissioners*, 1843, xxiv, Tables of Deaths, facing p. 182.)
[2] The mortality material of this census was collected in a table inserted in the census form in which the head of the family was required to give certain particulars relating to all deaths which had occurred in his family in the previous

they do not allow us to measure Irish mortality by the yardstick of experience in England (or in any other country). The Census Commissioners arrived at a crude death-rate for Ireland for the years 1836–40 of 16·8 per 1,000.[1] The Fifth Annual Report of the Registrar-General gave a crude death-rate for England and Wales for the period 1838–41 of 22·2 per 1,000.[2] It would, however, be quite illegitimate to take these figures as evidence of a higher expectation of life in Ireland. Apart from the adequacy of the crude death-rate as a measure of mortality in populations which may have different age-compositions, and apart from any doubts there may be concerning the reliability of the figure for England, we can have no confidence in the accuracy of the Irish figure. It would indicate 1 death per year for every 59·5 persons living, but, in the words of the Census Commissioners, 'as there can be no reason for supposing the mortality less than 1 to 45—on the contrary many circumstances would appear to place it higher— we are led to apprehend a deficiency in the death returns amounting to about one-fourth'.[3]

The expectation-of-life tables included in the 1841 Census, together with contemporary English tables, suggested a second way in which it might be possible to compare Irish with English mortality. The Irish tables were compiled from the data gathered on the ages at death of the 1,187,000 people whose deaths in the preceding ten years were reported in 1841. That the total number of deaths returned was substantially less than the real number does not necessarily take from the accuracy of the life tables: providing the omissions were scattered proportionately throughout all ages the returns would give an accurate figure for the average age at

---

ten years: he was asked for the date and cause of death, and the age and occupation of the deceased person. Similar returns were required from hospitals and other institutions. The Census Commissioners recognized that the resulting figures were likely to be defective for three leading reasons: first, because they made no attempt to include deaths in families which had left Ireland at the time of the enumeration; second, because they omitted deaths which resulted in the extinction of a family, and, third, because householders forgot, or for other reasons omitted, a certain number of deaths. Although the error from these sources was likely to be less for 1840 than for any other year, the Commissioners thought that they could obtain the most satisfactory death-rate by relating the average number of deaths per year over the period 1836–40 to the estimated mean population of those years. (Ibid., 'Report of Census Commissioners', pp. xlvii ff.)

[1] Ibid., p. xlix.
[2] *Reports from Commissioners*, 1843, xxi. 379.
[3] Census of Ireland, 1841, op. cit., p. xlix.

death. The Census Commissioners felt that the chief danger of error in their tables lay in the particularly defective records of the deaths of old people, people who had been heads of families and whose deaths were omitted by their successors whose responsibility it was to fill in the census form. The Irish life tables showed for males in rural districts an expectation of life at birth of 29·58 years.[1] The Registrar-General's figure for males in England and Wales two years later was 40·19.[2] These figures, however, no more show that life was shorter in Ireland than the crude death-rates

TABLE 24

'Expectation of Life' (erroneously deduced from Deaths alone) in Ireland and England and Wales, 1831–41[*]

Expectation of Life

Age	Ireland		England and Wales	Surrey	London	Liverpool
	Rural districts	Civic districts				
Birth	29	24	29	34	29	20
5	41	35	42	44	42	36
20	33	28	35	37	33	28
40	23	19	26	27	22	19
60	13	11	14	15	12	11

[*] *Fifth Annual Report of the Registrar-General, Reports from Commissioners,* 1843, xxi. 372.

show that it was longer. The Registrar-General commented on the Irish tables. He pointed out that they could be correct only if the number of births and deaths in the period from which their material was drawn had been equal, and if there had been no emigration. The departure from both of these assumptions meant that the tables were not true life tables and that, in fact, they underestimated the real expectation of life to an unknown extent. The Registrar-General constructed for England and Wales, and for certain divisions of the country 'expectation of life' tables on the same principle as those for Ireland. The figures are given above, in Table 24: they show the same 'expectation of life' at birth in rural Ireland as in England, and at later ages a rather less favourable position in Ireland. As the Registrar pointed out, the

[1] Census of Ireland, 1841, op. cit., p. lxxx. The corresponding figure for civic districts was 23·99.
[2] *Fifth Annual Report of the Registrar-General,* op. cit., p. 359.

Irish rural figures for all ages are remarkably similar to those for London.[1]

Can we accept this table as evidence of broadly similar mortality experience in rural Ireland and England? Providing the data on which the figures are based were accurate it would be legitimate to make comparisons between the two countries on two assumptions; first, that the population of each, over a considerable period, had increased at the same rate, and, second, not only that each had lost by emigration the same proportion of its population, but also that the emigrants from both countries showed the same age-composition. To endeavour to determine the extent to which these conditions were fulfilled would be a statistical labour of considerable complexity, based on material so insecure that little confidence could be placed in its conclusions. We are obliged, it seems, to leave undetermined the relative mortality of Ireland and England in the 1840s.

Our second problem, to investigate differential mortality within Ireland, presents fewer difficulties than the problem of comparing Irish with English mortality. Data drawn up under the same headings and by the same process are available for the whole of Ireland: the Census Commissioners say they had no reason to suspect peculiar inaccuracy in any one part.[2] They compiled the following table showing the average age at death in the provinces

TABLE 25

*Average Age at Death in the Rural and Civic Districts of the Provinces of Ireland, 1831–41**

	Average age at death									
	Leinster		Munster		Ulster		Connaught		Ireland	
	Rural	Civic	Rural	Civic	Rural	Civic	Rural	Civic	Rural	Civic
Males . . .	32·0	25·0	28·2	23·6	31·8	23·8	26·1	22·6	29·6	24·1
Females . .	31·5	25·4	27·0	23·7	32·0	23·6	24·3	22·4	28·9	24·3

* Census of Ireland, 1841, op. cit., p. l.

by dividing the sum of the ages of all the deceased by their number. On the assumption that the age-distribution of the deaths that were omitted from the census returns were similar for every province to those that were recorded, this table would seem to give us

[1] Ibid., p. 372.
[2] Census of Ireland, 1841, op. cit., p. l.

a measure of mortality in the four provinces providing the age-distribution in each province was broadly similar. Table 26 shows us that, in fact, this was not the case. In Connaught, for instance, there were 428 people per 1,000 aged 15 or less, while in Leinster there were only 380; in Connaught there were 173 people aged 41 or over, while in Leinster there were 198. It is improbable, then,

TABLE 26

Age-Distribution of the Population of the Rural and Civic Districts of the Provinces of Ireland in 1841*

Age	Number per 1,000 of the total population				
	Leinster	Munster	Ulster	Connaught	Ireland
5 and under	143·28	153·84	153·25	161·86	152·46
6–10	123·36	130·56	138·45	143·07	132·13
11–15	113·73	115·81	130·45	122·63	119·51
16–20	115·50	116·45	110·94	119·12	116·06
21–30	187·70	186·35	151·28	168·48	176·15
31–40	117·35	120·03	113·82	111·49	115·66
41–50	93·32	78·54	83·20	79·65	84·16
51–60	60·81	61·82	62·85	57·88	60·59
61–70	29·09	24·00	34·20	23·64	27·65
71–80	11·49	9·45	15·85	9·07	11·54
Over 80	3·61	2·45	4·64	2·35	3·29
Not specified	0·76	0·70	1·06	0·75	0·80

* Census of Ireland, 1841, op. cit., pp. lxvi–lxvii.

that on this foundation we should be justified in accepting the Census Commissioners' conclusion that there was a 'remarkable difference in the duration of life in favour of Leinster and Ulster'.

Can we find confirmation or refutation of this conclusion elsewhere? Table 27 shows the number of deaths recorded for 1840 for various age-groups per 1,000 persons of those ages in 1841. As previously pointed out it is likely that fewer deaths were omitted for the year 1840 than for any other year: for 1840, also, as the enumeration took place in the following year, the recorded ages at death probably tend to be most nearly accurate. The validity of the table is most likely to be impaired by differences from province to province in the disparity between the age-distribution of the persons whose deaths were recorded and that of those whose deaths were omitted. On the extent of this differential we can do little more than repeat the opinion of the

TABLE 27

Proportion of Deaths in 1840 at various Ages per 1,000 Persons living at those Ages in 1841 in the Rural Districts of the Provinces, and in the Rural and Civic Districts of Ireland*

	Under one year			2–5		
	No. of person living in 1841	Deaths in 1840	Deaths per 1,000	No. of persons living in 1841	Deaths in 1840	Deaths per 1,000
Leinster, R.D.	64,267	4,764	74·13	159,615	2,711	16·98
Munster, R.D.	89,498	8,006	89·45	225,403	4,459	19·78
Ulster, R.D.	95,035	6,567	69·10	238,125	3,338	14·02
Connaught, R.D.	62,255	6,003	96·43	156,170	2,914	18·66
Ireland, R.D.	311,055	25,304	81·35	779,313	13,422	17·22
Ireland, C.D.	50,369	6,952	138·02	105,676	4,807	45·49
Ireland, R. and C.D.	361,424	32,256	89·25	884,989	18,229	20·60
	6–15			*16–25*		
Leinster, R.D.	378,675	1,974	5·21	314,636	2,294	7·29
Munster, R.D.	506,672	2,495	4·92	411,650	2,669	6·48
Ulster, R.D.	569,531	2,171	3·81	412,886	2,566	6·21
Connaught, R.D.	358,727	1,539	4·29	264,488	1,680	6·35
Ireland, R.D.	1,813,605	8,179	4·51	1,403,660	9,209	6·56
Ireland, C.D.	243,551	2,383	9·78	242,237	2,399	9·90
Ireland, R. and C.D.	2,057,156	10,562	5·13	1,645,897	11,608	7·05
	26–35			*36–45*		
Leinster, R.D.	213,873	1,876	8·77	158,916	1,895	11·92
Munster, R.D.	297,311	2,440	8·21	192,485	2,238	11·63
Ulster, R.D.	279,592	2,217	7·93	217,061	2,172	10·01
Connaught, R.D.	182,393	1,587	8·70	128,499	1,661	12·93
Ireland, R.D.	973,169	8,120	8·34	696,961	7,966	11·43
Ireland, C.D.	181,208	2,418	13·34	132,481	2,441	18·42
Ireland, R. and C.D.	1,154,377	10,538	9·13	829,442	10,407	12·60
	46–55			*56–65*		
Leinster, R.D.	115,514	2,054	17·78	77,296	2,687	34·76
Munster, R.D.	139,218	2,349	16·87	96,705	3,524	36·44
Ulster, R.D.	154,568	2,365	15·30	111,692	3,134	28·06
Connaught, R.D.	89,547	1,762	19·68	63,131	2,466	39·06
Ireland, R.D.	498,847	8,560	17·16	348,824	11,811	33·39
Ireland, C.D.	89,552	2,187	24·42	56,930	2,361	41·47
Ireland, R. and C.D.	588,399	10,747	18·26	405,754	14,172	34·93
	66–75			*Over 75*		
Leinster, R.D.	32,433	2,306	71·10	15,469	2,449	158·32
Munster, R.D.	33,827	2,326	68·76	15,187	2,254	148·41
Ulster, R.D.	53,308	3,014	56·54	26,956	3,472	128·80
Connaught, R.D.	22,363	1,445	64·62	10,157	1,360	133·90
Ireland, R.D.	141,931	9,091	64·05	67,769	9,535	140·71
Ireland, C.D.	21,575	1,572	72·40	9,894	1,357	137·15
Ireland, R. and C.D.	163,506	10,663	65·21	77,663	10,892	140·25
	Ages not specified					
Leinster, R.D.	412	113	··			
Munster, R.D.	1,264	60	··			
Ulster, R.D.	1,944	31	··			
Connaught, R.D.	905	14	··			
Ireland, R.D.	4,525	218	··			
Ireland, C.D.	1,992	1,244	··			
Ireland, R. and C.D.	6,517	1,462	··			

* Census of Ireland, 1841, op. cit., pp. 150–1, 260–1, 362–3, 428–9, 438–9, and Table of Deaths, facing pp. 65, 105, 153, 181, and 183.

Commissioners: they 'had no reason to suspect peculiar inaccuracy in any one part'.

What conclusions on the question of differential mortality does the table suggest? First, quite unequivocally, that mortality in the civic districts was higher than mortality in the country-side: in every age-group, with a single exception (and that in the oldest and smallest group), the town-dweller stood a smaller chance of survival than the countryman. The three age-groups which, in the country as a whole, were responsible for the largest numbers of deaths were those of infants under 1, children of from 2 to 5 and men and women of from 56 to 65: in the first of these groups (and the one that accounted for more deaths than the other two together) proportionate mortality in civic districts was 70 per cent. higher than in rural districts; in the second it was 165 per cent. higher, and in the third, 24 per cent. Second, in conjunction with the evidence of Table 28 (which shows the proportion of total deaths which took place at various ages), it supports the conclusion the Census Commissioners drew from inadequate data that mortality in Connaught and Munster was higher than in Leinster and Ulster. Table 27 shows that the age-groups of highest mortality in the rural districts of Ireland were those of infants under 1, children from 2 to 5, and adults from 56 to 65: these groups accounted respectively for 22·71, 12·05, and 10·6 per cent. of total mortality. In the largest of these groups, Table 27 shows that mortality in rural Connaught was 40 per cent. greater than in rural Ulster; in the next group 34 per cent. greater, and in the smallest group 39 per cent. greater. In each of these age-groups Munster approached or exceeded the mortality of Connaught, while Leinster approached (though not always closely) the more favourable position of Ulster. In every other age-group Ulster had a lower mortality than Connaught, though the greater expectation of life in the larger age-groups in Leinster as compared with Munster was partially offset by a higher proportion of deaths in Leinster in most of the smaller age-groups.

The available mortality figures have not allowed us to say whether the expectation of life in Ireland before the Famine was unusually long or unusually short, and they give us, therefore, no guidance at all on whether part of the reason for the quickening in the rate of population-increase towards the end of the eighteenth century was that people were living longer: for evidence on this point we shall be obliged to rely on the equivocal testimony of the existence of forces that tended to depress or raise the death-rate. On differential mortality within Ireland the statistics are more

TABLE 28

Percentage of Total Deaths in 1840 at various Ages in the Rural Districts of the Provinces of Ireland*

Rural districts	Ages							
	Under 1		*2–5*		*6–15*		*16–25*	
	Num-ber	*Per cent.*	*Num-ber*	*Per cent.*	*Num-ber*	*Per cent.*	*Num-ber*	*Per cent.*
Leinster	4,764	18·96	2,711	10·79	1,974	7·86	2,294	9·13
Munster	8,006	24·37	4,459	13·57	2,495	7·59	2,669	8·12
Ulster	6,567	21·15	3,338	10·75	2,171	6·99	2,566	8·26
Connaught	6,003	26·80	2,914	13·01	1,539	6·87	1,680	7·50
Ireland	25,304	22·71	13,422	12·05	8,179	7·34	9,209	8·26

	26–35		*36–45*		*46–55*		*56–65*	
Leinster	1,876	7·47	1,895	7·54	2,054	8·18	2,687	10·69
Munster	2,440	7·43	2,238	6·81	2,349	7·15	3,524	10·73
Ulster	2,217	7·14	2,172	7·00	2,365	7·62	3,134	10·09
Connaught	1,587	7·09	1,661	7·42	1,762	7·87	2,466	11·01
Ireland	8,120	7·29	7,966	7·15	8,560	7·68	11,811	10·60

	66–75		*Over 75*		*Age unspecified*		*Total deaths*	
Leinster	2,306	9·18	2,449	9·75	113	0·45	25,123	
Munster	2,326	7·08	2,254	6·86	60	0·18	32,850	
Ulster	3,014	9·71	3,472	11·18	31	0·10	31,047	
Connaught	1,445	6·45	1,360	5·83	14	0·06	22,395	
Ireland	9,091	8·16	9,535	8·56	218	0·20	111,415	

* Census of Ireland, 1841, op. cit., Tables of Deaths, facing pp. 65, 104, 153, 181, and 183.

helpful: their indications are clear, consistent, and of sufficient authority to warrant our accepting their guidance unless there is strong literary evidence to the contrary. They suggest as problems worthy of investigation the greater expectation of life in rural Ulster and Leinster than in rural Connaught and Munster, and, in particular, the greater likelihood in these more favoured provinces of a child's surviving infancy.

VIII

HOSPITALS AND DISPENSARIES

WOULD it be legitimate for us to attribute any considerable part of the growth of population in Ireland in the late eighteenth and early nineteenth centuries to the prolongation of life as a result of treatment given in hospitals and dispensaries? There is some contemporary comment that would encourage us to do so. Bicheno, Secretary of the Linnaean Society and author of *Ireland and its Economy*, told the Select Committee of 1830 that 'it appeared to me that the provisions were larger in Ireland than in England for the sick poor. Their infirmaries, fever hospitals and lunatic asylums are often on a magnificent scale. Those which I saw at Cork, Waterford, Limerick, Dublin and Belfast were all well managed, as far as my cursory observation went.' The system of providing for the sick poor 'is certainly more complete in Ireland than in England, far more complete. The infirmaries which we have in England are only erected in very large towns and cities; whereas in Ireland, they are become a system, a part of the law of the land.'[1] Bishop Doyle, so often uninhibited in his criticism of Irish institutions, thought that the system of relief provided in the way of medicine and medical attendance for the poor was 'fully adequate'. 'Perhaps in some portions of those districts to which my examination refers [and he regarded his knowledge of Carlow, Queen's, and Kildare as particularly intimate], there may not be a sufficient supply of means of relief for persons afflicted with fever; but, making that exception I am confident the dispensaries throughout all the country are well managed, that they are more than sufficient in number, and that there is no person having a just claim to relief who is not attended to.'[2]

Does an examination of the dissemination of medical institutions support this favourable comment? Did they appreciably lessen the chance of death? Certainly, in the sixty years before the Famine, hospitals and dispensaries, hitherto practically non-existent beyond

[1] *Rep. S.C. S.P.I.*, 1830, op. cit., qq. 4224–5.
[2] Ibid., q. 4375.

Dublin, were opened in every county. The only seventeenth-century hospitals to which any reference has been found were for the treatment of soldiers. The Royal Hospital of Charles II 'for the relief and maintenance of ancient and maimed Officers and Soldiers of the Army in Ireland' was founded in 1680 at Kilmainham and maintained by a levy of 6*d*. in the pound from the pay of every soldier in Ireland.[1] Of the 10,000 troops that Schomberg embarked at Hoylake in 1689 to quell the Irish rebellion, 3,762 are said to have died in hospital in Belfast.[2] The Infirmary for the Sick and Wounded Soldiers of the Army, established towards the middle of the eighteenth century, continued to tend members of the Dublin Garrison until the Royal Military Infirmary was opened in Phoenix Park in 1788.[3] The first non-military hospital of which there is record was founded on a tiny scale—it had beds for four patients— in 1726.[4] Sixteen years earlier Dr. Steevens had died and made available in his will the property which led to the opening in 1733 of the hospital named after him. Richard Steevens was the son of an incumbent of Athlone, a royalist clergyman who thought it wise to leave England to avoid the punishment that threatened him for preaching against Cromwell. While practising medicine in Dublin, Richard is said to have acquired both a fortune and a sympathy with the sick poor of the city. On his sister's promising that she would never marry he felt able in his will to direct that after her death property yielding some £600 a year should be used for the foundation of a hospital. In 1733 the hospital was opened and was able to admit forty poor patients, chosen without distinction of religion or disease (except that their complaints had to be neither venereal nor infectious). For the rest of the eighteenth century, gifts and bequests allowed the hospital to expand considerably: in the following fifty years the process continued, but then it was largely nourished by public money. In 1737 Lord Primate Boulter fitted up a ward of ten beds which he maintained until his death five years later. In the forties ten additional beds were made available, partly by private generosity, partly by the proceeds of a lottery. Anonymous donations of £23,000 in the early eighties did not bring the hospital's income up to its expenditure. A number of

[1] 1851 Census, *Report on the Status of Disease, Accounts and Papers*, 1854, lviii. 95–6.
[2] C. Creighton, *History of Epidemics in Britain*, ii, 1894, p. 234.
[3] *Rep. on Status of Disease*, 1851, op. cit., p. 95.
[4] Ibid., p. 92.

wards was closed and the situation created which induced the Governors to appeal to Parliament for funds in 1801. Ten thousand pounds were granted for repairs and, in return for some wards which the Government took over for use as a military hospital, an additional £200 a year were promised. This amount was increased to nearly £1,500 by 1812 and more was added when the hospital admitted patients suffering from fever and venereal disease. By 1835 Steevens' had an operating theatre, a lecture-room, and an apothecary's shop: its wards, 'large, lofty and well-ventilated', had accommodation for 250 patients. Something over 2,000 in-patients were admitted annually: 16,000 were treated by the out-patients' department and a maternity section attended mothers in their homes. 'After-care' had developed to the extent of establishing a relief and clothing fund and giving necessitous discharged patients the railway fare to their homes. The Commissioners of 1829, appointed to inquire into the state of the charitable institutions of Dublin, reported that Steevens' was in much repute: it was attended by some of the most eminent surgeons of the city; it gave the poor advice and assistance with judgement and skill not exceeded in any similar establishment; its medical department was most respectably conducted, though accommodation for surgical cases was insufficient for the wants of the city. In addition to its other benefits, the hospital helped Dublin by assisting in the training of students in the medical schools.[1] Again in 1842 Steevens' was commended by a public commission: 'the patients appear to be extremely well taken care of; they have the benefits of the best medical and surgical attendance which Dublin affords, and the institution stands as high at present in public opinion as it did at any former period, both as an hospital for the relief of patients, and as a school for surgical instruction.'[2]

Dr. Steevens was the first of a line of people who, by gift or bequest, established hospitals in Dublin. In 1734 Mrs. Mary Mercer founded the hospital named after her. Ten years later the Charitable Musical Society opened a hospital for incurables. In the following year Dr. Bartholomew Mosse established the first maternity hospital in the United Kingdom.[3] Sixteen thousand pounds were voted by the Irish Parliament to help repay the costs

[1] C. Brady, *History of Steevens' Hospital*, Dublin, 1865, *passim*.
[2] *Rep. Comms. to inspect Charitable Institutions in Dublin, Accounts and Papers*, 1842, xxxviii. 95.   [3] *Rep. on Status of Disease*, 1851, op. cit., p. 96.

of its erection and equipment. In 1785 the Governors were granted the proceeds of a tax on sedan chairs to supplement subscriptions already raised for the purpose of erecting public rooms as a source of income for the hospital. In 1842 it was accommodating ninety-four patients: its wards were reported to be 'spacious and well ventilated, and kept in a most creditable manner'.[1] In 1752 St. Mark's Hospital was founded as the New Charitable Infirmary. The Westmoreland Lock Hospital came in 1755 and the Charitable Venereal Hospital three years later. The Meath Hospital, opened in 1756 for the benefit of poor artisans of the Earl of Meath's Liberty, became, in 1774, the County Dublin Infirmary.[2] In 1842 it had thirteen wards, with, in all, 100 beds: the patients were said to be extremely well attended to.[3] The Dublin House of Industry started its hospital in 1774 with two wards, one for medical and one for surgical cases. In 1814, a century after Sir Patrick Dun had died, the hospital named after him was opened. He had bequeathed money for the establishment of professorships in connexion with the College of Physicians, but the Irish Parliament in 1800 had altered his intentions and allowed the building of a hospital. In 1804, as the result largely of voluntary contributions, partly of a parliamentary grant, the Cork Street Fever Hospital and House of Recovery was opened. The Professors of the Royal College of Surgeons of Ireland founded the City of Dublin Hospital in 1832; the Sisters of Charity of the Order of St. Vincent de Paul opened St. Vincent's Hospital in 1834.[4]

The history of hospital building in the metropolis doubtless has its place in a discussion of rural population history, but it is a limited place. Hospitals in Dublin could accommodate some of the sick of the neighbouring country-side: they could help train doctors who practised in the provinces: they could act as an example to the benevolent or public-spirited in less fortunate areas: there was the probability that improvements in medicine, originating in the metropolitan hospitals, would find their way to the country-side. Such indirect benefits of the Dublin hospitals cannot, of course, be measured, but the provincial hospitals were undoubtedly in a much stronger position to cure the sick peasant or farm labourer.

---

[1] *Rep. Comms. Char. Institutions*, 1842, op. cit., pp. 62–4.
[2] *Rep. on Status of Disease*, 1851, op. cit., p. 95.
[3] *Rep. Comms. Char. Institutions*, 1842, op. cit., p. 142.
[4] *Rep. on Status of Disease*, 1851, op. cit., p. 97.

The Committee on the Poor of Ireland reported in 1804 that almost every county had its infirmary.[1] It was private individuals who showed the initiative that led to the establishment of these hospitals and it was from private contributions that most of their funds were drawn. Nonetheless, especially after the Act of Union, they were granted considerable financial assistance from public funds. The generosity with which the sick poor of Ireland were relieved by the more fortunate members of society, as well as by the poor themselves, was often commented on. There are indications, too, that in a country where infectious diseases were unusually prevalent, more than philanthropy induced men to subscribe to hospitals. In the 1820s, with small-pox and fever prevalent, there were more subscriptions than usual to the Belfast General Hospital.

It cannot be concealed [says the historian of the hospital] that a material agency in the augmentation of funds was the very prevalent dread of fever. . . . The Hospital was looked upon universally as the safety-valve which prevented the general explosion of the epidemic; and this view was ever strongly impressed upon the minds of the public, both by the reports of the Committee and the frequent instances of infection observed by the Medical Officers.[2]

Rogan, the physician to the Strabane Fever Hospital, pointed out to the 'higher classes' in 1819 that there was 'sufficient proof that inattention on their parts, to the comfort of the lower orders, among whom the disease usually originates, is sure to bring its own punishment. They would perceive the necessity of using every means for bettering the condition of the poor as the only certain method of protecting themselves from this formidable disease, which the experience of the late epidemic has proved to be peculiarly fatal in the upper ranks of society. They would learn that, by mitigating the distresses of the indigent, they increase their own prospect of enjoying, for a longer period, the goods of this world; and might, therefore, be induced to contribute a more liberal portion of them towards supporting the different institutions which have been formed for relieving the poor in sickness, or increasing their comforts in health.'[3] Harty, discussing the same epidemic a little later, thought that even British assistance during fevers in Ireland was 'not a question of mere duty or humanity . . . self-

---

[1] Reprinted as Appendix M to *Rep. S.C. S.P.I.*, 1830, op. cit., p. 150.
[2] A. G. Malcolm, *History of the General Hospital, Belfast*, Belfast, 1852, p. 82.
[3] F. Rogan, 1819, op. cit., pp. x–xi.

defence and self-interest combine to give it every adventitious importance that can be desired; because it is, in truth, impossible that fever should rage in Ireland, and that England should altogether escape its pernicious influence'.[1] In the words of the man who both wrote the history of Steevens' Hospital and appealed for funds on its behalf, 'no-one can say he does not owe his preservation from contagious diseases . . . to the fact that their progress has been checked . . . by means of public hospitals.'[2]

The State was not entirely indifferent to the development of medical institutions in the eighteenth century. It made provision for only trivial contributions to their funds, but it helped them to deal with some of their legal and constitutional problems. In the nineteenth century, *laissez-faire* notwithstanding, Parliament authorized the Grand Juries in Ireland to make presentments for hospitals and dispensaries and it made contributions to them from the national exchequer. The principle of State assistance to Irish hospitals was excused, partly because wealth in Ireland had not increased in proportion to population, partly because the Act of Union had tended to lessen the volume of private subscriptions: while, after the Union, Dublin remained a metropolis of the poor it was no longer a metropolis of the wealthy.[3]

An Act of 1765 made the clergy of the established Church a perpetual corporation for the erection of infirmaries; the qualifications of governors by subscription were fixed; a system of internal government was decided on and Grand Juries were empowered to make presentments of up to £100. This sum, after 1805, could be increased by £500: two years later it was made available in cities and towns which had local government.[4] The need for fever hospitals was hardly less apparent than the need for general hospitals. In the last quarter of the eighteenth century, following the establishment of the Hospital of St. John in Limerick in 1773, a number of Acts provided for the establishment and endowment of fever hospitals. In 1807 Grand Juries were empowered to make contributions of up to £100 to their funds. In 1818, with the stimulus of a serious outbreak of fever, the powers of the Grand Juries were widened: they might present for fever hospitals sums up to double

---

[1] W. Harty, *Historic Sketch of the Causes . . . of the Contagious Fever . . .*, Dublin, 1820, pp. xi–xii.
[2] Brady, op. cit., p. 30.
[3] *Reps. Comms. Char. Institutions*, 1842, op. cit., p. 11.
[4] *Rep. S.C. S.P.I.*, 1830, op. cit., p. 24.

the amount of the private subscriptions they received and at the same time the problems of the hospital builders were eased by the provision of government loans repayable by instalments.[1]

Parallel with the increasing State encouragement of the establishment of infirmaries and fever hospitals, institutional treatment was provided for lunatics. In the eighteenth century they were in a lamentable plight. Dublin, Cork, Waterford, and Limerick had accommodation, mostly in the Houses of Industry, for under 200 lunatic paupers, but this was wholly inadequate for the number of people who needed admission.[2] Of those who could not get to asylums, some wandered the country, some were taken in by the prisons, others stayed in their homes. The Select Committee of 1817 which considered the state of the lunatic poor was told by one of its members that 'when a strong young man or woman gets the complaint, the only way they have to manage is by making a hole in the floor of the cabin not high enough for a person to stand up in, with a crib over it to prevent his getting up, the hole is about five feet deep, and they give this wretched being his food there, and there he generally dies'.[3]

An Act of 1787 empowered the Grand Juries to present the sums necessary for establishing wards for lunatics, but little notice was taken of it.[4] In 1810 a grant was made to the Dublin Richmond Lunatic Asylum. But it was not until the 1817 Committee on the Lunatic Poor had made its recommendations that there was any real attempt by the State to alleviate the lot of lunatics. The Lord-Lieutenant was empowered to arrange for the construction of whatever asylums he considered necessary. By 1827 seven, designed to accommodate over 800 patients, were built or being built. They certainly impressed the Inspectors-General of Prisons, whose duty it was to visit asylums: 'the present asylums of Ireland', they reported, 'are superior to anything of the kind in Europe. . . . The whole system of cure, chiefly consisting of employment, kindness, moral government, and freedom from restraint, is worthy of examination as a good example.'[5]

The dispensary movement, like the hospital movement, found

---

[1] *Rep. S.C. S.P.I.*, 1830, op. cit., pp. 25–6.

[2] *Report from the Committee respecting the Poor in Ireland*, 1804, reprinted as Appendix M, *Rep. S.C. S.P.I.*, op. cit., p. 150.

[3] *Rep. S.C. on the Lunatic Poor in Ireland, Reports (Ireland)*, 1817, viii. 55.

[4] *Report from the Committee respecting the Poor in Ireland*, 1804, op. cit., p. 150.

[5] Quoted in *Rep. S.C. S.P.I.*, op. cit., p. 29.

its impetus partly in private contributions, partly in legislative action. The origin of most dispensaries is obscure; an exception is the Belfast Dispensary. An appeal to the well-to-do, launched in the Belfast *Newsletter* in 1792, started with the easily defended proposition that 'the importance and utility of the industrial poor to a civilised and commercial nation are indisputable, yet little attention has been paid in this country to the preservation of their lives and health'. Three great benefits, it was expected, would be derived from a dispensary: there would be fewer beggars; inoculation would be made more general, and Ireland would be enabled to emulate other nations by adopting schemes for the recovery of persons apparently drowned. Later, the relief of lying-in women was added as a fourth service a dispensary might render.[1] In 1805, Parliament, realizing that many of the Irish poor were unable to benefit from the county infirmaries because they lived too far away from them, empowered Grand Juries to double any private contributions made to dispensaries. Originally the legislation was interpreted as compulsory, later as discretionary.[2]

Table G, Appendix VI,[3] makes it clear that in the three-quarters of a century before the Famine, coinciding closely enough with the rapid increase of population, there was a remarkable extension throughout Ireland in the provision of infirmaries, fever hospitals, and dispensaries. With the possible exception of Waterford, every county had its infirmary by 1821: 6 were set up before the legislation of 1765; 15 in the following 10 years. The 60 fever hospitals that survived in 1851 were mostly of a more recent foundation: 14 dated from the decade of the 1817 epidemic, 10 from the 1820s and 21 from the 1830s. By 1851 there were dispensaries in every county—and not infrequently more than 20 to a county. Private gifts and State grants impelled the spread of medical institutions: both were motivated by a desire to alleviate suffering and save life. How far was the contemporary steep increase in population a measure of their success? Any precise answer would require a medical criticism of the treatment given in these institutions. This must be regarded as beyond the scope of the present work: nonetheless, we can find in the statistics and in contemporary comment some indications of the direction in which the solution may be found.

[1] Malcolm, op. cit., pp. 34–5.
[2] *Rep. S.C. S.P.I.*, 1830, op. cit., p. 27.   [3] pp. 274–5.

The evidence given before the 1830 Committee pointing to the fuller provision of hospitals in Ireland than in England is not easily substantiated. Judging merely by the number of provincial hospitals, Ireland seems to have been outdistanced. Even including 61 fever hospitals, Ireland in 1835 had only 99 provincial hospitals[1] as compared with 114 in England 5 years later.[2] A medical statistician calculated that in the provinces of Ireland, apart from accommodation for maternity cases and for patients suffering from fever and opthalmic and venereal diseases, there was one hospital bed for 5,827 persons, while in the English counties there was one for 2,692 people (apart from provision in workhouses, which was greater in England than in Ireland): in England the provincial infirmaries took one patient per year for every 403 people in the population, in Ireland one for 746.[3] Apart from the relative adequacy of the Irish and English hospitals there is no doubt that the accommodation in Ireland was wholly insufficient to meet the needs of the people. The infirmary in Queen's County was the only one that published figures for the number of patients it was obliged to refuse for want of funds: in the four years from 1828 to 1832, 2,212 sick people were turned away, compared with the 2,406 who were admitted.[4] As we can dismiss the possibility that Leinster had a surfeit of hospitals we can conclude from figures collected in the 1841 Census that Connaught (probably needing more) had to be content with a grossly inadequate number: in Leinster there were 3·64 hospitals per 10,000 inhabitants, in Connaught, 0·63.[5] In 1851 Leinster had one hospital bed (for all types of patient) for every 517 in the population: in Connaught the corresponding figure was 2,476.[6] The tragedy was that it was often the poorest districts, those most likely to need an infirmary or fever hospital, that were left unprovided. Fever hospitals after 1818 qualified for grants according to the amount of private subscriptions they attracted. Private subscriptions were notoriously hard to find where

[1] D. Phelan, *Statistical Inquiry into the present State of the medical Charities of Ireland*, Dublin, 1835, p. 2.

[2] G. T. Griffith, *Population Problems of the Age of Malthus*, Cambridge, 1926, p. 221.

[3] Phelan, 1835, op. cit., pp. 11 and 14.

[4] Ibid., p. 13.

[5] 1841 Census, *Reports from Commissioners*, 1843, xxiv, *Report on Table of Deaths*, p. xii. The corresponding figures for Munster and Ulster were 2·62 and 1·29, respectively.

[6] See below, Table G, Appendix VI, pp. 274–5.

landlords were not resident, but there can have been little positive correlation between non-residence and immunity from fever.

The inadequacy of the hospitals was apparent in other ways than the shortage of accommodation: their sites, usually in the assize towns, were often chosen in complete disregard of the convenience of the people from whom they were to draw their patients; Wexford's infirmary was in the extreme east of the county, Antrim's in its south-eastern corner. Sometimes unfriendly relations between local doctors and the infirmaries did not increase the usefulness of either: a majority of the doctors practising in Ireland were trained in Great Britain and resented being largely disbarred from hospital work by the legal requirement that at least three-quarters of the infirmary doctors should be Dublin-trained. Hospital patients were often neglected because there was no resident doctor. Nonetheless, the medical officers, according to Phelan, were

generally, I may say universally, fully capable of discharging their professional duties, being excellent anatomists, good surgeons, and from the course of their professional studies, and a rigid examination, well qualified to prescribe in mere medical cases. . . . I believe the medical officers of the county infirmaries of Ireland, are, at least, as well educated, and as capable of discharging their mixed professional duties as any others in similar institutions in England or elsewhere.[1]

Even though a medical inquirer might show that some of the practices these hospitals trusted in could do little to save life, it is difficult to avoid the conclusion that on balance they tended to lower mortality. Removal to hospital normally gave the patient clean surroundings and fresh air, both remedial measures that he was far from certain to find at home; it gave medical care up to the standard of the day, and that, too, was only exceptionally available in the Irish cabin: with infectious cases, moreover, removal to hospital meant that the patient's relatives and friends were less likely to contract disease, partly because a source of infection was removed, partly because they were not obliged to deny themselves food and clothes to procure the requirements of the patient. That the hospitals of Ireland were on a 'magnificent scale' and that there was 'no person having a just claim to relief that was not attended to' it is impossible to believe: the thirty-four provincial infirmaries had between them less than 2,000 beds, and, in a year of unusually

---

[1] Phelan, 1835, op. cit., p. 43.

heavy mortality their entire income, together with that of all the other hospitals, fever hospitals, and dispensaries in the country, was under £112,000.[1]

The dispensaries, like the hospitals, were too few in number to meet the needs of the people. In 1835, for the country as a whole there was one dispensary for 13,520 people, but this average figure hid both the relative abundance of dispensaries in parts of Leinster and the enormous number of people who had to make do with a single institution elsewhere: in Down, Longford, and Leitrim there was not a dispensary for every 20,000 of the population.[2] Vast parts of the poorer and more desolate districts of Donegal, the Devon Commission was told, were not only without dispensary doctors, but without doctors of any sort.[3] Phelan was not so satisfied with the care and competence of the medical officers of the dispensaries as he was in the case of their colleagues in the infirmaries: often they had no legally recognized qualifications, and, though there was no accoucheur who could take their places, many did not practise midwifery. Some were enticed to stint their patients by a regulation obliging them to find their remuneration in whatever funds remained when medicines were paid for: perhaps this helps to explain why at Trim dispensary medicine cost less than 2d. per patient, while elsewhere it cost as much as 2s. 5d.[4] Some doctors lived so far from their dispensaries that they visited them only once or twice a week: some refused to visit patients living more than a mile or two from their centre; others spent so much time on more lucrative private practice that they had little opportunity of caring for dispensary patients.[5] Jobbery seems to have been partially responsible for the poor quality of the medical attendance in some of the dispensaries;[6] but it was probably more often the result of sheer lack of funds to pay a more competent officer. In Limerick, in the early forties, the funds of the city dispensary were so low 'that they have not for many years paid any salary to the medical officers, except the apothecary . . . [they] have not even been able, except very partially, to pay for any one for visiting the sick poor at their

[1] See below, Table G, Appendix VI, pp. 274–5.
[2] *Report of the Poor Law Commissioners on the Medical Charities, Ireland, Reports from Commissioners*, 1841, xi. 3.
[3] *Reports from Commissioners*, 1845, xix. *278*, 34.
[4] *Rep. . . . on Medical Charities*, 1841, op. cit., p. 3.
[5] Ibid., p. 4.
[6] *Rep. Devon Com.*, 1845, op. cit., *28*, 84.

homes'.[1] Not only distance prevented people in need of treatment from using the dispensary: some were discouraged by a fee that could be as high as 2s. 6d.,[2] others were debarred by rules which allowed treatment to be given only to the tenantry of subscribers, and subscriptions in some places were expected only from members of one party.[3]

The dispensaries, then, both because there were too few of them and because of shortcomings in their administration, did not attain the standards we would have to find before we could regard them as of outstanding importance in contributing to the rapid growth of population. Sometimes, indeed, they were blamed for spreading infection by bringing together the sick from various maladies, but on balance, by giving medical advice to people who, otherwise, would have had none, and, perhaps, occasionally, by convincing people that it was worthwhile to struggle with dirt, they doubtless allowed some of their patients to live longer.

[1] Ibid., *Reports from Commissioners*, 1845, xx. *622*, 14.
[2] Ibid., *Reports from Commissioners*, 1845, xix. *200*, 31.
[3] *Rep. . . . on Medical Charities*, 1841, op. cit., pp. 2 and 5.

IX

SMALL-POX, INOCULATION, AND VACCINATION

ALTHOUGH we lack statistical confirmation it is probable that in the half-century before the Famine the greatest contribution made by medical advance to the growth of the population of Ireland was by the lessening of the incidence of small-pox. Small-pox had for centuries been one of the deadliest of diseases in Ireland. Rogers, a Cork physician, writing of it in 1734, said that 'though of foreign Growth, and by *Transplantation* brought in amongst us, it is now become a *Weed* of our own *Soil*, and a *Native* of our *Country*. 'Tis well known that *Arabia* and the adjoining *Southern* Regions were the *Mother Countries*, the unhappy *Parents* of this *Contagious Disease*; and that it can claim no longer a Descent with us, than about two *Centuries*.'[1] Sir William Wilde, in the 1851 Census, gives it a more remote Irish pedigree, one beginning in the eighth century.[2] Although the sources of Irish epidemiology for the seventeenth and eighteenth centuries are limited, and, unfortunately, too little concerned with the health of the country-side, we have accounts of frequent ravages of small-pox. In 1648 'the Small-pox spread a pestilence through Galway city and carried off multitudes of the citizens'.[3] In Cork and its neighbourhood in 1708–9 it was 'very frequent' and it lingered on, though less severely, for several more years.[4] In 1718 it flared up again to epidemic proportions and did not disappear for ten years.[5] 'Early in the Winter of the Year 1728, and soon after our *Endemial Epidemic Fever* raged, the *Small Pox* of all the Kinds before mentioned, began to show themselves again, very *Epidemic*; and as the *Fever* continued to increase through the Winters of the Years 1729, 30, and 1731, so did they. From thence the *Small Pox* and their contemporary

---

[1] Joseph Rogers, M.D., *Essay on Epidemic Diseases*, Dublin, 1734, p. 82.
[2] 1851 Census, *Reports from Commissioners*, 1856, xxix. 686.
[3] *Life of Bishop Kirwan*, quoted in 1851 Census, op. cit., p. 372.
[4] J. Rogers, *Essay on Epidemic Diseases*, 1734, p. 91.
[5] Ibid., p. 108; M. O'Connell, *Observationes Medicales*, quoted in 1851 Census, op. cit., p. 383.

Fever, began sensibly to abate, both in Frequency and Violence, and at last, were little heard of.'[1] In Dublin, in the early summer of 1738 there was small-pox of a bad kind, frequently mortal, though by August it was becoming milder.[2] In the Famine years, 1740–1 small-pox was generally prevalent. In Cork, in April 1740, 'Epidemic Small-pox of the worst type spreading universally came on. This gradually increasing reached the greatest intensity and extent in the month of July, from which time declining by degrees it was seldom seen at the time of the autumnal equinox'.[3] In Dublin the disease began to rage in May and increased so rapidly during the summer that in August thirty-three died from it in a single week.[4] Five years later Dublin suffered again: scarcity in the north drove many beggars to Dublin and their children, full of small-pox, were exposed in the streets and were regarded as the cause of a 'remarkable increase' in small-pox.[5]

That mortality from small-pox was high in Dublin even in years not singled out by contemporary comment as periods of notable epidemics is shown by four surviving bills of mortality for years between 1743 and 1754. In 1743 there were recorded 272 deaths from small-pox out of a total of 2,193; in 1752, 251 out of 1,844; in 1753, 241 out of 1,825; and in 1754, 292 out of 1,897.[6] As a measure of total deaths these figures are grossly deficient. They may well, in addition, under-assess the proportion of total deaths to be attributed to small-pox: the minority to whom the figures referred— almost all members of the established Church—were doubtless immune from the worst of the overcrowding which allowed epidemic diseases to spread so rapidly among the poor.

From 1765, Dr. James Sims, of Tyrone, continues the history of disease in Ireland. Towards the end of September 1766, in Tyrone, bilious disorders gave way to the small-pox 'that, with unheard of havock, desolated the close of this year, and the succeeding spring of 1767. They had appeared above a year before along the eastern coast of the kingdom, and proceeded slowly westward with so even a pace, that a curious person might with ease have computed the rate of their progress. . . . As they had not visited the

---

[1] J. Rogers, *Essay on Epidemic Diseases*, 1734, p. 108.
[2] Rutty, 1770, op. cit., p. 70.
[3] O'Connell, *Observationes Medicales*, quoted in 1851 Census, op. cit., p. 391.
[4] Rutty, op. cit., p. 81.
[5] Ibid., p. 126.
[6] 1851 Census, op. cit., pp. 398, 400–1.

country for some years, numberless subjects were grown up for them to exercise their fury upon, and many blooming infants were just opening to the sun, in vain, since they were so soon to be cropt by this unfeeling spoiler. Of thousands who caught the infection in this and the neighbouring counties, scarcely one-half escaped, and even of these, some with the loss of one or both eyes, and several with faces so altered, as to be known with difficulty by their most intimate acquaintance.'[1] In the early summer of 1770 there was a fresh outbreak: that it was less mortal than that of 1766 was rather to be attributed to 'the want of subjects for them to exercise their fury upon, the preceding disorder having left few who had not undergone the malady, than to any abatement in their malignancy'.[2] In September 1776 the *Hibernian Magazine* reported that 'small-pox has been so rife and fatal in Cork for five or six weeks past that it is almost pestilential, the children dying in great numbers'.[3] 1817 and 1821 are referred to by contemporaries as years of unusually heavy mortality from small-pox in Dublin.[4] The Dublin Cow Pock Institution reported that in 1823 a 'most malignant small-pox prevailed in many parts of this island'.[5]

In spite of much discussion in medical circles on the respective merits of the warm and the cool régime in treating small-pox patients, if Sims is to be trusted, there was little the eighteenth-century doctor could do for them. In the 1766 epidemic

some persons were bled in the beginning, others were kept warm and sweated, and others followed the cool regimen, and used laxatives; some took cordials at first, others not until after the sixth day; large quantities of the bark were given to some during the state of maturation, to others opiates or claret and water; some were blistered on the secondary fever arising, others were purged, and others took James's powders, and others antimonials; in vain! in vain were most things which the art of man could devise called in to their assistance, the mortality still continued.[6]

Doctors had more promising results when they devoted their energies to prevention rather than to cure. Inoculation was no novel practice when, early in the eighteenth century, it was noticed in the British scientific press and when, in 1717, Lady Mary Wortley Montague's *Letters* from Turkey brought it to the atten-

---

[1] J. Sims, M.D., *Observations on Epidemic Disorders . . .*, 1773, pp. 36–8.
[2] Ibid., pp. 134–5.
[3] Quoted in 1851 Census, op. cit., p. 413.   [4] Ibid., p. 686.
[5] Ibid., p. 461.   [6] Sims, 1773, op. cit., p. 43.

tion of a wider public. Lady Mary reported that 'they take the smallpox here by way of diversion, as they take the waters in other countries'. She knew of no case of anybody dying from deliberate infection and she felt 'patriot enough to take pains to bring this useful invention into fashion in England'. Her son was successfully inoculated in Constantinople and her daughter is said to have been the first person to be inoculated by a surgeon in Britain. Yet more publicity resulted from Princess Anne's severe attack of small-pox in 1725. Queen Caroline, then Princess of Wales, concerned for her other children, secured permission to have seven condemned criminals reprieved on condition that they allowed themselves to be inoculated. None of the prisoners had reason to regret his boldness: six suffered only from mild small-pox and the seventh survived a more severe attack. Caroline, further reassured by the successful inoculation of eleven charity children, offered two princesses to the inoculators. The result was satisfactory and the practice was more widely accepted.[1]

In the scientific comment stimulated by these celebrated cases of inoculation it was made plain that however ignorant London had been of inoculation, 'buying the pox' had long been a custom in remote parts both of Wales and Scotland. Dr. Perrot Williams, a physician in Haverfordwest, reported in the *Philosophical Transactions* for 1722 that in parts of South Wales 'they either rub the matter taken from the pustules when ripe on several parts of the skin of the arm, etc., or prick these parts with pins, or the like, first infected with the same matter. And notwithstanding they omit the necessary evacuations, such as purging, etc., yet, as I am informed, they generally come off well enough; and, what's remarkable, I cannot hear of one instance of their having smallpox a second time'.[2] The Scottish highlanders had long inoculated their children by tying round their wrists worsted threads, moistened with variolous matter or by putting them to bed with a child who had the disease mildly.[3] No evidence has come to light of any similar traditional practice in Ireland. The first recorded inoculation there, performed by Mr. Hannibal Hall, a Dublin surgeon, did not take

[1] W. Woodville, M.D., *History of the Inoculation of the Small-pox in Great Britain*, 1796, i. 37–108.

[2] J. Jurin, *A Letter . . . containing a Comparison between the Mortality of the Natural Small-pox and that given by Inoculation*, 1723, p. 23.

[3] Woodville, op. cit. i. 42; James Moore, *History of the Small-pox*, 1815, p. 225.

place until 1723, until after, that is, the earlier of the celebrated English experiments.[1] The practice spread slowly: only twenty-five cases are recorded in the whole of Ireland by 1729 and, indeed, the early results were not encouraging.[2] Dr. Bryan Robinson published an account of his inoculation in 1725 of five children of a Dublin gentleman: three recovered, but a 'strong lusty boy' and a 'strong healthy boy who had never had any sickness' died.[3]

In rural Ireland inoculation was diffused with a momentum independent of its advance in England. In England, and, doubtless, in Dublin, the approbation that followed the successful inoculation of princes of the blood or the members of a bishop's household, or the notoriety following the death after inoculation of a peer's son or butler, put the practice in or out of vogue. The effect of the argument, reasoned or unreasoned, of the case for or against inoculation could also be noticed. Some avoided it because they thought it the inspiration of the devil, others because they felt it promoted vice or immorality, or because they suspected that with the variolous matter there could be introduced into the body syphilis, scrofula, or consumption.[4] Maitland, the original practitioner, claimed that inoculated small-pox was not only invariably milder than in a natural attack, but that it was not infectious. The widely published disproval of his claims did not help the cause: much was made of the epidemic of small-pox in London in 1723 and the great mortality from it in Hertford, both, it was said, the result of the introduction of the disease by inoculated people.[5] Others, however strongly they wanted inoculation, found it beyond their means. By the 1750s in England it had become a serious and expensive affair: the surgeon would not act until the patient was fortified by a month's preparatory treatment and medical attendance was often continued for five or six weeks afterwards. 'Consequently', says an early historian of small-pox, 'the practice of inoculation, though widely diffused, was in a great measure confined to the opulent'.[6]

In Ireland, by the early nineteenth century, inoculation was cer-

---

[1] Woodville, op. cit., p. 200.

[2] J. G. Scheuchzer, M.D., F.R.S., *Account of the Success of Innoculating the Small-pox for the years 1727 and 1728*, 1729, p. 41.

[3] B. Robinson, M.D., *The Case of Five Children who were Inoculated in Dublin on the 26th of August 1725*, Dublin, 1725, pp. 4–6.

[4] General Board of Health, *Papers relating to the History and Practice of Vaccination, Accounts and Papers*, 1857, sess. 2, xxxv. 154.

[5] Moore, op. cit., pp. 242–4.

[6] Ibid., p. 265.

tainly not the monopoly of the well-to-do. Its diffusion seems mainly to have been the work of itinerant quacks, a body of men in whom the Irish had great faith. There is evidence that ten, twenty, and even fifty, years after enlightened opinion, aware of the advantages of vaccination, had endeavoured to undermine the position of the travelling inoculators, they retained the confidence of much of the peasantry. Sir William Wilde said that inoculation had been practised 'very extensively' in Ireland from 1725 to the 1850s.[1] In a Derry parish, in 1812, village surgeons were popularizing vaccination, but they were hampered by 'the ignorance and injudicious management of some itinerant quacks [which] have not only tended to discredit, with the common people, this happy discovery, but have raised an outcry against the whole system of inoculation'.[2] The Report of the Board of Health, published in 1822, dealt with the counties of Munster, and showed that in every one the inoculators were still active, often with disastrous results.[3]

Inoculation, then, seems to have been common in Ireland by the beginning of the nineteenth century, but we cannot, for that reason, regard it as one of the causes of the growth of population: indeed it may well have had a depopulating influence. There was much to make the individual want to be inoculated, but the practice was one of which the community might well be wary. The individual, when deliberately infected by small-pox, usually had a mild attack, and he was, in general, safe from reinfection in time of an epidemic. Rogers, the Cork epidemiologist, knew well the attractions of inoculation: 'it appears', he wrote in 1734, 'by a *Computation* of 42 Years past . . . that of those who are taken ill of the Natural Small Pox, there dies one in five or six, or nearest, two in Eleven. That of persons who have been *Inoculated* in *England* for some Years past, there have died but one in ninety one. From these Facts, which may be looked upon as unquestionable, (being with great Accuracy and Exactness stated by the Learned Dr. *Jurin*,) the Inference is natural, and admits for no Doubt.'[4] The individual's immunity was gained at the cost of increasing the risk of his neighbour's infection—and the disease picked up from the inoculated person was of normal virulence. The danger of such an extension of small-pox was increased in England towards the end

[1] 1851 Census, op. cit., p. 686.   [2] Mason, op. cit. i, 1814, p. 313.
[3] *First Report of the General Board of Health in the City of Dublin*, pp. 94–7.
[4] Rogers, 1734, op. cit., pp. 176–7.

of the eighteenth century by the growing practice amongst doctors of discouraging the patients they inoculated from keeping to their beds. In Ireland, with the more widespread inoculation of the poor, it can never have been the rule for the patient to be isolated, and many of the social habits of the Irish increased the risks from any source of infection. In 1822, in Co. Waterford, there were 'complaints of itinerant inoculators who bring small-pox into the district'; in Cork, Kerry, and Clare, small-pox was said to be frequently introduced by itinerant inoculators; in Limerick 'small-pox would appear but seldom, but for the busy inoculation of empirics'.[1] Sir Gilbert Blane, writing in 1811, while admitting that inoculation gave the individual a milder form of small-pox, thought that on balance there was an increase of mortality by 'inoculation destroying more than it saved, by spreading it [the disease] to places which would otherwise have escaped'.[2] In Paris inoculation was forbidden in 1763 after a serious outbreak of small-pox, generally attributed to infection by inoculated persons.[3]

Vaccination, like inoculation, was new to the doctors but not to the country-side, when the public began to read about it. There was a tradition in cow-keeping districts, on the Continent as well as in England, that if dairy-maids, or other people, handling cows suffering from a certain pustular disease were infected by them, they themselves would acquire immunity from small-pox. Jenner, as a doctor's apprentice near Bristol, became interested in this piece of folk medicine, and in 1798 published a paper in which he collected the accounts of many people who, by accidental infection from cows had become immune from small-pox. He showed, too— and in this he was anticipated by the country people of Holstein— that there was no need to wait for accidental infection: immunity was readily acquired by deliberate inoculation with cow-pox, or, as Jenner discovered, by lymph taken from a person already so inoculated.[4]

Some of the arguments in the public discussion of the merits of vaccination were attractive to a people with so firm a belief in the power of magic in medicine as the Irish. They might well have been troubled by the questions of the London pamphleteers. Would not the human character undergo strange mutations if the

[1] *First Rep. Gen. Board of Health*, op. cit., pp. 94–7.

[2] G. Blane, 'On the Practice of Vaccination', in *Reports of the Society for bettering the Condition and increasing the Comforts of the Poor*, 1815, vi. 305–7.

[3] General Board of Health, *Papers relating to . . . Vaccination*, op. cit., p. 157.

[4] Ibid., pp. 157–9.

body were polluted with fluid taken from a cow? What security was there against the growth of horns from the human head? The questions were made the more worrying by the 'authenticated examples' of the pamphleteers. There was 'the child at Peckham [who] had its former natural disposition absolutely changed to the brutal, so that it ran upon all fours like a beast, bellowing like a cow, and butted with its head like a bull'. There were faces distorted until they resembled those of oxen: there was the lady's daughter who coughed like a cow and the boy who grew patches of cow's hair.[1] That the Irish countryman was frequently confronted with any of these examples in the original is open to doubt, but that many of them were influenced by such considerations at second-hand is certain. The itinerant inoculators, afraid for their profession, did not scruple in the arguments they used in its defence. In a country, too, which many of its educated class believed to be over-populated, there was room for resistance to vaccination by those who might be expected to disseminate the practice, on the ground that the more sure it was as a safeguard against small-pox, the more certain its harm to the country. Small-pox, being a 'merciful provision on the part of Providence to lessen the burthen of a poor man's family', was it not 'impious and profane to wrest out of the hands of the Almighty these divine dispensations'?[2]

It was not only prejudice—and prejudice was strong until the second half of the century[3]—that hindered the progress of vaccination in Ireland. The remoteness of many districts made it difficult for people to get vaccinated, and difficult, even, to get pure virus to them.[3] Nonetheless, progress there was. In 1804 the Dublin Cow Pock Institution was opened 'for the purposes of securing a succession of cow pock matter, of inoculating gratuitously the children of the poor and supplying the different parts of the kingdom with genuine infection'.[4] By 1809 it had vaccinated 12,000 people in Dublin, but it believed that twice as many Dubliners had been immunized elsewhere.[5] Although small-pox was far from being exterminated in Dublin, the Institution believed that the general substitution of vaccine for variolous infection had considerably diminished the number of patients brought to hospital. The

---

[1] Ibid., pp. 163–4.   [2] Ibid., p. 163.   [3] 1851 Census, op. cit., p. 423.
[4] T. Bernard, 'Account of the Dublin Cow Pock Institution', in *Reports of the Society for bettering the Condition . . . of the Poor*, 1815, vi. 132.
[5] *Papers relating to Vaccination in Dublin, Reports, etc. (Ireland)*, 1810–11, vi. 1140.

following year it was able to refer to the 'most satisfactory accounts' it had received from its correspondents of the progress of vaccination throughout the interior of Ireland: its directors had 'great pleasure in observing the zeal and disinterestedness of the Country Practitioners, who sacrifice private interest to the public good, in strongly recommending the practice'.[1]

The zeal of the medical profession was further demonstrated by a series of resolutions unanimously passed by a meeting of the Royal College of Surgeons of Ireland in 1811. The College agreed that there was not a physician or surgeon in Ireland who did not approve and practise vaccination; that inoculation was scarcely practised by respectable practitioners, except as a means of testing the efficacy of vaccination; that vaccination had increased in Ireland beyond the expectations of the most sanguine supporters, and that in consequence the mortality from small-pox had materially decreased.[2] From the country, too, came evidence of the dissemination of vaccination. The incumbent of Ballintoy, Co. Antrim, wrote in 1812 that 'since the prejudice against inoculation has in a great measure been removed, and that the people have become acquainted with the happy effect of the cow-pock, that loathsome and deadly disease, the small-pox, is but little known. In the propagation of the cow-pock I am the principal practitioner, and have inoculated many hundreds with the greatest success.' In Co. Cork, in 1816 the ravages of the small-pox 'in consequence of the practice of vaccination [have] been much less frequent of late years than formerly'. In Dungiven, Co. Derry, 'vaccination has been making considerable progress under the hands of our village surgeons'. In a Tipperary parish there was no prejudice against vaccination when the case in its favour was fairly stated, but in more remote districts the practice was not as general as it deserved to be because the itinerant inoculators clung to variolous inoculation as the serum was more readily obtained. From Kilmactige, Co. Sligo, came the report that 'inoculation has saved the lives of thousands . . . as scarcely any child dies of it; but at this time a great many, whom the suspicion of their parents kept from inoculation, are dying of the natural pock, and scarcely one of them survives'.[3]

[1] *Papers relating to Vaccination in Dublin, Reports, etc. (Ireland)*, 1810–11, vi. 1141–4.
[2] *Reports of the Society for bettering the Condition . . . of the Poor*, vi. 281–2.
[3] Mason, op. cit. i. 156, 313; ii. 112, 131, 368.

Before the Famine the State did little directly to encourage the spread of vaccination, although, doubtless, the dispensaries, which public money helped to finance, played their part by the free vaccination which many of them offered. The only legislation on vaccination was passed in 1840 and 1841. It charged the Poor Law Boards of both Ireland and England and Wales with the duty of seeing that the guardians arranged with local doctors for the vaccination, at the expense of the rates, of anybody living in their unions who wished for it. At the same time inoculation with variolous matter was made an offence.[1] The Act came too late to have any substantial effect before the Famine, and, indeed, 'notwithstanding the daily and manifest breach of the law, there has scarcely been an instance', twelve years after the passing of the Act, of conviction of an inoculator.[2]

The mortality statistics of the thirties and forties show that small-pox, in spite of vaccination, remained, next to fever, the greatest single cause of mortality in Ireland.[3] Some saving of life undoubtedly followed the spread of vaccination, but it may well be that this gain was offset, in the dozen years before the Famine, by the repeated shortage of food and the associated factors which then contributed to the spread of disease.[4] Certainly, if the statistics give even general guidance, Ireland was far outstripped by other countries in combating small-pox. In Sweden, it is said, that in the forty years following the introduction of vaccination in 1801, 158 people died of small-pox per million of the total population; in Westphalia, from 1816 to 1850, only 114.[5] Yet in Ireland, from 1831 to 1841, there were, on an annual average, 710 deaths from small-pox per million of the 1841 population. By English standards, too, small-pox remained very deadly in Ireland. From 1831 to 1841, of every 1,000 deaths in Ireland, 49 were from small-pox, while in England and Wales, from 1843 to 1851, the comparable figure was 22.[6]

---

[1] *Report on the State of Small-pox and Vaccination . . . presented . . . by the Small-pox and Vaccination Committee*, 1853. *Accounts and Papers*, 1852–3, ci. 84.

[2] 'Report on the State of Smallpox and Vaccination in Ireland' made by William Wilde to the Lord Lieutenant. *Accounts and Papers*, 1852–3, ci. 103.

[3] 1841 Census, Table of Deaths, *Reports from Commissioners*, 1843, xxiv, facing p. 182.   [4] See below, Chapter X, pp. 227–37.

[5] General Board of Health, *Papers relating to . . . Vaccination*, op. cit., pp. 168, 171.

[6] *Report . . . by Small-pox and Vaccination Committee*, 1853, op. cit., p. 80. None of these comparisons can be regarded as at all precise. They are partially

Looking at the regional distribution of mortality from small-pox, we see that Leinster suffered least and Connaught most. Table 29 shows the number of deaths in each province from small-pox per 1,000 deaths from all causes: in Connaught relative mortality was

TABLE 29

Deaths from Small-pox, 1831–41, as a Proportion of Total Deaths*

Rural and civic districts	Deaths from small-pox	Total deaths	Small-pox deaths per 1,000 total deaths
Leinster . . .	10,762	323,695	32·97
Munster . . .	18,505	363,907	50·85
Ulster . . .	15,184	294,550	51·54
Connaught . . .	13,555	205,222	66·05
Ireland . . .	58,006	1,187,374	48·85

* 1841 Census, op. cit., Table of Deaths, facing pp. 64, 104, 152, 180, 182.

TABLE 30

Proportion of Small-pox Deaths, 1831–41, at various Ages*

Rural and civic districts	Under one year		1–5		6–10	
	No.	No. per 1,000 of total small-pox deaths	No.	No. per 1,000 of total small-pox deaths	No.	No. per 1,000 of total small-pox deaths
	(i)	(ii)	(i)	(ii)	(i)	(ii)
Ireland . .	24,188	417	24,850	428	6,004	104

11–20		21–30		31 and over		Total deaths
(i)	(ii)	(i)	(ii)	(i)	(ii)	
2,208	38	578	10	141	2	58,006

* 1841 Census, op. cit., Table of Deaths, facing pp. 65, 105, 153, 181, 183.

just over twice as high as in Leinster. The table, however, is partially invalidated by differences between the provinces in the age-distribution of their inhabitants. Small-pox mortality, as Table 30 shows, was almost confined to infants and young children. In the country as a whole, of all people dying from small-pox, 84·5 per cent. were under six and 95·9 per cent. were under eleven: Leinster,

invalidated by differential inaccuracies in enumeration, by different rates of population growth, and so forth: nonetheless, the consistency of their indication of substantially greater small-pox mortality in Ireland is of interest.

as Table 26 in Chapter VII[1] shows, was the province with the smallest proportion of children under eleven, and Connaught the province with the greatest.[2] Table 31 has been compiled to overcome this difficulty. It relates for each province small-pox deaths

TABLE 31

Deaths from Small-pox, 1831–41, at various Ages, per 1,000 People at those Ages in 1841*

Rural and civic districts	5 and under			6–10		
	Deaths from small-pox	*Total population*	*Deaths from small-pox per 1,000*	*Deaths from small-pox*	*Total population*	*Deaths from small-pox per 1,000*
	(i)	(ii)	(iii)	(i)	(ii)	(iii)
Leinster	8,916	282,804	31·5	1,200	243,481	4·9
Munster	15,821	368,618	42·9	1,861	312,838	5·9
Ulster	12,522	365,332	34·3	1,617	320,828	5·0
Connaught	11,779	229,659	51·3	1,326	202,989	6·5
Ireland	49,038	1,246,413	39·3	6,004	1,080,136	5·6

	11–20			21–30†		
	(i)	(ii)	(iii)	(i)	(ii)	(iii)
Leinster	477	452,430	1·1	136	370,464	..
Munster	602	556,534	1·1	153	446,528	..
Ulster	749	573,863	1·3	242	384,002	..
Connaught	417	343,006	1·2	47	239,055	..
Ireland	2,208	1,925,833	1·2	578	1,440,049	..

* 1841 Census, op. cit., Table of Deaths, pp. lxvi–lxvii and facing pp. 65, 105, 153, 181, 183.

† Only 0·24 per cent. of all people dying from small-pox were over thirty.

at various ages, in the ten years before 1841, to the total number of people of those ages in 1841. It shows that in the five-and-under age-group (which, Table 30 shows, accounted for 84·5 per cent. of total small-pox mortality) in Leinster there were 31·5 small-pox deaths per 1,000 children of this age, while in Connaught there were 51·3. In the next age-group, that of children from six to ten (and this, with 10·35 per cent. of all deaths from small-pox, is the only other age-group suffering a considerable mortality) Leinster is again the most-favoured province, with 4·9 deaths per 1,000, and Connaught the least-favoured, with 6·5.

[1] p. 192.

[2] Leinster in 1841 had 267 children under eleven per 1,000 of its total population: Connaught had 305; Munster, 284, and Ulster, 292.

In the eighteenth century, small-pox, because of the extent and nature of mortality from it, was of outstanding importance amongst the factors restraining the growth of population: in spite of the limited sources of Irish eighteenth-century epidemiology, many contemporary accounts underline the magnitude of its ravages, and these losses were of more than transitory influence on the growth of population. Small-pox did not merely anticipate deaths that might have been expected within a year or two: the people who died were infants and young children who, had they survived, might reasonably have reinforced the population personally for years to come, and by their offspring, indefinitely. The eighteenth-century doctor could do little for small-pox patients; perhaps, indeed, his activities increased their number. In the new century, as shown by the experience of England and other countries, vaccination could greatly reduce the incidence of the disease. Vaccination was practised in Ireland shortly after its introduction to England, but, retarded by the wildness of the country, the prejudice of the people, and a social environment more favourable to the spread of disease, only in Dublin, by the time of the Famine, had it brought small-pox deaths down to anything approaching the English level.[1] Elsewhere, in the rural areas, it is broadly true to say that the more highly developed the characteristic features of Irish economic life, the greater the mortality from small-pox: the provinces, when arranged according to the incidence of small-pox deaths show the grouping that has been typical in our discussion and tables—Connaught at one extreme, Leinster at the other and Munster and Ulster not far apart, often inclining more closely towards Connaught than towards Leinster.

We can come to no precise conclusion on the extent to which vaccination lowered mortality from small-pox in Ireland in the forty years before the Famine. Some positive effect there undoubtedly was, especially in the towns and less remote country districts, but, nonetheless, in the much smaller proportion of Irish lives saved by vaccination, we have another item to add to the series of contrasts between the mortality experience of Ireland and England.

---

[1] In Dublin from 1831 to 1841 there were 28·0 deaths from small-pox per 1,000 deaths from all causes: from 1841 to 1851 there were 25·66. In England and Wales from 1843 to 1851 the corresponding figure was 21·9. (*Report . . . by Small-pox and Vaccination Committee*, 1853, op. cit., pp. 80 and 104.)

X

THE INCIDENCE OF FEVER

FEVER in our period, and for centuries before, was almost continuously present in Ireland. Dr. Crampton, who reported on the health of Connaught to a Select Committee in 1819, said that 'fever is always to be met with in the western district of Ireland, in the towns, in the villages, and amongst the scattered population throughout the country'. That it was not only the west that suffered was made clear by one of his colleagues: in Leinster 'it was universally admitted by everyone acquainted with the condition of the poor, that fever is never altogether absent; that at all times there are cases of it to be met with in every populous or extensive district'.[1] With any aggravation of the hardships of the people, the fever, never entirely suppressed, flared up as an epidemic. Shortage of food was the great precipitating cause of epidemics. It was not merely that during a famine hunger reduced people's resistance to disease; then, too, an admirable environment was created for the spread of the typhus-carrying louse. Excessive rain, which was frequently the cause of the shortage of food, led also to a shortage of fuel as the turf could not be dried. The cottage fires went out: hot water became scarce, and clothes and bodies were washed less frequently. To keep out the cold, windows and doors were shut, the poor wrapped themselves in all their available rags, and kept them on day and night. Whole families huddled together under the same covering at night and few remained free from infestation. 'The rotted potatoes, nettles and dock leaves, eaten raw for lack of firing brought on famine diarrhoea and predisposed to dysentery. Typhus, always smouldering somewhere, flared up.'[2] Once it flared up in any district, insanitary houses, overcrowding, and dirt were ably assisted by other features of Irish social life in causing it to spread far and wide. The sociability

[1] *First Report from the Select Committee on the State of Disease . . . in Ireland*, Reports from Committees, 1819, viii. 414, 433.
[2] W. MacArthur, 'Famines and Fevers in England and Ireland', Appendix to a paper by Dr. Bonser in *J.B. Arch. Ass.*, 3rd ser., 1944, ix. 67.

and hospitality which the traveller found such endearing traits in the Irish temperament doubtless did much to make tolerable a life that was poor in material comforts: the sick man had seldom to forgo either the solace of having a neighbour to sit and smoke with him, or the comfort of knowing that, should he die, his friends from far and wide would gather in his house to mark their loss in the traditionally proper manner. But visiting the sick, and waking the dead, spread the fever. The Irishman's hospitality was not reserved for his friends: he 'thinks himself accursed if he refuses admission to a begging stranger'[1]—and the greater the appearance of sickness or distress, the more nearly irresistible was the beggar's claim.[2] The beggars, if not themselves infected, were, doubtless, frequently carriers of infection, and they were carriers, too, of their sick children. An Act of 1819 gave magistrates power to apprehend vagrants during the existence of contagious diseases, and to cause their persons and apparel to be cleansed, but little is to be heard of its enforcement.[3] Weekly markets, and cultivation in common, both social as well as economic institutions, frequent holidays, and dirty schools, were amongst the host of other factors which, by throwing people together, the sick with the healthy, help to explain the high mortality from epidemic and contagious diseases. Once fever got a foothold the soup-kitchens and the other relief measures of the kind-hearted, by causing people to collect together, may have done something to extend the distress they were designed to curb.[4] The poverty which often made the peasant family desperately short of clothes affected its health not only by making cleanliness unattainable. Bundles of second-hand clothing were imported to Ireland for sale among the peasants, and with them came the germs of disease.[5] Shopkeepers and the pawnbrokers to whom any spare clothes went in bad times were said seldom to escape infection in an epidemic, and frequently after redeeming its clothes a family would suffer from a fresh attack of fever.[6] The fever patient was often covered with the overcoats and cloaks of his neighbours, and little sterilizing was

---

[1] *First Report of the General Board of Health in the City of Dublin*, 1822, p. 77.
[2] Rogan, op. cit., p. 85.
[3] 59 Geo. III, c. 41. *First Rep. Gen. Board of Health*, op. cit., p. 127.
[4] Rogan, op. cit., p. 152.
[5] Lord George Hill, in evidence before the Devon Commission. *Reports from Commissioners*, 1845, xxi. *1055*, 35.
[6] *First Rep. Gen. Board of Health*, op. cit., pp. 34–5.

done before they were returned to their normal use. In some places it was the custom for nurses to appropriate for themselves the clothes of the patients who died under their care.[1]

The major problem concerning fever that we must inquire into in a discussion of the growth of population is whether there was any diminution in its incidence in the two or three generations before the great outburst of 1845 which would help us to explain, in terms of lower mortality, the doubling of population in these years. Once more, of course, we lack the statistics that would give us a ready answer. But what records we have of eighteenth- and early-nineteenth-century epidemics make it almost certain that, even in proportion to the larger population, far more lives were lost by fever in the sixty years after 1780 than in the sixty years before. In the early years of rapid population-increase, up to 1816, there was, it is true, only one major flare-up of fever. But as this relative immunity was no improvement on the experience of preceding years, which, since 1741 had been as free from major outbreaks, it is of no direct help to us in explaining the new impetus to population growth in the 1780s. After 1816 population-expansion stubbornly persisted in spite of unparalleled mortality from fever in the repeated famines which set the Irish economic body trembling as it staggered towards 1845. Whatever the causes of population-increase they were strong enough to sweep over mounting losses from fever, with, apparently, their vigour little diminished.

From 1700 to 1739 there seem to have been major epidemics of fever between 1708 and 1710, between 1718 and 1721, and between 1728 and 1734. Rogers's observations from twenty-four years practice in Cork showed him that the

Fever hath, within the above-mention'd Space of time, made its Appearance amongst us *three* several times in a very signal manner: Not that it was during any of the successive Intervals intirely extinguish'd: The Fire only for that time long lay buried under its Embers, to blaze out with more or less Violence, just as the concurring Causes afforded Fuel in such respective Proportions. 'Twas in the Year 1708, I had occasion first to make my Observations on this *Fever*; how long it had been in the Town before, I can't tell; but it seem'd in the Winter of that Year to have attain'd to its State; declining sensibly for a Year or two and then disappear'd. . . . The Year 1718, very remarkably usher'd in a Fever in all respects the *same*, raging greatly from *November* to

[1] Ibid., p. 71.

February and *March*: And it so continued to do the latter Parts of the years 1719, 1720, and 1721. From that time it abated of its Severity, dwindling insensibly away till at length 'twas rarely to be met with. . . . From the Year 1721, to the Year 1728, this Fever was little heard of; but from that time hath visibly every Year gain'd ground: and seems to have been this last *Winter* at its full heighth.[1]

We have Lecky's testimony and references to bear out that in the years 1708–10 and 1718–21 there was great distress far beyond Cork City,[2] but apart from that of O'Connell, a colleague of Rogers's in Cork, no additional medical evidence has come to light on the prevalence of fever in these years.[3] The epidemic beginning in 1728 is more fully documented: these are the years of Swift's *Modest Proposal* and of his *Short View of the State of Ireland*. Rutty, the Dublin epidemiologist, pointed out that the fever Rogers had called the 'endemial epidemic' of Cork was, in these years, 'far from being peculiar to Cork'.[4] The author of *The Groans of Ireland* gives one of the most vivid descriptions of the ravages of fever in 1741—the first major disaster Ireland suffered from a deficiency of potatoes.[5] He pointed out that the country was subject to frequent wants and famines: 'this (the worst so far) is the third I have seen in the compas of twenty years'.

I have been absent from this country for some years and on my return to it last summer found it the most miserable scene of universal distress that I have ever read of in history: want and misery in every face; the Rich almost unable, as they were unwilling, to relieve the poor; the roads spread with dead and dying bodies; mankind the colour of the docks and nettles they fed on; two or three, sometimes more, on a car going to the grave for want of bearers to carry them, and many buried only in the fields and ditches where they perished. . . . This universal scarcity was ensued by fluxes and malignant fevers which swept off multitudes of all sorts; whole villages were laid waste by want and sickness, and death in various shapes; and scarce an house in the whole island escaped from tears and mourning. . . . It were to be wished, sir,

---

[1] J. Rogers, M.D., *An Essay on Epidemic Diseases* . . ., Dublin, 1734, pp. 3–5.

[2] Lecky, i. 183–4.

[3] 'About the vernal equinox of 1719, a certain continued epidemic fever commenced, increasing more and more daily, attacking almost every family and spreading most widely beyond all which have hitherto come under my observations.' (M. O'Connell, *Observationes Medicales*, quoted in 1851 Census, *Reports from Commissioners*, 1856, xxix. 383.)

[4] Rutty, 1770, op. cit., p. 24.

[5] See above, Chapter V, p. 144.

that some curious enquirer had made a calculation of the number lost in this terrible calamity: If one for every house in the kingdom died (and that is very probable when we consider that whole families and villages were swept off in many parts together) the loss must be upwards of 400,000 souls: if but one for every other house (and it was certainly more) 200,000 have perished. A loss too great for this ill-peopled country to bear; and the more grievous as this loss was mostly of the grown up part of the working people.[1]

In Cork, about August 1740 or a little earlier, 'griping diarrhoeas and epidemic dysenteries broke out, which, gradually increasing through the entire autumn, caused great and incredible mortality during all the ensuing winter. At the end of August a certain epidemic continuous fever appeared, which in some localities raged exceedingly, chiefly among the lower classes, and prevailed to the approach of winter, attacking many epidemically. But severe frost and snow then supervening, this fever gave way to violent dysentery, until at length, on the thawing of the frost, and the arrival in due course of a dry and stormy spring, the same continuous fever broke out again, and, more widely spread, indiscriminately attacked nearly all the people—predominating over all other epidemics at that time.'[2] In Dublin, small-pox, fever, and dysentery raged from 1740 to 1742.[3]

We may be certain that there was no repetition of fever on the scale of 1741 in the remainder of the eighteenth century: the records, admittedly, are imperfect, but had such a disaster been repeated they could not have left us unaware of the fact. It is difficult, however, with the available material, to draw up a history of fever in these years: in particular, we miss for the last quarter of the century records such as Rogers and O'Connell, Rutty, and Sims kept for earlier years. It seems probable that, while fever remained endemic, there was only one serious outbreak—in 1771 —and that that, from the paucity of references to it, was on a smaller scale than some of its predecessors and successors. For the years between 1742 and 1766 Rutty records few serious outbreaks. There was a 'remarkable increase' in the incidence of fever in 1745 and in the following year 'inflammatory fevers, though interspersed with those of the low kind, continued to be frequent

[1] *The Groans of Ireland in a Letter to a Member of Parliament*, Dublin, 1741, pp. 3–4.
[2] O'Connell, op. cit., quoted in 1851 Census, op. cit., p. 391.
[3] Rutty, op. cit., pp. 81–2.

through the winter', but in the records for the next twenty years, though fever is mentioned frequently enough, it is never referred to in terms to suggest that it had assumed disastrous proportions.[1]

In Tyrone, throughout the fifties, the seasons were cold and wet, and the disorders which 'revelled with unbridled fury' included 'low, putrid or nervous fevers throughout the year'. The year 1761–2 was dry and the disorders abated. The spring of 1765 was uncommonly healthful: the doctor was required only for a few petechial fevers, and not knowing what course to take, he left them to nature—'people must perceive that the patients of nature come easier off than those of the doctor'. In 1770 there were some low fevers among adults, and a more severe worm fever among children, especially those highly pampered with luxuries. In the summer of 1771, severe weather brought fever which

as autumn advanced raged with the greatest violence, nor was it overcome by a severe winter, but in its irresistible course finished the circle of a year. This disorder was entirely different from any of those formerly mentioned, claiming the prerogative of the plague, almost all others vanishing from before its sovereign presence. It had showed itself, as I am informed, above twelve months sooner in the eastern parts of the kingdom, pursuing a regular career from east to west in the same manner as all the epidemics which I have seen. In relating this progress it must not be omitted that they made most rapid strides in marshy overflowed grounds, so that they had often got a great way onward in such places, when they were only beginning to attack the hills of the more eastern parts; and as low damp grounds were soonest seized they were likewise more severely handled.[2]

In 1800 and the following year, Ireland suffered from what appears to have been a worse epidemic than any since 1740–1. Indeed, though there are many records of the 1816–17 outbreak, and few of its predecessor, the early disaster may bear comparison with the later. The deaths recorded in the Dublin House of Industry in 1800–1 nearly approached the number in all the Dublin fever hospitals from 1817 to 1819. In Cork City, in 1800, 4,000 fever cases were treated in the dispensary alone: in Limerick things were said to have been as bad as in 1817. In 1797 fever had appeared in several cantonments of troops and a wet summer and autumn brought conditions that encouraged its spread amongst

---

[1] Rutty, op. cit., pp. 126, 135.
[2] Sims, 1773, op. cit., pp. 10, 11, 14, 16, 134, 155, 181–2.

the peasants. In 1799 bad weather again led to a deficient harvest, and disease, aggravated by the aftermath of the rebellion of the previous year, spread more widely: Wexford, the principal seat of the rebellion, appears to have suffered most severely. In 1800 there was yet another bad harvest: the shortage of food became more acute and fever and dysentery reached their peak. An abundant harvest in 1801 quickly put an end to the epidemic.[1]

The first of the series of famines and fevers that afflicted Ireland with gathering frequency in the generation before the Great Famine, broke out in 1816. Not only was the disaster the worst the Irish remembered,[2] but according to one of its historians, a doctor of some eminence, it may 'without fear of any charge of exaggeration be asserted that a more general Epidemic never, perhaps, existed in any country of equal dimensions and population; for according to every account, whether public or private, it would appear that not only every city, town, and village was visited by the disease, but that even very few of the isolated cabins of the poor escaped.'[3]

There is general agreement on what the causes of the trouble were. For more than half a century the relationships of rural society in Ireland had been adapted to the dependence of her people upon a single foodstuff, and that a crop, both more liable to fail than its common alternatives, and more disastrous in failure. When the potato failed, there was no substitute for it. None could be grown because it was too late in the year. None could be bought because there was only the most rudimentary distributive apparatus, because to many the potato was money as well as food, and because those who had money knew that if they diverted it from rent to food, eviction would bring upon them utter and permanent disaster for what might be a tightening of the belt. Even when the Government and the public were moved to open their purses, there was no certainty that a substitute would be found: the relief agencies had hastily to improvise means of distributing food in a wild country that lacked mills and ovens, and amongst people whose digestion, conditioned to a diet of potatoes and milk, was already further weakened by lack of it.[4]

---

[1] Creighton, op. cit., ii., 1894, pp. 248–50.
[2] *First Rep. S.C. State of Disease . . .*, 1819, op. cit., p. 20.
[3] Harty, 1820, op. cit., p. 10.
[4] See above Chapter V, pp. 142–4.

The wonder, then, is not that famine broke out in 1816, but that there had not been earlier repetitions of the disaster of 1741. The winter of 1815 was hard and long; the potato was sown late the following spring, and incessant rains in the summer rotted much of the seed, and retarded ripening. Partial failure was general: in mountainous districts it was almost complete. When some potatoes were obtained, starving people ate them half cooked, when there were none they fell back on nettles, hips, and wild mustard, eked out with what oatmeal they could get: either way, inadequate food led to dysentery, and dysentery to fever.[1] Lesser hardships aggravated the distress. With the end of the French wars, the army was reduced in size and a source of income lost; the price of agricultural produce fell, sometimes to a third of its war-time level; with the failure of banks, shopkeepers and dealers suffered; in the north, the linen industry, in the south the stuff manufacture was depressed; in Munster the fisheries did badly. Everywhere the rain which rotted the potatoes kept the turf wet: we have seen already that when the fires went out, food was eaten raw and dysentery increased, people huddled together for warmth at night time, more clothes were piled on, fresh air was kept out of the cabins, less washing was done, and disease quickly spread from sick members of the family to healthy. As the distress increased, so did the number of beggars who exchanged disease for alms. Magnifying the effect of all these privations in increasing the susceptibility to disease was the intense anxiety engendered both by the hardships themselves and by the fever that followed them. 'Hope, confidence, enthusiasm, and an ardent, enterprising spirit, will enable men to support great fatigues and privations', a Dublin fever-hospital doctor wrote,[2] but none of these safeguards could thrive in the peasant's family in the best of times, let alone during a famine. Well might the people be terrified of the fever: there was the fear, not only of death but of acute suffering. The symptoms of the disease varied from place to place and in the course of the epidemic, but the type of suffering it entailed is described by a physician at one of the Cork Fever Hospitals. The disease, he said, was preceded, in almost every instance by trembling and nausea, or, as the victim expressed it, by an 'empty

[1] Rogan, op. cit., p. 69.
[2] R. Grattan, M.D., 'Medical Report of the Fever Hospital, Cork Street, Dublin', *Trans. K. & Q. Coll. of Physicians in Ireland*, 1820, iii. 365.

straining'. During the first few days after its onset, the patient complained of headache, pains in the back and limbs, stupor, oppression of the chest, nausea, bleeding from the nose, and a great thirst. His pulse was quick and feeble, his tongue was a milky white, and there was a peculiar foetor from his skin. On the fourth or fifth day petechiae appeared on the body and limbs: patients took on what their friends described as the appearance of a turkey-egg. Delirium and raving began two or three days later. Deafness was the most unerring symptom that the patient was going to recover: in favourable cases the crisis was normally perspiration on the fourteenth or fifteenth or twentieth day. Removal of the fever was generally followed by considerable debility: relapses were frequent, but they were milder and less fatal than the original disease. When fatal the disease rarely lasted beyond the eleventh or thirteenth day: the indications of death were a low muttering, comatose delirium, a picking of the bed-clothes and convulsions of the muscles of the face. Shortly before death the entire body frequently changed to a deep livid or black colour, as if scorched by gunpowder. Towards the end of the summer and in the autumn the symptoms of the fever became even more distressing.[1]

That shortage of food and fuel, dirt, and worry were the causes of fever is borne out by the experience of the various groups of the population which were more or less insulated both from these hardships and from the worst of the fever. Inmates of institutions, whatever the reason for their leading regular lives, with some assurance of adequate food and a certain minimum of cleanliness, were little affected by fever: soldiers, prisoners, lunatics, and orphans, all escaped, wholly or in part.[2] Even in the outside world, where there were pockets of local prosperity and not too much contact with affected areas, there was a happier health history. In Ulster, fever was general except in Rosstrevor, 'a town out of the common thoroughfare, situated in a remarkably dry soil, with wide and airy streets, devoid of those miserable habitations where the lower orders of travellers and mendicants are lodged . . . [and] much resorted to in Summer by sea bathers and other visitors,

---

[1] W. Pickels, M.B., 'Report of the South Fever Asylum, Cork . . .', *Trans. K. & Q. Coll. of Physicians in Ireland*, 1820, iii. 195–210.

[2] Ibid., p. 227; *Rep. S.C. State of Disease*, op. cit., p. 12; F. Page, *Obs. on the State of the indigent Poor in Ireland*, 1830.

who circulate a great deal of money among the inhabitants'.[1] In Wexford and Dingle fever appeared later than in the rest of the country: the position of Wexford meant that it was less troubled with beggars than much of the rest of Ireland, and its dry soil meant that the potato suffered less from excessive rains: Dingle, too, was isolated; the linen trade and fishing helped to keep up income, and the savings of a notoriously thrifty people were generously used.[2]

That, in fact, few parts of the country were spared a most intimate knowledge of the nature of the fever is made clear by all accounts of its incidence. In Leinster it raged throughout six counties; of the remaining eight, Longford and King's had a 'remarkable increase' and, in many parts of Westmeath, which suffered less than any other county with the exception of Wexford, 'scarcely a cabin escaped'. In Munster, 'fever had prevailed in almost every district, with scarcely an exception . . . sufferers cannot be rated at less than one ninth of the total population': in parts of Cork, bordering on Kerry, where, admittedly, conditions were peculiarly favourable to the progress of the disease, a half, or even two-thirds of the population suffered. In Ulster, by the summer of 1817, fever was general, apart from tiny local exceptions: in Monaghan 'among the lower orders' scarcely a h use escaped; in Armagh and Tyrone it was 'universal'. In Connaught 'there were no places which derived an exemption from fever from their local situation'.[3]

Harty has estimated in the table reproduced below the number, both of sufferers and deaths from fever during the course of the epidemic, in the four provinces. He was quite aware of the inadequacy of many of the returns upon which he had to base his work. He made allowances for these deficiencies, which do not seem unreasonable, and which we certainly are in no position to amend: doubtless we can accept his figures as a fair guide. The 'registered sick' in the table are the sum of Harty's records of the patients received in hospitals and those who were attended from the dispensaries: not all hospital and dispensary records were available to him, and those that were were often incomplete. In

---

[1] *Rep. S.C. State of Disease*, op. cit., p. 423.

[2] Harty, op. cit., p. 5.

[3] Quoted from the accounts of the doctors who reported to the 1819 Committee on the extent of the disease in the various provinces. *Rep. S.C. State of Disease*, op. cit., pp. 373–446.

many places where there were hospitals not a sixth of the infected cases could be received, and in vast areas there was no medical establishment of any sort. Wherever the sick were regularly registered, their proportion to the total population was at times 1 : 3, it seldom fell short of 1 : 6:[1] Harty, therefore, thought the

TABLE 32

*Estimated Number of Fever-cases and Deaths from Fever, 1817–19**

	Probable population	Registered sick	Total probable sick	Registered deaths	Total probable deaths	Relative proportion of sick, 1:	Relative proportion of deaths, 1:
Leinster	1,520,000	65,650	202,000	2,696	9,050	7½	22½
Munster	1,815,000	51,807	258,000	1,935	14,200	7	18¼
Ulster	1,671,000	22,648	206,500	2,224	17,500	8	12
Connaught	826,000	9,667	70,500	246	3,550	11	20
Ireland	5,832,000	149,772	737,000	6,101	44,300	8	16⅔

* Harty, op. cit., p. 21. Presumably the surprising lowness of the figures for both patients and deaths in Connaught is the result of the exceptionally inadequate facilities there for the treatment of the disease, with the result that 'registered sick' and 'registered deaths' were a smaller proportion of the totals than elsewhere.

proportion he accepted, 1 : 8, not exaggerated. As to the number of deaths Harty had full, and probably reliable, statistics showing that of the registered sick one in twenty-five died. But registered patients had a better chance of survival than unregistered: not only did they receive medical attention, but most of them, as many hospitals were opened and others extended in the course of the epidemic, were ill in 1818, when mortality was small in comparison with that of the previous year. If, then, one in twenty-five of the registered sick died, one in fifteen does not seem unreasonable for the unregistered. We arrive, then, at 737,000, as the number of cases of fever, and at 44,000 as the number of deaths. But these figures are dependent on Harty's population estimate, which is deficient by something approaching a sixth: he assumes the population of Ireland to be 5,832,000, while the census figure for 1821, itself probably below the truth, put it at 6,802,000.

[1] Doubtless the regular registrations more frequently applied to urban than to rural districts: the incidence of fever, however, may well have been as great in the country as in the towns. The overriding cause of the epidemic, the shortage of potatoes, must have caused greater distress in the country, where there was more nearly exclusive dependence upon the potato as an article of food: dirt, bad ventilation, overcrowding, and the indiscriminate mixing of sick and healthy must, even in the country, have approached optimum conditions for the spread of disease.

Perhaps we should inflate his figure of cases of fever to something approaching 850,000 and his figure of mortality to about 50,000.

We are fortunate in possessing for this, the first well-documented famine-fever in Ireland, some indications of the differential incidence of the disease and of mortality from it, in various groups of the population. Women, there is some (though restricted) evidence for believing, suffered more than men. In the Strabane area, where, thanks to the zeal of its dispensary doctor, we have the fullest regional account of the epidemic, nearly two-thirds of the dispensary patients were female, a fact attributed by the doctor to the amount of women's time spent indoors and to their being responsible for so much of the nursing of the sick.[1] The medical reports, almost without exception, say that while the poor contracted fever much more generally than those living in comfortable circumstances, the well-to-do, when infected, were more likely to die: in Strabane, one in twenty of the poor patients died, but one in ten of those in the 'upper classes'.[2] That the well-to-do were less frequently infected would seem to be the result of their insulation from the hunger, the dirt and the overcrowding that spread the disease: that their mortality was so high may, perhaps, be the result of the rarity of the disease in their families; amongst the poor, we have seen, the disease was ever present and perhaps familiarity bred resistance. At Strabane children were more frequently attacked than middle-aged people, and the younger the children, the more likely they were to be attacked: infants, nonetheless, as well as persons of advanced years were peculiarly exempt.[1] The report of the Cork Street Fever Hospital for 1819 gives the data tabulated below on the ages of patients admitted during the year, and on mortality in various age-groups.[3] Unfortunately, the first line of the table tells us little about the incidence of the disease in the various age-groups: the report points out that the two groups sending most cases to hospital were the largest, though by what amount is not known, in Dublin. If the second line of the table can be taken as giving any guide to the ages of the 50,000 who died from fever in the country as a whole, it suggests, in conjunction with the Strabane evidence, that young

---

[1] Rogan, op. cit., p. 28.
[2] *Rep. S.C. State of Disease*, 1819, op. cit., p. 423; Pickels, loc. cit., pp. 223 and 231; Barker and Cheyne, op. cit., Rogan, op. cit., p. 28.
[3] *Trans. K. & Q. Coll. of Physicians in Ireland*, 1820, iii. 481.

people were peculiarly liable to infection, that those who died
from fever were not, in general, people whose expectation of life
was brief, and who were not likely again to become parents, but
the young, who, had they escaped infection could have looked
forward, both to a considerably longer life and to children, or
more children, of their own.

TABLE 33

*Ages of Fever-patients entering and of Fever-patients dying in Cork
Street Fever Hospital, Dublin, 1818–19*

	1–10	10–20	20–30	30–40	40–50	50 and over
No. of patients admitted .	465	1,111	1,012	664	388	281
Proportion of deaths to admissions . . .	1:20	1:15	1:22	1:12	1:10	1:47

There is a wealth of material for the history of fever in Ireland
in the years after 1817: the economy of the country was so starkly
diseased that the politicians and the economists, the philanthro-
pists and the patriots, were driven, if they shirked trying to mend
its constitution, at least to try to hide the sores. Investigation was
not infrequently thought a proper preliminary to prescription,
and, though the country benefited little from the palliatives prescribed by those with power, or from the utopian schemes of those
without, the historian gains by the skill and industry with which
many of the investigators compiled their blue-books, *Tours*, and
'statistical enquiries'. Almost year by year both the energy and
the shape of Irish social life were pruned of what was irrelevant
or counteractive, and acquired, as if with design, what was still
wanting to make the country the classic field for unrestrained
fever to breed havoc. Ever more exclusively the structure of rural
life was shaped by the concern of the landlords to swell their rents
and by the morbid rate of population-growth: that this was so
is shown by the stubborn maintenance, even extension, of an
unnaturally large quantum of arable when the market, as well as
soil and climate, demanded a reversion to pasture: it is shown in
the continued subdivision of holdings when it was only in the
occasional good year that the already fragmented farms could
satisfy both the landlord's demand for rent and a family's demand
for food: it is shown in the ever more exclusive, and ever more
precarious dependence of the people on the potato.

By the thirties the double insistence of the insatiable demand for rent and the hunger of an ever-increasing population, had forced peasant farming into the dilemma that was to be resolved only by famine, fever, and emigration on a scale unparalleled, even in Ireland. On the one hand, farming had to be so organized that a maximum area of good land was producing the cash crops that paid the rent; on the other hand, in a gamble to get food, too little land, much of it indifferent, was sown with potatoes of a type that was chosen because it promised a heavy yield, even though at the cost of greater susceptibility to disease. To look for escape from the dilemma in more efficient farming, or in ambitious works of reclamation, is to forget the significance of absenteeism in Irish society: it gave a double guarantee—that the peasants should lack not only guidance to a less precarious farming, but the enterprise and the means to secure it for themselves.

We have already seen that a shortage of food, while lowering resistance to disease, aggravated the dirt, the overcrowding, and the mendicancy which caused it to spread: we have seen that in times of famine, the fever that was always endemic flared up to epidemic proportions. By the thirties the degeneration of the varieties of the potato in common use increased the risk of food shortage and a series of bad seasons turned risk into chronic famine. Persistent famine meant persistent fever. We need not piece together the story of the famines and fevers from 1821 to 1845: the work has already been done[1] and recapitulation would show that, in essentials, the prototype of 1817 was followed. Shortage of food and unsuitable food led to dysentery; shortage of fuel set in motion the train of circumstances which gave the typhus-carrying louse something approaching optimum conditions for breeding: as the distress became acute the more beggars were obliged to tramp the country and the greater the chance of people being herded together to receive relief; either way the fever was helped to saturate the country.

For the thirties we can measure, with some assurance of accuracy, the extent of mortality from fever. From 1831 to 1841 112,072 deaths, or 9·4 per cent. of the total, were attributed to fever. Table 34 shows that fever deaths were by no means confined to a narrow range of age-groups: in only the smallest group, that

---

[1] See 1851 Census, op. cit., pp. 455–99; Creighton, 1891–4, op. cit.; O'Rourke, 1875, op. cit.

of people over seventy, were there less than 3·6 per cent. of total fever deaths: each of the three ten-yearly groups between eleven and forty accounted for more than 15 per cent.

TABLE 34

*Proportion of Fever Deaths, 1831–41, at various Ages**

Rural and civic districts	Under one year		1–5		6–10		11–20		21–30		31–40	
	No. of fever deaths	No. per 1,000 of total fever deaths	No. of fever deaths	No. per 1,000 of total fever deaths	No. of fever deaths	No. per 1,000 of total fever deaths	No. of fever deaths	No. per 1,000 of total fever deaths	No. of fever deaths	No. per 1,000 of total fever deaths	No. of fever deaths	No. per 1,000 of total fever deaths
Ireland	4,083	36	6,274	56	6,276	56	17,656	158	20,279	181	18,571	166

Rural and civic districts	41–50		51–60		61–70		70		Unspecified	Total
	No. of fever deaths	No. per 1,000 of total fever deaths	No. of fever deaths	No. per 1,000 of total fever deaths	No. of fever deaths	No. per 1,000 of total fever deaths	No. of fever deaths	No. per 1,000 of total fever deaths		
Ireland	16,252	145	12,190	109 .	5,066	45	2,154	19	3,271	112,072

* 1841 Census, op. cit., Table of Deaths, facing pp. 65, 105, 153, 181, 183.

Table 35 relates fever deaths at particular ages in the years from 1831 to 1841 to the total number of people of those ages in each of the provinces. It points to two significant conclusions. First, in every age-group, Ulster made the best showing;[1] this is notably the case in the three groups of highest mortality: 18·1 per cent. of all fever deaths occurred within the age-group 21–30; here Ulster had 13 deaths per 1,000 while Leinster and Connaught both had over 15: 16·6 per cent. of all deaths were within the 31–40 group; here Ulster had 15·7 deaths per 1,000, while the other provinces all had more than 20: in the 11–20 age-group, with 15·7 per cent. of total mortality, the figures are close; Ulster had 8·8 deaths per 1,000, while Leinster, at the other extreme, had 10·0. Second, in spite of the characteristic immunity of Leinster from the more extreme evils of Irish social life, for all ages below 41 (and these included the three groups of heaviest fever mortality) Leinster

[1] With the exception that in the 51–60 age-group Munster had the same proportion of fever deaths as Ulster.

TABLE 35

Deaths from Fever, 1831–41, at various Ages, per 1,000 People of those Ages in 1841*

Rural and civic districts	5 and under			5–10		
	Deaths from fever	Total population	Deaths from fever per 1,000	Deaths from fever	Total population	Deaths from fever per 1,000
Leinster	2,402	282,804	8·5	1,550	243,481	6·4
Munster	3,596	368,618	9·8	2,188	312,838	7·0
Ulster	2,272	365,332	6·2	1,458	320,828	4·5
Connaught	2,087	229,659	9·9	1,080	202,989	5·3
Ireland	10,357	1,246,413	8·3	6,276	1,080,136	5·8
	11–20			21–30		
Leinster	4,526	452,430	10·0	5,679	370,464	15·3
Munster	5,258	556,534	9·4	6,028	446,528	13·5
Ulster	4,848	573,863	8·4	4,973	384,002	13·0
Connaught	3,024	343,006	8·8	3,599	239,055	15·1
Ireland	17,656	1,925,833	9·2	20,279	1,440,049	14·1
	31–40			41–50		
Leinster	5,012	231,622	21·6	4,082	184,182	22·2
Munster	5,763	287,614	20·0	4,823	188,193	25·6
Ulster	4,199	268,103	15·7	3,979	202,668	19·6
Connaught	3,597	158,186	22·7	3,368	113,010	29·8
Ireland	18,511	945,525	19·64	16,252	688,053	23·6
	51–60			61–70		
Leinster	2,826	120,020	23·5	1,284	57,409	22·4
Munster	3,613	148,130	21·1	1,376	57,502	23·9
Ulster	3,059	145,044	21·1	1,454	77,568	18·7
Connaught	2,692	82,126	32·8	952	33,548	28·4
Ireland	12,190	495,320	24·6	5,066	226,027	22·4

Rural and civic districts	70 and over			Ages not specified	
	Deaths from fever	Total population	Deaths from fever per 1,000	Deaths from fever	Total population
Leinster . .	541	29,820	18·1	1,913	1,499
Munster . .	565	28,522	19·8	851	1,682
Ulster . .	705	46,691	15·1	291	2,274
Connaught	343	16,218	21·1	216	1,062
Ireland . .	2,154	121,251	17·8	3,271	6,517

* 1841 Census, op. cit., pp. lxvi–lxvii, and Table of Deaths, facing pp. 65, 105, 153, 181, 183.

suffered nearly as severely, if not more so, than Connaught, characteristically the most afflicted province.

The history of fever, we must conclude, is of no direct assistance in helping to explain the vigour of the growth of population. As we found in discussing emigration, population rose, in spite of an increasing wastage. The early years of rapid population-increase, it is true, were free from serious epidemics; but so also were the preceding years. In 1817 there began the series of epidemics, precipitated by scarcity of potatoes, which culminated in the Great Famine. In the thirties, when statistics become available, in the country as a whole, nearly one death in ten was attributed to fever: in no province was the proportion less than one in eleven. Ulster, in every age-group, suffered least from fever, and, significantly, it was in Ulster that there was the widest range of supplements to the potato in the dietary of the people. In Leinster there was heavy mortality from fever, doubtless because the proportion of town-dwellers was higher in Leinster than elsewhere. Fever, indeed, may have contributed in these years of its heavy incidence to a rapid replacement of the population, but the causal link was not a lowering of mortality: the more tenants who died, the more settlements were vacated, and there was some easing of the difficulty that was commonly reported in the thirties of finding the holding that was the prerequisite to marriage.

XI

CONCLUSION

WE began this study with an attempt to measure the rate of population-growth in Ireland in the century and a half before the Famine. We collected a number of estimates put forward, sometimes as little more than guesses, sometimes as the result of elaborate calculation, by a series of writers who were curious to know the size of the population of Ireland before the 1821 Census gave an authoritative figure. Later writers have accepted, without radical revision, the trend of these early estimates: on their evidence there has been general agreement that the startling feature in Irish demographic history before the Famine is a spectacular acceleration in the rate of growth beginning in the 1770s. In the sixty years before 1778 the traditional estimates show an increase of 38 per cent.: in the next fifty-three years, from Arthur Young in 1778 to the Census of 1831, they show an increase of 159 per cent. The foundation of population estimates which show so violent a leap demanded examination. We saw that, with few exceptions, the pre-census estimates were based on the hearth-money collectors' returns of the number of houses in the country, together with an estimate of the average number of occupants in a house. For a variety of reasons the collectors were likely to underestimate the number of houses and we were able to suggest that there was a more restrained rate of population-increase after 1780 than has been thought. For 1781 we have put forward a figure of rather over 4 millions. This, on the evidence presented, would seem to err in the direction of underestimating the real population; the increase of 92 per cent. which it shows for the following fifty years is likely, therefore, to exaggerate the rapidity of the growth of population[1]—but it may,

---

[1] That the exaggeration in this percentage may still be substantial is suggested by the risk of error in the evidence which we used to reduce Bushe's figure for the average number of residents in a house in 1788 from 6·25 to 5·65. Bushe's figure is the only national average for the entire century which can claim any approach to a scientific foundation. (See above, Chap. I, pp. 18–22.) We modified it, however, because its inconsistency with later census figures and with a host

nonetheless, be a wholly insufficient measure of the natural increase of the Irish. The excess of births over deaths in the sixty years before the Famine added (on our figures) not only 4 million to the population of Ireland, but one and three-quarter million to the population of Britain and North America.[1]

Our initial inquiry, then, left us with imprecise information on the dimensions of our problem: but it left us certain that in the causation of either a rising birth-rate or a falling death-rate there was scope for an investigation of quite central importance not only to the political and economic history of the years of increase, but to the history of the great disaster, largely shaped by the pressure of population, which abruptly reversed expansion and inaugurated a century during which Ireland, alone among the nations, has experienced a continuously declining population.

When statistics are lacking in what should be a statistical inquiry, presumption must take the place of assertion: we cannot prove that little or none of the quickening of the rate of population-growth resulted from a prolongation of life: certainly our examination of the social habits and the housing of the Irish, the dissemination of hospitals and dispensaries, the spread of vaccination and the incidence of fever does not support the proposition that in Ireland, as is said to have been the case in England, greater cleanliness and medical advances led to a substantial lowering of mortality. One great potential cause of a falling death-rate was undoubtedly present: in the first forty years of rapid population-increase there was an abundant supply of nutritionally adequate food. This was not an entirely new development: famines are not conspicuous in the records of the years after 1742, and over much of the country the potato was known, at least as a supplement to the traditional foodstuffs, long before the 1780s. In so far as foodstuffs were readily obtained before 1780 we must discount the influence of the potato in the following decades as a cause of falling mortality. Moreover, between 1820 and the Famine, when the shortage of

of contemporary opinions and local calculations, conflicted with our aim of giving only a conservative revision of figures which did not appear improbable to contemporaries. Bushe's figure may, nonetheless, be correct. In conjunction with the upward revision suggested in Chapter I (p. 12) of the estimate which he used of the number of houses in the country it would give a population estimate for 1788 of 4,855,344. This would put the increase from 1788 to 1831 at 60 per cent.

[1] See above, Chapter II, pp. 27–9.

potatoes became chronic, still there was rapid population growth: certainly, for these years, the prolongation of life as a result of the improvement of food supplies can have had little influence in increasing population. If abundance of food did, in fact, lead to the growth of population, there is no reason why the mechanism should have been a falling death-rate. The greater the assurance with which a couple could look forward to being able to maintain a family, the more readily would people marry young: the earlier the average age at marriage, the higher was the birth-rate likely to be.

It is not only the flimsiness of the evidence that there was any considerable prolongation of life that encourages us to place the weight of our explanation of rapidly rising population upon factors influencing the birth-rate. Statistics of some authority are available for the closing decades of our period: they suggest that fertility in Ireland was high by contemporary, and subsequent, English standards. Of greater authority is the evidence of the series of contemporary writers who were interested in population history. They thought, with unbroken unanimity, that more births were the prime cause of the acceleration in the rate of population growth, and their writings, together with the general sources of Irish social and economic history, furnish a coherent explanation of how, in the Irish country-side in these years, there were both the desire and the opportunity to conceive almost as many children as it was possible for the mother to bear. The desire was direct and indirect. Directly (apart from emotional satisfactions, which, if they grew stronger or weaker, did so without leaving traces in the material with which the historian must work) children were wanted because of their unusual value to their parents. Indirectly, youthful marriage, which led inescapably to a large family, was irresistibly attractive to Irishmen and Irish women. In a country where the margin between the yield of a man's labour and his family's subsistence found its way to pockets other than his own, and where there was no poor law, a numerous family was the only sort of protection against destitution in sickness and old age. Nor, when boys and girls worked on the land, did men have to wait until they were old before enjoying the fruits of parenthood. There was little parents had to deny themselves to secure these advantages. A cabin was cheaply built, and overcrowding was too common to be resented: with trifling labour the potato supplied an abundance of food. No strand of evidence suggests that the bearing and rearing of children were regarded as a sacrifice, and, indeed, with motherhood looked upon as an irremoveable feature of a married woman's life, this is not surprising. Indirectly, the utter poverty and hopelessness of life for Irish men and women made them eager to marry young: to defer marriage gave a couple not the least promise of being able to rear their children in less strained circumstances; to marry young was the accepted thing to do; it meant no added privations and might make existing hardships more easily borne; it might, in years to come, be a safeguard against destitution.

It is unlikely, however, that the acceleration in the rate of population growth was a result of a change in the Irishman's attitude towards marriage: except that before the 1780s the force of example doubtless encouraged men and women to remain single for a longer period, there is every reason for believing that then, too, youthful marriage had its appeal. Once more, positive evidence is elusive: by the nineteenth century, to the British Government and to the literate public, Ireland was a social problem, and in the blue books and the travellers' accounts a peasant's own comments will occasionally dissect for us the motivation of his habits: before the nineteenth century Ireland was less a problem to be investigated than a colony to be ruled and exploited by methods too heavy to require understanding. Unless, indeed, the peasant's attitudes and motives are reflected in his folklore we can only guess what they were by examining the society which helped to shape them. In this society life was no less wretched, nor the future less grim, than in the generation after 1780—perhaps, even, the reverse—and it is not unreasonable to conclude that the answer to our problem is to be found elsewhere than in a change in the attitude of the peasant's children towards marriage. They always wanted to marry young, but, increasingly, in the half-century after 1780 they were able to gratify their desire. These years were a period of radical revision in the relationships of rural society and the conspicuous features of the pattern that was emerging were calculated to allow earlier marriage and (with no evidence to suggest that contraception was a force to be reckoned with) to allow, therefore, the more rapid growth of population. Without doubt, when the initial years were passed, the growth of population did not remain only the effect of social and economic

changes: it became one of their major causes and a cause, therefore, of the perpetuation of population-growth. But the movement
was no purely demographic phenomenon. It was not merely that
a growing population provided for its continued growth. Back of
the whole problem was the availability of food. Malthus was an
accurate observer: it was platitudinous, but topically platitudinous, for an early nineteenth-century writer to point to food-supply
as the limit to population-growth. Ireland for fifty and more years,
in spite of, and partly because of, a wretched standard of living,
hardly knew what the positive check was: her peculiar political
and economic history had driven her to depend on the potato
when, in neighbouring countries, it was still an occasional delicacy,
or a local supplement to the traditional foodstuffs; or when,
indeed, it was the dread of the poor who saw in it the menace of
an Irish standard of living, or the hope of reformers who saw in
the reduction of the cost of the labourer's subsistence, the promise
of national well-being. The extent to which the potato dominated
the Irishman's table varied from region to region, but, by and
large, for half a century, it was only in exceptional seasons that
the Irish family could not count on getting its fill of potatoes, an
immense quantity, which, with the accompanying foods, made a
diet that could be criticized for its monotony, but not for its
nutritional adequacy.

Early marriage, then, was discouraged by no fear of being unable
to feed a family: a minimum of effort would safeguard the largest
family from death by starvation and even from death by malnutri-
tion—and such a contention focuses an element of uniqueness in
Irish history. But the role of the potato was not confined to the
mere supply of plenty of food; it provided abundantly from a
fraction of the land required to get its nutritional equivalent from
grain or pastoral products; it thrived on mountain and bog that
was useless in other branches of arable farming; increasingly, in
the years before the Famine, the planting of a more prolific potato
meant that a family could gain its food from an even more confined
area. The potato, then, provided food for an expanded population,
and it provided the mechanism of expansion. In every way that it
reduced the area from which a family could gain its living, it increased the chances that a son or a daughter could early find the
settlement that was the preliminary (though not, to an improvident
population, the indispensable preliminary) to marriage. Nationally,

the more extra-marginal land which the potato made productive, and the more it reduced the area from which a family could gain its subsistence, the more families could the country support: the Malthusian doctrine of the pressure of population showed that it was merely a matter of time before the possibility of an increase in population became an actual increase.[1] Locally, when a father found he could support his customary way of life with something less than the yield of his entire holding, and when to better this way of life seemed merely to seek permission to pay a higher rent, he would agree to allow a son or daughter to establish a family on part of his land, supplemented, perhaps, with a scrap of mountain or bog.

Reinforcing the effect of the potato in releasing the restraints to population-growth were the swing from pasture farming to arable and the improvement of waste land.[2] The extension of arable coincided with the acceleration in the rate of population-growth and was related to it as both cause and effect. A number of external reasons account for the increased prominence of arable. When Britain ceased to export corn and became anxious for imports, her requirements from her Irish colony changed: formerly Irish corn exports, a menace to the English landed interests, were discouraged: Irish politicians, harassed though they were by mercantilist anxieties

[1] Unless, indeed—and this was, perhaps, the major restraint to population-growth—as the area of land required to win a family's subsistence shrank, the area needed to buy the title to a subsistence holding grew. Nominal rents (and almost certainly the amounts actually paid, though this might be difficult to prove) increased in the decades after 1780. Rents were paid very largely from the produce of the land, apart from potatoes. As there was no considerable increase in the efficiency of grain or pastoral farming, more rent meant that more land had to be devoted to cash crops, and that, therefore, less was available for the settlement of new families. Any attempt to assess the overall effect of rising rents in restraining population-growth would, of course, have to take into account their contrary tendency in depriving the peasant of the fruits of his labour, in making his future hopeless, and, therefore, of encouraging him to marry young, careless of the consequences.

[2] Professor O'Brien thinks that in the half-century before the Famine reclamation of waste land was of little consequence: 'the main fact', he says, 'is that from one cause or another, avoidable or unavoidable, the waste lands of Ireland were not reclaimed.' (Op. cit., 1921, p. 127.) I am unable to accept this conclusion. There is much evidence that at least during the French wars and in the thirties and early forties reclamation of a very considerable amount was carried out by the peasants in spite both of the indifference of the landlords and of the discouragement given to works of improvement by the system of land-tenure. The evidence on which this conclusion is based and a discussion of the influence of reclamation on population history will be found in my paper, *The Colonisation of waste Land in Ireland, 1780–1845*, shortly to be published in *The Economic History Review*.

at the necessity of importing grain, dared, or were allowed, to do no more to encourage arable than subsidize native corn-growers according to their remoteness from the Dublin market. A national Parliament in 1783 was able to tax grain imports and offer bounties on exports, but it took the food scares of thirteen years of war to induce the British Parliament to allow the grain merchants of Ireland access to the English market with the freedom enjoyed by her sister nations in the United Kingdom. Then the extravagant corn prices that promised wealth to the farmers of England if they increased their output of corn, extended arable in Ireland also, though in Ireland it was less the chance of profit that stimulated the peasant than his realization that if he did not produce grain he would lose his land to the man who would promise more rent by doing so.

As in the case of the increased dependence upon the potato, the shift from pasture to arable relaxed the limits to population-growth by facilitating subdivision. When a family which had formerly looked for its rent to butter and bacon, cows and calves, found it by marketing the decreasing quantity of grain which, in the war years, would make up a fixed payment, it needed to earmark a smaller proportion of its holding for the requirements of the landlord. The landlord's endeavour was to increase rent, with the result that the tenant was again left with only his conventional subsistence. The landlord was well equipped to put his wishes into practice. Nonetheless, there were limits to the extent to which he could absorb the entire margin between the produce of the rent-producing pasture and of the same land when tilled. One was the, perhaps occasional, existence of a lease which the peasant could enforce and which defined the rent; another, more powerful, was that a given area of pasture needed more people to work it when it was put under the spade or plough. The old unit of holding, appropriate to a largely pastoral agriculture, was unwieldy for impoverished corn growers. If landlords were to tap the profits of the corn trade, they had to break up their estates, even though doing so meant increasing the population the land had to sustain. The peasants, like their class elsewhere, perennially beset with the problem of establishing their younger sons, and already, with the greater yield of tillage, prepared to believe that they had more land than they required, co-operated with the landlords by transferring portions of their holdings to their sons or to outsiders.

The peasant's sons had traditionally wished to marry young: now the overwhelming obstacle, the difficulty of procuring a holding, was broken down.

To treat Ireland as a unit in discussing its social history, and to treat more than half a century of this history as though it displayed uniformity in cause and effect is to compress or inflate the facts until they fit the mould of convenience. The price of the plausibility of an argument erected on such a foundation may be the overlaying of the pattern of reality by the pattern of the analyst. The peril is clear, but the limitations of the material make escape uncertain. Irish demographic history, when the particularism of natural features was bolstered up by primitive means of communication, and by a stubborn retention of traditional social and technical practices, should be local history, yet the statistics, over most of the period, are too inadequate and insecure to point with any certainty to regional trends in population-growth. The literary material, while it allows an account of overall trends to be pieced together, leaves us uncertain whether large divisions of the country outstripped the national rate of change or ran counter to it, and, moreover, while national population history is obscured by uncertainty about emigration, regional history is bedevilled by ignorance of the volume and course of the many streams of internal migration.

The problem, then, is difficult, and our inquiry is unlikely to be rewarded by more than probabilities. Nonetheless, a number of central issues must at least be raised. First, how uniform was the national rate of population-growth between 1780 and the Famine? Second, in what periods and in what districts were there the greatest divergences from the national trend? Third, what differences were there between district and district in the relative contributions of rising fertility and falling mortality to population-growth?

As guides to the answer to the first question we have only the population estimates of Chapter I[1] and what we know of the tendency of particular estimates to inflate or deflate the real population. On the authority of these figures an increase of 17 per cent. between 1781 and 1791 was succeeded by an increase of 43 per cent. in the following thirty years, and then by 14 and 5 per cent. in the first and second inter-censal periods. The method of calculating the

[1] See above, Table 4, p. 25.

estimates for 1781 and 1791 suggests that the percentage increase they show may not distort the real position too wildly: the estimates are not widely separated in time; they are based on similar material, similarly revised. Less may be said for the smaller rate of increase shown for the next thirty years. As with all the revised estimates put forward in Chapter I, that for 1791 was conservatively calculated: its error, which may well be substantial, almost certainly makes it something below the real figure. It is true that the first census may also have been defective, but there can be little doubt that it was more nearly correct than the pre-census figures. We must, therefore, regard the real rate of increase between 1791 and 1821 as very probably falling short of the 43 per cent. suggested by our figures. For 1821–31 the tendency of the census figures, as pointed out in Chapter I,[1] was to inflate the rate of increase. While in 1821, the error lay in overlooking part of the population, ten years later the danger was that the enumerators returned people who did not exist. The 1841 Commissioners, whose authority must be respected, were confident that errors in enumeration led to no serious distortion of the rate of increase. They thought, too, that this inter-censal increase of 14 per cent. might be applied to the rate of natural increase in the following decade, when, on the census figures, population increased by only 5 per cent. The thirties were the first decade of substantial emigration, and the first decade, therefore, when even the most accurate population figures are seriously misleading if taken as a measure of the rate of natural increase.[2] Our conclusions must be, first to underline that we do not possess material that would allow us to point confidently to the nature of any shifts in the curve of natural increase; and, second, that the statistics, such as they are, suggest that a remarkably steep rate of increase in the 1780s may not have been maintained in the war-years, but was nearly reached again in the generation before the Famine.

The second question we raised concerned the extent to which certain districts made themselves conspicuous in population history by a rate of increase markedly greater or less than that of the country as a whole. Table 36 presents some statistical material bearing on this problem. The second column doubtless complies with the standards of accuracy we have any reason to impose. Less may be

[1] pp. 1–3.
[2] 1841 Census, *Reports from Commissioners*, 1843, xxiv, p. viii.

said in support of the other figures in the table: indeed, so riddled are they with almost the certainty of gross error that they might be better discarded. As a measure of relative population growth they suffer by ignoring any differential changes in the provinces in the average number of people residing in one house, and by ignoring

TABLE 36

Percentage Increases in Houses, 1791–1821, and in Population, 1821–31, in the Provinces of Ireland*

		Percentage increase of houses 1791–1821	Percentage increase of population 1821–31
Leinster	.	51	9
Munster	.	63	15
Ulster .	.	67	14
Connaught	.	99	21
Ireland	.	66	14

* *Journals of the House of Commons of Ireland*, 1792–4, xv, App. p. ccii; 1821 Census, *Accounts and Papers*, 1824, xxii. 411; J. R. McCulloch, 1854, op. cit., 4th ed. pp. 437–8. The percentage increases in the population of the provinces for the inter-censal years 1831–41 are, Leinster, 3; Munster, 8; Ulster, 4; Connaught, 5; and, for the whole of Ireland, 5 (ibid.). These figures, however, are too distorted by differential emigration to be of any use as a guide to the provincial rates of natural increase.

the doubtless substantial range of deficiency between the provinces in the hearth-money collectors' returns. (Almost certainly, for instance, the collectors of Leinster, unless grossly more negligent than their colleagues in Connaught, presented a more nearly accurate return of the houses in their districts.) Offsetting, to a certain degree, the extent of error from this source, is the probability that the areas where the tax-collectors had encountered the greatest difficulties were also the areas for which the census returns were most deficient. The figures, then, are treacherous: nonetheless, so gross is the disparity they show between the rates of increase of Leinster and Connaught that they are of some weight in supporting the proposition that the greater than average rate of increase in Connaught in the twenties, and the smaller than average rate of increase in Leinster, perpetuated the relative position of these two provinces in the population history of the previous thirty years. The literary evidence enables us both to point to some possible causes of the later discrepancies, and to strengthen the evidence of their earlier existence.

To deal with these two points together, the central argument of this work has been that an unusually rapid growth of population must be attributed very largely to the increase of fertility that followed earlier marriage. Earlier marriage was made possible by a number of developments which, by and large, in the earlier as well as the later part of the period were pushed farthest in Connaught and least far in Leinster. The wretched and hopeless condition of the people predisposed them to marry early: without doubt, if the provinces could be grouped according to the standard of living of their peasants, or their chances of bettering their lot, Leinster would be at the head of the table and Connaught at the foot. It is only for the closing years of our period that anything approaching proof of this proposition is available, but contemporary accounts make it indisputable that it is to the belatedness of the first detailed census, rather than to a changed order of the provinces that this must be attributed. The value of agricultural holdings, the quality of housing, the incidence of deaths from fever, the proportion of the population able to read and write, the proportion attending school, are all matters bearing on the well-being and prospects of the community. On every count, Leinster appears in a favoured position and Connaught in an unfavoured. Only 44 per cent. of all holdings in Leinster in 1846 were valued at under £4, as compared with 59 per cent. in Connaught.[1] In 1841, in Leinster, 31 per cent. of all houses were classified by the Census Commissioners as either Class I or Class II; in Connaught, only 10 per cent.[2] The incidence of fever as a measure of wretchedness is likely, because of the higher urbanization of Leinster, to underestimate the contrast between it and Connaught: nonetheless the disparity is striking; between 1831 and 1841 fever deaths per 1,000 total deaths were 92 in Leinster and 102 in Connaught.[3]

In so far as education was an asset in allowing the peasant or his children to better their lot, there is no doubt that the prospect of material advance was more remote in the western than in the

[1] See above, Table 23, p. 165. The corresponding figures for Munster and Ulster are 44 and 42.

[2] 1841 Census, op. cit., pp. lvi ff. In Munster and Ulster the corresponding figures were 21 and 26.

[3] Ibid., Table of Deaths, facing pp. 64, 104, 152, and 180. The corresponding figures for Munster and Ulster were 94 and 93.

eastern counties. Table 37 shows that throughout the country there was little enough schooling. Even in Leinster fewer than a quarter of the children in rural districts between the ages of six

TABLE 37

Proportions of Children from 6 to 15 attending Primary and Superior Schools in the Rural Districts of the Provinces and in the Rural and Civic Districts of Ireland in 1841*

	Children 6–15	Children 6–15 attending primary schools		Children 6–15 attending superior schools	
		Number	Per cent.	Number	Per cent.
Leinster, R.D. . .	378,675	87,310	23·06	2,102	0·55
Munster, R.D. . .	506,672	104,698	20·66	1,395	0·27
Ulster, R.D. . .	569,531	96,769	16·99	4,543	0·80
Connaught, R.D. . .	358,727	38,994	10·87	752	0·21
Ireland, R.D. . .	1,813,605	327,771	18·07	8,692	0·48
Ireland, C.D. . .	243,551	87,372	35·87	13,003	5·34
Ireland, R. and C.D. .	2,057,156	415,143	20·18	21,695	1·05

* 1841 Census, op. cit., pp. 150–1, 260–1, 362–3, 428–9, and 438–9.

and fifteen were reported to be attending primary schools in 1841: in Connaught the proportion was under one-ninth. It was the country children of Ulster who had the most favourable chance of enjoying higher education: four-fifths of 1 per cent. of them were reported to be attending 'superior' schools in 1841; in rural Connaught two out of every 1,000 children were able to profit in after-life from the opportunities provided by such institutions. The effect of the more general schooling enjoyed by Leinster children is, doubtless, reflected in the literacy figures. Table 38 shows that while in rural Leinster over 40 per cent. of the male population

TABLE 38

Percentage of the total Male Population, 5 Years old and upwards, in the Rural Districts of the Provinces, unable to Read or Write, 1841*

Rural districts

Leinster	.	.	.	.	. 42·2
Munster	.·	.	.	.	. 55·8
Ulster	.	.	.	.	. 36·9
Connaught .	.	.	.	. 65·8

* 1841 Census, op. cit., pp. lvi–lix.

aged at least five was unable to read or write, the proportion in
Connaught was half as much again.

The ability to marry young, we have emphasized more than
once, was probably more influential than the desire, and we have
seen that for the people to be able to marry young they had to be
able readily to acquire settlements. The acquisition of a settlement
became a matter of minimal difficulty in the years of rapid population-increase because of the swing from pasture to arable, because
of the general dependence upon the potato, and because of the subdivision of holdings. It is not easy to trace the relative potency of
these three forces in the provinces. The influence of the first we are
quite unable to assess: we know too little of changes in the distribution of arable and pasture in the four provinces to make the
attempt. Ulster's more limited dependence upon the potato, as a
restraint to the rate of population growth was, perhaps, offset by
the importance of the linen industry: if holdings could not there
reach the extremes of parcellation because of the people's reluctance
to forsake grain and meat in their diet, their earnings from spinning
and weaving allowed them to buy in more of their requirements,
and, in fact, by 1841, Ulster was second only to Connaught in the
extent of subdivision. Leinster, next to Ulster, in all probability,
was the province where there were the most considerable supplements to the potato; Munster lived on it hardly less exclusively
than Connaught, but its dependence appears to have had a longer
history, and had, doubtless, lost some of its force as a release to the
restraints on population-growth: for both these reasons it would be
legitimate to attribute to the influence of the potato some part of
the more rapid rate of population-increase in Connaught than in
Leinster or Munster. It was through the subdivision of holdings
that the influence of most of the factors facilitating early marriage
was felt: the statistics of the 1840s leave us in no doubt that it was
in Connaught that subdivision was pressed farthest, and in Leinster
least far. In the whole of Ireland, in 1841, 45 per cent. of all holdings above one acre were under five acres; in Connaught 64 per
cent., and in Leinster 37 per cent.[1] That, in fact, Connaught's more
rapidly rising population is to be associated with developments
which made it easier for couples to marry—and to marry young—
is confirmed by the marriage statistics collected in the 1841 Census.

[1] See above, Table 22, p. 164. The percentages for Munster and Ulster were
35 and 43.

In rural Connaught, in 1841, 54 per cent. of women above sixteen were married; in Leinster, only 45 per cent.[1] In 1831, 84 per cent. of the brides in all first marriages in the rural districts of Connaught were under twenty-six; in Leinster the corresponding figure was 69.[2]

We have, then, in earlier and more general marriage, a reasonable, though, perhaps insufficient, explanation of Connaught's outstripping Leinster in the rate of population-growth; and we are able to associate these differences in marriage-customs with social and economic developments which made both marriage and early marriage more desirable and more possible in Connaught than in Leinster. How far did differential mortality-experience reinforce, how far did it offset, the tendency for earlier marriage to lead to the most rapid rate of increase in Connaught? Any conclusions we can come to here will clearly throw some light on the third problem we raised above, concerning differences between the provinces in the relative contribution made to population-increase by rising fertility and falling mortality. We are fortunate, in dealing with this problem, in possessing statistical guidance of such a nature that there is no apparent reason for disputing its validity. We saw, in Chapter VII,[3] that while the mortality data of the 1841 Census are too defective to bear comparison with later Irish, or overseas figures, the probability is that they have sufficient internal consistency to allow comparisons between different regions of Ireland. We saw, too, that these data point unequivocally to Ulster and Leinster as the regions of relatively low mortality, and, especially, of relatively low infantile mortality. Infants under 1 accounted for 23 per cent. of all deaths in rural Ireland in 1840: in rural Connaught 96 infants died for every 1,000 living in 1841; in Leinster 74, and in Ulster 69. Children from 2 to 5 accounted for 12 per cent. of all deaths: in Connaught 19 per 1,000 died, in Leinster 17, and in Ulster 14. People from 55 to 65 were the only other age-group accounting for more than 10 per cent. of total deaths: in Connaught 40 per 1,000 died, in Leinster 35, and in Ulster 29.[4]

At the end of our period, the conclusion is plain, regional

[1] See above, Table 13, p. 38. In Munster the percentage was 50, and in Ulster, 49.
[2] See above, Table 15, p. 40. In Munster the percentage was 77, and in Ulster, 75.
[3] pp. 188–95.
[4] See above, Tables 27 and 28, pp. 193, 195.

mortality differences, far from helping to explain the differential rates of population growth, tended to lessen them. Connaught achieved its fastest rate of population growth in spite of heavier general mortality, and, more significantly, in spite of heavier infantile mortality. This conclusion would become the more striking if it applied to the earlier as well as to the later years of rapid population-growth: the momentum of a population which had been increasing rapidly for more than two generations might well have withstood a short-lived rise in the death-rate, but Connaught's excess fertility would indeed have been remarkable if, over sixty years, it were able to override infantile mortality continuously more than a quarter as heavy again as Leinster's. There is, of course, no statistical guidance on differential mortality at the beginning of the century: we are driven, yet again, to inform a guess at probabilities with what knowledge we have of the social history of these years. There can be little doubt that Leinster's lower mortality in 1840 was associated with her greater success in resisting small-pox, with the escape of her rural areas from the worst consequences of the famines and fevers of the twenties and thirties, with better housing, and, perhaps, indeed, with her lower fertility. There is no reason for believing that either the gap between standards of living in Leinster and Connaught, or the gap between fertility in the two provinces narrowed in the half-century before the Famine, but in controlling small-pox, and in resisting famine and fever, Leinster was more successful than Connaught: what contribution, moreover, was made in these years to the saving of life, by the extension of hospitals, fever hospitals and dispensaries was concentrated disproportionately in Leinster. There is, then, some probability that infantile mortality in the early years of population-increase was less markedly lower in Leinster than in Connaught than it was in 1840. Similar reasoning would apply to mortality at higher ages, and incline us to the conclusion that, while in the decades before 1840 the expectation of life of persons past infancy was lower in Connaught than in Leinster it was less markedly so than in 1840.

We have, then, some support for the proposition that throughout our period, in Connaught, where the rate of population-increase was probably steepest, there was not only a higher level of fertility than in the other provinces, but also higher infantile and general mortality. This apparent association of high fertility with high

mortality led Mr. E. C. Large, in his discussion of the influence of
the potato in Ireland, to suggest that perhaps 'a natural provision
for the perpetuation of the species' caused times of high mortality
and danger to be times also of high fertility.[1] This type of reasoning
was anticipated by contemporary commentators. J. B. Bryan
pointed out that 'it is an extraordinary circumstance in physiology,
that persons who have been afflicted with epidemic diseases which
arise from want, etc. have a strong tendency to procreation. . . .
Hence immediately after famine and pestilence, there is a great
increase of births.'[2] Lavergne thought that in Ireland there were
two 'mysterious causes of this unlimited propagation, both proceeding from the miserable condition of the people.' 'The first is the
inexplicable physiological law which ordains, for all living species,
that the means of reproduction increase in proportion to the chances
of destruction. . . . As the chances of death increase, births also
increase. . . . The second cause was altogether political. Ireland
under its state of oppression, instinctively felt that it had no other
power to depend upon than numbers, and that it was only in this
way it could defend itself.'[3] No evidence can be offered here to
support the proposition that there was a physiological connexion
between high mortality and high fertility, but that there was a
social link is easily shown. Connaught was a district of high fertility
partly because it was a district of high mortality: high fertility, we
have repeatedly underlined was a function of the ease with which
a couple could find the holding that would promise to sustain their
marriage and their children. The availability of holdings, and the
age at marriage, were partly determined by the time in a father's
life when a son could hope to succeed to his holding. To-day, in
rural Ireland, with subdivision the exception, holdings are normally
passed intact from father to son, and marriage is unusually late
because the son has reached his thirties before his father dies or is
willing to pass on his land to him. A century or more ago fathers
aged more rapidly: they died, or yielded control of their farms at a
sufficiently early age for the sons who succeeded them to marry
young: high mortality thereby became a cause of high fertility.
Similarly, it is not impossible that high infantile mortality tended

[1] E. C. Large, *The Advance of the Fungi*, 1940, p. 24.

[2] J. B. Bryan, *A Practical View of Ireland, from the Period of the Union*, Dublin,
1831, p. 308.

[3] L. de Lavergne, *The Rural Economy of England, Scotland, and Ireland*,
Edinburgh, 1855, pp. 366-7.

towards high fertility: we have attributed early marriage, in part, to the esteem with which parents regarded a numerous family both as their provision for old age and as a reserve of labour: with the high infantile mortality of Connaught it is possible that young men and women learnt from example, if not from teaching, that if a couple were to be survived by a large family, they had to marry betimes.

APPENDIX I

THE CONSTRUCTION OF THE TRADITIONAL ESTIMATES OF THE POPULATION OF IRELAND FROM THE TIME OF PETTY UNTIL THE CENSUS OF 1821

THE differences between the traditional estimates of the population of Ireland and the revised estimates given in Table 4 are easily explained. Nine of the traditional estimates (the four for 1712, 1718, 1725, and 1726, attributed to Arthur Dobbs, and the five for 1754, 1767, 1777, 1785, and 1791, attributed to the hearth-money collectors) have been obtained by the simple procedure of multiplying the hearth-money returns by six. The use of an unjustifiably high figure for the average number of people per house prevents their being deficient in the same proportion as the hearth-money returns. Several other estimates employ a technique no more, or scarcely more, refined. Dobbs, to arrive at his estimate for 1725, deducted from the hearth-money returns 8,800 'waste' houses and arrived at the figure of 377,339 inhabited houses. But this, he thought, was short of the truth, as incomplete returns were made of houses inhabited by persons not paying hearth-money. For the equivalent of 13·3 counties no returns had been made of these houses: if they had pauper's houses at the same rate as the remaining counties there would be 5,607 houses not returned. These added to his figure of inhabited houses would bring the total to 382,846, which he felt was still an underestimate because he had 'often known hearth-money collectors fall short, but never any who have given too large returns of the poor-houses', and because the returns did not purport to include public buildings. This figure for houses he multiplied by 4·36 to arrive at a population estimate which he believed to be 'within the truth', and apparently was so to a greater extent than its author realized. The author of the *Abstract* simply multiplied the 1732 return by five and added 65,000 to make up for omissions.[1] Price multiplied the 1767 return by 4·5.[2] Laffan rounded the 1777 return of 448,426 to 450,000 and allowed 5·5 persons per house.[3] Arthur Young, writing in 1780, was fully aware

---

[1] *Abstract of the Number of Protestant and Popish Families in Ireland*, Dublin, 1736. Reprinted in *Tracts and Treatises illustrative . . . of Ireland*, Dublin, 1861, ii. 536.　　　　　　　　　　　　[2] Price, 1783, op. cit. ii. 253.

[3] J. Laffan, *Political Arithmetic of the Population . . . of Ireland . . .*, Dublin, 1785, p. 1.

of the value of knowledge of a country's population, and he earnestly recommended 'to the legislature of Ireland to order an actual enumeration of the whole people'. He protested that he did not 'pretend to compute' the people of Ireland 'because there are no satisfactory data whereon to found any computation . . . all computations based on taxes must be erroneous, they may be below, but they cannot be above the truth'. Nonetheless he reported the 'common idea' 'that there are something under three millions in Ireland',[1] and he even went so far as to say that £61,646, the amount of the hearth-money in 1778, 'cannot indicate a less population, exceptions included, than three millions'.[2] Howlett raised the 1781 return from 477,602 to 500,000 and gave alternative estimates based upon households of 5 and 5·5.[3] Bushe, we have already seen, went to considerable pains to produce an accurate figure for the average number of persons living in a household. He was as careful in the corrections he made of the official returns of the number of houses in the country. He was aware that the 1788 figures, much more accurate though they were than those for 1785, were 'far short of the truth'. He was able to arrive at some estimation of the deficiency in thirteen counties in which he arranged for the supervisors of the hearth tax to make check surveys in parishes selected at random from the walk of each collector. On the assumptions that the supervisors concerned made accurate returns and that the deficiencies in other parishes in these counties were equal to those in the parishes where check surveys were made, the number of houses in these counties not included in the official returns would be about 24,800. To the omissions for these counties had to be added the omissions for the rest of the country. Bushe's opinion, 'formed on a variety of circumstances', was that they amounted to 20,000. Besides the addition of these 44,800 houses Bushe wanted allowance made for the deliberate exclusion from the returns of public buildings. These omissions, added to the official return of 621,484 houses, would have put the total well above 650,000, but it is upon this figure that Bushe based his population estimate. This figure, still apparently substantially deficient, he multiplied by the unjustifiably high figure of 6·25 persons per household to arrive at a population estimate not seriously divergent from that given in the table.[4]

Three years after the publication of Bushe's paper, Dr. Beaufort in his *Memoir of a Map of Ireland* gave estimates of the population of Ireland in 1790 and 1791. He arrived at the estimate for the earlier year by multiplying each[5] of the county totals of houses returned by the

---

[1] Young, 1780, op. cit. ii. 199–200.   [2] Ibid. ii. 354.

[3] J. Howlett, *An Essay on the Population of Ireland*, 1786, pp. 15–17.

[4] Bushe, 1789, op. cit., facing pp. 143 and 145.

[5] The only exception is for Co. Tyrone for which Beaufort omitted estimates both of the number of persons per house and of the total population. To allow

hearth-money collectors for 1790 by what he thought an appropriate figure for the number of persons per house. Even though the total number of houses[1] upon which he worked was greater than Bushe's amended hearth-money returns, the total of his figures for the population of each county amounts only to 3,750,344, a figure 289,656 less than Bushe's estimate, which itself seems to be deficient. The explanation of the deficiency is to be found, of course, in the lower estimates of the number of persons per house that Beaufort uses. For his estimate for 1791 Beaufort multiplied the uncorrected hearth-money returns by five. This gave him a figure of roughly 3,500,000, which he raised to 3,850,000 to make allowance for public buildings and the overcrowding of poor cottages and city houses.[2]

Duigenan was convinced that the population of Ireland was not more than 3 millions in 1799. He thought that the estimates of Bushe and his followers overestimated both the number of houses in the country and the average number of residents in a house. Ireland, he thought, had not the manufactures and commerce that would allow the growth of her population to rival that of England. Simple observation, moreover, showed him that Ireland was less densely peopled than the high estimates suggested.[3] Eden, having no proof of the inaccuracy of the number of houses returned by the hearth-money collectors in 1791, accepted their figures, and assumed, with Beaufort,[4] that there were, on the average, five-and-a-half persons to a house. After allowing for what he, almost alone among the writers of his time, believed to be a net loss in the following years (the result of civil war and emigration), he put the population in 1800 at 3,800,000.[5] The anonymous author of the *Essays on the Population of Ireland* used the authority of Petty and South for estimating the population in 1700 at about 1 million. He found 'no difficulty in affirming, that on an average, since the year 1700, they have experienced an increase of one-fifth or thereabout every eleven years', and that there were, therefore, above 5 million people in 1800.[6]

an estimate for the whole country to be based upon Beaufort's figures, an estimate for Tyrone is arrived at here by multiplying the figure Beaufort gives for the number of houses in Tyrone by six. MacEvoy in his *Tyrone* (1802, p. 142) says: 'From a great number of views that I have taken in different parishes I find the average of persons to each house rather exceeds six.'

[1] On p. 14 Beaufort gives the return of the hearth-money collectors for 1790 as 677,094, but the total of the figures he gives for each county is 683,359. He gives no explanation of this discrepancy.

[2] Beaufort, 1792, op. cit., p. 142.

[3] P. Duigenan, *Fair Representation of the Present Political State of Ireland*, 1799, App., pp. 236–9.   [4] In making his estimate for 1790. See above, p. 19.

[5] F. M. Eden, *An Estimate of the Number of Inhabitants in Great Britain and Ireland*, 1800, p. 41.

[6] *Essays on the Population of Ireland* . . ., by a Member of the last Irish Parliament, 1803, pp. 2–5.

The estimate in Table I for 1813 appears in the 'Preliminary Observations' to the Census of 1821, signed by W. Shaw Mason. In 1812, he said, an Act was passed for taking an account of the population of Ireland. It was largely copied from that of 1810 for Great Britain 'to the provisions of which it adhered in all practical details, more closely than the different circumstances of the two countries would justify'. After two years during which the enumeration had proceeded it was found that only ten counties or counties of towns had furnished complete returns, and that the remaining thirty had either ignored the Act, or sent in particulars that were inaccurate or defective. The county returns, as published in 1822, come to a total of 4,598,284 persons.[1] 'By the aid of comparative calculations founded on previous enquiries, and on the partial results of the Act, the amount of the Population in 1813 has been conjectured to be 5,937,856.'[2]

The estimate for 1731, made from returns submitted by the parochial clergy and the magistracy to the House of Lords, is of particular interest because it is the only one of the eighteenth-century estimates not based upon the hearth-money returns. It gives[3] the Protestant and Roman Catholic population of each province and puts the national total at 2,010,219. There are different opinions of the accuracy of this figure. McCulloch says 'the result is not believed to be entitled to much confidence'.[4] But, on the other hand, Newenham[5] says that 'of the accuracy of this return there is not sufficient reason to doubt', and Tighe, in his Kilkenny, gives tables based upon the parochial returns for the see of Ossory which, he says, were 'drawn up with great accuracy'.[6] The confidence of Newenham and Tighe is almost certainly misplaced. It is hardly to be expected that the parochial clergy, ministering by their own figures to little more than a third of the population, would be either accurately informed, or without bias on the subject of the households attached to the religion of the majority. Perhaps we may treat their figures for their own parishioners with some degree of confidence: not only was it the duty of the incumbent to know his congregation, but the Protestants tended to be concentrated in the more accessible parts of the country, and, having less justification for fearing oppression, they may have been less unwilling than the Catholics to disclose their numbers. But, however complete the return of Protestants, it is likely that the much greater Catholic population is seriously underestimated. The conclusion that the estimate is below the truth is supported by the official

[1] *Reports (Ireland)*, 1822, xiv. 737 f.
[2] *Accounts and Papers (Ireland)*, 1824, xxii. 417.
[3] As quoted by Newenham, 1809, op. cit., App., p. 19.
[4] McCulloch, 4th ed., 1854, op. cit., ii. 435.
[5] Newenham, 1805, op. cit., p. 93.
[6] Tighe, 1802, op. cit., p. 454.

returns of the number of houses. The nearest return to 1731 that we possess is that of 386,902 for 1732. The lowest estimate we have used for the average number of persons per house would put the total population at 2,011,890, a figure slightly in excess of the parochial return, but, since it takes no account of the deficiency of the hearth-money returns, a serious understatement of actual numbers.

The estimate of Captain South[1] for 1695 is based upon returns made for the poll-tax.[2] South was one of the 1,415 Protestant Commissioners of His Majesty's Revenues appointed to collect the tax.[3] His estimate gives what he claims are exact returns of the population of Armagh, Louth, and Meath, distinguishing persons assessed for the tax from persons exempt. To these county totals he added a figure for the city of Dublin and a figure for the other counties. How he arrived at these figures is not clear. He says nothing of the computations from which the Dublin figure emerged, and of those for the counties, merely that 'In the rest of the Kingdom, according to the First Quarter's assessment of the Poll there are in proportion to the above three counties which were returned exactly 907,432'. McCulloch, discussing South, says 'it is impossible to say what credit should be given to his statement'.[4] Judging it in comparison with estimates before and after it, it seems to be even more widely deficient than the majority of eighteenth-century figures.

The earliest population estimates given in Table 1 are those of Sir William Petty. In the *Political Anatomy* he devoted considerable attention to Irish population problems. He not only gave an estimate of the total population, but tables purporting to show the division of the people by age, nationality, religion, and occupation. In spite of his virtually complete reserve on the procedure that allowed him to arrive at his estimate, there is little doubt that Newenham was right in regarding it as 'rather a rough conjecture than anything else'.[5] Most probably Petty here, like the later writers on Irish population, and as in his own later work, based his figure on data derived from the administration of the hearth-money. This may well have led him into more pitfalls than his successors. In the 1670s the hearth-money was still farmed, and the Government's fiscal officials can have had only the haziest idea of the number of houses in the country. In the *Treatise of Ireland* Petty gave a population estimate for 1687 of 1,300,000, a figure that showed an increase of 200,000 in fifteen years. Again he estimated the numbers of Catholics and Protestants, and he included calculations showing that it was 'naturally possible' for the population of Ireland to double in twenty-

[1] South, 'An Estimate of the number of people that were in Ireland, January 10th 1695', *Phil. Trans. R.S.*, 1700, xxii. 520.

[2] Imposed by 7 Wm. III, c. 15.

[3] Newenham, 1809, op. cit., App., p. 19.

[4] McCulloch, 1854, op. cit. ii. 436.   [5] Newenham, 1805, op. cit., p. 89.

five years. He explained more fully than in the *Political Anatomy* how he arrived at his estimate. The proceeds of the hearth-money, he said, were £30,000. With each hearth taxed at 2*s.* this meant 300,000 hearths. 'By a good estimate from the hearth books' he assumed there were 20,000 houses with more than one hearth, and that they averaged three apiece. Deducting these hearths from the total left 240,000 single-hearth houses. On the assumption that each house with more than one chimney had an average of six occupants, and that each 'cabineer' family averaged five, Petty reached his figure of 1,300,000.[1] It is very insecurely based. Not only does it make no allowance at all for hearths on which no tax was paid either because of the evasion of their owners or because of the inefficiency of the tax-gatherers, but it completely omits persons exempt from the tax, and persons living in houses with no hearths. The fifty per cent. deficiency which we have assumed to be present in the hearth-money returns from 1712 to 1785 must account for only part of the shortcomings of Petty's figure. If we accept his estimate of the number of people per house (and there is no contemporary evidence available to warrant our modifying it, nor does it seem improbable when considered by the side of later evidence) the population estimate should be increased by substantially more than 50 per cent. to approach accuracy. The figure of 2,167,000 given in Table 4 was arrived at by assuming that the number of households, as given by Petty, was deficient by two-thirds.

[1] Petty, 1687, op. cit., p. 141.

APPENDIX II

CRUDE BIRTH-RATE AND FERTILITY

TABLE A

Crude Birth-rate, Counties of Ireland, 1832–41*

Rural and civic districts	Births per 1,000 mean population, 1832–41	Rural and civic districts	Births per 1,000 mean population, 1832–41
Carlow	29·7	Clare	36·6
Dublin	30·4	Cork	32·2
Kildare	30·3	Kerry	36·6
Kilkenny	30·5	Limerick	34·1
King's	31·3	Tipperary	33·7
Longford	31·5	Waterford	33·4
Louth	32·5	Munster	33·9
Meath	31·7		
Queen's	30·6	Antrim	33·9
Westmeath	31·1	Armagh	33·3
Wexford	30·6	Cavan	34·2
Wicklow	31·8	Donegal	33·1
Leinster	31·0	Down	30·3
		Fermanagh	32·6
Galway	35·1	Londonderry	30·5
Leitrim	36·4	Monaghan	31·1
Mayo	36·8	Tyrone	31·7
Roscommon	35·3	Ulster	32·1
Sligo	35·2		
Connaught	35·7	Ireland	33·0

* 1841 Census, *Reports of Commissioners*, 1843, xxiv. 459.

TABLE B

Fertility to 6 June 1841 of first Marriages taking place 1838–40; Rural and Civic Districts of the Provinces of Ireland and Large Towns**

Number of births taking place before 6 June 1841 per 100 marriages taking place 1838–40 in which neither partner married before.

Column (a) gives the number of marriages; column (b) the number of births; and column (c) the number of births per 100 marriages.

	Age of wife at time of marriage					
	Under 17			17–25		
Rural districts	(a)	(b)	(c)	(a)	(b)	(c)
Leinster						
1838	74	68	92	4,617	6,129	133
1839	43	29	67	4,413	4,066	92
1840	47	9	19	3,935	1,845	47
1838–40	164	106	65	12,965	12,040	93
	26–35			36–45		
	(a)	(b)	(c)	(a)	(b)	(c)
1838	2,111	2,656	125	225	144	64
1839	2,356	2,158	92	231	133	58
1840	2,034	935	46	171	47	27
1838–40	6,501	5,749	88	627	324	52
	Under 17			17–25		
	(a)	(b)	(c)	(a)	(b)	(c)
Munster						
1838	189	155	82	8,089	10,322	128
1839	142	71	50	7,300	6,599	90
1840	131	21	16	6,177	3,032	49
1838–40	462	247	53	21,566	19,953	92
	26–35			36–45		
	(a)	(b)	(c)	(a)	(b)	(c)
1838	3,302	4,267	129	176	121	69
1839	3,248	2,991	92	178	114	64
1840	2,548	1,336	52	108	30	28
1838–40	9,098	8,594	94	462	265	57
	Under 17			17–25		
	(a)	(b)	(c)	(a)	(b)	(c)
Ulster						
1838	135	136	100	6,645	8,691	131
1839	126	85	67	6,283	5,685	90
1840	125	24	19	5,916	2,645	45
1838–40	386	245	63	18,844	17,021	90

* 1841 Census, op. cit., pp. 460 ff.

Rural districts	Age of wife at time of marriage					
	26–35			36–45		
	(a)	(b)	(c)	(a)	(b)	(c)
Ulster, *cont.*						
1838	2,016	2,469	122	250	172	69
1839	2,079	1,881	90	217	106	49
1840	1,675	690	41	169	33	19
1838–40 . . .	5,770	5,040	87	636	311	49
	Under 17			17–25		
	(a)	(b)	(c)	(a)	(b)	(c)
Connaught						
1838	138	127	92	5,666	7,171	126
1839	131	81	62	5,093	4,449	87
1840	98	18	18	4,290	2,011	47
1838–40 . . .	367	226	62	15,049	13,631	91
	26–35			36–45		
	(a)	(b)	(c)	(a)	(b)	(c)
1838	1,608	1,971	123	117	59	50
1839	1,547	1,369	88	96	48	50
1840	1,073	512	47	71	14	20
1838–40 . . .	4,228	3,852	91	284	121	43
	Under 17			17–25		
Civic districts	(a)	(b)	(c)	(a)	(b)	(c)
Leinster						
1838	16	12	75	811	1,048	129
1839	13	11	85	759	659	87
1840	10	4	40	678	282	42
1838–40 . . .	39	27	69	2,248	1,989	88
	26–35			36–45		
	(a)	(b)	(c)	(a)	(b)	(c)
1838	310	477	154	40	16	40
1839	305	247	81	40	25	62
1840	273	107	39	29	9	31
1838–40 . . .	888	831	93	109	50	46
	Under 17			17–25		
	(a)	(b)	(c)	(a)	(b)	(c)
Munster						
1838	40	35	87	1,241	1,564	126
1839	39	24	61	1,232	1,076	88
1840	27	2	7	1,149	458	39
1838–40 . . .	106	61	57	3,622	3,098	85
	26–35			36–45		
	(a)	(b)	(c)	(a)	(b)	(c)
1838	426	551	129	37	23	62
1839	478	401	84	54	25	46
1840	413	178	43	43	10	23
1838–40 . . .	1,317	1,130	86	134	58	43

Civic districts				Age of wife at time of marriage					
				Under 17			17–25		
				(a)	(b)	(c)	(a)	(b)	(c)
Ulster									
1838 .	.	.	.	21	16	76	496	618	124
1839 .	.	.	.	10	9	90	525	430	82
1840 .	.	.	.	9	..	..	505	219	43
1838–40	.	.	.	40	25	62	1,526	1,267	83
				26–35			36–45		
				(a)	(b)	(c)	(a)	(b)	(c)
1838 .	.	.	.	124	134	108	15	2	13
1839 .	.	.	.	167	130	78	18	4	22
1840 .	.	.	.	129	50	39	17	3	18
1838–40	.	.	.	420	314	75	51	9	18
				Under 17			17–25		
				(a)	(b)	(c)	(a)	(b)	(c)
Connaught									
1838 .	.	.	.	21	25	119	339	436	129
1839 .	.	.	.	11	10	91	299	253	85
1840 .	.	.	.	8	1	12	272	111	41
1838–40	.	.	.	40	36	90	910	800	88
				26–35			36–45		
				(a)	(b)	(c)	(a)	(b)	(c)
1838 .	.	.	.	81	106	131	5	3	60
1839 .	.	.	.	91	87	96	9	4	44
1840 .	.	.	.	66	26	39	5	2	40
1838–40	.	.	.	238	219	92	19	9	47
				Under 17			17–25		
Large towns				(a)	(b)	(c)	(a)	(b)	(c)
Dublin City									
1838 .	.	.	.	37	37	100	1,006	1,169	116
1839 .	.	.	.	24	15	62	1,052	826	78
1840 .	.	.	.	22	3	14	1,049	346	33
1838–40	.	.	.	83	55	66	3,107	2,341	75
				26–35			36–45		
				(a)	(b)	(c)	(a)	(b)	(c)
1838 .	.	.	.	298	291	98	37	24	65
1839 .	.	.	.	335	275	82	53	27	51
1840 .	.	.	.	280	78	29	32	10	31
1838–40	.	.	.	913	644	70	122	61	50
				Under 17			17–25		
				(a)	(b)	(c)	(a)	(b)	(c)
Cork City									
1838 .	.	.	.	7	7	100	361	437	121
1839 .	.	.	.	5	3	60	347	304	88
1840 .	.	.	.	4	..	..	313	108	35
1838–40	.	.	.	16	10	62	1,021	849	83

Civic districts	Age of wife at time of marriage					
	26–35			36–45		
	(a)	(b)	(c)	(a)	(b)	(c)
Cork City, *cont.*						
1838	118	130	110	14	12	86
1839	113	101	89	16	9	56
1840	108	28	26	4	1	25
1838–40 . . .	339	259	76	34	22	65
	Under 17			17–25		
	(a)	(b)	(c)	(a)	(b)	(c)
Belfast Town						
1838	13	11	85	355	430	121
1839	18	12	67	399	331	83
1840	13	4	31	387	133	34
1838–40 . . .	44	27	61	1,141	894	78
	26–35			36–45		
	(a)	(b)	(c)	(a)	(b)	(c)
1838	75	76	101	11	5	45
1839	83	67	81	10	2	20
1840	72	30	42	10	1	10
1838–40 . . .	230	173	75	31	8	26
	Under 17			17–25		
Ireland	(a)	(b)	(c)	(a)	(b)	(c)
Rural districts						
1838	536	486	92	25,017	32,313	129
1839	442	266	60	23,089	20,759	90
1840	401	72	79	20,318	9,533	47
1838–40 . . .	1,379	824	60	68,424	62,605	91
	26–35			36–45		
	(a)	(b)	(c)	(a)	(b)	(c)
1838	9,037	11,363	126	768	496	65
1839	9,230	8,399	91	722	401	55
1840	7,330	3,473	47	519	124	24
1838–40 . . .	25,597	23,235	91	2,009	1,021	51
	Under 17			17–25		
	(a)	(b)	(c)	(a)	(b)	(c)
Civic districts						
1838	155	143	92	4,609	5,702	124
1839	120	84	70	4,615	3,879	84
1840	93	14	15	4,350	1,657	38
1838–40 . . .	368	241	65	13,574	11,238	83
	26–35			36–45		
	(a)	(b)	(c)	(a)	(b)	(c)
1838	1,432	1,631	114	159	85	53
1839	1,572	1,308	83	200	96	48
1840	1,341	507	38	139	36	26
1838–40 . . .	4,345	3,446	79	498	217	44

Ireland	Age of wife at time of marriage					
	Under 17			17–25		
	(a)	(b)	(c)	(a)	(b)	(c)
Rural and civic districts						
1838	691	629	91	29,626	38,015	128
1839	462	350	76	27,704	24,638	89
1840	494	86	17	24,668	11,190	45
1838–40 . . .	1,747	1,065	61	81,998	73,843	90
	26–35			36–45		
	(a)	(b)	(c)	(a)	(b)	(c)
1838	10,469	12,994	124	927	581	63
1839	10,802	9,707	90	922	497	54
1840	8,671	3,980	46	658	160	24
1838–40 . . .	29,942	26,681	89	2,507	1,238	49

TABLE C

Proportion of Births in 1840 and Children under 6 in 1841 per 100 women 16–45 in 1841; Rural Districts of the Counties of Ireland and Rural and Civic Districts of the Provinces*

Rural districts	Women 16–45	Births in 1840	Children under 6 in 1841	Proportion per 100 women 16–45 of	
				Births	Children under 6
Carlow . .	16,990	1,895	10,422	11·1	61
Dublin . .	28,807	3,749	16,465	13·0	57
Kildare . .	23,332	2,710	14,720	11·6	63
Kilkenny .	41,255	4,795	25,481	11·6	62
King's . .	29,092	3,912	19,902	13·4	66
Longford .	23,055	3,136	15,845	13·6	68
Louth . .	22,701	3,122	14,623	13·7	64
Meath . .	38,755	4,914	25,422	12·7	65
Queen's .	32,218	4,357	20,074	13·5	65
Westmeath .	29,077	3,379	19,136	11·6	66
Wexford .	40,511	5,167	24,595	12·7	61
Wicklow .	25,984	3,864	17,897	14·9	69
Leinster .	351,777	45,000	223,882	12·8	64
Clare . . .	59,030	7,681	43,310	13·0	73
Cork . . .	153,297	20,164	105,457	13·1	69
Kerry . .	58,012	8,497	44,434	14·6	77
Limerick .	62,030	8,776	42,950	14·1	69
Tipperary .	83,354	10,571	56,699	12·7	68
Waterford .	34,815	4,180	22,051	12·0	63
Munster .	460,538	59,869	314,901	13·0	70

* 1841 Census, op. cit., pp. lxii ff. and 458–9.

Rural districts	Women 16–45	Births in 1840	Children under 6 in 1841	Proportion per 100 women 16–45 of	
				Births	Children under 6
Antrim . .	57,710	8,008	39,047	13·9	68
Armagh . .	47,193	6,145	33,046	13·0	70
Cavan . .	50,858	7,728	37,555	15·2	74
Donegal . .	62,588	8,960	46,086	14·3	74
Down . .	74,531	10,316	49,004	13·8	66
Fermanagh . .	32,788	4,356	23,925	13·3	73
Londonderry .	44,040	5,697	29,167	12·9	66
Monaghan . .	43,523	5,720	28,302	13·1	65
Tyrone . .	64,065	8,697	46,127	13·6	72
Ulster . .	478,590	65,798	333,160	13·7	70
Galway . .	89,849	11,752	64,169	13·1	71
Leitrim . .	33,850	5,303	25,626	15·7	76
Mayo . .	79,717	11,225	61,554	14·1	77
Roscommon .	53,473	8,236	40,269	15·4	75
Sligo . . .	36,346	5,365	26,807	14·8	70
Connaught .	293,235	41,881	218,425	14·3	74
Civic districts					
Leinster . .	127,100	14,494	58,922	11·4	46
Munster . .	106,232	12,676	53,717	11·9	51
Ulster . .	59,833	7,241	32,172	12·0	54
Connaught . .	21,127	2,579	11,234	12·2	53
Ireland					
Rural districts .	1,574,150	212,548	1,090,368	13·5	69
Civic districts .	314,392	36,990	156,045	11·8	50
Rural and civic districts . .	1,888,542	249,538	1,246,413	13·2	66

APPENDIX III

IMPORTS AND EXPORTS

TABLE D

Annual Average Exports from Ireland of Grain, Oatmeal, and Flour,
1726–8 to 1830–9*

	Wheat (qrs. of 40 stone)	Oats (qrs. of 22 stone)	Barley (qrs. of 24 stone)	Oatmeal (barrels)	Flour† (cwt.)	Value of produce of corn £000s
1726–8‡	670	8,359	31,208§	2,813	..	..
1744–9	2,437	1,427	14,493	4,649	..	..
1750–9	318	5,237	6,262	..	..	..
1751–7	..	..	..	8,522	..	..
1760–9	1,022	9,662	6,216	..		
1764–9	..	..	..	21,592		
1768–9	..	..	..	..	9,951	..
1770–3	771	12,647	2,932	17,163	117	..
	(Barrels)‖	(Barrels)‖	(Barrels)‖	(cwt.)		
1772–9	13,358	95,887	22,116	51,407	11,746	65
1780–9	65,704	210,964	76,425	71,833	49,890	252
1790–9	69,620	557,254	26,638	81,396	32,928	382
1800–9	85,928	388,546	24,033	47,794	23,360	416
1810–19	249,068	1,036,629	140,086	64,140	115,322	..
					Wheatmeal and flour (cwt.)	
1820–9	552,233	1,913,828	127,517	184,780	377,880	..
1830–9	654,492	2,373,235	274,160	753,822	922,031	..

* 1726–8 from *Journals of the House of Commons of Ireland*, iii, 1715–30, App., p. ccclxviii; 1744–55, ibid. ix, App., p. ccxlvii; 1755–7, ibid. vi, App., p. xxx–xxxi; 1758–65, ibid. viii, App., p. lxxviii; all figures for value of produce of corn, 1772–1809, *Estimates, Accounts and Papers* 1823, xvi. 519; 1766–73, *Ireland: Exports and Imports, 1764–1773*, manuscript in British Library of Political and Economic Science; 1774–1822, *Estimates, Accounts and Papers*, 1823, xvi. 519; 1823–39, *Accounts and Papers*, 1840, xliv. 60. During the years 1726–8 the quarter of wheat, oats and barley, for official purposes, appears to have been 8 bushels. (See 6 Anne, c. 18, 1707.) The half-quarter of 4 bushels, according to 13 & 14 Geo. III, c. 11, 1773–4, was to *continue* to be 224 lb. It seems, therefore, that the quarter of 1726–8 contained 448 lb. or 32 stone. Continuously from 1738 (11 Geo. II, c. 11, 1737) until 1774 (13 & 14 Geo. III, c. 11, 1773–4) the official quarter of wheat contained 40 stone, that of oats, 22 stone and that of barley, 24 stone. The exports for 1726–8 are here given in terms of these quarters in force after 1738.

† From 1726 to 1769 there are records of the exports of barrels of wheatmeal: they exceed 400 on only one occasion (in 1745). From 1823 the figures in this column include wheatmeal.

‡ From 1726 to 1800 the years referred to are those ending on 25 March in the year in question, from 1801 to 1819, those ending on 5 January in the year in question: from 1820 to 1839 they are the years ending on the following 5 January.

§ Barley, malt, and rye.

‖ 23 & 24 Geo. III, c. 19, 1783–4, enacted that a legal barrel of wheat should weigh 20 stone, of oats 14 stone, and of barley 16 stone.

TABLE E. *Annual Average Imports to Ireland of Wheat, Oats, Barley and Malt, Oatmeal, and Flour, 1726–8 to 1820–1**

	Wheat (qrs. of 40 stone)	Oats (qrs. of 22 stone)	Barley and malt (qrs. of 24 stone)	Oatmeal (barrels)	Flour (cwt.)
1726–8	17,850	615	3,844	368	(Barrels 3,949)
1743–9	30,517	4,192	51,023	..	37,368
1750–9	26,713	1,002	61,474	..	65,887
1760–9	14,979	493	30,857	..	52,285
1770–3	28,002	568	30,119	..	67,539
1786–7	752	5	8,828	..	531
	(Barrels)	(Barrels)		(cwt.)	
1792–9	13,203	..	..	..	..
1800–9	9,758	..	..	..	..
1810–19	14,639	..	..	..	..
1813–19	..	1,054	2,340	5,286	56,490
	Wheat and wheat flour (qrs.)	Oats and oatmeal (qrs.)	Barley and barleymeal (qrs.)	Indian corn and meal (qrs.)	
1842–5	107,390	10,038	26,843	16,019	
1846–51	790,949	28,928	81,255	1,693,228	

* 1726–8 from *Journals of the House of Commons of Ireland*, iii. 1715–30, App. p. ccclxvi; 1743, ibid. iv, 1731–48, p. cclviii; 1744–54, ibid. ix, App. p. ccxlvi; 1755–7, vi, App. p. xxix; 1758–65, ibid. viii, App. lxxvi; 1766–73, *Ireland: Exports and Imports, 1764–1773*, manuscript in British Library of Political and Economic Science; 1786–7, *J.H.C.I.* xxv, 1788, p. cliv; 1792–1821, wheat, *Estimates, Accounts and Miscellaneous Papers*, 1821, xx. 106 and 111; 1813–19, oats, barley, oatmeal, and flour, *Accounts and Papers*, 1819, xvi. 323; 1842–51, *Accounts and Papers*, 1852, li. 484.
For definition of measures, see notes * and ||, Table D, above.

TABLE F. *Annual Average Export from Ireland of Linen Yarn and Linen Cloth, 1725–9 to 1810–19**

	Linen yarn (cwts.)	Linen cloth (yds.) 000s.	Value of produce of flax-seed £000s.
1726–9	14,525	1725–9: 4,325	..
1730–9	15,014	5,254	..
1740–9	20,854	7,494	..
1750–9	26,094	12,715	..
1760–1 and 1764–9	32,938	16,163	..
1772–9	31,752	20,311	1,613
1780–9	32,155	25,007	1,877
1790–9	20,484	40,720	2,857
1800–9	12,657	38,178	2,647
1810–19	16,122	41,858	..

* Yarn, 1726–57, from *Journals of the House of Commons of Ireland*, vi, App., p. lxvii; cloth, 1725–49, *J.H.C.I.*, v, App., p. xxiv; 1750–7, ibid., vi, App., p. lxvii; cloth and yarn, 1758–61, ibid., vii, App., p. xlv; 1774–1819, *Estimates, Accounts and Papers*, 1823, xvi. 505, 519; 1764–73, *Ireland: Exports and Imports, 1764–73*, manuscript in British Library of Political and Economic Science.

APPENDIX IV

THE BOUNTIES ON THE TRANSPORT OF
GRAIN TO DUBLIN

'An Act for better supplying the City of Dublin with Corn and Flour',
31 Geo. II, c. 3, authorized the payment of a bounty to everybody who,
after 1 June 1758, brought 'sound, clean, well saved, merchantable' corn
and flour by land carriage to Dublin from any place more than ten miles
distant where it grew or was made, and sold it publicly in the city. The
bounty was to be paid at the rate of 5*d*. per 5 miles per 40 stone, subject
to the proviso that the bounty in respect to any forty stone should not
exceed 10*s*. however far it was carried. Ten years later there was passed
'An Act to explain and amend the laws made for the better supplying
the city of Dublin with corn and flour', 7 Geo. III, c. 12. Its preamble
explained that the premiums payable for flour under the earlier act were
much bigger than the cost of transport: it went on, however, to increase
the premium payable for wheat flour from 5*d*. per 40 stone to 3*d*. per
8 stone for every 5 miles it was carried: the bounty was in future to be
paid on flour coming from between five and ten miles from the capital.
The grain payments were similarly extended to produce coming 5 miles
from the capital, and a payment of $\frac{1}{2}$*d*. per mile per 40 stone was to be
made in addition to the earlier bounty. In the same year, 'An act for the
encouragement of tillage and navigation by granting a bounty on the
carriage of corn coastways', 7 Geo. III, c. 24, gave a bounty of 4*d*. per
hundredweight on grain brought by sea from any place south of Dublin
between Wicklow and the Tuscar, or north between Drogheda and
Carrickfergus and sold in the markets of Dublin: produce coming from
south of the Tuscar or north of Carrickfergus qualified for an additional
1*d*. per hundredweight. Grain brought from south of Cooley Point, near
Carlingford, by water to Newry, Belfast, or Londonderry, was to receive
4*d*. per hundredweight. 'An Act for explaining a doubt arising upon
the laws for supplying the city of Dublin with corn and flour; and also
for lessening the expenses of supplying the said city with the articles
aforesaid', 17 & 18 Geo. III, c. 29, referred to the uncertainty as to how
far persons bringing corn and flour to Dublin, partly by canal and partly
by cart, were entitled to the premiums. It explained that, as the charge
by canal was less than by road it would be unreasonable for the State
to pay the full bounty for produce brought by canal: accordingly from
1 January 1779, for all corn and flour coming by inland navigation two-

thirds of the premiums offered for land-carriage should be payable: oatmeal was made an exception; it continued to qualify for the full bounty when brought by canal. 'An act for the encouragement of tillage and rendering the carriage of corn to the city of Dublin less expensive', 17 & 18 Geo. III, c. 34, provided that anybody who imported wheat, flour, or oatmeal from any place south of Dublin between Wicklow and the Tuscar, or north of Dublin between Drogheda and Carrickfergus should receive 4d. per hundredweight of grain and oatmeal, and 12d. per hundredweight of flour: an additional penny per hundredweight was to be paid on grain coming from south of the Tuscar or north of Carrickfergus, and an extra 2d. on flour. The Act was to continue until 1 June 1782 and to the end of the next session. In 1779–80, the benefits of this act being apparent, it was extended (by 19 & 20 Geo. III, c. 34), with certain modifications of the bounties, to 24 June 1784 and to the end of the next session from then: the former duties remained for produce coming from between Carrickfergus and the Tuscar: grain shipped between the Tuscar and Cape Clear, or between Carrickfergus and Doonaff Head, Co. Donegal, was to receive 5d. per hundredweight and flour 1s. 2d. per hundredweight; grain coming from between Cape Clear and Doonaff Head was to receive 10d. per hundredweight, and flour 1s. 6d. 'An act for the better regulating the Corn trade of this Kingdom', 19 & 20 Geo. III, c. 17, was primarily concerned with extending the bounties payable on the export of grain and flour, but it made, from 29 September 1780, certain reductions in the bounties on inland carriage to help finance the export subsidies: no bounty was to be payable on flour on behalf of which the recipient did not testify that every hundred-weight, and not the average, actually sold for at least 6s. per hundred-weight, nor on malt, unless sold in barrels of a prescribed size for at least 11s.: bounties on land carriage of wheat and flour were not to exceed 1d. or 2d., respectively, per hundredweight for five miles. Bounties payable for carriage by inland navigation were not to be affected by this Act.

APPENDIX V

ACTS, OTHER THAN THE BOUNTIES ON THE INTERNAL CARRIAGE OF GRAIN, DESIGNED TO ENCOURAGE TILLAGE IN IRELAND, FROM 1707 TO FOSTER'S CORN LAW OF 1783

NOT all of the eighteenth-century Acts of the Irish Parliament nominally intending to encourage tillage adopted the contemporary English policy of subsidizing exports and penalizing imports. Apart from that 'most singular [of] measures that have anywhere been adopted'[1]—the bounty on inland carriage—an Act of 1727 (1 Geo. II, c. 10) harked back to Elizabethan precedent and imposed penalties on the owner or occupier of any land of at least 100 acres, of which any was fit for ploughing, who did not 'annually till, plough, and sow with corn or grain' at least 5 per cent. Two years later, taxes were levied on carriages, cards, and dice to finance the improvement of bogs and inland transport in the interest of employment and tillage (3 Geo. II, c. 3). In 1765 eight premiums of £200 were offered to the landholders and farmers of each county who had the greatest quantity of corn reaped from their own land and 'preserved so that air may pass beneath, and so as to be defended against vermin'[2] (5 Geo. III, c. 18). In 1772 there followed 'An act for punishing such persons as shall do injuries or violence to the persons or properties of His Majesty's subjects, with intent to hinder the exportation of corn' (11 Geo. III, c. 7).

The first of the series of acts subsidizing corn exports was passed in 1707 (6 Anne, c. 18). Its preamble said that it had been found 'that exportation of grain when its price is low is an advantage to owners of land and to trade in general': the deduction, Newenham pointed out, was drawn from British, not Irish experience. British experience, he also showed, made plain that bounties of the order of magnitude offered by the Irish law were unlikely to be of serious effect. The English cornexporter was offered 5s. a quarter on wheat when the price was under 48s.; the Irish 1s. 6d. when the price was under 14s. The average price of wheat in England in the twenty-two years ending in 1707 was 33s. 11d. a quarter, about fourteen shillings below the qualifying price for the

---

[1] Young, 1780, op. cit. ii. 243.
[2] Payments under this Act from 1769 to 1771 amounted to £8,532 (*J.H.C.I.*, 1771–2, xv. 25, 27) and in 1772 to £10,974 (ibid., 1773–4, xvi. 24).

bounty. What the price was in Ireland at the time of the act Newenham was unable to discover, but he felt he might safely assume that it did not fall below the English price by the 20s. that would have been necessary to make the offer of the bounty effective.[1]

Other acts professing similar objectives and offering varying bounties were passed in 1755, 1765, 1773–4, and 1779–80. The frequency with which they were passed and the volume of contemporary opinion lamenting the encroachments of the graziers are not the only indications of the ineffectiveness of this legislation. The statute-book itself admits defeat, first in the preamble of the Act of 1773–4 and ten years later in Foster's Corn Law which begins with the words 'whereas the laws heretofore made have not proved sufficient for the effectual encouragement of agriculture'. Most emphatically, however, defeat is shown by the tiny amounts recorded as having been paid in bounties. A return covering the nine years from 1757 to 1765 reports that in five of them no grain at all qualified for the premiums: in the other four years the total amount of the bounty paid, in all the Irish ports on all kinds of grain, was £757.[2] By 1781 the annual payment had increased to nearly £15,000,[3] but even with subsidies of this order of magnitude the legislation can have made only a derisory contribution to the extension of arable.

[1] T. Newenham, 1809, op. cit., pp. 124–5.
[2] *J.H.C.I.*, vii. App., p. lxxv.
[3] Ibid., x. App., p. cclxxvi.

APPENDIX VI

TABLE G

*Provincial Hospitals and Dispensaries, 1845–51**

		Infirmaries		Fever hospitals†		Proportion of hospital accommodation to population‡ (1 bed:) (v)	Number of dispensaries for which co. present-ments made in 1845 (vi)	Total income of infirmaries, fever hospitals, and dispensaries in 1845 (vii)
		Date of opening (i)	Accommodation in 1851 (ii)	Date of opening (iii)	Accommodation in 1851 (iv)			
Leinster								£
Carlow .	.	1767	40	1827	35	355	8	2,750
				1829	50			
				1832	60			
Drogheda								
Town	.	1811	10	..	..	1,681	..	178
Dublin .	.	..	..	1835	32	232§	7	1,489
Kildare	.	1769	70	1819	24	396	16	2,983
				1841	60			
Kilkenny	.	1760	50	..	..	3,034	20	3,016
King's .	.	1788	50	1838	100	714	12	1,508
Longford	.	1767	39	..	..	2,005	6	992
Louth .	.	1755	50	..	..	1,776	7	1,305
Meath .	.	1754	40	1817	80	1,122	28	3,251
Queen's	.	1766	64	1838	34	1,099	14	3,628
Westmeath	.	1729	43	1819	12	1,957	18	2,096
Wexford	.	1769	72	1809	50	848	21	5,217
				1815	60			
Wicklow	.	1766	30	1814	12	413	15	2,323
		1817	16	1814	30			
				1817	30			
				1817	50			
				1818	24			
				1836	28			
				1841	12			
Total	.	13	574	19	783	517	172	30,736
Munster								
Clare .	.	1785	100	..	..	1,923	24	3,982
Cork City	.	1750	90	1802	200	796§	2	2,515
		1777	80					
Cork Co.	.	1784	36	1825	32	..	68	5,526
				1828	68			
				1832	84			
				1838	54			
Kerry .	.	?	48	1800	100	757	26	4,443
				1814	130			
Limerick City		1759	120	1780	500	226§	?	?
Limerick Co.	.	..	..	1830	20	..	30	6,477
				1831	25			
				1831	60			
				1838	60			
Tipperary	.	1768	70	1811	300	512	41	10,111
				1815	40			
				1825	150			
				1825	24			

	Infirmaries		Fever hospitals†		Proportion of hospital accommodation to population‡ (1 bed:) (v)	Number of dispensaries for which co. presentments made in 1845 (vi)	Total income of infirmaries, fever hospitals, and dispensaries in 1845 (vii)
	Date of opening (i)	Accommodation in 1851 (ii)	Date of opening (iii)	Accommodation in 1851 (iv)			
							£
Waterford City	?	160	..	..	843§	1	775
Waterford Co.	..	..	1818	18	..	13	2,138
Total	8	544	17	1,865	573	205	35,967
Ulster							
Antrim .	1767	53	..	..	1,115	19	2,939
Carrickfergus	..	..	..	..	..	1	11
Armagh .	1766	72	1827	30	1,140	15	1,581
			1834	28			
			1847	40			
Cavan .	1767	60	1824	40	1,493	19	3,261
			1832	14			
Donegal .	1773	88	1832	60	1,126	30	3,866
			1832	36			
			1845	40			
Down . .	1767	50	1834	30	2,126	17	3,306
			1839	70			
Fermanagh .	1821	51	..	..	2,239	13	2,055
Londonderry.	1806	83	1806	48	1,449	18	3,403
Monaghan .	1768	60	1833	6	766	14	3,307
			1836	30			
			1838	30			
			1843	40			
			1844	14			
Tyrone. .	1809	72	1838	32	1,753	22	3,761
			1844	40			
Total .	9	589	18	628	1,341	168	27,490
Connaught							
Galway City .	?	80	1822	50	2,333§	1	666
Galway Co. .	..	..	..	..		24	4,541
Leitrim .	1805	40	1842	18	1,888	10	1,581
Mayo . .	1765	50	..	..	5,227	23	4,236
Roscommon .	1767	52	..	..	3,213	17	2,963
Sligo . .	1765	50	1822	50	1,251	11	3,320
Total	5	272	3	118	2,476	86	17,307
Ireland (total)	35	1,979	57	3,394	787	631	111,500

* Columns (i) to (v) are derived from the 1851 Census, *Report on the Status of Disease, Accounts and Papers*, 1854, lviii. 100–3; columns (vi) and (vii) from *Accounts and Papers*, 1849, xlix. 212–21. In addition to the hospitals listed in this table and the Dublin City hospitals, there were in 1851 seven provincial lying-in hospitals: in all they had accommodation for seventy-four patients. (*Rep. on Status of Disease*, 1851, op. cit., pp. 100–3.)

† The number of fever hospitals open varied according to the incidence of fever and the availability of funds. In 1845 County Presentments were made in Leinster for 32 fever hospitals, as compared with the 19 open in 1851: in Munster, for 42, as compared with 17; in Ulster, for 20, as compared with 18, and in Connaught, for 6, as compared with 3. The great outbreak of fever in 1845 led to the opening of a number of new, short-lived hospitals.

‡ The accommodation of the Dublin hospitals and of the provincial lying-in hospitals referred to in note * is taken into account in arriving at the figures in this column.

§ City and County considered together.

BIBLIOGRAPHY

I. OFFICIAL PUBLICATIONS

The Journals of the House of Commons of Ireland.

Report from the Lords' Committees appointed to enquire into the State of Tillage in this Kingdom . . ., Dublin, 1757.

Report of the Select Committee appointed to take into Consideration the Means of promoting the Cultivation and Improvement of the Waste . . ., 1795, *Reports from Committees of the House of Commons, 1774–1802*, ix.

Report of the Committee on the Corn Trade between Great Britain and Ireland, 1802, *Reports of the Committees of the House of Commons, 1774–1802*, ix.

Report from the Committee respecting the Poor in Ireland, 1804, reprinted in *Reports from Committees*, 1830, vii.

First–Fourth Reports of the Commissioners . . . to enquire into the Nature and Extent of the Several Bogs of Ireland, Reports, &c. (Ireland), 1810, x; 1810–11, vi; 1813–14, vi.

Papers relating to Vaccination in Dublin, Reports, &c. (Ireland), 1810–11, vi.

Census of Ireland, 1813 (incomplete), *Reports (Ireland)*, 1822, xiv.

Report of the Select Committee on the Lunatic Poor in Ireland, Reports (Ireland), 1817, viii.

First and Second Reports from the Select Committee on the Contagious Fever in Ireland, Reports from Committees, 1818, vii.

First and Second Reports of the Select Committee on the State of Disease and Condition of the Labouring Poor in Ireland, Reports from Committees, 1819, viii.

Census of Ireland, 1821, *Reports (Ireland)*, 1822, xiv; *Accounts and Papers*, 1824, xii.

First Report of the General Board of Health in the City of Dublin, Dublin, 1822.

Report from the Select Committee on the Employment of the Poor in Ireland, Reports from Committees, 1823, vi.

Report of the Select Committee on the State of Ireland, 1825, reprinted in *Reports from Committees*, 1830, vii.

Report from the Select Committee on Emigration from the United Kingdom, Reports from Committees, 1826, iv.

Report of the Select Committee on Tolls and Customs in Ireland, 1826, reprinted in *Reports of Committees*, 1830, vii.

First–Third Reports from the Select Committee on Emigration from the United Kingdom, Reports from Committees, 1826–7, v.

Report of the Select Committee on the State of the Poor in Ireland, Reports from Committees, 1830, vii.

Reports of the Commissioners on certain Charitable Institutions in the City of Dublin, Accounts and Papers, 1830, xxvi.

Census of Ireland, 1831, *Accounts and Papers*, 1833, xxxix.

Report from the Select Committee on Agriculture, Reports from Committees, 1833, v.

First and Second Reports from the Select Committee on the Advances made by the Commissioners of Public Works in Ireland, Reports from Committees, 1835, xx.

Reports of the Commissioners for inquiring into the Condition of the Poorer Classes in Ireland, Reports from Commissioners, 1836, xxx–xxxiv.

Annual Reports of the Registrar-General for England and Wales, 1838– .

Report of the Poor Law Commissioners on Medical Charities, Ireland, Reports from Commissioners, 1841, xi.

Census of Ireland, 1841, *Reports of Commissioners*, 1843, xxiv.

Report of the Commissioners . . . to inspect certain Charitable Institutions in Dublin, Accounts and Papers, 1842, xxxviii.

Report from Her Majesty's Commissioners of Inquiry into the State of the Law and Practice in Relation to the Occupation of Land in Ireland, [*Report of the Devon Commission*], *Reports from Commissioners*, 1845, xix–xxiii.

Census of Ireland, 1851, *Accounts and Papers*, 1852–3, xci–xcii; 1854, lviii; *Reports from Commissioners*, 1856, xxix–xxxi.

Report on the State of Small-pox and Vaccination . . . presented . . . by the Small-pox and Vaccination Committee, Accounts and Papers, 1852–3, ci.

General Board of Health, *Papers relating to the History and Practice of Vaccination, Accounts and Papers*, 1857, sess. 2, xxxv.

Fertility Census, 1911, *Reports of Commissioners*, 1917–18, xxxv.

II. CONTEMPORARY BOOKS, PAMPHLETS, ETC.

An Abstract of the Number of Protestant and Popish Families in the several Counties and Provinces of Ireland, . . . in the years 1732 and 1733, Dublin, 1736. Reprinted in *A Collection of Tracts and Treatises illustrative . . . of Ireland*, Dublin, ii, 1861, pp. 529–41.

The Act for permitting the free Importation of Cattle from Ireland considered with a View to the Interests of both Kingdoms, 1740.

ALCOCK, T., *The Tenure of Land in Ireland considered*, 1848.

ALISON, A., *The Principles of Population and their Connection with human Happiness*, 1840.

ANDREWS, W. G., 'An Essay on the Properties, Habits, and Culture of the Potato', included in *Prize Essays on the Potato*, Dublin, Royal Dublin Society, 1835.

ANKETEL, W. R., *The Conduct of the Resident Landlords of Ireland, contrasted with that of the Absentees*, 1844.

—— *The Effects of Absenteeism*, 1843.

ARCHER, J., *Statistical Survey of the County of Dublin*, Dublin, 1801.

ATKINSON, A., *Ireland in the Nineteenth Century*, 1833.

BAKER, JOHN W., *Considerations upon the Exportation of Corn written at the Request of the Dublin Society*, Dublin, 1771.

—— *The Reclaiming and Cultivation of a Bog in the County of Kildare . . .*, Dublin, 1773.

BARKER, F., and CHEYNE, J., *An Account of the Rise, Progress, and Decline of the Fever lately epidemical in Ireland . . .*, 1821.

BARNES, GEORGE, *Statistical Account of Ireland founded on Historical Facts*, Dublin, 1811.

BEAUFORT, D. A., *Memoir of a Map of Ireland*, 1792.

BEAUMONT, G. DE, *Ireland: Social, Political, and Religious*, ed. W. C. Taylor, 1839.

BELL, R., *Description of the Condition and Manners . . . of the Peasantry of Ireland . . . between the years 1780 and 1790*, 1804.

BELLEW, R., *Thoughts and Suggestions on the Means . . . towards improving the Condition of the Irish Peasantry*, 1808.

BENNETT, WILLIAM, *Narrative of a Recent Journey of Six Weeks in Ireland*, 1847.

BERKELEY, G., *The Querist . . .*, Dublin, 1752, reprinted in *Tracts and Treatises illustrative . . . of Ireland*, op. cit., ii, pp. 143–202.

—— *A Word to the Wise*, Dublin, 1752, reprinted in *Tracts and Treatises illustrative . . . of Ireland*, op. cit., ii, pp. 203–24.

BERNARD, THOS., 'Dublin Cow Pock Institution', *Reports of the Society for bettering the Condition and Increasing the Comforts of the Poor*, vi, 1815, pp. 132 ff.

—— 'Progress of Dublin House of Recovery', *Reports of the Society for . . . the Poor*, op. cit., vi, 1815, pp. 147 ff.

BICHENO, J. E., *Ireland and its Economy . . .*, 1830.

BLANE, G., 'On the Practice of Vaccination', *Reports of the Society for . . . the Poor*, op. cit. vi, 1815, pp. 305 ff.

BOATE, G., *Ireland's Natural History*, 1652, reprinted in *Tracts and Treatises illustrative . . . of Ireland*, i, 1860, pp. 1–148.

BRAKENRIDGE, W., 'A Letter to George Lewis Scot, Esquire, concerning the present Increase of the People in Britain and Ireland', *Phil. Trans.*, 49, Pt. ii, 1756, pp. 877–90.

BRYAN, J. B., *A Practical View of Ireland, from the Period of the Union*, Dublin, 1831.

BUCKLEY, JAMES, (ed.), 'A Tour in Ireland in 1672–4', *J. Cork Hist. and Arch. Soc.*, 2nd Series, x, 1904, pp. 85–100.

BUSHE, G. P., 'An Essay towards ascertaining the Population of Ireland', *Trans. R.I. Acad.*, 1789.

CAMPBELL, T., *A Philosophical Survey of the South of Ireland*, 1777.

COBBETT, W., *Letters of William Cobbett to Charles Marshal*, reprinted in *Rural Rides*, ed. G. D. H. and M. Cole, 1930, iii, pp. 882–916.

Commentaries on National Policy and Ireland, Dublin, 1831.

COOPER, G., *Letters on the Irish Nation*, 1801.

COOTE, C., *Statistical Survey of the County of Armagh*, Dublin, 1804.

—— *Statistical Survey of the County of Cavan*, Dublin, 1802.

CROKER, T. C., *The Popular Songs of Ireland*, 1839.

CROLY, D. O., *An Essay . . . on Ecclesiastical Finance*, Cork, 1834.

CURWEN, J. C., *Observations on the State of Ireland*, 1818.

Dissertation on the present Bounty Laws for the Encouragement of Agriculture in Ireland, Dublin, 1780.

DOBBS, ARTHUR, *An Essay on the Trade and Improvement of Ireland*, Dublin, 1729–31.

DOYLE, JOHN, *Speech of Gen. Sir John Doyle . . . President at the First Anniversary Meeting of the Society for Improving the Condition and Increasing the Comforts of the Irish Peasantry*, London, 1823.

DUBLIN, Association for the Suppression of Mendicity, *Report for the year 1818*.

DUBOURDIEU, J., *Statistical Survey of the County of Antrim*, Dublin, 1812.

—— *Statistical Survey of the County of Down*, Dublin, 1802.

DUIGENAN, P., *A Fair Representation of the Present Political State of Ireland*, 1799.

DUNDONALD, Earl of, *Letters by the Earl of Dundonald on making Bread from Potatoes*, Edinburgh, 1791.

DUNTON, J., *The Dublin Scuffle . . . also some Account of his Conversation in Ireland*, 1699.

DUTTON, H., *Observations on Mr. Archer's Statistical Survey of the County of Dublin*, Dublin, 1802.

—— *Statistical Survey of the County of Clare*, Dublin, 1808.

EDEN, F. M., *An Estimate of the Number of Inhabitants in Great Britain and Ireland*, 1800.

ELLY, S., *Potatoes, Pigs, and Politics, the Curse of Ireland . . .*, 1848 (?).

FLETCHER, J., *A Charge delivered to the Grand Jury of the County of Wexford at the Summer Assizes, 1814*, 1814.

FORSTER, J., *England's Happiness Increased . . . by a Plantation of the Roots called Potatoes*, 1664.

FOSTER, THOMAS C., *Letters on the Condition of the People of Ireland*, 1846.

Four Letters, originally written in French relating to the Kingdom of Ireland, Dublin, 1739.

FRASER, ROBERT, *General View . . . of the County of Wicklow*, Dublin, 1801.

GAMBLE, JOHN, *Views of Society and Manners in the North of Ireland*, 1819.

LE GOUZ, DE LA BOULLAYE, *The Tour of the French Traveller M. de la Boullaye le Gouz in Ireland, A.D. 1644*, ed. T. C. Croker, 1837.

The Groans of Ireland in a Letter to a Member of Parliament, Dublin, 1741.

H., W. (WALTER HARRIS?), *Remarks on the Affairs and Trade of England and Ireland*, 1698.

HANCOCK, W. N., *Impediments to the Prosperity of Ireland*, 1850.

HARTY, W., *An Historic Sketch of the Causes, Progress, Extent, and Mortality of the Contagious Fever epidemic in Ireland during the years 1817, 1818, and 1819*, Dublin, 1820.

HEBERDEN, W., Jun., *Observations on the Increase and Decrease of Different Diseases and Particularly of the Plague*, 1801.

'Hibernicus', *Practical Views and Suggestions on the present Condition and Permanent Improvement of Ireland*, Dublin, 1823.

HILL, Lord GEORGE, *Facts from Gweedore*, Dublin, 1846.

HOWARD, G. E., *A Treatise of the Exchequer and Revenue of Ireland*, Dublin, 1777.

HOWLETT, J., *An Essay on the Population of Ireland*, 1786.

HUTCHINSON, J. HELY, *The Commercial Restraints of Ireland*, Dublin, 1779.

INGLIS, H. D., *Ireland in 1834*, 1835.

'Irish Catholic', *Letter on the present State of Ireland*, Dublin, 1846.

'The Irish Crisis', *Edinburgh Review*, 87, Jan. 1848, pp. 229 ff.

J.K.L. (Rt. Rev. Dr. James Doyle), *Letters on the State of Ireland, addressed by J.K.L. to a Friend in England*, Dublin, 1825.

JURIN, J., *A Letter to the learned Caleb Cotesworth M.D. . . . containing a comparison between the Natural Small Pox and that given by inoculation*, 1723.

KANE, R., *The Industrial Resources of Ireland*, Dublin, 1844.

KEATING, M., *Letter to Rt. Hon. Lord Morpeth, M.P.*, 1836.

King's and Queen's College of Physicians in Ireland, *Transactions*, i, 1817 to v, 1828, for reports on fever, fever hospitals, &c.

KOHL, J. G., *Ireland, Scotland, and England*, 1844.

LAFFAN, J., *Political Arithmetic of the Population, Commerce, and Manufactures of Ireland . . .*, Dublin, 1785.

LARCOM, T. A., 'Observations on the Census of the Population of Ireland in 1841', *J. Stat. Soc.* vi, 1843, pp. 323–51.

LAVERGNE, L. DE, *The Rural Economy of England, Scotland, and Ireland*, Edinburgh, 1855.

LEDWICH, E., *A Statistical Account of the Parish of Aghaboe*, Dublin, 1796.

LEIGH, R., 'A Chorographic Account of the Southern Part of the County of Wexford, written anno 1684 by Robert Leigh . . .', ed. H. F. Hore, *Proc. and Papers of Kilkenny and South East of Ireland Arch. Soc.*, New Series, ii. 24, Nov. 1859, pp. 451–67.

Letters from the Irish Highlands of Cunnemarra, 1825.

LEWIS, G. C., *On Local Disturbances in Ireland*, 1836.

LEWIS, S., *A topographical Dictionary of Ireland*, 1846.

LONGFIELD, A. K. (ed.), *The Shapland Carew Papers*, Dublin, 1946.

McCULLOCH, J. R., *A Descriptive and Statistical Account of the British Empire*, 2nd ed., 1839; 4th ed., 1854.

—— *On the State of Ireland*, 1825.

McEVOY, J., *Statistical Survey of the County of Tyrone*, Dublin, 1802.

M'PARLAN, J., *Statistical Survey of the County of Donegal*, Dublin, 1802.

—— *Statistical Survey of the County of Leitrim*, Dublin, 1802.

—— *Statistical Survey of the County of Mayo*, Dublin, 1802.

—— *Statistical Survey of the County of Sligo*, Dublin, 1802.

MADDEN, S., *A Letter to the Dublin Society on the Improving their Fund; and the Manufactures, Tillage, etc., in Ireland*, Dublin, 1739.

—— *Reflections and Resolutions proper for the Gentlemen of Ireland*, Dublin, 1738.

MALCOLM, A. G., *The History of the General Hospital, Belfast, and other Medical Institutions*, Belfast, 1851.

—— *The Sanitary State of Belfast*, Belfast, 1852.

MALTHUS, T. R., *Essay on the Principle of Population*, 1798–1805.

—— *Principles of Political Economy*, 1820.

—— Review of T. Newenham's *Population of Ireland*, *Edinburgh Review*, xii, July 1808, pp. 336–55.

MARTIN, ROBERT M., *Ireland, as it was,—is,—and ought to be*, 1833.

—— *Ireland before and after the Union with Great Britain*, 3rd ed., 1848.

MARTINEAU, H., *Letters from Ireland*, 1852.

MASON, WM. SHAW, *Statistical Account, or Parochial Survey of Ireland*, Dublin, i, 1814; ii, 1816; iii, 1819.

MAUNSELL, W., *Letter on Culture of Potatoes*, Dublin, 1794.

'Member of the last Irish Parliament', *Essays on the Population of Ireland, and the Character of the Irish*, 1803.

MOORE, JAMES, *The History of the Small Pox*, 1815.

MOREAU, C., *Past and Present Statistical State of Ireland*, 1827.

MOUNTMORRES, Lord, *The History of the Principal Transactions of the Irish Parliament from the year 1634 to 1666*, 1792.

NEWENHAM, T., *A Statistical and Historical Inquiry into the Progress and Magnitude of the Population of Ireland*, 1805.

NEWENHAM, T., *A View of the Natural, Political, and Commercial Circumstances of Ireland*, 1809.

NOEL, B. W., *Notes of a Short Tour through the Midland Counties of Ireland in the Summer of 1836*, 1837.

O'BRIEN, G. (ed.), *Advertisements for Ireland, 1623*, Dublin, 1923.

Observations on the habits of the Labouring Classes in Ireland suggested by Mr. G. C. Lewis' Report on the State of the Irish Poor in Great Britain, Dublin, 1836.

O'CONNELL, J., *Argument for Ireland*, Dublin, 1844.

O'DRISCOL, JOHN, *Views of Ireland, Moral, Political, and Religious*, 1823.

PAGE, FREDERICK, *Observations on the State of the indigent Poor in Ireland*, 1830.

PAGE, J. R., *Ireland: its Evils traced to their Source*, 1836.

PARKER, W., *A Plea for the Poor and Industrious*, Cork, 1819.

PARMENTIER, A. A., *Observations on such nutritive Vegetables as may be substituted in the place of ordinary food in Times of Scarcity*, 1783.

PENDER, S., *A Census of Ireland (c. 1659)*, Dublin, 1939.

PETTY, W., *The Political Anatomy of Ireland*, 1691.

—— *Political Arithmetic*, 1690.

—— *Treatise of Ireland*, 1687.

PHELAN, D., *Statistical Enquiry into the present State of the Medical Charities of Ireland*, Dublin, 1835.

PIM, J., *The Condition and Prospects of Ireland*, Dublin, 1848.

A Plan for the Improvement of Ireland by the Union of English and Irish Capital, 1834.

PORTER, J. G. V., *Some agricultural and political Irish Questions calmly discussed*, 1843.

PRICE, R., *Observations on the Reversionary Payments*, 4th ed., 1783.

PRIOR (ARTHUR DOBBS?), *A List of the Absentees of Ireland . . .*, Dublin, 1729, reprinted in *Tracts and Treatises illustrative . . . of Ireland*, op. cit. ii, pp. 225–304.

RAWSON, T. J., *Statistical Survey of the County of Kildare*, Dublin, 1807.

Refutation of Dr. Duigenan's Appendix or an attempt to ascertain the extent, population and wealth of Ireland, 1800.

REID, THOS., *Travels in Ireland in the year 1822*, 1825.

A Reply to Mr. Montgomery Martin's 'Ireland before and after the Union with Great Britain . . .', Dublin, 1844.

'Resident Native', *Lachrymae Hiberniae, or The Grievances of the Peasantry of Ireland, especially in the western counties*, Dublin, 1822.

REVANS, J., *Evils of the State of Ireland*, 2nd ed., 1837.

RICHARDSON, WM., *Plan for reclaiming the Bog of Allen and the other great Morasses in Ireland*, Dublin, 1809.

—— 'Simple Measures by which the recurrence of Famines may be prevented', *Pamphleteer*, viii, no. xv, 1816.

ROBINSON, BRYAN, *The Case of Five Children who were Inocculated in Dublin on the 26th of August 1725*, Dublin, 1725.

ROGAN, F., *Observations on the Condition of the Middle and Lower Classes in the North of Ireland . . .*, 1819.

ROGERS, JASPER W., *An Appeal for the Peasantry of Ireland, and the objects of the Irish Amelioration Society*, 2nd ed., 1847.

—— *Facts for the Kind-Hearted of England!* 1847.

—— *The Potato Truck System of Ireland*, 2nd ed., 1847.

ROGERS, JOSEPH, *An Essay on Epidemic Diseases*, Dublin, 1734.

RUTTY, J., *A Chronological History of the Weather and Seasons, and of the prevailing Diseases in Dublin*, 1770.

—— *Essay towards a natural History of the County of Dublin*, Dublin, 1772.

SADLER, M. T., *Ireland; its Evils and their remedies . . .*, 1828.

SAMPSON, G. V., *Statistical Survey of the County of Londonderry*, Dublin, 1802.

SCHEUCHZER, J. G., *Account of the Success of Inoculating the Small-Pox, for the years 1727 and 1728*, 1729.

SENIOR, N. W., *Journals, Conversations, and Essays relating to Ireland*, 1868.

SHEFFIELD, JOHN, Lord, *Observations on the Manufactures, Trade and Present State of Ireland*, 1785.

SHORT, T., *New observations . . . on City, Town, and Country Bills of Mortality*, 1750.

SIMS, J., *Observations on epidemic Disorders with Remarks on nervous and malignant Fevers*, 1773.

Sketch of the State of Ireland, Dublin, 1808.

Some Thoughts on the Tillage of Ireland . . ., 3rd ed., Dublin, 1741.

SOUTH, Captain, 'An Estimate of the Number of People that were in Ireland January 10th 1695', *Phil. Trans. Roy. Soc.* xxii, 1700.

SPENSER, EDMUND, *View of the State of Ireland*, Dublin, 1633, reprinted in *Tracts and Treatises illustrative . . . of Ireland*, op. cit. i, pp. 407–592.

STAPLETON, A. G., *The real monster Evil of Ireland*, 1843.

STEVENS, JOHN, *Journal of John Stevens . . . 1689–1691*, ed. R. H. Murray, Oxford, 1912.

A Stipendiary Romish Priesthood, being a review of an 'Essay on Ecclesiastical Finance', Dublin, 1834.

STOKES, W., *Observations on the Population and Resources of Ireland*, Dublin, 1821.

SWIFT, JONATHAN, *An Answer to a Paper called 'A Memorial of the poor Inhabitants, tradesmen and labourers of the Kingdom of Ireland'*, Dublin, 1735.

—— *The Drapier's Letters*, 1724–5.

—— *A Modest Proposal . . .*, Dublin, 1729.

SWIFT, JONATHAN, *A Proposal for the Universal use of Irish Manufacture*, Dublin, 1720.
—— *Short View of the State of Ireland*, Dublin, 1727–8.
THOMPSON, R., *Statistical Survey of the County of Meath*, Dublin, 1802.
TIGHE, W., *Statistical observations relative to the County of Kilkenny*, Dublin, 1802.
TOWNSEND, H., *Statistical Survey of the County of Cork*, Dublin, 1810.
TUKE, J. H., *A Visit to Connaught in the Autumn of 1847*, 1847.
WAKEFIELD, E., *An account of Ireland, Statistical and Political*, 1812.
WARBURTON, J., WHITELAW, J., and WALSH, R., *History of the City of Dublin*, 1818.
WEBSTER, W. B., *Ireland, considered as a Field for Investment or Residence*, Dublin, 1852.
WELD, I., *Statistical Survey of the County of Roscommon*, Dublin, 1832.
WHITELAW, J., *Essay on the Population of Dublin*, Dublin, 1805.
WIGGINS, J., *The 'Monster' Misery of Ireland . . .*, 1844.
WILDE, W. R., 'The Food of the Irish', *Dublin University Magazine*, xlii, Jan.–June 1854, pt. i, no. ccliv, Feb. 1854, pp. 127–46; pt. ii, no. cclv, March 1854, pp. 317–33.
—— 'The Introduction and time of the general use of the Potato in Ireland', *Proc. R.I. Acad.* vi, 1853–7, pp. 356 ff.
—— 'Short Account of the Early Bills of Mortality in Dublin', *Assurance Magazine*, iii, no. xi, April 1853, pp. 248–51.
WOODVILLE, W., *The History of the Inoculation of the Small-Pox in Great Britain*, 1796.
YOUNG, ARTHUR, *A Tour in Ireland . . .*, 2nd ed., 1780.

III. BOOKS, ARTICLES, ETC., WRITTEN SINCE 1860

ADAMS, WILLIAM F., *Ireland and Irish Emigration to the New World*, New Haven, 1932.
ARENSBERG, C. M., *The Irish Countryman*, 1937.
—— and KIMBALL, S. T., *Family and Community in Ireland*, Cambridge, Mass., 1940.
BRADY, C., *History of Steevens' Hospital*, Dublin, 1865.
CAMPBELL, G., *The Irish Land*, 1869.
CARR-SAUNDERS, A. M., *World Population*, Oxford, 1936.
Combined Food Board, *Food Consumption Levels*, 1944.
CREIGHTON, C., *A History of Epidemics in Britain*, 1891–94.
DAVIDSON, W. D., 'History of Potato Varieties', *J. Dept. of Agri.*, Irish Free State, xxxiii, 1935, pp. 57–81.
—— 'The "Champion" Potato, History and Possibilities of its Revival', *J. Dept. Lands and Agri.*, Irish Free State, xxvi, 1926, pp. 109 ff.

DUNCAN, J. M., *Fecundity, Fertility, Sterility and Allied Topics*, Edinburgh, 1871.

FERENCZI, I., and WILLCOX, W. F., *International Migrations*, New York, 1929–31.

FITZPATRICK, WM. J., *The Life, Times, and Correspondence of the Right Rev. Dr. Doyle*, Dublin, 1861.

FROUDE, J. A., *The English in Ireland in the Eighteenth Century*, 1895.

GEARY, R. C., 'The Future Population of Saorstat Eireann and some observations on Population Statistics', *J. Stat. and Soc. Inq. Soc. of Ireland*, xv, 1935–6.

—— 'Irish Population Prospects Considered from the Viewpoint of Reproduction Rates', *J. Stat. and Soc. Inq. Soc. of Ireland*, xvi, 1940–1.

GRIFFITH, G. T., *Population Problems of the Age of Malthus*, 1926.

HANDLEY, JAMES E., *The Irish in Scotland, 1798–1845*, 2nd ed., Cork, 1945.

HARDINGE, W. H., 'Observations on the earliest known manuscript Census Returns of the People of Ireland', *T.R.I.A.* xxiv, 1865.

KERR, B., *Irish Immigration into Great Britain, 1798–1838* (unpublished B.Litt. Thesis in Oxford University).

LARGE, E. C., *The Advance of the Fungi*, 1940.

LECKY, W. E. H., *History of Ireland in the Eighteenth Century*, new ed., 1892–1909.

MACARTHUR, WM., 'Famines and Fevers in England and Ireland', Appendix to paper by Dr. Bonser published in *J.B. Arch. Assoc.*, 3rd ser., ix, 1944, pp. 66–71.

McCANCE, R. A., and WIDDOWSON, E. M., *The Chemical Composition of Foods*, 1942.

MAXWELL, CONSTANTIA, *Country and Town in Ireland under the Georges*, 1940.

MURRAY, ALICE E., *A History of the Commercial and Financial Relations between England and Ireland from the Period of the Restoration*, 1903.

O'BRIEN, G., *The Economic History of Ireland in the Eighteenth Century*, 1918.

—— *The Economic History of Ireland in the Seventeenth Century*, 1919.

—— *The Economic History of Ireland from the Union to the Famine*, 1921.

O'BRIEN, R. B. (ed.), *Two Centuries of Irish History*, 1907.

O'ROURKE, J., *The History of the great Irish Famine of 1847 with Notices of earlier Irish Famines*, Dublin, 1875.

SALAMAN, R. N., *The Influence of the Potato on the Course of Irish History*, Dublin, 1943.

—— 'The Potato—Master or Servant?', *New Biology*, 1, 1945, pp. 9–28.

SIGERSON, G., *History of the Land Tenures and Land Classes of Ireland*, 1871.

THOMPSON, WILLIAM J., 'The Development of the Irish Census and its national Importance', *J. Stat. and Soc. Inq. Soc. of Ireland*, xii, 1911, pt. xci, pp. 474–88.

WOOD, HERBERT, 'Methods of registering and estimating the Population of Ireland before 1864', *J. Stat. and Soc. Inq. Soc. of Ireland*, xii, 1909, pt. lxxxix, Dec. 1909, pp. 219–29.

INDEX

Swift, J., on extension of pasture, 91; on food of the Irish, 128.

Tillage, extension of, after 1770s, 95–7; suggested by trade and excise statistics, 97–9; causes of, 99–113, 243; influence of relative proportions of factors of production in leading to, 101; whether cause or effect of rising population, 95, 99, 117; tended to facilitate early marriage, 90, 243; whether cause or effect of subdivision, 100; facilitated subdivision of holdings, 161, 166; tended to increase rents, 69; whether tillage receding after 1815, 113–15; why proportion of tillage remained high after 1815, 115–20, 233.

Tithes, method of collection after 1735 favoured pastoralist, 93.

Townsend, H., on difficulties of census enumerators, 2; on fecundity, 47; on value of children to parents, 15; on peasants' reckless marrying, 79; on tendency of rent to leave peasant with only subsistence, 82–3; on food of Irish, 133; on quantity of potatoes consumed by Irish, 148–9; on leases, 68, 71; on partnership leases, 77; on transport bounties on corn, 105; on extension of tillage, 96, 99; on division of father's farm amongst his sons, 165.

Trade, exports of pastoral products, 1753–1819, Table 18, p. 109, 108–9; exports of grain, &c., 1726–1839, Table D, App. III, p. 268; imports of grain, &c., 1726–1821, Table E, App. III, p. 269; exports of linen yarn and linen cloth, 1725–1819, Table F, App. III, p. 269.

Transport bounties, on the carriage of grain to Dublin. See Legislation.

Vaccination. See Small-pox.

Wages, level of, in 1830s, 76 n. 2; payment of, in land, 166.

Wakefield, Edward, on form of marriage, 55, 56; on value of children to

their parents, 79; on priests' encouraging early marriage, 80; on division of father's farm amongst his daughters, 165; on landlords' encouragement of subdivision as a means of increasing rent, 166; on value of potato as food, 152; on aims of Irish landlords, 63; on leases, 68, 72; on letting land by auction, 73–4; on 'hanging gale', 75; on 'rundale', 76–7, 78; on middlemen, 67, 82; on prosperity of graziers during wars, 116.

War, 1793–1815; tendency for living conditions to improve during, 87–9; influence of, in allowing free import of Irish grain to Britain in 1806, 102; influence of, on wheat prices, 112–13.

Waste land, reclamation of, 56, 243; considerable extent of, 1793–1845, 243 n. 2; influence of potato upon, 119, 124, 124–5, 135, 156–9; tended to facilitate early marriage, 90, 243.

Wilde, Sir William, on chronology of dependence of Irish on potato, 134 n. 2; on failures of potato crop, 1741–1845, 144–6; on quantity of potatoes consumed by Irish, 149; on method of preparing potatoes, 152; on origin of small-pox in Ireland, 208.

Wray, T., Inspector-General of Hearth-money, on frauds of collectors, 7; on accuracy of their returns, 11, 13.

Young, Arthur, on size of population of Ireland, 255–6; on value of children to parents, 15; on food of Irish, 133, its abundance, 146–7; on quantity of potatoes consumed by Irish, 147–8; on milk consumed by Irish, 150; on value of potato as food, 151; on increase in potato-culture after 1760, 133; on relative productivity of potato- and corn-land, 122; on extension of tillage, 95; on transport bounties on corn, 104, 106, 107, 108, 109; on middlemen, 66–7; on administration of justice, 68 n. 1.

PRINTED IN
GREAT BRITAIN
AT THE
UNIVERSITY PRESS
OXFORD
BY
CHARLES BATEY
PRINTER
TO THE
UNIVERSITY